THIRD EDITION

SOCIAL MARKETING

This book is dedicated to Ned Roberto, the Coca-Cola Professor of International Marketing at the Asian Institute of Management in the Philippines and our coauthor of the first and second editions of Social Marketing. *We are indebted to you, Ned, for your guidance and wisdom in codeveloping the field of social marketing.*

THIRD EDITION

SOCIAL MARKETING

Influencing Behaviors for Good

Philip Kotler
Northwestern University

Nancy R. Lee
Social Marketing Services, Inc.

SAGE Publications
Los Angeles • London • New Delhi • Singapore

Cover Credits:

5 A Day: Produce for Better Health Foundation
Save the Crabs. Then Eat 'Em. Academy for Educational Development and ChesapeakeClub.org
Click It or Ticket: Tennessee Governor's Highway Safety Office
Mutt Mitt: Intelligent Products, Inc.

For information:

Sage Publications, Inc.
2455 Teller Road
Thousand Oaks, California 91320
E-mail: order@sagepub.com

Sage Publications India Pvt. Ltd.
B 1/I 1 Mohan Cooperative Industrial Area
Mathura Road, New Delhi 110 044
India

Sage Publications Ltd.
1 Oliver's Yard
55 City Road
London EC1Y 1SP
United Kingdom

Sage Publications Asia-Pacific Pte. Ltd.
33 Pekin Street #02-01
Far East Square
Singapore 048763

Printed in the United States of America

Library of Congress Cataloging-in-Publication Data

Kotler, Philip.
Social marketing: Influencing behaviors for good/Philip Kotler, Nancy R. Lee. — 3rd ed.
    p. cm.
Includes bibliographical references and index.
ISBN 978-1-4129-5647-5 (pbk.: alk. paper)
    1. Social marketing. 2. Behavior modification. I. Lee, Nancy, 1932– II. Title.

HF5414.K67 2008
658.8—dc22   2007039239

This book is printed on acid-free paper.

07   08   09   10   11   10 9 8 7 6 5 4 3 2 1

Acquisitions Editor:	Al Bruckner
Editorial Assistant:	MaryAnn Vail
Production Editor:	Diane S. Foster
Copy Editor:	Barbara Coster
Typesetter:	C&M Digitals (P) Ltd.
Proofreader:	Jenifer Kooiman
Indexer:	Terri Corry
Marketing Manager:	Nichole M. Angress
Cover Designer:	Gail A. Buschman

Contents

PART IV: Developing Social Marketing Strategies

Foreword

This third edition of a pioneering book on social marketing comes out as the field is showing dramatic growth. A noticeably increasing number of nonprofit organizations and government agencies have come to recognize the power of sophisticated marketing concepts and tools drawn from the commercial sector in making the world a better place. Organizations such as the Centers for Disease Control and Prevention have set up specific departments to apply social marketing approaches to daunting and important challenges to individual and social well-being.

Perhaps most dramatically, the Department of Health in the United Kingdom has decided to apply social marketing approaches to every health challenge they face where individual behavior is a source of a problem or can be a contributor to solutions. It has helped create the National Social Marketing Centre to provide advice, training, and resources to those who can use these powerful tools. The centre joins a galaxy of social marketing entrepreneurs, scholars, and funders in over 40 countries around the world. Social marketing activities are particularly active in Canada, Australia, and New Zealand—as well as the United Kingdom.

This book is, therefore, very valuable to all those who wish to understand what social marketing is all about and how to carry it out most effectively. It is written by two of the leaders in the field. Philip Kotler, along with Gerald Zaltman, coined the term back in 1971 and has been an active conceptualizer, writer, and supporter of the field ever since. Nancy Lee is both a hands-on practitioner and a teacher, speaker, and publisher. Both authors have penned significant contributions to this field and to the broader domain of nonprofit marketing and management.

What distinguishes this book from others in the field is its excellent combination of the conceptual and practical. Its core includes careful definitions and frameworks. Its structure follows the classical approach to devising and launching effective social marketing campaigns. Perhaps its greatest value lies in the rich trove of examples, checklists, and warnings that provide both students and practitioners the kind of hands-on guidance they need to do social marketing well.

I urge both neophytes and experienced veterans to use this volume as a guide to creating powerful social marketing campaigns. Furthermore, I recommend it to others who might not even realize that social marketing approaches might apply to their own challenges. I and others have long argued that, at base, social marketing is all about influencing behavior. Sometimes this is getting people not to behave—not to smoke, do drugs, or abuse others. Sometimes it is getting them to take up a new behavior like eating less or continuing a behavior like sticking with their high blood pressure treatment regimen.

And social marketing concepts and tools can also be used for other behavioral challenges besides influencing people who are engaging—or might engage—in problem behaviors. Social marketers and academics have recognized that solutions to social problems often require attention to environmental challenges that make desired behaviors difficult or impossible to carry out. So, tackling childhood obesity means influencing school principals and magazine editors. It means getting parents to model desired behaviors and have the right food and exercise options available. It may mean getting a city council to build more playgrounds and foundations to provide funds for equipment and supervisors. And, of course, it will mean getting the food, restaurant, and recreation industries to play their roles.

In each case, it is a matter of getting someone to do something.

That's where social marketing comes in. Those who face these behavioral challenges or who may do so in their future careers are well advised to make this volume one of the key resources in their library as they move forward.

—Alan R. Andreasen
Georgetown University

Part I

UNDERSTANDING SOCIAL MARKETING

CHAPTER 1

Defining Social Marketing

I believe the genius of modern marketing is not the four Ps, or audience research, or even exchange, but rather the management paradigm that studies, selects, balances and manipulates the 4Ps to achieve behavior change. We keep shortening "The Marketing Mix" to the 4Ps. And I would argue that it is the "mix" that matters most. This is exactly what all the message campaigns miss—they never ask about the other 3Ps and that is why so many of them fail.

—Bill Smith
Executive Vice President
Academy for Educational Development

Social marketing, as a discipline, has made enormous strides and has had a profound positive impact on social issues in the area of public health, safety, the environment, and community involvement. Fundamental principles at the core of this practice have been used to help reduce tobacco use, decrease infant mortality, stop the spread of HIV/AIDS, help eradicate guinea worm disease, make wearing bike helmet a social norm, decrease littering, increase recycling, and persuade pet owners to license their pets and "scoop their poop."

Social marketing as a term, however, is still a mystery to most and misunderstood by many. A few even worry about using these words with their colleagues and elected officials, fearing the association some have with manipulation and sales. This chapter is intended to create clear distinctions and to answer common questions. How does this differ from commercial marketing, nonprofit marketing, cause marketing, and public education? Everyone argues it is more than communications, but what's the "more"? Do people who do social marketing actually call themselves social marketers? Where do they work?

We also join the voices of many who are advocating for an expanded role for social marketing and social marketers, challenging professionals to take this technology "upstream" and influence other factors that affect positive social change, including laws, enforcement, public policy, built environments, business practices, and the media. We agree the time has come.

We begin this and all chapters with an inspiring case story from a social marketing expert, highlighting the focus of the chapter. We conclude with one of several Marketing Dialogues that feature discourses among social marketing practitioners seeking to shape, evolve, and transform this discipline, intended at its inception to improve the quality of life.

Save the Crabs. Then Eat 'Em (2005–2006)

BILL SMITH

Executive Vice President
Academy for Educational Development

Background

The Chesapeake Bay is the largest estuary in the United States. A complex ecosystem, it includes the bay itself, its rivers, wetlands, trees, and land that encompass parts of six states and the entire District of Columbia. Under pressure for years to address the bay's demise, regulation and education programs are nothing new to the residents of Virginia and Maryland—two of the states most identified with the bay. The bay is a source of continual public scrutiny. The concept of yet another "campaign" to save the bay would have to fight message fatigue and skepticism about its messages and motives.

In 2004, the Chesapeake Bay Program funded the nonprofit Academy for Educational Development (AED) to design and implement a communications campaign targeting an untapped source of potential nutrient reductions—the residents of the greater D.C. area. This campaign would strive to change personal behaviors that impact bay water quality and heighten awareness of bay pollution among this audience of busy yet socially aware and often influential individuals.

Target Audiences

- Residents of the Chesapeake Bay area who fertilize their lawns primarily in the spring
- Lawn care services
- Lawn care product providers
- Decision makers

Behavior Objectives

Given the history of environmental action in favor of the bay, the program created and implemented by AED was a small, highly targeted effort with three specific purposes:

1. To refresh attention to the bay's problems in a large-scale population suffering from message fatigue

2. To bring a new group of stakeholders to the table

3. To popularize a new target behavior with significant potential to improve water quality if implemented on a large scale

The campaign's behavior objective (product) is a simple behavior that requires homeowners with lawns to fertilize their lawns in the fall rather than in the spring to avoid fertilizer runoff, which is damaging to many bay species, including the Chesapeake Bay blue crab.

Strategies

The blue crab is a regional icon. For centuries, Chesapeake Bay blue crabs were considered the best blue crabs in the world. Chesapeake blue crab harvests declined to near record lows at the end of the 20th century. The 3-year (2001–2003) commercial harvest average of 50 million pounds is 32% below the long-term average (from 1968 to 2003) of about 73 million pounds per year. In 2003, the Chesapeake blue crab harvest hit a near historic low.

With this knowledge at hand, the campaign theme of "saving the seafood" was born. While people in the D.C. area may have only limited concern for the bay, many are passionate about their seafood, as is evidenced by the many thriving seafood restaurants throughout D.C. and its Maryland and Virginia suburbs. *Reframing the problem of a polluted bay as a culinary, not an environmental, problem was the cornerstone of the campaign.*

Lawn care partners were a critical part of the strategy. Messages to fertilize in the fall would fail if there was no fertilizer available in the fall. Meeting with the major lawn care providers in the region met with resistance, but the strategy of promoting specific brands on the campaign Web site helped reduce the resistance. Print collateral was developed to support several campaign components. A color brochure promoting the Chesapeake Club lawn care option was developed and provided to all participating lawn care partners.

The campaign was branded as the Chesapeake Club in order to create a sense of membership, participation, and practice of a behavior that is the accepted social norm—a sense that "this is what people like me do"—for distribution to existing and potential customers. Mass media messaging focused on "wait until fall to fertilize," as this was the desired behavior for 84% of the target audience. Three television ads (two 15-second spots and one 30-second spot) were developed under the direction of Marketing for Change Creative Director David Clemans, each encouraging viewers to wait until fall to fertilize their lawns and each using humor to lighten the

message. One ad explains that "no crab should die like this . . . ," and as he bites into a lump of crabmeat, opines that "they should perish in some hot, tasty butter." Each ad ends with the tagline "Save the Crabs. Then Eat 'Em" and the Web site address. An additional 30-second public service announcement (PSA) was also developed and offered to the Washington television stations, but it is unclear how often it ran, if at all.

A total of 1,200 rating points of air time was purchased on Washington's four major broadcast television networks over the 7 weeks of the campaign, beginning with a 2-week launch at 250 rating points a week. This translates into reaching 83% of intended television audience an average of 14 times over the period, or about twice a week.

In addition, five similarly themed out-of-home executions were also developed as posters inside the cars on two Washington Metro lines (blue and orange) that reach suburban Virginia and to blanket the kiosks and banner space in Union Station, the final stop for the Maryland and Virginia commuter trains. Print ads also ran once a week in the Sunday *Washington Post* and in a free tabloid handed out at Metro stops called *Express* (also owned by the Washington Post Company) (see Figure 1.1).

Branded "Save the Crabs. Then Eat 'Em" drink coasters were printed and distributed without charge to local seafood restaurants, to use and hand out to patrons (see Figure 1.2). The coasters sported the "fertilize in the fall" message on the back, and restaurant waitstaff were informed regarding the purpose of the campaign and why fall fertilizing is more environmentally sound. In this way, restaurants also became partners in disseminating the campaign message and, as an extra incentive, were also promoted on the campaign Web site.

Media opportunities were pitched to local news outlets and national newswires throughout

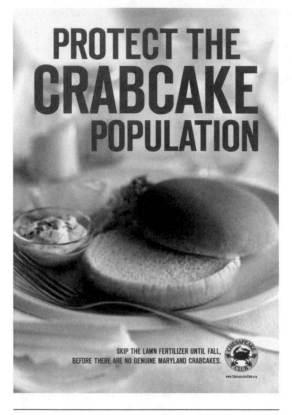

Figure 1.1 Out-of-Home Ad Promoting Fertilizing in the Fall

Figure 1.2 Drink Coasters Distributed to Local Seafood Restaurants

the 7-week ad run, and a number of stories ran as a result. Several media outlets were interested in the angle of a nonenvironmental theme for an environmental campaign, and others focused on the partnership with lawn care companies, which they deemed an unlikely but beneficial partnership.

Results

A postintervention random-digit-dial telephone survey was administered over 2½ weeks beginning the last week of the television buy, again reaching 600 area residents who reported they cared for their lawn or hired someone to do it. Respondents were asked the same

questions regarding environmental concern and practices as in the preintervention survey, with the addition of a few others. Homeowners were also asked whether they plan to fertilize this year and, if so, when they plan to do so.

- When asked when they planned to fertilize that year, 52% of those surveyed in spring 2004, before the campaign, reported that they planned to fertilize that spring. When asked the same question, only 39% of those surveyed in spring 2005, after the campaign, reported that they would fertilize in the spring.
- Of those surveyed, 44% were able to recall the Chesapeake Club brand and/or the

"Save the Crabs, Then Eat 'Em" tagline, without any prompt other than asking if they'd heard anything this year about fertilizer use and the Chesapeake Bay.

- Of those surveyed who recalled the phrase "Save the Crabs. Then Eat 'Em," 51% liked the tagline and 42% had no opinion, while only 7% disliked it. Of those who recalled the Chesapeake Club brand, 34% reported liking the name, 65% had no opinion, and only 1% disliked it.
- Postcampaign survey data indicated that respondents remembered seeing the ads on television (29%), in the newspaper (18%), on billboards (17%), on subway cars (10%), and/or on a flyer or drink coaster (4%). Again, these responses were unprompted. (It is worth noting, however, that 26% also recalled hearing messages on the radio, when no radio ads were produced.)
- The campaign's use of partnerships significantly enhanced the penetration and overall success of the campaign.

By recruiting a potentially adversarial group of stakeholders (lawn care companies) and making them campaign spokespeople, the campaign gained reach and legitimacy.

- The campaign approach of reframing the issue to appeal to the target audience's stomachs rather than their environmental consciousness was sufficiently newsworthy to gain significant media coverage, also enhancing the campaign's reach and legitimacy.
- Several components of the campaign were disappointing, including the following:
  o Insufficient time was allotted for development and distribution of print collateral to support the lawn care partners.
  o An effort to partner with Scotts, a major manufacturer of lawn chemicals, to develop a product for use in the springtime in place of lawn fertilization did not result in a plan to come up with a replacement product.

WHAT IS SOCIAL MARKETING?

Social marketing is a distinct marketing discipline, one that has been labeled as such since the early '70s and refers primarily to efforts focused on influencing behaviors that will improve health, prevent injuries, protect the environment, and contribute to communities. Though several definitions are widely used, themes are similar, as evidenced in the following—beginning with one we have adopted for this text:

> Social marketing is a process that applies marketing principles and techniques to create, communicate, and deliver value in order to influence target audience behaviors that benefit society (public health, safety, the environment, and communities) as well as the target audience. (Philip Kotler, Nancy Lee, and Michael Rothschild, 2006)[1]
>
> Social marketing is a process for creating, communicating and delivering benefits that a target audience(s) wants in exchange for audience behavior that benefits society without financial profit to the marketer. (Bill Smith, 2006)[2]

Social marketing is the application of commercial marketing technologies to the analysis, planning, execution, and evaluation of programs designed to influence the voluntary behavior of target audiences in order to improve their personal welfare and that of their society. (Alan Andreasen, 1995)[3]

Social marketing is the systematic application of marketing concepts and techniques to achieve specific behavioral goals relevant to a social good. (Jeff French and Clive Blair-Stevens, 2005)[4]

It seems clear there is agreement that social marketing is about influencing behaviors, that it utilizes a systematic planning process and applies traditional marketing principles and techniques, and that its intent is to deliver a positive benefit for society. It is considered by many, as Bill Smith's definition aludes, to be an activity most often conducted by nonprofit organizations or public sector agencies. Table 1.1 provides examples illustrating the definition that will be used in this text. Subsequent discussions in this section elaborate on common elements in all definitions.

This chapter will also discuss how social marketing is distinct from traditional commercial sector, nonprofit, and public sector marketing, and you will find a description of 50 social issues that can benefit from social marketing efforts.

We Focus on Behaviors

Similar to commercial sector marketers who sell goods and services, social marketers are selling behaviors. Change agents typically want to influence target markets to do one of four things: (1) *accept* a new behavior (e.g., composting food waste), (2) *reject* a potentially undesirable behavior (e.g., starting smoking), (3) *modify* a current behavior (e.g., increasing physical activity from 3 to 5 days of the week), or (4) *abandon* an old undesirable one (e.g., talking on a cell phone while driving). It may be the encouragement of a one-time behavior (e.g., install a low-flow showerhead) or the establishment of a habit and the prompting of a repeated behavior (e.g., take a 5-minute shower).

Although benchmarks may also be established for increasing knowledge and skills through education, and efforts may need to be made to alter existing beliefs, attitudes, or feelings, the bottom line for the social marketer will be whether the target audience "bought" the behavior. For example, a specific behavior that substance abuse coalitions want to influence is for women to avoid alcohol during pregnancy. They recognize the need to inform women that alcohol may cause birth defects and convince them that this could happen to their baby. In the end, however, their measure of success will be whether the expectant mother abstains from drinking.

The Behavior Change Is Typically Voluntary

Perhaps the most challenging aspect of social marketing (also its greatest contribution) is that it relies heavily on "rewarding good behaviors" rather than "punishing bad ones" through legal, economic, or coercive forms of influence. And in many cases, the

Table 1.1   Examples Illustrating Definition Elements

SOCIAL ARENA: *Social Issue*	*HEALTH:* *Obesity*	*SAFETY:* *Falls*	*ENVIRONMENT:* *Water Supply*	*COMMUNITY:* *Voting*
Influence a Target Market	Parents of children in elementary school	Seniors 75+	Homeowners	College students living out of state
Potential Behaviors to Promote				
Accept a New Behavior	Support your child to walk to school at least 1 day a week.	Take a special strength and balance fitness class.	Test toilets for leaks.	Apply for an absentee ballot.
Reject a Potential New Behavior	Do not offer after-school snacks high in fat and sugar.	Don't buy the latest flip-flop shoes.	Install water softening systems only when necessary.	Do not submit an application if you have a permanent absentee ballot.
Modify a Current Behavior	Encourage your child to order sliced fruit instead of french fries with a fast-food meal.	Rise slowly from a sitting position.	Time your shower to keep it under 5 minutes.	Read details about candidates and issues before voting.
Abandon an Old Behavior	Use fat-free cooking methods like baking or steaming.	Don't walk downstairs without holding onto a handrail.	Use a broom instead of a hose to clean your driveway or sidewalk.	Don't wait until the last minute to mail your ballot.
Use Marketing Principles and Techniques (4Ps)	Product: Organized walking programs such as "Walking School Bus"	Price: Coupons for free first fitness class	Place: Order a toilet test kit online.	Promotion: "Rock the Vote" tour bus visiting college campuses around the country
Benefit	Healthier children	Seniors living independently longer	Reduced water bills and sustainable water supplies	Youth experience having a voice

social marketers cannot promise a direct benefit or immediate payback in return for adopting the proposed behavior change. Consider, for example, the task of increasing voter turnout—especially among youth. Can an organization such as RockTheVote.org really promise voters their vote will make a difference? Or should they instead promise satisfaction for self-expression (see Figure 1.3)? As you will read in subsequent chapters, this is why a systematic, rigorous, and strategic planning process is required—one that is inspired by the wants, needs, and preferences of target audiences and focuses on real, deliverable, and near-term benefits. It should be noted, however, that many believe this heavy reliance on individual voluntary behavior change is outdated and have moved on to applying social marketing technologies to influence other change factors in the environment as well (e.g., laws, policies, media), ones elaborated upon later in this chapter.

We Use Traditional Marketing Principles and Techniques

The American Marketing Association defines marketing as "an organizational function and a set of processes for creating, communicating and delivering value to customers and for managing customer relationships in ways that benefit the organization and its stakeholders."[6] The most fundamental principle underlying this approach is to apply a *customer orientation* to understand barriers target audiences perceive to adopting the desired behavior and benefits they want and believe they can realize. The process begins with *marketing research* to understand market segments and each segment's potential needs, wants, beliefs, problems, concerns, and related behaviors. Marketers then select *target markets* they can best affect and satisfy. They establish clear *objectives and goals*. The product is *positioned* to appeal to the desires of the target market, and the game requires that they do this more effectively than the competition. They then use four major tools in the marketer's toolbox, the "4Ps," to influence target markets: product, price, place, and promotion, also referred to as the *marketing mix*. Once a plan is implemented, *results are monitored and evaluated,* and strategies are altered as needed.

Figure 1.3 RockTheVote .org Encourages Young Adults to Vote, Even Provides Application for Absentee Ballots Online[5]

We Select and Influence a Target Market

Marketers know that the marketplace is a rich collage of diverse populations, each having a distinct set of wants and needs. They know that what appeals to one individual may not appeal to another and therefore divide the market into similar groups (market segments), measure the relative potential of each segment to meet organizational and marketing objectives, and then choose one or more segments (target markets) for concentrating their efforts and resources. For each target, a distinct mix of the 4Ps is developed, one designed to uniquely appeal to the targeted segment.

Considering, again, a more expanded view of social marketing, Robert Donovan and Nadine Henley, among others, advocate for also targeting individuals in communities who have the power to make institutional policy and legislative changes in social structures (e.g., school superintendents). In this case, efforts will move from (just) influencing an individual with a problem or potentially problematic behavior to influencing those who can facilitate individual behavior change.[7] Techniques, however, remain the same.

The Primary Beneficiary Is Society

Unlike commercial sector marketing, in which the primary intended beneficiary is the corporate shareholder, the primary beneficiary of the social marketing program is society. The question many pose and banter about is, who determines whether the social change created by the program is beneficial? Although most causes supported by social marketing efforts tend to draw high consensus that the cause is good, this model can also be used by opponents who have the opposite view of what is good. Abortion is an example of an issue where both sides argue that they are on the "good" side, and both use social marketing techniques to influence public behavior. Who, then, gets to define "good"? Donovan and Henley propose the U.N. Universal Declaration of Human Rights (www.unhchr.ch) as a baseline with respect to the common good, while other perspectives and discussions are elaborated upon in the Marketing Dialogue at the end of Chapter 2.

WHERE DID THE CONCEPT ORIGINATE?

When we think of social marketing as "influencing public behavior," it is clear that campaigning for voluntary behavior change is not a new phenomenon. Consider efforts to free slaves, abolish child labor, influence women's right to vote, and recruit women into the work force (see Figure 1.4).

Launching the discipline formally more than 25 years ago, the term *social marketing* was first introduced by Philip Kotler and Gerald Zaltman, in a pioneering article in the *Journal of Marketing,* to describe "the use of mar-

Figure 1.4 "Rosie the Riveter," Created by the War Ad Council to Help Recruit Women[8]

keting principles and techniques to advance a social cause, idea or behavior."[9] In intervening decades, growing interest in and use of social marketing concepts, tools, and practices has spread from public health and safety to use by environmental and community advocates, as is evident in the partial list of seminal events, texts, and journal articles in Box 1.1. (See Appendix B for additional resources.)

Box 1.1
Social Marketing: Seminal Events and Publications

1970s

1971: A pioneering article, "Social Marketing: An Approach to Planned Social Change," in the *Journal of Marketing* by Philip Kotler and Gerald Zaltman, coins the term *social marketing*.

More distinguished researchers and practitioners join the voice for the potential of social marketing, including Alan Andreasen (Georgetown University), James Mintz (Federal Department of Health, Canada), Bill Novelli (cofounder of Porter Novelli Associates), and Bill Smith (Academy for Educational Development).

1980s

World Bank, World Health Organization, and Centers for Disease Control start to use the term and promote interest in social marketing.

1981: An article in the *Journal of Marketing* by Paul Bloom and William Novelli reviews the first 10 years of social marketing and highlights the lack of rigor in the application of marketing principles and techniques in critical areas of the field, including research, segmentation, and distribution channels.

1988: An article in the *Health Education Quarterly,* "Social Marketing and Public Health Intervention," by R. Craig Lefebvre and June Flora, gives social marketing widespread exposure in the field of public health.

1989: A text, *Social Marketing: Strategies for Changing Public Behavior,* by Philip Kotler and Eduardo Roberto, lays out the application of marketing principles and techniques for influencing social change management.

1990s

Academic programs are established, including the Center for Social Marketing at the University of Strathclyde in Glasgow and the Department of Community and Family Health at the University of South Florida.

1992: An article in the *American Psychologist* by James Prochaska, Carlo DiClemente, and John Norcross presents an organizing framework for achieving behavior change considered by many as the most useful model developed to date.

1994: A publication, *Social Marketing Quarterly,* by Best Start Inc. and the Department of Public Health, University of South Florida, is launched.

1995: A text, *Marketing Social Change: Changing Behavior to Promote Health, Social Development, and the Environment,* by Alan Andreasen, makes a significant contribution to both the theory and practice of social marketing.

1999: The Social Marketing Institute is formed in Washington, D.C., with Alan Andreasen from Georgetown University as interim executive director.

1999: A text, *Fostering Sustainable Behavior,* by Doug McKenzie-Mohr and William Smith, provides an introduction to community-based social marketing.

2000s

2003: A text, *Social Marketing: Principles & Practice,* by Rob Donovan, is published in Melbourne, Australia.

2005: The National Social Marketing Centre is formed in London, England, headed by Jeff French and Clive Blair-Stevens.

2005: The 10th annual conference for Innovations in Social Marketing is held.

2005: The 16th annual Social Marketing in Public Health conference is held.

2006: A text, *Social Marketing in the 21st Century,* by Alan Andreasen, describes an expanded role for social marketing.

HOW DOES SOCIAL MARKETING DIFFER
FROM COMMERCIAL SECTOR MARKETING?

There are a few important differences.

Most agree that a major distinguishing factor lies in the type of product sold. In the case of commercial sector marketing, the marketing process revolves primarily around selling *goods* and *services*. In the case of social marketing, the marketing process is used to sell a *desired behavior*. Yet, the principles and techniques to influence this are the same.

In the commercial sector, the primary aim is *financial gain.* In social marketing, the primary aim is *societal gain*. Given this focus on financial gain, commercial marketers often favor choosing primary target market segments that will provide the greatest volume of profitable sales. In social marketing, segments are selected based on a different set of criteria, including prevalence of the social problem, ability to reach the audience, readiness for change, and others that will be explored in depth in Chapter 6 of this text. In both cases, however, marketers seek to gain the greatest returns on their investment of resources.

Although both social and commercial marketers recognize the need to identify and position their offering relative to the competition, their competitors are very different in nature. Because, as stated earlier, the commercial marketer is most often focused on selling goods and services, the *competition is often identified as other organizations offering similar goods and services* or ones that satisfy similar needs. In social marketing, since the focus is on selling a behavior, *the competition is most often the current or preferred behavior of our target market* and the perceived benefits associated with that behavior, including the status quo. This will also include any organizations selling or promoting competing behaviors (e.g., the tobacco industry).

For a variety of reasons, social marketing is more difficult than commercial marketing. Consider the financial resources the competition has to make smoking look cool, yard cleanup look easy by using a gas blower, and weed-free lawns the norm. And consider the challenges faced when trying to influence people to do any of the following:

- Give up an addictive behavior. (Stop smoking.)
- Change a comfortable lifestyle. (Reduce thermostats.)
- Resist peer pressure. (Be sexually abstinent.)
- Go out of their way. (Take unused paint to a hazardous waste site.)
- Be uncomfortable. (Give blood.)
- Establish new habits. (Exercise 5 days a week.)
- Spend more money. (Buy recycled paper.)
- Be embarrassed. (Let lawns go brown in the summer.)
- Hear bad news. (Get an HIV test.)
- Risk relationships. (Take the keys from a drunk driver.)
- Give up leisure time. (Volunteer.)

- Reduce pleasure. (Take shorter showers.)
- Give up looking good. (Wear sunscreen.)
- Spend more time. (Flatten cardboard boxes before putting in recycling bins.)
- Learn a new skill. (Compost food waste.)
- Remember something. (Take your bags to the grocery store and reuse them.)
- Risk retaliation. (Drive the speed limit.)

Despite these differences, we also see many similarities between the social and commercial sector marketing models:

- *A customer orientation is critical*. The marketer knows that the offer (product, price, place) will need to appeal to the target audience, solving a problem they have or satisfying a want or need.
- *Exchange theory is fundamental*. The target audience must perceive benefits that equal or exceed the perceived costs they associate with performing the behavior.[10] As Bill Smith at AED often purports, we should think of the social marketing paradigm as "Let's make a deal!"[11]
- *Marketing research is used throughout the process*. Only by researching and understanding the specific needs, desires, beliefs, and attitudes of target adopters can the marketer build effective strategies.
- *Audiences are segmented*. Strategies must be tailored to the unique wants, needs, resources, and current behavior of differing market segments.
- *All 4Ps are considered*. A winning strategy requires an integrated approach, one utilizing all tools in the toolbox, not just relying on advertising and other persuasive communications.
- *Results are measured and used for improvement*. Feedback is valued and seen as "free advice" on how to do better next time.

HOW IS IT DIFFERENT FROM NONPROFIT MARKETING, PUBLIC SECTOR MARKETING, AND CAUSE PROMOTIONS?

As you will read, social marketing efforts are most often initiated and sponsored by those in the public and nonprofit sectors. However, in the nonprofit sector, marketing is more often used to support utilization of the organization's services (e.g., ticket sales), purchases of ancillary products and services (e.g., at museum stores), volunteer recruitment, advocacy efforts, and fundraising. In the public sector, marketing activities are also used to support utilization of governmental agency products and services (e.g., the post office and community clinics) and engender citizen support and compliance. In summary, social marketing efforts are only one of many marketing activities conducted by those involved in nonprofit or public sector marketing.

Cause promotions are primarily focused on efforts to raise awareness and concern for a social issue (e.g., global warming, domestic violence) but typically stop short of charging itself with changing behaviors. This change in knowledge and belief may be a necessary prelude to changing behaviors, and social marketers may contribute to this awareness building and attitude change—but the ball their eyes will be on is the one indicating the desired behavior was "bought."

WHO DOES SOCIAL MARKETING?

In most cases, social marketing principles and techniques are used by those on the front lines responsible for improving public health, preventing injuries, protecting the environment, and engendering community involvement. It is rare when they have a social marketing title. More often, they are program managers or those working in community relations or communication positions. Efforts usually involve multiple change agents who, as Robert Hornik points out, may or may not be acting in a consciously coordinated way.[12] Most often organizations sponsoring these efforts are *public sector agencies*, international ones such as the World Health Organization (WHO), national ones such as the Centers for Disease Control and Prevention (CDC), Departments of Health, Departments of Social and Human Services, the Environmental Protection Agency, the National Highway Traffic Safety Administration, Departments of Wildlife and Fisheries, and local jurisdictions, including public utilities, fire departments, schools, parks, and community health clinics.

Nonprofit organizations and foundations also get involved, more often supporting behaviors aligned with their agency's mission, as does the American Heart Association when they urge women to monitor their blood pressure, the Kaiser Family Foundation with their Know HIV/AIDS campaign promoting testing, and the Nature Conservancy when they promote actions that protect wildlife habitats.

Professionals working in a for-profit organization in positions responsible for corporate philanthropy, corporate social responsibility, marketing, or community relations might support social marketing efforts, often in partnership with nonprofit organizations and public agencies that benefit their communities and customers. Though the primary beneficiary is society, they may also find their efforts contribute to organizational goals as well, such as a desired brand image or even increased sales. Safeco Insurance, for example, provides households with tips on how to protect rural homes from wildfire; Crest supports the development of videos, audiotapes, and interactive lesson plans to influence good oral health behaviors; and thousands of customers at Home Depot's stores have attended weekend workshops focusing on water conservation basics, including drought-resistant gardening (see Figure 1.5).

Finally, there are marketing professionals who provide services *to organizations engaged in social marketing campaigns,* firms such as advertising agencies, public relations firms, marketing research firms, and marketing consulting firms—some that specialize in social marketing.

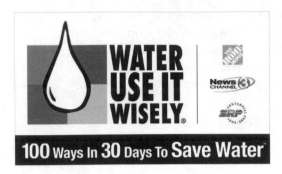

Figure 1.5 Home Depot's Arizona Stores Offered Weekend Workshops on Water Conservation Basics, Including Drought-Resistant Gardening. More Than 3100 Consumers Attended

WHAT SOCIAL ISSUES CAN BENEFIT FROM SOCIAL MARKETING?

Table 1.2 presents 50 major social issues that could benefit from the application of social marketing principles and techniques. It is only a partial list but is representative of the four major arenas mentioned earlier that social marketing efforts are usually focused on: health promotion, injury prevention, environmental protection, and community involvement. For each of the social issues listed, the status could improve if and when we are successful in increasing the adoption of desired related behaviors.

Relative to circumstances most eminent and real, social marketing principles and techniques were present in the aftermath of the terrorist attack on September 11, 2001. Behavior change strategies included the following:

- Those near the site of the wreckage in New York City were provided with cloth face masks and encouraged to *wear them to protect your lungs*.
- Those who had walked in debris from the collapsed buildings were warned to *wash asbestos off your shoes so you don't track it into your home*.
- Postal workers began *wearing gloves to protect from potential anthrax*.
- Some who reported walking down the stairwells of the World Trade Center towers after the attacks reported the benefit they experienced by *putting an arm on the shoulder of the person in front of you to guide yourselves through the rubble and barriers*.
- Airline pilots were reported to have encouraged brave passengers to protect themselves and others and *throw something (anything) at someone who stands up and threatens to hijack the plane*.
- An extra plea was made for volunteers to find and *donate extra-large sizes of clothing for firefighters* so they could continue their work without disruption.
- Those who had rare and valuable blood types were able to *move to the front of the line*.
- At airport security, officials pleaded for travelers to *have your computer out of your bag and your change in your carry-on* in exchange for a speedy pass through.

Interestingly, a variety of news and special programs then seized an opportunity to reinforce benefits realized from adopting behaviors promoted by existing social marketing efforts:

- If you really want to protect yourself from a premature death, you should stop smoking, buckle your seatbelt, and exercise at least five times a week.
- Yes, there were more than 3,000 people killed on 9/11, but each year in the United States more than 16,000 people are killed in traffic collisions involving drunk driving.

WHAT ARE OTHER WAYS TO IMPACT SOCIAL ISSUES?

Social marketing is clearly not the only approach to impacting a social issue, and social marketers are not the only ones who can be influential. Other forces and organizations, ones some describe as upstream factors, can influence individual behaviors downstream—even make personal change unnecessary. Included are technological innovations, scientific discoveries, economic pressures, laws, improved infrastructures, changes in corporate business practices, new school policies and curricula, public education, and the media.

Technology: Some new gas pumps inhibit the ability to top off the tank, thus avoiding ozone-threatening spillage. Some cars have automatic seatbelts that wrap around the passenger when the door is closed. In some states, ignition locks require Breathalyzers for serious offenders, and Mothers Against Drunk Diving (MADD) is advocating to require automobile manufacturers to include high-tech alcohol sensors in all new cars. Imagine the impact on trip reduction if cars were designed to give feedback on how much that trip to the grocery store just cost, given the current price of a gallon of gas.

Science: Medical discoveries may eventually provide inoculations for certain cancers, such as one recently released for 11 to 26-year-olds to help prevent cervical cancer. And in 2006, researchers at the Mayo Clinic announced they felt they were close to discovering a shot that could be given that would help (if not ensure) a smoker to quit.[13]

Legal/Political/Policy Making: Sometimes when all else fails, the laws have to get tougher, especially when the vast majority of the market has adopted the behavior and only the most resistant are still holding out (late adopters and laggards, as they are labeled in marketing). In some states, for example, booster seats are now required for children until they are 6 years old or until the child weighs 60 pounds. Many U.S. states have passed a 0.08% blood alcohol level limit for drinking and driving. Some states have considered laws requiring deposits on cigarettes similar to those requiring deposits on beverage containers (and rewarding their return). And in a policy statement published in December 2006 in the journal *Pediatrics*, the American Academy of Pediatrics asked Congress and the Federal Communications Commission to impose severe limits on children-targeted advertising, including banning junk food ads during shows viewed predominantly by those under age 8.[14]

Table 1.2   50 Major Issues Social Marketing Can Impact

Health-Related Behaviors to Impact	
Tobacco Use	One in five (20.5%) adults 18+ smokes cigarettes.[a]
Heavy/Binge Drinking	More than a fourth (26%) of 18- to 24-year-olds binge drink (have five or more drinks on one occasion).[b]
Fetal Alcohol Syndrome	2.7% of pregnant women binge drink and 3.3% drink frequently.[c]
Obesity	More than half (51.3%) of adults do not exercise at recommended levels.[d]
Teen Pregnancy	37% of sexually active 9th- to 12th-graders did not use a condom during their last sexual intercourse.[e]
HIV/AIDS	About a fourth (24%–27%) of Americans living with HIV are unaware of their infection.[f]
Fruit and Vegetable Intake	More than three out of four adults (76.8%) do not consume the recommended five or more servings a day. [g]
High Cholesterol	23% of adults have never had their cholesterol checked.[h]
Breastfeeding	86% of mothers do not meet recommendations to breastfeed infants until they reach at least 6 months.[i]
Breast Cancer	25% of females 40+ years have not had a mammogram within the past 2 years.[j]
Prostate Cancer	48% of men aged 40+ have not had a PSA test within the past 2 years.[k]
Colon Cancer	47% of adults aged 50+ have never had a sigmoidoscopy or colonoscopy.[l]
Birth Defects	60% of women of childbearing age are not taking a multivitamin containing folic acid.[m]
Immunizations	19% of 29- to 35-month-old children are not receiving all recommended vaccinations.[n]
Skin Cancer	Only 9% of youth wear sunscreen most of the time.[o]
Oral Health	30% of adults have not visited a dentist or dental clinic in the past year.[p]
Diabetes	One third of 20.8 million Americans with diabetes are not aware that they have the disease.[q]

Blood Pressure	30% of the estimated 60 million Americans with high blood pressure don't know they have it.[r]
Eating Disorders	57% of college students cite cultural pressures to be thin as a cause of eating disorders.[s]
Injury-Related Prevention Behaviors to Impact	
Drinking and Driving	29% of high school students report having ridden one or more times in the past year in a car driven by someone who had been drinking.[t]
Other Vehicle Crashes	20% to 30% of all motor vehicle crashes can be linked to driver distraction.[u]
Seatbelts	Observation surveys nationwide indicate at least 18% of people do not wear a seatbelt.[v]
Head Injuries	More than a third (35%) of children riding bicycles wear helmets improperly.[w]
Proper Safety Restraints for Children in Cars	83% of children ages 4 to 8 ride improperly restrained in adult safety belts.[x]
Suicide	8.4% of 9th- to 12th-graders attempted suicide one or more times during the past 12 months.[y]
Drowning	Alcohol is a major contributing factor in up to 50% of drownings among adolescent boys.[z]
Domestic Violence	Around the world, at least one woman in every three has been beaten, coerced into sex, or otherwise abused in her lifetime. Most often the abuser is a member of her own family.[aa]
Gun Storage	An estimated 3.3 million children in the United States live in households with firearms that are always or sometimes kept loaded and unlocked.[bb]
School Violence	5% of students in high schools reported carrying a gun onto school property during a given month.[cc]
Fires	Roughly half of home fire deaths result from fires in the small percentage (4%) of homes with no smoke alarms.[dd]
Falls	More than one third of adults 65 and older fall each year. In 2003, more than 13,700 people 65+ died from injuries related to falls.[ee]

(Continued)

Table 1.2 (Continued)

Household Poisons	More than 4 million accidental poisonings are reported each year. 65% of those involve children, and the most common forms of poisoning among small children are vitamins, aspirins, cleaning products, and beauty supplies.[ff]
Environmental Behaviors to Impact	
Waste Reduction	Only 50% of all paper, 45% of all aluminum beer and soft drink cans, and 34% of all plastic soft drink bottles is recycled.[gg]
Wildlife Habitat Protection	Roughly 70% of the major marine fish stocks depleted from overfishing are being fished at their biological limit.[hh]
Forest Destruction	About 15 million trees are cut down annually to produce the estimated 10 billion paper bags we go through each year in the United States.[ii]
Toxic Fertilizers and Pesticides	An estimated 76% of households use harmful insecticides, and an estimated 85% have at least one pesticide in storage.[jj]
Water Conservation	A leaky toilet can waste as much as 200 gallons a day.[kk]
Air Pollution From Automobiles	An estimated 76% of commuters in the United States drive alone to work.[ll]
Air Pollution From Other Sources	If every household in the United States replaced their five most frequently used light fixtures with bulbs that have the ENERGY STAR® label, more than 1 trillion pounds of greenhouse gas emissions would be prevented.[mm]
Composting Garbage and Yard Waste	30%–50% of all trash that ends up in a landfill in the United States could have been composted.[nn]
Unintentional Fires	An average of 106,400 wildfires are estimated to break out each year in the United States, with about 9 out of 10 started by carelessness.[oo]
Energy Conservation	Only about 6% of total energy consumption in the United States in 2003 came from renewable resources; 86% of all energy came from fossil energy sources.[pp]
Litter	Each year, over 4.5 trillion nonbiodegradable cigarette butts are littered worldwide.[qq]
Watershed Protection	At least 40% of Americans don't pick up their dogs' waste.[rr]

Community Involvement Behaviors to Impact	
Organ Donation	As of January 2007, 94,875 patients were on a waiting list for an organ transplant.[ss]
Blood Donation	60% of the U.S. population is eligible to give blood, but only 5% do in a given year.[tt]
Voting	Only 55.3% of the eligible voting-age population voted in the 2004 U.S. presidential election.[uu]
Literacy	Only 16% of children have a bedtime story every night compared to 33% of their parents' generation.[vv]
Identity Theft	About 3.6 million U.S. households (3%) were victims of at least one type of identity theft during a 6-month period in 2004.[ww]
Animal Adoption	Over 10 million animals in shelters are not adopted and are euthanized each year.[xx]

NOTE: Estimated/approximate statistics. Data are for the United States, unless otherwise noted.

Improved Infrastructures and Built Environments: If we really want more people to ride bikes to work, we'll need more bike lanes, not just bike paths. If we really want to reduce cigarette butt littering on roadways, perhaps automobile manufacturers could help out by building in smoke-free cigarette butt containers so that disposing a cigarette inside the car is just as convenient as tossing it out the window. If we want to reduce electrical consumption, perhaps lights in hotel rooms could only be turned on when the room key is inserted in a master switch and therefore automatically turned off when guests leave the room with their key. And if we want more people at work to take the stairs instead of the elevators, we may want to have elevators skip the first three floors except in cases of emergency or to accommodate those with a physical disability, and we certainly want to take a look at the cleanliness and lighting of the stairway. How about a little music? And social marketers can play a huge role in influencing policymakers and corporations to make these changes.

Changes in Corporate Policies and Business Practices: In 2004, Kraft Foods announced a decision to eliminate all promotions in schools, reduce the amount of trans fats in many of its products, and limit the size of single portions. In the same year, Ford came out with a hybrid SUV, and in 2006 Starbucks introduced a new disposable cup containing 10% post-consumer recycled content, a move anticipated to save 78,000 trees and reduce 3,000,000 pounds of solid waste a year.[15] Each of these efforts will positively impact the same social issues that social marketers are trying to address.

Schools: School district policies and offerings can contribute significantly in all social arenas, providing channels of distribution for social marketing efforts: health (e.g., offering healthier options in school cafeterias and regularly scheduled physical activity classes), safety (e.g., requiring students to wear ID badges), environmental protection (e.g., providing recycling containers in each classroom), and community involvement (e.g., offering school gymnasiums for blood donation drives).

Education: The line between social marketing and education is actually a clear one, with education serving a useful tool for the social marketer, but one that does not work alone. Most often, education is used to communicate information and/or build skills but does not give the same attention and rigor to creating and sustaining behavior change. It primarily applies only one of the four marketing tools, that of promotion. Many in the field agree that when the information is motivating and "new" (e.g., the finding that secondhand tobacco smoke increases the risk of sudden infant death syndrome), it can move a market from inaction—even resistance—to action very quickly. This, however, is unfortunately not typical. Consider the fact that death threats for tobacco use have been posted right on cigarette packs for decades, and yet the World Health Organization estimates that 29% of youth/adults (age 15+) worldwide still smoke cigarettes.[16] Marketing (benefits in exchange for behaviors) has often been missing in action.

Media: News and entertainment media have powerful influences on individual behaviors as they shape values, are relied upon for current events/trends, and create social norms. Many argue, for example, that the casual and sensational attitude of movies and television toward sex has had a major contribution to the problems we see among young people today.[17] On the flip side, the media was a powerful factor influencing people to donate time and resources to victims of Hurricane Katrina.

WHAT IS THE SOCIAL MARKETER'S ROLE IN INFLUENCING UPSTREAM FACTORS?

As noted earlier, many believe that to date we have been placing too much of the burden for improving the status of social issues on individual behavior change and that social marketers should direct some of their efforts to influence upstream factors. We agree.

Alan Andreasen, in his book *Social Marketing in the 21st Century,* describes this expanded role for social marketing well. "Social marketing is about making the world a better place for everyone—not just for investors or foundation executives. And, as I argue throughout this book, the same basic principles that can induce a 12-year-old in Bangkok or Leningrad to get a Big Mac and a caregiver in Indonesia to start using oral dehydration solutions for diarrhea can also be used to influence politicians, media figures, community activists, law officers and judges, foundation officials, and other individuals whose actions are needed to bring about widespread, long-lasting positive social change."[18]

Consider the issue of the spread of HIV/AIDS. Downstream, social marketers focus on decreasing risky behaviors (e.g., unprotected sex) and increasing timely testing (e.g., during pregnancy). If they moved their attention upstream, they would notice groups and organizations and corporations and community leaders and policymakers that could make this change a little easier or a little more likely, ones that could be a target market for a social marketing effort. The social marketer could advocate with others to influence pharmaceutical companies to make testing for HIV/AIDS quicker and more accessible. They could work with physician groups to create protocols to ask patients whether they have had unprotected sex and, if so, encourage them to get an HIV/AIDS test. They would advocate with offices of public instruction to include curriculums on HIV/AIDS in middle schools. They would support needle exchange programs. They would provide the media with trends and personal stories, maybe even pitch a story to producers of soap operas or situation comedies popular with the target audience. They might look for a corporate partner that would be interested in setting up testing at their retail location. They could organize meetings with community leaders such as ministers and directors of nonprofit organizations, even provide grants for them to allocate staff resources to community interventions. If they could, they would visit hair salons and barbershops, engaging owners and staff in spreading the word with their clients. They would testify before a senate committee to advocate for increased funding for research, condom availability, or free testing facilities.

The marketing process and principles are the same as ones used for influencing individuals: utilizing a customer orientation, conducting marketing research, establishing clear objectives and goals, crafting a positioning statement, developing a marketing mix, and conducting monitoring and evaluation efforts. Only the target market has changed.[19]

Chapter Summary

Social marketing is a process that applies marketing principles and techniques to create, communicate, and deliver value in order to influence target audience behaviors that benefit society (public health, safety, the environment, and communities) as well as the target audience.

There are a few important differences between social marketing and commercial sector marketing. Social marketers are focused on selling a behavior, while commercial marketers are more focused on selling goods and services. Commercial sector marketers position their products against those of other companies, while the social marketer competes with the audience's current behavior and associated benefits. The primary benefit of a "sale" in social marketing is the welfare of an individual, a group, or society, whereas in commercial marketing it is shareholder wealth.

Social marketing principles and techniques are most often used to improve public health, prevent injuries, protect the environment, and increase involvement in the community. Those engaged in social marketing activities include professionals in public sector agencies, nonprofit organizations, corporate marketing and community relations and advertising, public relations, and market research firms. A social marketing title is rare and is most likely to fall within the responsibility of a program manager, community relations, or communications professional.

Other approaches to changing behavior and impacting social issues include technological innovations, scientific discoveries, economic pressures, laws, improved infrastructures, changes in corporate business practices, new school policies and curricula, public education, and the media. Many agree these factors and audiences are well within the purview, even responsibility, of social marketers to influence.

MARKETING DIALOGUE

Are we really the same as commercial marketing?

Do we want to be?

Do we care?

There are social marketing practitioners who believe that it's time for social marketing to declare its own identity, develop its own definition, and distinguish itself as a unique and separate discipline. They argue as follows:[20]

We have been at this for three decades now and it's about time to define our discipline uniquely, rather than as a subset of commercial marketing. Our missions and motives and means and markets have very little in common.

We have a very different marketplace than commercial marketers and therefore need different tools. The 4P model that is at the cornerstone of commercial marketing exaggerates our role. Let's stop kidding others and ourselves. Most professionals in this field have very few opportunities for influencing product design, pricing, and distribution channels. We don't really do everything. In the end, isn't 90% of what we do persuasive communication (at best)?

I resent the notion that social marketing has the same motivations and therefore the same processes as those in for-profit organizations. Commercial ventures are in it for the shareholders. We're in it for the public good. I don't like the association.

There are others on the Social Marketing Listserv who think it is crucial that social marketing stay connected to the marketing discipline, in theory and in practice. Their counterpoints include the following:

We need to move closer to, not further from, the disciplines and practices of commercial marketers. Marketing has been a powerful addition to the set of tools used in influencing public health and safety, protecting the environment, and encouraging community participation. We desperately need to be constantly reminded that we are not just educators or social advertisers who "may be content to work at the information or attitudinal level. Social marketers aim to bring about purchase and use and to close the sale."[21] We must begin to look at participating in product development, suggesting pricing strategies, and understanding and recommending distribution channels.

What's wrong with making a profit? And what's wrong with using practices that have been around longer than many of us have that have been tried and tested and enhanced? Commercial marketers have spent billions of dollars learning what works and what doesn't. We should be benefiting from this, not reinventing it.

We need to encourage (even challenge) expert marketers from the commercial sector to join us, to specialize in this exciting niche of the marketing field. We should be proud of the rigor our field requires and demonstrate we understand the contribution marketing can make.

CHAPTER 2

Steps in the Strategic Marketing Planning Process

Traditional planning models rely too much on tactical interventions and too little on strategy needed to sustain long-term change. In social marketing, consumer research provides the gene pool and strategy serves as the DNA structure needed to bring that information to life.

—Carol Bryant
University of South Florida

Although most agree that having a formal, detailed marketing plan for a social marketing effort "would be nice," the practice doesn't appear to be the norm. Those in positions of responsibility who could make this happen frequently voice common perceptions and concerns such as these:

- We just don't have the time to get this all down on paper. By the time we get the go-ahead, we just need to spend the money before the funding runs out.
- The train already left the station. I believe the team and my administrators already know what they want to do. The target market and communication channels were chosen long ago. It seems disingenuous, and quite frankly a waste of resources, to simply prepare a document to justify these decisions.

We begin this chapter with an inspiring case story that demonstrates the positive potential return on your investment in the planning process. Ten steps to developing a compelling social marketing plan will then be outlined—ones we hope will demonstrate that the process can be simple and efficient and that those who have taken the time to develop a formal plan realize numerous benefits. Readers of your plan will see evidence that recommended activities are based on strategic thinking. They will understand why specific target audiences have been recommended. They will see what anticipated costs are intended to produce in specific, quantifiable terms that can be translated into an associated return on investment. They will certainly learn that marketing is more than advertising and will be delighted (even surprised) to see you have a system, method, timing, and budget to evaluate your efforts.

We conclude with comments on why a systematic, sequential planning process is important and where marketing research fits in the process. The Marketing Dialogue at the end of the chapter gives a glimpse at the ongoing, passionate debate over the first step in the planning process—deciding "what is good."

VERB™ Summer Scorecard (2003–2006)

CAROL BRYANT, ANITA COURTNEY, JULIE BALDWIN,
ROBERT McDERMOTT, MARILYN PETERSON, AND DIANA KOONCE

Background and Situation

Since 1980, overweight has more than tripled among youth 12–19 years of age and more than doubled for children 2–11.[1-2] In addition to the problem of young people eating unhealthy foods or quantities, a major contributor to childhood overweight and obesity is physical inactivity. However, despite compelling evidence supporting its benefits,[3,4,5] the 2005 National Youth Risk Behavior Surveillance Survey data indicate that 64% of youth in grades 9–12 do not meet recommended physical activity guidelines and 10% are sedentary.[6]

Given the consequences of physical inactivity and obesity, many communities seek ways to increase youth physical activity levels. This case story describes how a community coalition in Lexington, Kentucky, used social marketing principles to address this challenge.

Objectives

Formed in 2003, the coalition included over 50 people representing public health, social service, and other community-based organizations, businesses, and concerned principals, teachers, coaches, physicians, and parents. The Florida Prevention Research Center (FPRC) provided technical assistance as coalition members used social marketing principles to design a behavior change intervention and modify state and local policies. Local health department employees convened and staffed the coalition. One of our first tasks was to select physical activity as a target behavior and tweens (youth aged 9–13 years) as the population they would give their greatest priority. Our objectives for the project described in this case study were to (a) develop opportunities for tweens to be physically active during the summer months, (b) offer new and exciting ways for tweens to be physically active, and (c) increase physical activity.

Target Audience

Tweens were selected as the target audience because physical activity levels decline dramatically during these years and we wanted to capitalize on the marketing information and media materials assembled by the national campaign targeting this population: "VERB–It's what you do."[7] Within the tween market, we selected two segments to receive the highest priority in their planning efforts: *moderately actives* (i.e., those active but not yet passionate about any of the physical activities in which they participate) and *passives* (i.e., those uninvolved in physical activity and who do things mostly out of boredom). High-risk youth (i.e., those lacking parental support and other resources needed to participate in physical activities outside of school) and superstars (i.e., those already involved in multiple activities) were given less attention but not ignored or excluded. We also attempted to address differences between boys and girls and between younger (8–10 years of age) and older (11–13 years of age) tweens.

Strategy

Consumer research provided the foundation for our marketing strategy. After a careful review of existing literature and marketing data assembled by the VERB program, our research team conducted 10 individual interviews with principals and other program partners, six focus groups with tweens, and two focus groups with parents. Results were presented to the coalition for their use in developing a comprehensive marketing plan based on the 4Ps. Key elements of the plan that served as a blueprint for program design and implementation are summarized below.

Product

Program activities were designed to offer a bundle of benefits (i.e., core product) to satisfy tweens' major motivators: have fun, spend time with their friends, explore new and adventurous activities, and master new skills. Health benefits were not offered; in fact, program partners were asked to avoid making any references to obesity prevention or health benefits associated with physical activity to protect the VERB brand's position. An augmented product was also created—the VERB Summer Scorecard—to encourage tweens to monitor their physical activity

throughout the summer and try new ways to be physically active. The Scorecard had 24 squares that could be stamped each time a tween was physically active at one of the Summer Scorecard sites offering special deals to cardholders (e.g., free admission to public pools, reduced admission prices to commercial facilities, free sports clinics for beginners) (see Figure 2.1). Parents and other adults also could initial as many as 12 squares to acknowledge when tweens were physically active for at least 1 hour (see Figure 2.1). Tweens who filled all 24 squares before the end of summer received small prizes and gained entrance into a grand finale event in which they were entered into a drawing for physical activity–related prizes (e.g., bicycles, scooters, and karate lessons).

Price

Project activities were designed to overcome tweens' fear of embarrassment in front of their peers and their parents' fears about children's safety, and to provide free or discounted opportunities to be active.

Place

A wide variety of action outlets (special opportunities for tweens to be physically active with friends and try new activities) were offered around the community during the summer. Special efforts were made to provide free or low-cost opportunities in or near economically disadvantaged neighborhoods. Scorecards were distributed by public libraries and swimming pools, schools, McDonald's restaurants, the YMCA, day camps, faith-based organizations, and other nonprofit and private business partners.

Figure 2.1 Scorecard Tweens Used to Get Great Prizes and Deals

Promotion

Free and paid media were used to promote the program. The Scorecard and all promotional materials included the VERB logo and followed the national program's branding guidelines. In addition to the Scorecard intervention aimed at tweens, the marketing plan included plans to advocate for policy changes at the county and state level to increase funding for community facilities and mandate increased physical activity in public schools.

The coalition then created an implementation plan for the Scorecard and other related marketing interventions designed by the Tweens Nutrition and Fitness Coalition that served as a blueprint for program implementation. Additional information about the Scorecard program and information on how to implement it are available at the FPRC and Centers for Disease Control and Prevention (CDC) Web sites:

http://hsc.usf.edu/nocms/publichealth/prc/

http://www.cdc.gov/youthcampaign/partners/spotlights/lexington_spotlight.htminsert

Results

The Scorecard program was pilot tested in 2004 and implemented again in 2005 and 2006 in Lexington. It also has been adapted by 16 other communities in the United States to promote physical activity during the summer months, over the winter vacation, or during other time periods.[8] Although it has proven impossible to document the number of tweens who have participated in all Scorecard activities, a survey of 2,974 students conducted in 27 Lexington elementary schools in May 2005 revealed that 31.3% had participated during the summer of 2004. A count of the Scorecards entered into the grand finale drawings shows an increase from 335 in 2004 to 838 in 2005 and a slight decline to 738 in 2006. Telephone interviews conducted with 35 parents whose children participated in the 2005 summer program suggested that the program increased physical activity levels during the summer months and that these gains were sustained into the fall when parents were contacted. A survey of over 5,000 fourth- to eighth-graders who completed surveys in May 2006 showed that almost 59% of elementary school students and 61% of middle school students reported "having seen, read, or heard something about VERB Summer Scorecard" the previous summer. Of those who had heard about the Scorecard, 41.7% of elementary school students and 37% of middle school students said that they had filled out all or part of a Scorecard.

To examine the influence program participation may have had on physical activity, students who filled out all or part of a Scorecard were compared to those who did not complete a card. Results showed that students who participated in the Scorecard program were significantly more likely to have played the previous day than those who did not and also more likely to have tried a new activity in the last 2 months. The mean number of days of vigorous activity and the mean number of times a tween was active during the weekend were also significantly higher among those who filled out all or part of a card than among those who did not.

Finally, the coalition also was successful in advocating for increased funding for the county Parks and Recreation Department and the adoption and implementation of a state-of-the-art School Wellness Policy for the public school district. At the state level, the coalition played an instrumental role in passing some of the strongest school nutrition and physical activity legislation in the nation. As a result, Kentucky was ranked #1 in the nation in the *School Foods Report Card*, an evaluation of school food and beverage policies published by the Center for Science in the Public Interest (see report at http://cspinet.org/new/pdf/school_foods_report_card.pdf for more information).

In sum, the Lexington coalition has used social marketing to design a community-based intervention—the VERB Summer Scorecard—and modified state and local policies that hold great promise in the fight against childhood obesity.

MARKETING PLANNING: PROCESS AND INFLUENCES

To set the stage for developing a tactical social marketing plan, we begin with a description of the traditional marketing planning process, the evolution of the marketing concept, and a few of the most recent shifts in marketing management philosophy.

The Marketing Planning Process

In theory, there is a logical process to follow when developing a marketing plan—whether one for a for-profit corporation, nonprofit organization, or public sector agency. You begin with clarifying the purpose and focus for your plan; you move on to analyzing the current situation and environment, identifying target markets, establishing marketing objectives and goals, conducting research to deepen your understanding of your target audience, determining a desired positioning for the offer, and designing a strategic marketing mix (4Ps); and then you develop evaluation, budget, and implementation plans. Some conceptualize the process easier with these broader headings: Why are you doing this? Where are you today? Where do you want to go? How are you going to get there? How will you keep on track?

Evolution of the Marketing Concept

The cornerstone of the marketing concept is a customer-centered mind-set, one that sends marketers on a relentless pursuit to sense and satisfy target market wants and needs and to solve their problems—better than the competition. Marketers haven't always thought this way. Some still don't. This customer-centered focus didn't emerge as a strong marketing management philosophy until the 1980s and is contrasted with alternative philosophies in the following by Kotler and Keller.[9] We have added a few examples relevant for social marketers:

- *The Production Concept* is perhaps the oldest philosophy and holds that consumers will prefer products that are widely available and inexpensive, and therefore the organization's focus should be to keep costs down and access convenient. Early efforts to encourage condom use to prevent the spread of HIV/AIDS may have had this philosophical orientation, unfortunately falling on deaf ears for those who did not see this behavior as a social norm and feared their partner's rejection.

- *The Product Concept* holds that consumers will favor those products that offer the most quality, performance, or innovative features. The problem with this focus is that program and service managers often become caught up in a love affair with their product, neglecting to design and enhance their efforts based on customer wants and needs. It is otherwise known as the "build it and they will come" or "make it and it will sell" philosophy, one that may explain the challenges that community transit agencies face as they attempt to increase ridership on buses.

- *The Selling Concept* holds that consumers and businesses will probably not buy enough of the organization's products to meet goals if left alone, and as a result, the organization must undertake an aggressive selling and promotion effort. Communications (alone) encouraging adults to exercise and eat five or more servings of fruits and vegetables a day do not begin to address the barriers many in the target audience perceive—ones such as how to make time when holding down a full-time job or raising a family or simply not liking vegetables.

- *The Marketing Concept* is in sharp contrast to the product and selling concepts. Instead of a "make and sell" philosophy, it is a "sense-and-respond" orientation. Peter Drucker went so far as to proclaim, "The aim of marketing is to make selling superfluous. The aim of marketing is to know and understand the customer so well that the product or service fits him and sells itself."[10] If a city utility's natural yard care workshop is exciting, and better yet those who attend are able to keep their lawn weed-free without the use of harmful chemicals, they are bound to share their enthusiasm and this newfound resource with their neighbors—and go back for more!

- *The Holistic Marketing Concept* is a 21st-century approach, recognizing the need to have a more complete, cohesive philosophy that goes beyond traditional applications of the marketing concept. Three relevant components for social marketers include relationship marketing, integrated marketing, and internal marketing. The Farmers' Marketing Nutrition Program of the U.S. Department of Agriculture encourages clients in the Women, Infants, and Children (WIC) program to shop at farmers' markets for fresh, unprepared, locally grown fruits and vegetables. Keys to success include relationship building (e.g., counselors in WIC offices who work with clients to overcome barriers to shopping at the markets such as transportation), integrated marketing (e.g., farmers' stands at the market carry similar signage and messages regarding the program as clients see in WIC offices), and internal marketing (e.g., counselors in WIC offices are encouraged to visit the market themselves so they are more able to describe places to park and what clients are likely to find fresh that week).

Shifts in Marketing Management

Kotler and Keller also describe philosophical shifts in marketing management they believe smart companies have been making in the 21st century.[11] A few with relevance to social marketers in the planning process include the following:

- *From marketing does the marketing to everyone does the marketing*. Programs encouraging young partygoers to pick a designated driver are certainly supported (even funded) by more than public information officers within departments of transportation. Schools, parents, police officers, law enforcement, judges, health care providers, advertising agencies, bars, and alcohol beverage companies help spread the word and reinforce the program—even President Clinton was featured one year in public service announcements promoting the practice.

- *From organizing by product units to organizing by customer segments*. Clearly, an effective drowning prevention program plan would need to have separate strategies—even separate marketing plans—based on ages of children, with a potential separate focus on toddlers wearing life vests on beaches, young children taking swimming lessons, and teens knowing where they can buy cool life vests—ones that won't "ruin their tan."

- *From building brands through advertising to building brands through performance and integrated communications*. In the opening case story for this chapter, a national campaign called VERB– It's What You Do was mentioned, a campaign that, according to a 2006 article in the *Wall Street Journal,* not only had the "look and feel of slick ads from sports giants like Nike and Adidas" but also included unique interactive components. Five hundred thousand yellow balls were distributed at schools, camps, and family events around the country. Each 6-inch rubber ball was imprinted with a unique number, and kids were asked to play with the ball and then log on to www.verbnow.com, where they could fill out a blog about how they played with it. They were to then pass the ball on to a friend. The goal was to let kids track where their yellow ball went and who played with it. Follow-up surveys showed that 70% to 80% of schoolkids were aware of the VERB campaign, and, better yet, an article published in the medical journal *Pediatrics* reported that 9- and 10-year-old kids who had seen the VERB campaign reported one third more physical activity during their free time than kids who hadn't seen VERB.[12]

• *From focusing on profitable transactions to focusing on customer lifetime value.* We would consider the approach many city utilities take to increase recycling among residential households as one focused on building customer relationships and loyalty (to a cause). Many begin with just offering a container for recycling paper and then eventually offering those same households a separate container for glass and plastic. Some then take the next relationship-building step as they add containers for yard waste and food waste to the mix. A few are now providing pickup of used cooking oils, which can then be used to produce biodiesel fuel, and some cities (San Francisco for one) are considering collecting pet waste and turning it into methane to use for heating homes and generating electricity. At least one state (Minnesota) also suggests to customers that they put unwanted clean clothing and rags in a plastic trash bag and set it out for pickup on regular curbside recycling days.

• *From being local to being "glocal"—both global and local.* Efforts by the U.S. Environmental Protection Agency (EPA) to encourage households to use energy-saving appliances seems like a great example, where communications regarding ENERGY STAR® appliances and fixtures stress the link between home energy use and air pollution and at the same time provide detailed information on how these options can both save taxpayer dollars and lower household utility bills.

TEN STEPS TO DEVELOP A SOCIAL MARKETING PLAN

Our first of several primers in this book is presented in Table 2.1, outlining the 10 distinct and important steps that are described briefly in this chapter. Chapters 5–17 provide more detailed information on each step, and worksheets are also presented in Appendix A.

Although, for the most part, this outline mirrors marketing plans developed by product managers in for-profit organizations, three items in the model may jump out for some. First, that target markets are selected prior to establishing objectives and goals. In social marketing, our marketing objectives are to influence a behavior of a target market and therefore make it important to identify the target (e.g., seniors) prior to determining the specific desired behavior the plan will influence (e.g., join a walking group). Second, that the competition isn't identified in the situation analysis. Again, because we haven't decided at this point the specific behavior that will be influenced, we wait until Step 4, when we conduct audience research related to the desired behavior. Finally, that goals are the quantifiable measures of the plan (e.g., number of seniors you want to join a walking group) versus the broader purpose of the plan. In this model, the plan's purpose statement (e.g., increase physical activity among seniors) is included in Step 1. Certainly, labels for any part of the plan can and probably should be changed to fit the organization's culture and existing planning models. What is important is that each step is taken and developed sequentially.

Steps in the plan are described briefly in the following sections and are illustrated using excerpts from a marketing plan to reduce litter in Washington State.

Step 1: Describe the Plan Background, Purpose, and Focus

Begin by noting the social issue the plan will be addressing (e.g., climate change) and then summarize factors that have led to the development of the plan. What's the problem? What happened? It may include epidemiological, scientific, or other research data related to a public health crisis (e.g., increases in obesity), a safety concern (e.g., increases in cell phone use while driving), an environmental threat (e.g., water supply), or need for community involvement (e.g., blood donations). It might have been precipitated by an unusual event such as a tsunami or may simply be fulfilling an organization's mandate or mission (e.g., sustainable seafood).

A purpose statement is then developed that reflects the benefit of a successful campaign, and then a focus is selected to narrow the scope of the plan, choosing from the vast number of potential options to contribute to the plan's purpose (e.g., improved water quality) the one the plan will address (e.g., use of pesticides).

Litter Plan Excerpt: Every year in Washington State, over 16 million pounds of "stuff" are tossed and blown onto interstate, state, and county roads. Another 6 million pounds are tossed into parks and recreation areas. Programs funded through the Department of Ecology (Ecology) spend over $4 million each year, but staff estimate that only 25%–35% gets picked up. Litter creates an eyesore for motorists, harms wildlife and their habitats, and is a potential hazard for motorists, who may be struck by anything from a lit cigarette to an empty bottle of beer, even a bottle of "trucker's pee." In 2001, Ecology developed a 3-year social marketing plan with a *purpose* to decrease littering with a *focus* on intentional littering on roadways.

Step 2: Conduct a Situation Analysis

Relative to the purpose and focus of the plan, a quick audit of factors and forces in the internal and external environment is conducted—ones anticipated to have some impact on or relevance for subsequent planning decisions. Often referred to as a SWOT

Table 2.1   Social Marketing Planning Primer

Executive Summary

Brief summary highlighting plan purpose, target audiences, major marketing objectives and goals, desired positioning, marketing mix strategies (4Ps), and evaluation, budget, and implementation plans.

1.0 Background, Purpose, and Focus

2.0 Situation Analysis

1.1 SWOT: strengths, weaknesses, opportunities, threats

1.2 Past or similar efforts: activities, results, and lessons learned

3.0 Target Market Profile

3.1 Size

3.2 Demographics, geographics, related behaviors, psychographics

3.3 Stage of change (readiness to "buy")

4.0 Marketing Objectives and Goals

4.1 Social marketing objectives: behavior, knowledge, and beliefs

4.2 Goals: measurable and time sensitive

5.0 Target Market Barriers, Benefits, and the Competition

5.1 Perceived barriers to desired behavior

5.2 Potential benefits for desired behavior

5.3 Competing behaviors

6.0 Positioning Statement

How you want the target audience to see the desired behavior relative to competing behaviors

7.0 Marketing Mix Strategies (4Ps)

7.1 Product:
Core: benefit to target market of desired behavior
Actual: desired behavior and any name and sponsors
Augmented: tangible objects and services

7.2 Price:
Monetary fees, incentives, and disincentives
Nonmonetary incentives and disincentives

7.3 Place:
Where and when to promote that the target market perform the behavior
Where and when to acquire any tangible products and services

7.4 Promotion:
Messages
Messengers
Communication Channels

8.0 Evaluation Plan

8.1 Purpose and audience for evaluation

8.2 What will be measured: output/process, outcome, and impact measures

8.3 How and when measures will be taken

9.0 Budget

9.1 Costs for implementing marketing plan, including evaluation

9.2 Any anticipated incremental revenues or cost savings

10.0 Implementation Plan

Who will do what, when

(strengths, weaknesses, opportunities, and threats) analysis, internal (organizational) *strengths* to maximize and *weaknesses* to minimize are recognized, including factors such as available resources, expertise, management support, current alliances and partners, delivery system capabilities, agency reputation, and issue priority. Then a similar list is made of external forces in the marketplace that represent either *opportunities* your plan should take advantage of or *threats* it should prepare for. These forces are typically not within the marketer's control but must be taken into account, with major categories, including cultural, technological, natural, demographic, economic, political, and legal forces.[13]

Time taken at this point to contact colleagues, query Listservs, and conduct a literature, even Google, search for similar campaigns will be time well spent. Lessons learned from others regarding what worked and what didn't should help guide plan development, as would a reflection on prior similar campaigns conducted by the organization sponsoring this new effort.

Litter Plan Excerpt: The greatest strengths going into the campaign included the state's significant fines for littering, social marketing expertise on the team, management support, and other state agency support, including critical involvement and buy-in from the state patrol and Department of Licensing. Weaknesses to minimize included limited financial resources, competing priorities faced by law enforcement (traffic safety issues such as drinking and driving or use of seatbelts), and lack of adequate litter containers in public areas.

Opportunities to take advantage of included litterers not being aware of the significant fines for littering, strong environmental ethic of many citizens, and many businesses who were "part of the problem" that could be potential campaign sponsors (e.g., fast-food establishments, beverage companies, mini-marts). Threats to prepare for included the argument that litter was not considered a priority issue and litterers are not motivated by environmental concerns.

Step 3: Select Target Markets

In this critical step, the bull's-eye for your marketing efforts is selected. A rich description of your target market is provided using characteristics such as stage of change (readiness to buy), demographics, geographics, related behaviors, psychographics, and size of the market. A marketing plan ideally focuses on a primary target market, although additional secondary markets (e.g., strategic partners, target market opinion leaders) are often identified and strategies included to influence them as well. As you will read further in Chapter 6, arriving at this decision is a three-step process that involves first segmenting the market (population) into similar groups, evaluating segments based on a set of criteria, and then choosing one or more as the focal point for positioning and marketing mix strategies.

Litter Plan Excerpt: Surveys indicate that some of us (about 25%) would never consider littering. Some of us (about 25%) litter most of the time. Almost half of us litter occasionally but can be persuaded not to.[14] There were two major audiences for the campaign: litterers and nonlitterers. Target markets for littering include the five behavior-related segments creating the majority of intentional litter on roadways: (a) motorists or passengers who toss (1) cigarette butts, (2) alcoholic beverage containers, (3) food wrappers and other beverage containers out the window, and (b) those who drive pickup trucks and are (1) not properly covering or securing their loads and (2) not cleaning out the back of their pickup trucks prior to driving on roadways. Campaign strategies were to also be developed and aimed at nonlitterers traveling on Washington State roadways.

Step 4: Set Objectives and Goals

Social marketing plans always include a *behavior* objective—something we want to influence the target market to do. It may be something we want our target audience to accept (e.g., start composting food waste), reject (e.g., purchasing a gas blower), modify (e.g., water deeply and less frequently), or abandon (e.g., using fertilizers with harmful herbicides). Often our research indicates that there may also be something the market needs to know or believe in order to be motivated to act. *Knowledge objectives* include information or facts we want the market to be aware of (e.g., motor oil poured down the street drain goes directly to the lake)—ones that might make them more willing to perform the desired behavior (e.g., recycle motor oil). *Belief objectives* relate more to feelings and attitudes. Home gardeners may know the pesticide they are using is harmful, even that it works its way into rivers and streams, but may believe that using it once or twice a year won't make "that much difference."

This is also the point in the marketing plan where we establish quantifiable measures (goals) relative to our objectives. Ideally, goals are established for behavior objectives, as well as any knowledge and belief objectives—ones that are specific, measurable, attainable, relevant, and time sensitive (S.M.A.R.T.). You should recognize that what you determine here will guide your subsequent decisions regarding marketing mix strategies. It will also have significant implications for budgets and will provide clear direction for evaluation measures later in the planning process.

Litter Plan Excerpt: Campaign strategies were developed to support three separate objectives: (1) a short-term objective to create *awareness* that there are significant fines associated with littering and that there is a (new) toll-free number to report littering, (2) a longer-term objective to convince litterers to *believe* that their littering will be noticed and they could be caught, and (3) a long-term objective to influence litterers to *change their behaviors:* to dispose of litter properly, cover and secure pickup truck loads, and clean out the back of their trucks prior to driving on roadways. Telephone surveys to establish a baseline of public awareness and beliefs about the littering and field research that measured current quantities and types of litter were conducted.[15]

Step 5: Identify the Competition and
Target Market Barriers and Motivators

At this point you know who you want to influence and what you want them to do. You (theoretically) even know how many, or what percentage, of your target audience you are hoping to persuade. Before rushing to develop a positioning and marketing mix for this audience, however, you take the time, effort, and resources to understand what your target market is currently doing or prefers to do (the competition) and what real and/or perceived barriers they have to this desired behavior and what would motivate them to "buy" it. In other words, what do *they* think of your idea? What are some of the reasons they are not currently doing this or don't want to? What do they come up with when asked what would it take for them to do it? Do they think any of your potential strategies would work for them? Their answers should be treated like gold and considered a gift.

Litter Plan Excerpt: Focus groups with motorists who reported littering (yes, they came) indicated several perceived barriers to the desired behaviors of disposing of litter properly, covering pickup loads, and cleaning out backs of trucks: "I don't want to keep the cigarette butt in the car. It stinks." "If I get caught with an open container of beer in my car, I'll get a hefty fine. I'd rather take the chance and toss it." "I didn't even know there was stuff in the back of my truck. Someone in the parking lot keeps using it as a garbage can!" "The cords I have found to secure my load are just not that effective." "What's the problem, anyway? Doesn't this give prisoners a way to do community service?" And what would motivate them? "You'd have to convince me that anyone notices my littering and that I could get caught." "I had no idea the fine for littering a lit cigarette butt could be close to a thousand dollars!" (Notice their concerns were not about helping keep Washington green!)

Step 6: Craft a Desired Positioning

In brief, a positioning statement describes how you want your target audience to see the behavior you want them to buy—relative to competing behaviors. Branding is one strategy to help secure this desired position. Both the positioning statement and brand identity are inspired by your description of your target audience and their list of competitors, barriers, and motivators to action. It will also guide the development of a strategic marketing mix. The theory was first popularized in the 1980s by two advertising executives, Al Ries and Jack Trout, who contended that positioning starts with a product, but it isn't what you do to a product. "Positioning is what you do to the mind of the prospect. That is, you position the product in the mind of the prospect."[16] We would add "where you want it to be."[17]

Litter Plan Excerpt: We want motorists to believe that they will be noticed and caught when littering and that fines are steeper than they thought. In the end, we want them to believe disposing of litter properly is a better, especially cheaper, option.

Step 7: Develop a Strategic Marketing Mix (4Ps)

This section of the plan describes your product, price, place, and promotional strategies.

It is the blend of these elements that constitutes your marketing mix, also thought of as the determinants (independent variables) used to influence behaviors (the dependent variable). Be sure to present the marketing mix in the sequence that follows, beginning with the product and ending with a promotional strategy. After all, the promotional tool is the one you count on to ensure that target markets know about your product, its price, and how to access it. These decisions obviously, then, need to be made prior to promotional planning.

Product

Describe core, actual, and augmented product levels. The core product consists of benefits the target audience values that they believe they will experience as a result of acting and ones that you will highlight. Your list of motivators and positioning statement is a great resource for developing this component of the product platform. The *actual product* describes the desired behavior, usually in more specific terms. The *augmented product* refers to any additional tangible objects and/or services that you will include in your offer or that will be promoted to the target audience.

Litter Plan Excerpt: It was determined that a new service, a toll-free number, would be launched for motorists witnessing people throwing trash from vehicles or losing materials from unsecured loads. When they call the hotline, they will be asked to report the license number, description of the vehicle, time of day, type of litter, whether it was thrown from the passenger or driver's side of the car, and approximate location. Within a couple of days, the registered owner of the car will receive a letter from the state patrol, alerting the owner, for example, that "a citizen noticed a lit cigarette butt being tossed out the driver's side of your car at 3 p.m. on Interstate 5, near the University District. This is to inform you that if we had seen you, we would have pulled you over and issued a ticket for $1,025." All "Litter and it will hurt" campaign materials, from road signs (see Figure 2.2) to litterbags, stickers, and posters feature the campaign slogan and the litter hotline telephone number.

Figure 2.2 Road Sign for Reporting Littering[18]

Price

Mention here any program-related *monetary costs* (fees) the target audience will pay (e.g., cost of a gun lockbox) and, if offered, any *monetary incentives* such as discount coupons or rebates that you will make available. Also note any *monetary disincentives* that will be emphasized (e.g., fines for not buckling up), any *nonmonetary incentives* such as public recognition (e.g., plaques for backyard sanctuaries), and *nonmonetary disincentives* such as negative public visibility (e.g., publication of names of elected officials owing back taxes). As you will read in Chapter 11 on pricing, arriving at these strategies begins with identifying major costs the target market associates with adopting the behavior—both monetary (e.g., paying for a commercial car wash versus doing it at home) and nonmonetary (e.g., time it takes to drive to the car wash).

Litter Plan Excerpt: Fines for littering were to be highlighted in a variety of communication channels with an emphasis on targeted behaviors: lit cigarette butts ($1,025), food or beverage container ($103), unsecured load ($194), and illegal dumping ($1,000–$5,000 + jail time), with notes that fines are subject to change and may vary locally. The image in Figure 2.3 was used on billboards, posters, and litterbags.

Place

In social marketing, place is primarily where and when the target market will perform the desired behavior and/or acquire any campaign-related tangible objects (e.g., rain barrels offered by a city utility) or receive any services (e.g., tobacco quitline hours and days of the week) associated with the campaign. Place is often referred to as your delivery system or distribution channel, and you will include here any strategies related to managing these channels. These are very distinct from communication channels where promotional messages appear and are delivered (e.g., billboards, outreach workers, Web sites).

Figure 2.3 Washington State's Litter Campaign Focused on a Hotline and Stiff Fines[19]

Litter Plan Excerpt: The hotline will be available 24 hours a day, 7 days a week. Litterbags (printed with fines for littering) were to be distributed at a variety of locations, including fast-food restaurant windows, car rental agencies, and vehicle licensing offices. A litterbag was also enclosed with each letter sent in response to a litter hotline report.

Promotion

In this section, you will describe persuasive communication strategies, covering decisions related to *key messages* (what you want to communicate), *messengers* (any spokespersons, sponsors, partners, or actors you use to deliver messages), and *communication channels* (where promotional messages will appear). Decisions regarding slogans and taglines will be included as well. Information and decisions to this point will guide your development of this promotional plan—one that will ensure your target markets know about the offer (product, price, place), believe they will experience the benefits you promise, and are inspired to act.

Litter Plan Excerpt: Communication channels selected to spread the "Litter and it will hurt" message included roadway signs, television, radio, publicity, videos, special events, Web sites, and messages on state collateral pieces, including litterbags, posters, stickers, and decals. There were even special signs to be placed at trucker weigh stations targeting one of the state's "most disgusting" forms of litter—an estimated 25,000 jugs of urine found on the roadsides each year, (see Figure 2.4).

Figure 2.4 Washington State's Litter Poster at Truck Weigh Stations[20]

Step 8: Outline a Plan for Monitoring and Evaluation

Your evaluation plan outlines what measures will be used to evaluate the success of your effort and how and when these measurements will be taken. It is derived after first clarifying the purpose and audience for the evaluation and referring back to goals that were established for the campaign—the desired levels of changes in behavior, knowledge, and beliefs established in Step 4. Measures typically fall into one of three categories: *output* measures (campaign activities), *outcome* measures (target market responses and changes in knowledge, beliefs, and behavior), and *impact* measures (contributions to the plan purpose such as improved water quality).

Litter Plan Excerpt: A baseline survey of Washington State residents is planned to measure and then track (a) awareness of stiff fines associated with littering and (b) awareness of the toll-free number for reporting littering. Internal records will be used to assess the number of calls to the hotline, and periodic litter composition surveys will be used to measure changes in targeted categories of roadway litter.

Step 9: Establish Budgets and Find Funding Sources

On the basis of draft product benefits and features, price incentives, distribution channels, proposed promotions, and the evaluation plan, funding requirements will be summarized and compared with available and potential funding sources. Outcomes at this step may necessitate revisions of strategies, target audience, and goals or the need to secure additional funding sources. Only a final budget is presented in this section, delineating secured funding sources and reflecting any contributions from partners.

Litter Plan Excerpt: Major costs will be associated with campaign advertising (television, radio, and billboards). Additional major costs will include signage at governmental facilities and operating the toll-free litter hotline number. Funding for litterbag printing and distribution and retail signage is anticipated to be provided by media partners and corporate sponsors, who will also augment advertising media buys.

Step 10: Complete an Implementation Plan

The plan is wrapped up with a document that specifies *who* will do *what, when,* and for *how much.* It transforms the heretofore marketing strategies into specific actions. Some consider this section "the real marketing plan," as it provides a clear picture of marketing activities (outputs), responsibilities, time frames, and budgets. Some even use this as a stand-alone piece they can then share with important internal groups. Typically, detailed activities are provided for the first year of a campaign, with broader references for subsequent years.

Litter Plan Excerpt: Three phases were identified for this 3-year campaign. In summary, first-year efforts are concentrated on awareness building. Years 2 and 3 will sustain this effort, as well as add elements that are key for belief and behavior change.

A news release from the Department of Ecology in May 2005 regarding the results of Washington State's litter prevention campaign touted the headline "Ounce of prevention is worth 4 million pounds of litter." The results from a litter survey in 2004 found a decline from 8,322 tons to 6,315 tons (24%) compared to a similar survey conducted in 1999. This reduction of more than 2,000 tons represented 4 million pounds less litter on Washington's roadways. And calls to the hotline were averaging 15,000 a year.

WHY IS A SYSTEMATIC, SEQUENTIAL PLANNING PROCESS IMPORTANT?

Only through the systematic process of clarifying your plan's *purpose and focus* and *analyzing the marketplace* are you able to select an appropriate target market for your efforts. Only through taking the time to *understand your target market* are you able to establish realistic *objectives and goals.* Only through developing an *integrated strategy* will you create real behavior change, an approach that recognizes that it usually takes more than communications (promotion) and that you need to establish what product benefits you will be promising, what tangible objects and services you should offer, what pricing incentives and disincentives it will take, and how to make access easy. Only by taking time up front to establish how you will measure your performance will you ensure that this critical step is budgeted for and implemented.

The temptation, and often the practice, is to go straight to advertising or promotional ideas and strategies. This begs questions such as these:

- How can you know whether ads on the sides of buses (a communication channel) are a good idea if you don't know how long the message needs to be?
- How can you know your slogan (message) if you don't know what you are selling (product)?
- How can you know how to position your product if you don't know what your audience perceives as the benefits and costs of their current behavior compared with the behavior you are promoting?

Although planning is sequential, it might be more accurately described as spiral rather than linear in nature. Each step should be considered a draft, and the planner needs to be flexible, recognizing that there may be a good reason to go back and adjust a prior step before completing the plan. For example,

- Research with target markets may reveal that goals are too ambitious or that one of the target markets should be dropped, as you may not be able to meet their unique needs or overcome the specific barriers to change with the resources you have.
- What looked like ideal communication channels might turn out to be cost prohibitive or not cost effective when more carefully examined while preparing the budget.

WHERE DOES MARKETING RESEARCH FIT IN THE PLANNING PROCESS?

You may have questions at this point as to where marketing research fits into this process, other than at the step noted to conduct research regarding barriers and motivators. As you will read further in Chapter 4, and as is evident in Figure 2.5, research has a role to play when developing each step. And properly focused marketing research can make the difference between a brilliant plan and a mediocre one. It is at the core of success at every phase of this planning process, as it provides critical insights into the target market, the marketplace, and organizational realities. For those concerned (already) with resources available for research, we will also discuss in Chapter 4 Alan Andreasen's book *Marketing Research That Won't Break the Bank*.[21]

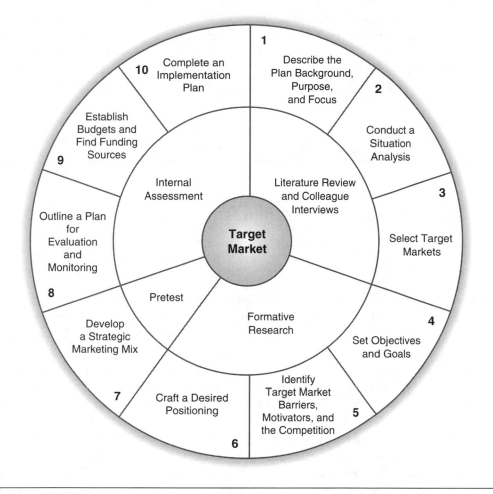

Figure 2.5   Summary of Marketing Planning Steps and Research Input

Chapter Summary

Marketing planning is a systematic process, and a 10-step model is recommended for developing social marketing plans. You begin with clarifying the purpose and focus for your plan; you move on to analyzing the current situation and environment, identifying target markets, establishing marketing objectives and goals, understanding your target audience's position, determining a desired positioning for the offer, designing a strategic marketing mix (4Ps), and then developing evaluation, budget, and implementation plans.

Although planning is sequential, the process is more accurately described as spiral rather than linear—a draft the first time around—as you may need to go back and adjust a prior step before completing the plan. Given the customer-centric nature of all great marketing programs, planning efforts will revolve around the target market, and research—both external and internal—will be essential to your success.

MARKETING DIALOGUE

Social Marketing Contributes to Social Good
"Good" Defined by Whom?

Most agree that social marketing is a technology that is used to influence behaviors that then benefit the individual and/or the society. What causes concern—even fury—is whether we should still call it social marketing if we (or even you) don't agree that the intended behaviors are good for the individual or society. Who gets to define good? Excerpts from the Social Marketing Listserv in 2006 present varied perspectives.

Many, like social marketing consultant Craig Lefebvre, say, "It is in the eye of the beholder. What I consider to be an absolute right and therefore worthy of extensive publicly funded social marketing campaigns, you may consider to be an absolute wrong. Organ donation is an absolute wrong for those whose religious beliefs preclude the desecration of bodies yet it is considered an important cause worthy of social marketing dollars by those not constrained by the same belief structure."[22]

Alan Andreasen's comments focused on the role of the social marketing consultant versus the client or funder. "We need to be clear that social marketers are 'hired guns' (excuse the metaphor). That is, give us a behavior you want influenced and we have some very good ways of making it happen. Each of us is free to work on behavior-influence challenges with which we feel comfortable and 'comfort' is both a matter of personal ethics and a matter of expertise. The decision about which behaviors ought to be influenced is not ours to make. Clients, or even societies or governments, make those judgments."[23]

Others, like Elisabeth Gleckler in Louisiana, expressed discomfort with the "neutral hammer tool of value-free hired guns" and suggested, "A good check and balance would be the inclusion of the 'target adopter' in the planning, implementation, and hopefully evaluation of the social marketing endeavor."[24] Additional ideas mentioned for deciding if the campaign is for good, and therefore should be considered and labeled as social marketing, would be to use public consensus (e.g., reducing drunk driving) or the U.N. Universal Declaration of Human Rights as a baseline (www.unhchr.ch).

CHAPTER 3

Discovering Keys to Success

We recognize that good health is the product of many complex factors—including Government policy, commercial marketing, education, and wealth—as well as individual lifestyle choices, and progress will depend on action on all these fronts. We will continue to seek the Holy Grail of joined-up public health policy.

—Gerard Hastings[1]

For a variety of reasons, social marketers have a tough job. You are (or will be) tackling huge social issues that have been around for decades, such as HIV/AIDS, teen pregnancy, malaria, senior falls, water quality, air pollution, traffic injuries, and colonies of feral cats. Your goliath competition (e.g., good-tasting trans fat, the tobacco industry, MTV, the status quo) usually have more resources, experience, expertise, distribution channels, and fans than you do. On top of that, you don't always (even often) have something you can give your customer in return for the exchange, especially in the near term. Your marketplace is diverse, and yet you may be forced to be equitable with your services, making them known and available to everyone, especially the hardest to reach. And to achieve real change, you can't usually do it on your own. You need partners in the legislature, school districts, law enforcement, local government, health care industry, and the corporate world—ones who take additional money, time, and patience to reach and influence.

This chapter presents 15 principles to make this job a little easier and to increase your chances of success. Some are simple, commonsense approaches. Others will take practice. Many are backed by theories that will be elaborated upon in subsequent chapters.

Our introductory case from the United Kingdom serves well to remind us of the role social marketing can play upstream—especially when using principles for success.

Competitive Analysis: A Fat Chance Pays Off (2006)

GERARD HASTINGS AND LAURA McDERMOTT

Institute for Social Marketing, U.K.

Background and Situation

Children's eating habits are causing as much concern in the United Kingdom as in the United States. The National Diet and Nutrition Survey conducted in 2000 reported that a vast majority of British children aged 4 to 18 years consume more than the recommended amount of saturated fat, sugar, and salt.[2] The Chief Medical Officer's report confirms that between 1996 and 2001, the number of overweight children between 6 and 15 years of age increased by 7% and obesity rates increased by 3.5%.[3]

The immediate response from social marketers might be to develop suitable healthy eating programs. However, *competitive analysis* is a valuable tool for social as well as commercial marketers, and this suggests that part of the problem here might be the influence of food promotion. Are British kids eating more energy-dense foods because the fast-food industry is actively encouraging them to do so? If the answer is yes, the best social marketing solution may be to constrain this unhealthy promotion, rather than try and mitigate it with countervailing activity.

The first need, then, was to review the evidence base around what, if any, impact food promotion has on children's dietary knowledge and behavior. The Institute for Social Marketing (http://www.ism.stir.ac.uk) was commissioned to do this by the U.K. government's Food Standards Agency (FSA).

Target Audience

This issue is an extremely contentious one. On one hand, the nongovernmental organization (NGO) community was adamant that food promotion was part of the obesity problem; on the other, the food and advertising industry argued strongly that it was not. This debate was taking place in very public forums, especially the media, so the general public also had a keen interest in the issue.

In reality, however, our review had just three key stakeholder targets: politicians, public health professionals (especially the FSA), and Ofcom, the U.K. body responsible for regulating food advertising. Their needs and the benefits they sought from the review are displayed in Table 3.1.

Objectives

The aim was to conduct a rigorous review of the research literature that would provide

Table 3.1   Stakeholder Needs and Benefits

Stakeholder	*Needs*	*Benefits sought from the ISM review*
Politicians	• Effective policies to combat childhood obesity • A political context that permitted enlightened debate	An objective, rigorous, and incontrovertible answer to the question: *What, if any, impact does food promotion have on children's dietary knowledge and behavior?*
The advertising regulatory body, Ofcom	• Recommendations and advice on policies • Governed by laws, political realities, public sentiments, budgets, licensing, etc.	
The Food Standards Agency and other public health professionals	• An intellectual context in which the role of food promotion was clearly delineated	

stakeholders with a reliable answer to two questions:

1. What is the extent and nature of food promotion to children?

2. What effect, if any, is this having on children's food knowledge, preferences, and behavior?

The review should be capable of withstanding the muscular scrutiny and criticism that would be leveled at it by vested interests, regardless of what it found. It should provide a firm foundation upon which a justifiable policy response could be built.

Strategy

For all three stakeholders, the vital need was for rigorous and reliable results. The medical community, which also has to make challenging, consensual decisions about a contested evidence base, has responded by developing the concept of "evidence-based decision making."[4] This is built around the "systematic review [SR],"[5] which strengthens traditional literature reviewing by making it comprehensive, rigorous, and transparent. The process starts by laying down a clear protocol for searching all relevant databases, the content and quality criteria that will be used to determine inclusion in the review, and the methods used to assess the relative quality of the included studies and their synthesis into conclusions. The contents of this protocol are included in the completed review and can therefore be subjected to detailed scrutiny and, if necessary, replicated by other researchers.

Our review adopted SR methods—the first time they had been applied to a marketing problem. These were further strengthened by consistent peer review, which scrutinized our work on no less than seven separate occasions.

In fact, we conducted two systematic reviews: The first examined the extent and nature of food promotion to children, and the second explored evidence on whether or not food promotion affects children's food knowledge, attitudes, and behavior.

Results

This first U.K. systematic review of the research literature found the following:

- *There is a great deal of food advertising to children*: Food is promoted to children more than any other type of product, with the exception of toys at Christmas.
- *The advertised diet is less healthy than the recommended one*: Television, the principal medium for food promotion, mostly supports the "big five" (presugared breakfast cereals, soft drinks, confectionary, savory snacks, and fast food) food sectors.
- *Children enjoy and engage with food promotion*: Fun, fantasy, and taste are the principal creative platforms, not health and nutrition.
- *Food promotion is having an effect:* It is affecting the food children express a preference for, buy, and ask their parents to buy. Weaker evidence also suggests that food promotion impacts children's long-term diet and health.
- *The effect is independent of other factors and operates at both a brand and category level:* Advertising can shift children's preferences not just between brands (e.g., Kit Kat versus Hershey) but also food categories (e.g., confectionary versus apples).

There were many challenges to these conclusions. The most sustained attack came from the Food Advertising Unit (FAU) of the Advertising Association, which commissioned both a rival review, which argued that commercial promotion of foods does *not* influence children,[6] and a critique of our review.[7]

The FSA assembled a seminar of leading academics under the chairmanship of Professor Nicholas Mackintosh of Cambridge University to discuss the conflicting assessments. The limited coverage of the FAU review was noted, as well as its contradiction of a review conducted by the same author in 1996 and its rejection of virtually all social science research as either too artificial (experimental studies) or having too little control (observational studies).[8] The seminar concluded: "It was not felt that further research was necessarily required as, on the balance of evidence, the Hastings review had provided sufficient evidence to indicate a causal link between promotional activity and children's food knowledge, preferences and behaviours."[9]

The criticisms of the Institute for Social Marketing review by Paliwoda and Crawford were also considered by the academic seminar[10] and were not felt to be substantiated. It was concluded that the review was "honest to the reality of the research landscape" and that the critique "did not make a sufficiently strong case to warrant re-examination of the conclusions."[11]

The review had stood up to scrutiny.

Ultimately, however, the proof of the review, as with any social marketing effort, is in whether it makes a difference. Has it changed behavior? In the case of our review, the answer is yes. Ofcom has accepted its findings and used them to guide their decision to introduce tighter regulation of food advertising on television. Specifically, they have now proposed to ban the advertising of energy-dense foods such as burgers and fried chicken "in and around all children's programming and on dedicated children's channels as well as in youth-oriented and adult programmes which attract a significantly higher than average proportion of viewers under the age of 16."[12]

Nonbroadcast advertising channels have also agreed to abide by these restrictions.

For us social marketers, it also reinforces the value of competitive analysis.[13]

FIFTEEN PRINCIPLES FOR SUCCESS

The sequence of the presentation of 15 principles for success is deliberate. It follows the marketing planning model outline, offering one or more principles to keep in mind when developing the related step in the marketing plan. Each is illustrated with an inspirational example.

Principle #1: Take Advantage of Prior and Existing Successful Campaigns

Beginning a social marketing campaign planning process with a search for similar efforts around the world is one of the best investments of a planner's time. Benefits can be substantial, including learning from the successes and failures of others, having access to existing research and detailed information on market segmentation and ideal targets, finding innovative and cost-effective strategies, and discovering ideas and materials for creative executions. And because most often social marketers are working with or for public sector agencies, chances are you may even be able to borrow campaigns that others have spent time and money to develop. The following exemplifies this opportunity.

Example: Pet Waste

Dog waste is more than a smelly and unsightly menace. It is also an environmental pollutant, with estimates that one average-sized dog dropping produces 3 billion fecal coliform bacteria.[14] When left on trails, sidewalks, streets, and grassy areas, it is then flushed into the nearest waterway when it rains. Individual pet owners may not think one little pile could be a problem, but when you multiply that by several thousand dogs in most communities, the impact on lakes, streams, rivers, and oceans is significant and creates a public health and wildlife hazard—on a daily basis.

Cities around the world seem united in their efforts to influence pet owners, with many campaigns using a common slogan—"Scoop the Poop"—circling the globe from Anchorage, Alaska, to Geelong, Australia, to Bristol, England, to Burlington, Vermont, to Charleston, South Carolina, to Austin, Texas, to Everett, Washington. Many campaigns go beyond a "mere" slogan, counting on additional tools in the marketer's toolbox as well. In Austin, Texas, for example, efforts are supported by an $86 fine (price). The city's Watershed Protection and Development

Figure 3.1 One City's Display of the Scoop the Poop Slogan Used Around the World

Review and Parks & Recreation departments makes the process of picking up for a pet "painless" by providing Mutt Mitts (product) in some 115 Scoop the Poop boxes throughout the city (place). In 2004, 540,000 Mutt Mitts were distributed. At an approximate 0.25 pounds of pet waste per bag, they believe they removed an estimated 135,000 pounds of waste and the related bacteria from watersheds in that year alone (see Figure 3.1).[15]

Principle #2: Start With Target Markets Most Ready for Action

In a nutshell, the social marketer's job is to influence some number of people to do some desired behavior, including potentially abstaining from an undesirable one. It would follow, then, that efforts and resources should be directed toward those market segments most likely to buy (the low-hanging fruit) rather than those least likely (hardest to reach and move).[16] Campaigns will increase their chances of success (actual number of behaviors "sold") when they start with market segments most ready for action, those that have one or more of the following ideal characteristics:

- Have a want or need the proposed behavior will satisfy or a problem it will solve (e.g., households wanting to reduce their water bill and contribute to sustainable water supplies)
- Have the knowledge/information regarding the benefits of the behavior and the costs of current alternative behaviors (e.g., hearing on the news about the new $86 fine for not picking up after a pet)
- Have the belief that they can actually perform the behavior and that they will experience important benefits (e.g., that exercising five times a week, 30 minutes at a time, can improve sleep)
- Are engaged in the desired behavior, but not on a regular basis, and have the perception of some initial benefit (e.g., trying to quit smoking)

The following example illustrates the increased marketing and operational efficiencies this organization achieves by focusing on a very attractive segment.

Example: Blood Donations

The Puget Sound Blood Center defines marketing as relationship building and places the highest value on the repeat donor segment, for good reasons. Their experience shows that it costs 10 times as much to acquire a new donor as it does to keep an established one. They know that if they can persuade just 10% of all donors to give blood just one more time each year, they will reach their annual donation goals, increase operational efficiencies, and reduce expenditures. They have identified clear benefits of targeting current donors: they are the most likely future donors, they have a lower reaction risk, they have a higher blood-usability rate, collection is more efficient, and they are the most credible recruiters of new donors.

Marketing tactics to increase repeat donations are aggressive and persuasive. Efforts are focused on making the first experience a pleasant one. Volunteers are the first and last persons a donor sees, and their sincerity is clear. After giving blood and sitting with a cup of juice and a cookie, donors are asked by volunteers whether they want to set up the next appointment, usually 2 months later. A reminder call or e-mail is placed the week prior to the next appointment.

First-time donors are mailed a donor card along with a message of thanks (scc Figure 3.2). After 56 days, they are called by a telerecruiting team, who know from the information on computer screens that their previous donations were their first with the blood center and recognize the donors for that.

In 2005, this center attracted 208,000 people to give blood, and 54% of those were repeat donors. Over time, 50% of first-time donors, on average, have become repeat donors, implying a 50% customer retention rate.[17]

The only lifesaving technique that involves eating a cookie.

Figure 3.2 Postcard Used to Thank and Remind Donors[18]

Principle #3: Promote Single, Simple, Doable Behaviors—One at a Time

In this world of information and advertising clutter, you often have only a few moments to speak with your target audience before they switch channels, click the mouse, hang up, leave the room, or turn the page. A simple, clear, action-oriented message is most likely to support your target market to adopt, reject, modify, or abandon a specific behavior. Your message should help the target audience know exactly what to do and whether it has been accomplished. Remember, as well, that if you are targeting those (most) ready for action, you won't have to spend as much time, money, and space convincing them they should do something. They are probably just waiting for clear instructions.[19]

Example: Crime Prevention

Back in 1980, a dog in a rumpled trench coat said, "You don't know me yet. But you will." Since then McGruff the Crime Dog™ has reached millions of people, addressing both persistent crimes and some of the latest crime trends and concerns, always giving Americans clear instructions on how to "Take a Bite Out of Crime." Through television, radio, and print commercials, activity books, video games, trading cards, live appearances, newspaper articles, and more, McGruff encourages Americans to take commonsense steps to reduce crime.

Going way beyond a "be safe" message, McGruff promotes simple, doable behaviors, from home security to bullying prevention for kids and parents to preventing identity theft and improving school safety. And in October 2006, news media across the country announced that McGruff is now fighting one of the largest safety problems, cyber crime. Through his new campaign, "Take a Bite Out of Cyber Crime," McGruff delivers information to protect home and business computers. His accompanying Web site, www.bytecrime.org, gives tips like "Be certain to install antivirus and firewall software" (see Figure 3.3).[20]

According to the National Crime Prevention Council, which serves as the day-to-day manager of the campaign, McGruff messages are catching on. "In 2004, violent and property crimes remained at their lowest levels since 1973 and criminal victimization is down. Today three out of four Americans believe they can personally do something to prevent crime. And most people know of McGruff, including nearly three quarters (73%) of adults, 79% of teens, and 76% of children 9 to 11."[21]

Figure 3.3 McGruff's Latest Effort to Combat Growing Plague of Computer Viruses, Worms, Spam, Spyware, Identity Theft, and Online Predators Includes a Web Site: www.bytecrime.org

Principle #4: Identify and Remove Barriers to Behavior Change

As mentioned in an earlier chapter, a list of concerns and real reasons why your target market members perceive they can't or don't want to do your desired behavior (their barriers) should be considered a gift. After all, when you have this, you are more likely to know what to say to them, what to do for them, and/or what to give them that will make it more likely they will adopt the desired behavior. Identifying these barriers can actually be as simple as asking your target audience (in groups or individually) a few questions relative to the desired behavior: What are some of the reasons you haven't done this in the past? What might get in the way of your doing this in the future? What do you prefer to do instead? Why?[22] As you will read in the following example, be prepared for an earful.

Example: Alternative Transportation

Employers encouraging employees to abandon their single occupant vehicles (SOVs) and take the bus, ride a bike, join a car pool, or walk to work—even one day a week—are likely to find one or more of the following "complaints." As discouraging as the list might be, consider the possibilities and strategic direction each barrier gives the marketer:

- I need my car to run personal errands during the day. (*Offer loaner cars.*)
- I have to drop off and pick up my child at day care. (*Provide on-site day care.*)
- I don't like all the chatter in a car pool. (*Give iPods to people committing for a year.*)
- I get all sweaty when I ride my bike. (*Provide showers and lockers.*)
- If I walk to work and it rains, I'll get soaked going home. (*Make ponchos and umbrellas available to borrow.*).
- I'll have to transfer buses, so it will take longer. (*Issue free bus passes and increase on-site parking rates.*)
- It's too hard to find a car pool partner. (*Develop an intranet match service.*)

Principle #5: Bring Real Benefits Into the Present

Benefits are something your target audience wants or needs that the behavior you are promoting can provide. Though simple in theory, your challenges and keys to success are to first ensure the benefits you select are real for the target audience— ones they truly value and believe your behavior will deliver. And the second is to highlight benefits that the target market is likely to realize sooner rather than later. Michael Rothschild at the University of Wisconsin asserts that this is because the rewards you promise are "worth less in the future" and at the same time "costs are less onerous in the future."[23]

Example: Smoke Alarms in Australia

In a 2002 *Social Marketing Quarterly* article authored by Michael Camit, he described an effort targeting Arabic, Chinese, and Vietnamese communities in New South Wales, Australia, to increase purchasing and installation of home smoke alarms. Background data showed that while 58% of total households surveyed had a smoke alarm installed, the target communities had substantially lower installation rates: Arabic-speaking community (39%), Chinese-speaking community (30%), and Vietnamese-speaking community (32%).

Formative research then revealed that the target groups did not really understand the benefits of the product. They were unaware that smoke inhalation in fact killed more people than fire in house fires and were not motivated by the current slogan, "Smoke alarms save lives." Feedback from focus groups suggested that this slogan was too vague, especially in view of the target audiences' lack of understanding of the benefit of a smoke alarm. Based on this insight, a more specific slogan, "Smoke alarms wake you up if there is a fire," was developed from the research, one promising a more tangible, believable benefit.

During the 8 weeks of the campaign, 3,433 smoke alarms were purchased by members of the target communities. Given an estimate of 50,000 target households, this was seen as representing a significant penetration of the target population in that time period.[24]

Principle #6: Highlight Costs of Competing Behaviors

Now you switch to the other side of the exchange equation and focus on identifying the competition for the desired behavior you are promoting and the costs your target market may (or may not yet) associate with them.

As mentioned earlier, the competition in social marketing is the behavior your target audience prefers, might be tempted to do, or is currently doing—instead of the one you would like them to do. It may also be defined as an organization or group that encourages or sells the competing behavior (e.g., the tobacco industry). As in commercial marketing, one key to attacking the competition is to highlight the downsides of this choice in an honest and credible way (e.g., according to the National Cancer Institute, cigarette smoking causes 87% of lung cancer deaths). Some concerned with fear appeal tactics stress the importance of quickly offering a solution (e.g., don't start smoking). Others suggest simply framing it as "choice and consequences," letting the market then decide (e.g., having middle school students touch and feel tumors in the lungs of persons who died from lung cancer and comparing them with the smooth and soft lungs of someone who hadn't smoked).

In many cases, your competition is the target market's inclination to "do nothing," as it was in the following example.

Example: Pet Adoption

On Saturday morning, October 14, 2006, an interview on a Seattle, Washington, radio station with a spokesperson for the Humane Society for Tacoma and Pierce County certainly highlighted the costs of doing nothing. "We have over a hundred cats and kittens that are likely to be euthanized tonight if they are not adopted today." Television news programs, newspaper articles, and blogs also helped spread the word to "*Skadoodle over to Kittenkaboodle* and help us end the heartache of euthanasia by adopting a homeless cat or kitten." The event promised to be festive and was decked out with balloons and offered free face paintings. An incentive topped off the offer with a $20 discount on the regular adoption fee and (today only) included spaying or neutering, a veterinary exam, a cat carrier, and even a cat toy.

On the following Monday, it was announced that a record-breaking 180 shelter pets found homes in just 8 hours! Follow-up news stories and Web site postings assured those who missed out, "No problem. The shelter will be open all week, and there is sure to be a new and ample supply of adoptable animals."[25]

Principle #7: Promote a Tangible Good or Service to Help Target Audiences Perform the Behavior

Although tangible goods like tablets to test for leaky toilets and services such as tobacco quitlines may be considered an optional component of a social marketing effort, they are sometimes exactly what are needed to help the target audience perform the behavior, provide encouragement, remove barriers, or sustain behaviors.[26] They can also enhance opportunities for branding campaign messages and measuring impact. Wiebe concluded from an analysis of more than four social change campaigns that "the more a campaign resembles a commercial product campaign, the more successful it is likely to be."[27] The following example certainly represents that opportunity.

Example: The Walking School Bus

Studies show that fewer children are walking and biking to school and more children are at risk of becoming overweight worldwide. Changing behaviors of children and parents requires creative solutions that are both safe and fun—ones like the Walking School Bus program.[28]

A walking school bus is essentially a group of children walking to school with one or more adults. It sounds simple. It is. And that's part of the beauty. It can be as informal as two families taking turns walking their children to school to as structured as having the kids wear fluorescent vests and developing a route with meeting points, a timetable, and regularly rotated schedule of trained volunteers. Parents often cite safety issues as one of the primary reasons they are reluctant to allow their children to walk to school. This addresses that barrier as well as offers additional attractive benefits, including reducing traffic congestion, air pollution, and getting people, parents, and students to work together for a common good.[29]

Successful programs have been implemented around the world, including one in Chicago where interested adults volunteer for the program by signing their name next to where they live on street maps displayed at the local school. Clusters of households are then identified and linked with one another. Safe and enjoyable routes are mapped out for the group. The involved adults become part of the problem-solving process in their neighborhood, as they can identify potential dangerous intersections along the route and monitor them so children can cross safely. In 2006, 175 schools in the Chicago area participated in the program.[30]

Principle #8: Consider Nonmonetary Incentives in the Form of Recognition and Appreciation

Pricing strategies in social marketing can utilize traditional monetary incentives such as discount coupons for compost and rebates for outdated car seats. The good news is that there are also effective ways to encourage changes in behavior that don't involve cash incentives and don't cost a lot of money. These nonmonetary incentives typically provide something else the target audience values—recognition or appreciation. This can be given to individuals by recognizing, for example, a household that commits to practicing natural yard care by putting a branded ladybug sticker on its yard waste container. It can also be a way to recognize organizations for supporting healthy, safe, or environmentally friendly behaviors. As you will read in the following example, this can also be popular in the private sector, as it can provide a way to do well by doing good.

Example: Ecolabels

Ecolabeling entered mainstream environmental policymaking in the late '70s when the German government established the Blue Angel program. According to the United Nations, "Since that time, ecolabels have become one of the more high-profile market-based tools for achieving environmental objectives."[31] There are now a variety of schemes in operation throughout the world, including a number within the European Union.

For one type of environmental labeling, ecolabels are awarded by an impartial third party that independently determines that certain products or services meet established environmental criteria. Labels are then granted to those products judged to be less harmful to the environment than others within the same product category. Ecolabels then indicate that a brand is more environmentally friendly than an unlabeled brand of the same type and are seen as a simple way to present complex environmental information to consumers. The rationale behind these systems is that credible environmental information will affect consumer brand choice and increase the market shares of companies with (more) environmentally friendly products.[32]

Many claim this is working for the common good: consumers, businesses, and the environment. The German Blue Eco Angel, for one, now covers over 4,000 products judged to have positive environmental features.[33]

Principle #9: Make Access Easy

In a society that places a premium on time, convenient access can be a deal breaker. Successful social marketing efforts provide target audiences *easy ways to sign up* (e.g., organ donation registration via the Internet), *convenient locations* to acquire tangible objects (e.g., gun lockboxes available at major retail outlets) and receive services (e.g., flu shots at grocery stores), and *reasonable hours and days of the week* for accessing services (e.g., natural yard and garden hotlines open on Saturdays, when homeowners are most likely doing their gardening).

Efforts to make adoption easy were worth it to the utility featured in the following example.

Example: Water Conservation

Seattle Public Utilities' Home Water Savers Program was designed to make things simple and extremely convenient for homeowners to conserve water.

During the summer of 1992, 300,000 showerheads were distributed door-to-door to about 90% of households in the utility's service area. A package was left at each doorstep with a high-quality showerhead and easy-to-follow installation instructions (see Figure 3.4).

Prior consumer research had tested several potential strategies to influence residents to do two things: (1) install this water-efficient model and (2) put their old showerhead in a bag provided in the package on their doorstep to be picked up within a few days. This was critical in order for program managers to know their installation rates. The messages from potential adopters were loud and clear: Make sure this showerhead is of high quality and make the process simple, easy, and convenient.

The simplicity and ease of participation of the program resulted in the highest rate of installation of water-efficient showerheads in the nation. The rate of installation was 65%, twice the expectation using national standards. And as an added benefit, approximately one third of residents reported in telephone surveys that they now take shorter showers and use less hot water for showering.[34]

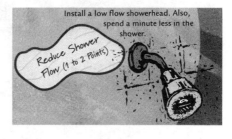

Figure 3.4 Promotional Materials Carried a Consistent Message[35]

Principle #10: Have a Little Fun With Messages

Using humor to influence public behaviors can be tricky, especially if a governmental agency is the messenger. There are times when it just isn't appropriate for the target audience (e.g., victims of sexual assault). There are agencies with a brand personality where humor doesn't quite fit (e.g., Homeland Security). There are some messages that are so complex they could be dismissed or lose their impact with a humorous approach (e.g., keeping household poisons away from children). And there are certain behaviors that are more likely to be inspired by an emotion other than humor (e.g., when getting people to evacuate their homes in the path of a wildfire).

You are encouraged, however, to look for opportunities where it might be appropriate and persuasive with your audience, where it wouldn't be inconsistent with your program or agency's brand, and where it might be just "the right emotion to garner the attention, appeal, and memorability you want in your campaign."[36] We think the following example fits that bill.

Example: Breastfeeding

Recent studies show that babies who are breastfed for 6 months are less likely to develop ear infections, diarrhea, and respiratory illnesses. And some studies suggest that infants who are not breastfed have higher rates of obesity, diabetes, leukemia, and asthma. Yet, in 2004 in the United States, only about 33% of mothers were breastfeeding at the recommended 6 months postpartum, one of the lowest breastfeeding rates in the developed world.[37] The Healthy People 2010 goal is to raise this to 50%. The U.S. Department of Health and Human Services, Office on Women's Health, has taken on this challenge.

Their precampaign research findings provided a direction and focus for the campaign, revealing that there was no clear understanding of the duration goal for breastfeeding and that there were no perceived real disadvantages of not breastfeeding. Campaign messages were designed to address this confusion and to highlight these misperceptions. A media campaign was launched in June 2004 with the support of the Advertising Council, with ads driving home the message "Babies were born to be breastfed" and highlighting real, tangible benefits—with a little humor (see Figure 3.5).[38]

In addition to mass media and the Internet, resources were also directed to support community-based demonstration

BREASTFEED FOR 6 MONTHS. YOU MAY HELP REDUCE YOUR CHILD'S RISK FOR CHILDHOOD OBESITY.

Recent studies show babies may be less likely to develop childhood obesity when exclusively breastfed for six months. Call 800-994-WOMAN or visit www.4woman.gov to learn more. Or talk to your healthcare provider. **Babies were born to be breastfed.**

U.S. Department of Health and Human Services

Figure 3.5 Poster for a Breastfeeding Campaign in Partnership With the Ad Council[39]

projects (CDPs) throughout the country, ones involving local coalitions, hospitals, universities, and other organizations that were funded to offer breastfeeding services, provide outreach to their communities, train health care providers, implement the media aspects of the campaign, and track breastfeeding rates in their communities.

Postcampaign research after the first year of the campaign was encouraging. Awareness about breastfeeding rose from 28% to 38%. More than half of respondents (63%) either correctly identified 6 months as the recommended length of time to exclusively breastfeed a baby or said the recommended duration was longer than 6 months. The number agreeing that babies should be exclusively breastfed in the first 6 months increased from prewave (53%) to postwave (62%). And, most important, more women surveyed had breastfed a child (any duration) in the 2005 study (73%) than in the 2004 study (63%).

Principle #11: Use Media Channels at the Point of Decision Making

Many social marketers have found that an ideal moment to speak to the target audience is when they are about to choose between alternative, competing behaviors. They are at a fork in the road, with your desired behavior in one direction and their current behavior, or potentially undesirable one, in the other. Being at this point of decision making with your offer can be powerful, giving you one last chance to influence their choice, even the choices of those around them, as demonstrated in the following example.

Example: Ask for Healthier Food in Singapore—And Get a Discount!

When a National Nutrition Survey in Singapore in 1998 showed that the majority (70%) of Singaporeans eat out at food courts and hawker centers, the Health Promotion Board knew right where to take more of their National Healthy Lifestyle Program messages.

By September 2002, 5,756 stall holders at hawker centers and 1,600 stall holders at food courts in Singapore were carrying point-of-purchase tent cards for tables, stickers, and posters with branded labels, including "Ask for more vegetables," "Ask for less gravy,"

"Ask for less oil," "Ask for less sugar," "Ask for less syrup," "Ask for plain rice," "Ask for skin to be removed" (see Figure 3.6). Stall vendors displaying the labels then respond to customers' requests for healthier choices (e.g., hawkers displaying the "Ask for more vegetables" label will give at least two Chinese spoonfuls of vegetables upon request).

By 2003, it looked like they were having even more fun with this, with Scotts Picnic Food Court announcing

Figure 3.6 A Point-of-Purchase Campaign in Singapore Influencing Healthier Choices

that it would be participating in its first-ever Great Singapore Sale by offering a 10% discount to customers who requested healthier food, and (from June 15 to June 30) that customers who asked for healthier food (e.g., with less oil, less gravy) would be entitled to a 10% discount on their favorite dishes.[40]

Principle #12: Try for Popular/Entertainment Media

Successful campaigns use media vehicles and formats that effectively reach target markets with appealing spokespersons, sponsors, and settings (e.g., situation comedies, rap songs, movies, entertainers, sports figures). For example, Bob Barker, host of daytime TV's longest running daily game show in the United States, was known for his passionate closing words each day: "Help control the pet population. Have your pets spayed or neutered." The following example also illustrates the impact that a small publicity stunt can have when a credible spokesperson is involved.

Example: Energy Conservation

During an energy crisis on the U.S. West Coast in the winter of 2001, a popular, well-respected radio talk show host, Dave Ross of 710 KIRO in Seattle, Washington, was intrigued when he heard of a successful conservation effort in Israel more than 20 years before. He then tried a similar strategy with his listening audience of several hundred thousand.

The campaign in Israel had taken place immediately after a popular television show dramatized Israel's overuse of electricity. The show's host asked the audience to leave the room and go around the house and turn off all extra lights. The viewers then saw the impact of their actions on their television screens, from a camera focused on the Israeli Electric Company's electricity consumption gauges. Within a few seconds, the gauges dropped sharply. The experiment that helped alter the belief that "my lights don't make a difference" saved an estimated 6% in aggregate electricity consumption during the 8 months of the campaign.[41]

Taking a similar approach, Dave announced on a preview for his show that he would try an experiment at 11:30 that morning and would be asking listeners to turn off and unplug anything electric that wasn't being used. He emphasized that he didn't want people to make any sacrifices. He just wanted them to turn off what they didn't need. At 11:28, the city's electric utility staff were standing by and read the current level of megawatts in use: "We're at 1,400 megawatts." At 11:30, the talk show host said "Go!" and for the next 5 minutes he walked around the studios of the station with a handheld microphone and turned off conference room lights and computer monitors in empty offices. He then called his daughter at home to make sure she was participating, all as an example for the listening audience.

At 11:35, the city utility public information officer came back on the air and reported impressive results. Usage had dropped by 40 megawatts, to 1,360. The decrease was enough to power 40,000 homes and represented $300,000 worth of electricity. The excitement over the success generated an hour-long program the next day on ways to conserve electricity (e.g., doing laundry in nonpeak hours and purchasing energy-saving appliances). Dave was presented a conservation award on air (an energy-saving lightbulb) by a member of the city council. For several weeks thereafter, local home and garden supply stores featured energy-saving appliances and lightbulbs.[42]

Principle #13: Get Commitments and Pledges

Gaining commitments and pledges to perform a behavior has been proven surprisingly effective, increasing the likelihood that your target market will actually follow through with a good intention. McKenzie-Mohr and Smith report this may work because "when individuals agree to a small request, it often alters the way they perceive themselves."[43] It also makes them even more likely to agree to a subsequent, more demanding activity, and to sustain it. Perhaps that's one of the reasons the following program is so successful.

Example: Teleworking

AT&T promotes teleworking as a way to achieve a good family balance, increase productivity, save money, and protect the environment. Its telework initiative launched in the United States in 1992 was, in part, a response to the new Clean Air act and provides information and support to all staff and management (part time and full time), corporate-wide, who are interested in teleworking. A simple but comprehensive Web site has been the primary means to promote and deliver the program and includes steps for setting up a telework location, tips, telework research, and links to employees and management involved in the program delivery. The initiative, which was launched using several pilot programs in different locations, includes a commitment (teleworking agreement) from each employee.

In 2000, reports indicated that since the program was initiated, 56% (36,000) of AT&T staff telework from home at least once a month. Consider, as well, the estimated environmental impact the program had that year alone:

- Avoided 110 million miles of driving to the office
- Saved 5.1 million gallons of gas
- Reduced 50,000 tons of carbon dioxide emissions

And despite the upfront cost incurred to set up teleworkers, AT&T estimates that the incurred costs are recouped within a year, through savings in real estate and related costs (e.g., energy) and the 15%–20% increases in productivity of teleworking employees due to enhanced morale and fewer meetings and interruptions.[44]

Principle #14: Use Prompts for Sustainability

According to McKenzie-Mohr and Smith, prompts are "visual or auditory aids which remind us to carry out an activity that we might otherwise forget. The purpose of a prompt is not to change attitudes or increase motivation, but simply to remind us to engage in an action that we are already predisposed to do." In other words, it works to address the most human of traits—simply forgetting.[45] And it can be a simple, lifesaving intervention, as illustrated in the following example.

Example: Sudden Infant Death Syndrome (SIDS)

SIDS is a term used to describe the sudden, unexplained death of an infant younger than 1 year of age. In the United States, it is the leading cause of death in infants between 1 month and 1 year of age. Some call it "crib death" because many babies who die of SIDS are found in their cribs. Health care providers don't know exactly what causes SIDS, but they do know that placing a baby on his or her back to sleep is one of the easiest ways to reduce the risk of SIDS.[46]

The Back to Sleep campaign along with other co-sponsors including the National Institute of Child Health and Human Development (NICHD), Maternal and Child Health Bureau, American Academy of Pediatrics, First Candle/SIDS Alliance, Association of SIDS, and Infant Mortality Programs. And Pampers, a strong and early partner of the program, helps to expand the reach of the campaign message by printing the Back to Sleep logo (a baby sleeping on its back) across the diaper-fastening strips of its newborn diapers (see Figure 3.7). This prompt helps ensure that every time caregivers change a baby's diaper, they will be reminded that back sleeping is best to reduce the risk of a baby dying from SIDS. Most important, the Back to Sleep logo on diapers is printed in three different languages—English, French, and Spanish.[47]

Figure 3.7   A Just in Time Reminder on Pampers' Newborn Diapers

In 2005, it was announced by the NICHD that since the campaign was launched in 1994, the percentage of infants placed on their backs to sleep increased dramatically and the rates of SIDS have declined by more than 50%.[48]

Principle #15: Track Results and Make Adjustments

Successful campaigns establish ways to monitor progress and make important adjustments so that current or planned strategies support objectives and goals. This effort is obviously most important when there is still time to alter the plan. In the following example, campaign target audiences and objectives were altered when research on audience perspective raised insurmountable barriers to desired behaviors.

Example: Eating Disorder Awareness and Prevention

GO GIRLS!™ (Giving Our Girls Inspiration & Resources for Lasting Self-Esteem) is an advocacy project launched in 1998 by the national nonprofit organization National Eating Disorders Association. The initial purpose of the effort was to encourage and support teens in influencing positive images of youth in advertising, television programs, fashion shows, and retail displays. Research by this organization and others has indicated that teenagers' self-esteem is significantly influenced by their images of their bodies compared with those portrayed in these industries.

An initial project began with a group of marketing students from three high schools who developed a plan to influence modeling agencies, advertising firms, and retail stores to use a diversity of body sizes and shapes in ads, fashion shows, and displays. Initial objectives were ambitious: to (a) persuade modeling agencies to use teen models of various weights and sizes, (b) persuade advertising agencies to request a diversity of models for ads, and (c) persuade retail department stores to use a variety of mannequins in teen displays. Planned efforts included interviews of executives in these industries at the beginning to understand any perceived barriers to using diverse images.

Initial interviews and presentations dampened the student marketers' enthusiasm as they listened to their target audience's problems. Modeling agencies provided models requested by advertisers, advertisers used models who fit into (small-sized) sample outfits from brand manufacturers, and retail executives indicated they had few, if any, options from mannequin manufacturers for teen displays.

The students adjusted their plan. They narrowed their audience to the merchandise managers of the retail stores, a segment with real decision-making authority and a problem they thought they could solve. Armed with media support from a local television station and a major newspaper reporter "at their side," they presented retail executives with a new idea, one they thought would help teens and would also work for the retailers. Given that factory-ordered mannequins would take several years to alter, they suggested stuffing existing soft-cloth mannequins so that they had larger-sized torsos.

The teens were jubilant when one of the department stores agreed to display mannequins with larger-sized torsos in their popular teen department. Local television and newspapers covered their successful efforts, spreading goodwill for one retail giant and casting a negative light over the other.[49]

Chapter Summary

The most credible and reliable indicator of success for your social marketing effort is the extent to which meaningful and relevant campaign objectives and goals are met. Fifteen principles that can contribute to achieving targeted results were presented in this chapter, illustrated with campaigns chosen to provide a balanced overview of the range and nature of successful campaigns:

1. Take advantage of prior and existing successful campaigns

2. Start with target markets most ready for action

3. Promote single, simple, doable behaviors—one at a time

4. Identify and remove barriers to behavior change

5. Bring real benefits into the present

6. Highlight costs of competing behaviors

7. Promote a tangible good or service to help target audiences perform the behavior

8. Consider nonmonetary incentives in the form of recognition and appreciation

9. Make access easy

10. Have a little fun with messages

11. Use media channels at the point of decision making

12. Try for popular/entertainment media

13. Get commitments and pledges

14. Use prompts for sustainability

15. Track results and make adjustments

Part II

ANALYZING THE SOCIAL MARKETING ENVIRONMENT

Determining Research Needs and Options

*We all know that good research is the foundation for the design and imple-
mentation of effective social marketing programs, but that isn't enough. The
marketer must continually check in with the target audience to monitor
changes in perception and behavior over time. Customers are not static or
formulaic. Their knowledge, attitudes, and behavior are susceptible to
change over time and marketing programs must evolve with them.*

—Gregory R. Niblett
*Senior Vice President and Director
The AED Social Change Group*

Alan Andreasen, a renowned marketing professor and social marketer at
Georgetown University, captures the mood of many regarding research with his
list of common myths below—coupled with his counterpoints for each:[1]

Myth 1: *"I'm Already Doing Enough Research."* Almost always, you aren't, but
there are simple decision frameworks that will help you find out.

Myth 2: *"Research Is Only for Big Decisions."* Research is not only for big decisions,
and sometimes big decisions do not even need it.

Myth 3: *"Market Research Is Simply Conducting Surveys, and Surveys Are
Expensive."* All research is not surveys, and even surveys can be done inexpensively.

Myth 4: *"Most Research Is a Waste."* Research can be a waste, but it need not be,
especially if you use a systematic approach to developing a plan, beginning with
determining key decisions to be made using the research results.

This chapter on research will only begin to debunk these myths further and only
scratch the surface of this important discipline and its contribution to successful campaigns. The focus is on ensuring you are familiar with some of the research jargon,
common research instruments and techniques, statistical procedures, sampling
methodologies, and the nature of focus groups. More detailed research case stories will
be presented in Chapters 6–14, intending to cover the range of research methodologies, as well as applications for social marketing campaigns. We open with an inspiring
case, where research not only helped guide the strategy, it *was* the strategy!

Research as Promotion

Jordan Water Efficiency Program (2000–2005)

GREGORY R. NIBLETT

Senior Vice President and Director
The AED Social Change Group

Municipal water shortages had reached emergency levels. Domestic and commercial rationing was in place year round. Raising the price of water to reduce demand would be the Jordanian government's next step. The assumption was that the consumer's behavior needed to change: turn off taps when brushing teeth or shaving, take shorter showers, don't take baths. But Jordanians were doing all these things and more, achieving one of the lowest per capita water usage rates on the planet. Research was key in helping AED find the right focus for the U.S. Agency for International Development (USAID)-supported Water Efficiency and Public Information for Action (WEPIA) program.

Background

When AED began WEPIA in 2000, little research existed that provided knowledge about consumer beliefs and attitudes toward water and water conservation in Jordan. Previous AED work in Jordan's schools noted that students were unaware that water shortages were endemic to Jordan and the Middle East, and had been so for centuries. Research

under a Middle East Peace Process grant to AED showed that students in neighboring countries were similarly unaware of limited water availability. A simple questionnaire administered in 1999 to students in environmental clubs managed by the Royal Society for the Conservation of Nature (RSCN) indicated that they blamed their shortages on political disputes with neighboring governments over access to the Jordan River, controlled by Israel, or to the Yarmouk River, controlled by Syria. No student mentioned the rapidly growing population from refugees, the high birth rate, or the growing industrial and hospitality/ tourism sectors as straining water resources. WEPIA relied on these and other data to guide programs, design messages, monitor success, and evaluate end results.

In 2000 the Ministry of Water and Irrigation's most useful research was a *Willingness and Ability to Pay* study conducted by the Market Research Organization (MRO), WEPIA's local research partner. This study became the basis for the demand management strategy used by WEPIA.

The study showed Jordanians reluctant to pay more for their water, no matter how scarce, unless they saw changes by the government:

improved infrastructure ("if the government can tolerate all these broken pipes in the street, they can't be serious about water shortage"); improved household measurement of water consumption ("I hardly use any water at all, but I still get huge bills because the meters are broken"); improved justice and equality to demand reduction ("I'm just a small user of water. Start with those people who have swimming pools and many bathrooms. Start with the big consumer"). The study showed that Jordanians felt ineffectual in the face of water shortages, and their financial resources were already strained. The national government focused on infrastructure repair and improved metering. WEPIA focused on equitable demand reduction.

Target Audience

Large consumers were targeted first, households second. A rapid survey of the Ministry of Water consumer billing data for the past 3 years yielded information on the largest water consumers in Jordan. Most of these were public buildings, universities, sports centers, private clubs, and a few private houses. Some large consumers could not be included for reasons of national security (e.g., police, military facilities, and palaces) but were passed on to the government to deal with directly. Some 760 subscriptions were identified as consuming upward of 500 liters (130 gallons) a day (less than the average daily amount used by a U.S. family). WEPIA then randomly selected 50 buildings and performed water audits to verify bills, ensure that consumption was not due to leaks, and note where any savings might be had. From there a simple water auditing tool was developed that highlighted weaknesses in the government's billing and provided information that helped improve it. Individual

interviews with an additional 86 large building owners were conducted to determine knowledge about water shortages in Jordan, methods of water conservation, and individual efforts, if any, that were being made to conserve water.

Results of the audits showed that consumption levels were primarily due to antiquated, poor quality, incorrect plumbing, not from individual excessive water use. Adding aerators to faucets would improve a building's water efficiency and reduce the water bill by 30%. Repairing leaks would create additional savings. Focusing on large-scale overhaul of plumbing systems was not viable. The Knowledge, Attitude and Practice (KAP) study results showed that appeals to civic pride would also be useless.

Behavior Objective

WEPIA focused on a simple message—add an aerator to your faucet and you can save 30% or more on your water bill. This message and the offer to perform free water audits became the core of WEPIA's demand management program initially targeting large consumers and later targeting individual households, rich or poor, through a variety of trained outreach volunteers (e.g., school students, female preachers). The appeal was to the pocketbook; the action recommended was the purchase and installation of a very cheap ($5) product that would, over time, lower the water bill. The objective measure of the success of the venture was water bills of buildings that had been retrofitted over a 1-year cycle (to avoid seasonal differences in water consumption) to ensure that there were savings of at least 30% (there were) and increases in sales of aerators from the several distributors that sold them.

Strategies

Despite the simple action, the task was still difficult. Install the wrong aerator and you alienate the user. Eventually the project worked to change the construction codes to standardize water flow rates and started work toward a uniform plumbing code. The consumer had to know the water pressure in the building on each floor, the kind of faucet one had and whether it had internal or external threads, and whether the aerator was intended for a kitchen or a bathroom. A test campaign using a lottery was developed to see if homeowners could correctly identify these items in their own homes. Prizes of computers and household appliances donated by the private sector were offered to the first 10 correct respondents. Colorful lottery cards were designed with questions on the back of the cards and distributed by a network of volunteers to grocery stores, neighborhood bakeries, and pharmacies (see Figure 4.1). This was *classic formative research* but conducted in a fun and entertaining way. It provided the answers WEPIA needed and began to create a buzz around water conservation. Suddenly people and organizations wanted to be associated with the project. It was research as promotion.

Figure 4.1 Arabic Lottery Card

Another innovative research tool used in WEPIA was the whole-system-in-a-room (WSR) conference used to launch the formal program. The fundamental principle is that if all members within a system are invited to sit in the same room and to bring their combined knowledge to work on a strategic plan, the need for formal research is obviated. In the case of our water conservation WSR, we invited university engineering faculty, Ministry of Water and Irrigation staff, staff from Ministries of Education and Health and other concerned ministries; nongovernmental organizations (NGOs) and private sector firms; donors; the general public; and groups such as women's groups, the media, teachers, and plumbers—85 people in all—further generating buzz throughout the media, the press, and word of mouth.

Results

The project used many classic research tools:

- Omnibus surveys every 6 months to monitor changes in perception and changes in behavior over time
- Desktop surveys to determine the increasing levels and kinds of coverage from all news and media sites
- Exit interviews as formative research that helped build a cartoon character as a logo for the project
- Pretests to review and improve all media materials
- Product testing to see if people could identify characteristics of aerators that would help in marketing
- Participatory research with civil society partners—imams, female householders, plumbers, high school students, and teachers

- In-depth interviews with industry leaders to determine trends
- Interviews and surveys to determine product packaging and placement
- Independent evaluations conducted by USAID to make sure the results they were hearing from the project were accurate

Research firms became partners working alongside us, not just as vendors. USAID called it the most successful project in Jordan, because WEPIA staff had successfully used research to design, implement, and monitor a trendsetting project. The Advertising Association in Jordan gave it the Golden Award for the best advertising campaign over a 2-year period in the country because we had done accurate formative research. The Minister for Water and His Highness King Abdullah congratulated the project for its water savings, because research had given social marketing the credibility it lacked at the start of the program. The best outcome of all—the general public started paying their own money to retrofit their homes.

MAJOR RESEARCH TERMINOLOGY

The first primer in this chapter presents some of the most commonly used research terms (see Table 4.1). They have been grouped by whether they are referring to the objective of the research, when the research is conducted in planning, the source of the data and information, the technique used, or approaches to collecting primary data. More detailed descriptions and an illustrative example are presented in the next several sections.

Research Characterized by Research Objective

Exploratory research has as its objective to gather preliminary information that helps define the problem.[2] It would be most characteristic of research conducted at the beginning of the marketing planning process, when you are seeking to determine the purpose and focus for your plan. A city wanting to persuade restaurants to recycle their cooking oil, for example, might begin by reviewing data on the estimated amount of cooking oil that is currently being dumped down drains or put in garbage cans and the impact it is having on infrastructures and the environment.

Descriptive research has an objective to describe factors such as the market potential for a product or the demographics and attitudes of potential target audiences.[3] It would be expected, for example, for the city developing the cooking oil recycling campaign to want to know the numbers, types, and locations of restaurants in the city that were generating the most cooking oil and where and how they were currently disposing of the oil.

Table 4.1   A Marketing Research Primer

Marketing Research is the systematic design, collection, analysis, and reporting of data and findings relevant to a specific marketing situation facing the organization.[a]

Characterized by Research Objective:

Exploratory research helps define problems and suggest hypotheses.

Descriptive research helps understand marketing problems, situations, or markets.

Causal research tests hypotheses about cause-and-effect relationships.

Characterized by Stage in Planning Process:

Formative research is used to help select and understand target markets and develop the draft marketing mix strategy.

Pretest research is used to evaluate draft marketing mix strategies and then make changes prior to finalizing the marketing plan and communication elements.

Monitoring research provides ongoing measurement of program outcomes through periodic surveys.

Evaluation research most often refers to research conducted at the conclusion of a campaign effort.

Characterized by Source of Information:

Secondary data were collected for another purpose and already exist somewhere.

Primary data are freshly gathered for a specific purpose or for a specific research project.

Characterized by Approach to Collecting Primary Data:

Key Informant interviews are conducted with colleagues, decision makers, opinion leaders, technical experts, and others who may provide valuable insight regarding target markets, competitors, and strategies.

Focus Groups usually involve 8-10 people gathered for a couple of hours with a trained moderator who uses a discussion guide to focus the discussion.

Surveys use a variety of contact methods, including mail, telephone, online/Internet, intercept, and self-administered surveys, asking people questions about their knowledge, attitudes, preferences, and behaviors.

Experimental research is used to capture cause-and-effect relationships, gathering primary data by selecting matched groups of subjects, giving them different treatments, controlling related factors, and checking for differences in group responses.[b]

Observation is the gathering of primary data by observing target audiences in action, in relevant situations.

Ethnographic research is considered a holistic research method, founded in the idea that to truly understand target markets, the researcher will need an extensive immersion in their natural environment.

Mystery Shoppers pose as customers and report on strong or weak points experienced in the buying process.

Characterized by Technique:

Qualitative research is exploratory in nature, seeking to identify and clarify issues. Sample sizes are usually small, and findings are not usually appropriate for projections to larger populations.

Quantitative research refers to research that is conducted in order to reliably profile markets, predict cause and effect, and project findings. Sample sizes are usually large, and surveys are conducted in a controlled and organized environment.

Causal research is to test hypotheses about cause-and-effect relationships.[4] We can now imagine the city managers "running the numbers" to determine how much oil they might be able to defray if they concentrated on Chinese restaurants in Phase 1 of their efforts and how this potential outcome stacked up against the suggested funding, at various cooperation (market penetration) levels.

Research Characterized by Stage in Planning Process

Formative research, just as it sounds, refers to research used to help form strategies, especially to select and understand target audiences and develop draft marketing strategies. It may be qualitative or quantitative in nature. It may be new research (primary data) that you conduct, or it may be research conducted by someone else that you are able to review (secondary data). In June 2002 in Washington State, for example, formal observation studies indicated that 82% of drivers wore seatbelts. Although some might think this market share seems adequate, others like the Washington Traffic Safety Commission were on a mission to save more lives and wanted to increase this rate. And formative research helped select target markets and form strategies. Existing data from the National Highway Traffic Safety Administration helped identify populations with the lowest seatbelt usage rates (e.g., teens and men 18–24, among others). Focus groups conducted around the state with citizens who didn't wear seatbelts on a regular basis presented clear findings that the current positive coaching messages like "We love you. Buckle up" were not motivating. A primary seatbelt law, tougher fines, and increased enforcement were what they said it would take.

Pretest research is conducted to evaluate a short list of alternative strategies and tactics, ensure that potential executions have no major deficiencies, and fine-tune possible approaches so that they speak to your target audiences in the most effective way.[5] It is most typically qualitative in nature (e.g., focus groups, intercept interviews), as you are seeking to identify and understand potential responses your markets may have to various campaign elements. It is most powerful when you can participate in, or at least observe, the interviews. Referring back to the Washington State seatbelt story, based on findings from the formative research, potential slogans, highway signs, and television and radio ad concepts were developed and then shared once more with focus groups. Among the concepts tested was a successful campaign from North Carolina called Click It or Ticket. Although focus group respondents certainly "didn't like it" (i.e., that they would be fined $82 for not wearing a seatbelt and that a part of the effort included increased law enforcement), their strong negative reaction indicated that it would certainly get their attention and likely motivate a behavior change. Findings indicated that elements of the North Carolina television and radio spots, however, left people with the impression that the enforcement effort was happening somewhere else in the country; hence they could psychologically dismiss the message. Advertisements were developed locally to counteract this.

Monitoring research provides ongoing measurement of program outputs and outcomes, often used to establish baselines and subsequent benchmarks relative to goals. Most important, it can provide input that will indicate whether you need to make course corrections (midstream), alter any campaign elements, or increase resources in order to achieve these goals. Once launched, the state's Click It or Ticket campaign was monitored using several techniques, including reviewing data from the state patrol on the number of tickets issued, analyzing news media coverage, and, most important, conducting periodic formal observation studies the first year. Findings indicated that in the first 3 months after the campaign launched, seatbelt usage rates had increased from 82% to 94%. Even though strategies appeared to be working, decisions were made to increase the fine from $82 to $101, and more grants were provided to support increased enforcement, hoping to sustain the rate in the years to follow.

Evaluation research, as distinct from monitoring, is described by Andreasen as research that "typically refers to a single final assessment of a project or program, and may or may not involve comparisons to an earlier baseline study."[6] Important attempts are made in this effort to measure and report in the near term on campaign outcomes and in the longer term on campaign impacts on the social issue being addressed—both relative to campaign outputs. Both monitoring and evaluation techniques will be discussed in depth in Chapter 15. Summarizing the results of the seatbelt campaign in Washington State, in August 2006 a press release from the Washington Traffic Safety Commission reported that results from the latest observational research survey of seatbelt use showed that the use rate had climbed to 96.3% (see Figure 4.2). It was the highest seatbelt use rate in the nation and the world, and research indicated that buckling up was attributed to seatbelt road signs, aggressive local law enforcement, and educational activities at all levels of government. Most important, in terms of impact on the social issue, vehicle occupant deaths dropped from 517 in 2002 to 421 in 2004, and an estimated 400 serious injuries were avoided in that same time period.

Figure 4.2 A Graphic on the Washington Traffic Safety Commission's Web Site, Celebrating the News That They Had the Highest Seatbelt Usage in the World in August 2006[7]

Research Characterized by Source of Information

Secondary research, or secondary data, refers to information that already exists somewhere, having been collected for another purpose at an earlier point in time.[8] It is always worth a first look. The agency's internal records and databases will be a good starting point. Searching through files for information on prior campaigns and asking around about what has been done before and what the results were is time well spent. It is likely, however, that you will need to tap a wide variety of external information sources, ranging from journal articles to scientific and technical data to prior research studies conducted for other, similar purposes. Some of the best resources are peers and colleagues in similar organizations and agencies around the world who often have information on prior similar efforts they are willing to share. Unlike those in commercial sector marketing competing fiercely for market shares and profits, social marketers are known to rally around social issues and to treat each other as partners and team players. Typical questions to ask peers responsible for similar issues and efforts include the following:

- What target audiences did you choose? Why? Do you have data and research findings that profile these audiences?
- What behaviors did you promote? Do you have information on what benefits, costs, and barriers your target audience perceived? Did you explore their perceptions regarding competing alternative behaviors?
- What strategies (4Ps) did you use?
- What were the results of your campaign?
- What strategies do you think worked well? What would you do differently?
- Are there elements of your campaign that we could consider using for our program? Are there any restrictions or limitations?

There may also be relevant Listservs to query (e.g., the Social Marketing Listserv at listproc@listproc.georgetown.edu and Fostering Sustainable Behavior at fsb@cbsm list.com), online database services (e.g., LEXIS-NEXIS for a wide range of business magazines, journals, research reports), and Internet data sources (e.g., Centers for Disease Control and Prevention's [CDC's] Behavioral Risk Factor Surveillance System [BRFSS], which will be described further in the research highlight in Chapter 6). (See Appendix B for additional resources.)

Primary research, or primary data, consists of information collected for the specific purpose at hand, for the first time. It is a journey to undertake only after you have exhausted potential secondary resources. A variety of approaches to gathering this data will be described in the following section. A hypothetical example of a water utility interested in a sustainable water supply will be used throughout.

Research Characterized by Approaches to Collecting Primary Data

Key informant interviews are conducted with decision makers, community leaders, technical experts, and others who can provide valuable insight regarding target markets, competitors, and potential strategies. They can be useful in helping interpret secondary data, explain unique characteristics of the target audience (e.g., in a country other than where you live), shed light on barriers to desired audience behaviors, and provide suggestions for reaching and influencing targeted populations. Though typically informal in nature, a standard survey instrument (questionnaire) is often used in order to compile and summarize findings. A water utility, for example, interested in persuading households to fix leaky toilets in order to conserve water might interview engineers on staff to understand more about what causes toilets to leak and options customers have to fix them. They might then want to interview a few retail managers of home supply and hardware stores to learn more about what types of questions customers come to them with regarding leaky toilets and what advice they give them.

Focus groups are a very popular methodology for providing useful insights into target markets' thoughts, feelings, and even recommendations on potential strategies and ideas for future efforts. Thought of as a group interview, a focus group usually involves 8 to 10 people "sitting around a table" for a couple of hours participating in a guided discussion—hence the term *focus group.* In terms of numbers of groups to conduct, Craig Lefebvre offers, "My rule of thumb is to plan to do as many as you can afford ONLY for segments that you will truly develop a specific marketing mix for. The advice I have gotten is to do at least three for any segment, but stop once you start hearing the same thing."[9] This chapter's second primer highlights focus group terminology and key components (see Table 4.2). For the leaky toilet project, focus groups with homeowners could help identify reasons for not testing their toilets (barriers) and what it would take to persuade them (benefits). Households living in targeted areas of the city might be contacted by a market research firm that would screen potential participants and then invite those to the upcoming group with the following profile: own their home, are the head of household most responsible for household maintenance and repairs, and have a toilet older than 1994 that has not been checked for leaks in the past 5 years.

Surveys use a variety of contact methods, including mail, telephone, online/ Internet, intercept, and self-administered surveys, asking people questions about their knowledge, attitudes, preferences, and behaviors. Findings are typically quantitative in nature, as the intent of the process is to project findings from a representative segment of the population to a larger population and to then have large enough sample sizes to enable the researcher to conduct a variety of statistical tests. These samples are designed by determining first *who* is to be surveyed (sampling unit), then *how many* people should be surveyed (sample size), and finally how the people will be *chosen* (sampling procedure).[10] Back to our leaky toilet example. A telephone survey might be conducted following the focus groups, intended to help prioritize and quantify barriers and benefits identified by participants in the groups. Findings would also be used to identify the demographic and attitudinal profile of target markets (those most likely/ready to test their toilets) and to test potential marketing strategies. How does interest increase (or not) if the utility were to host demonstrations on how to fix leaky toilets (product), provide monetary incentives to replace old high-water-using

Table 4.2   Focus Group Primer

Focus Groups: A research methodology where small groups of people are recruited from a broader population and interviewed for an hour to an hour and a half utilizing a focused discussion led by a trained moderator. Results are usually considered qualitative in nature and therefore not projectable to the broader population.

Planning: The first step in the focus group planning process is to establish the **purpose** of the group. What decisions will this research support? From there, **informational objectives** are delineated, providing guidance for discussion topics.

Participants: The ideal number of participants is between 8 and 12. With fewer than 8 participants, discussions may not be as lively nor input as rich. With more than 12 participants, there is not typically enough time to hear from each person in depth.

Recruitment: Ten to 14 participants are usually recruited in order to be assured 8 to 12 will show up. A marketing research firm is often involved in recruiting participants, using a **screener** developed to find participants with the desired demographic, attitudinal, and/or behavioral profile.

Discussion Guide: This detailed outline of discussion topics and related questions distributes the 60 to 90 minutes to ensure informational objectives are achieved. It usually begins with a welcome, statement of purpose, and ground rules and concludes with opportunities for the moderator and participants to summarize highlights of the discussion. It is likely to include time allowed for numerous *probes* (e.g., "Please say more about that") to achieve the intended in-depth understanding and insights.

Moderator: The group facilitator is usually (but doesn't have to be) a trained professional. Important characteristics include strong listening and group dynamics skills, knowledge of the topic, genuine curiosity for the findings, and ability to synthesize and report on findings relative to research objectives.

Facility: Many groups are held in designated focus group rooms at market research firms, which include two-way mirrors so that *observers* (e.g., the client for the research) can witness participants' expressions and body language, as well as slip notes to the moderator regarding additional questions or probes. Groups are often audiotaped and sometimes videotaped in order to prepare reports and share findings with others. Some focus groups are now conducted online, via the telephone, and/or video conferencing.

Incentives: Participants are usually provided monetary incentives for their time (e.g., $50–$60) and provided light refreshments when they arrive. The opportunity to share opinions, even contribute to an important social issue, is a strong motivator as well.

toilets that leak with new, more water-efficient ones (price), and offer to pick up old toilets (place)?

Experimental research is used to capture cause-and-effect relationships, gathering primary data by selecting matched groups of respondents (similar on a variety of characteristics), giving them different treatments (exposing them to alternative marketing strategies), controlling related factors, and checking for differences in group responses.[11] Some might even call it a pilot, where you measure and compare the outcomes of one or more potential strategies among similar market segments. Let's assume the utility, for example, was trying to decide whether they needed to provide the homeowner with dye tablets to use to test for a leak or whether it worked just as well to simply provide instructions on how to use ordinary food coloring from their household pantry. If the incidence of testing for leaks was not higher among households who were mailed a tablet than those who were simply mailed instructions, the utility would likely decide to roll out the campaign without the added costs of the tablet.

Observational research, as it would seem, gathers primary data by observing relevant people, actions, and situations. In the commercial sector, consumer packaged-good marketers visit supermarkets and observe shoppers as they browse the store, pick up products, examine the labels (or not), and then what purchase decisions they make.[12] In social marketing, it is more often used to provide insight into difficulties people have performing desired behaviors (e.g., recycling properly), to measure actual versus reported behaviors (e.g., seatbelt usage), or to simply understand how consumers navigate their environments in order to develop recommended changes in infrastructures (e.g., removing their computers from bags as they approach airport security screeners). It would be useful to the managers working on the leaky toilet project to watch people at local home supply stores as they check out repair kits for their toilets.

Ethnographic research is considered a holistic research method, founded in the idea that to truly understand target markets, the researcher will need an extensive immersion in their natural environment. It often includes observation as well as face-to-face interviews with study participants. For example, the utility might want to actually observe and interview people in their homes as they test their toilets for leaks and (if warranted) make decisions regarding repair or replacement. Findings can then be used to develop instructional materials that will be most helpful to others as they then engage in these behaviors.

Mystery shoppers pose as customers and report on strong or weak points experienced in the buying process. This may include interfacing with an agency's personnel, with an interest in observing and reporting on what the target audience sees, hears, and feels during the exchange and how personnel respond to their questions. Once launched, utility managers may want to call their own customer service center, for example, and ask questions regarding the mailer received on testing for leaky toilets and options for repairing and replacing them. They might also want to visit the Web site for the project, post a comment or question, and note how quickly their question is acknowledged.

Research Characterized by Technique

Sometimes a research project is characterized as either a qualitative or quantitative study. The differences between these two techniques are described in the following section. They will be illustrated with both qualitative and quantitative components of a research effort conducted to inform the development of a social marketing campaign to combat the spread of HIV/AIDS in Ethiopia, where the infection rate is one of the world's highest.

Qualitative research techniques generally refer to studies where samples are typically small and are not reliably projected to the greater population. It isn't their purpose. The focus, instead, is on identifying and seeking clarity on issues and understanding current knowledge, attitudes, beliefs, and behaviors of target markets. Focus groups, personal interviews, observation, and ethnographic studies are common tools that are used, as they are often qualitative in nature.[13]

In October 2005, an article titled "Managing Fear in Public Health Campaigns" by authors Cho and Witte appeared in *Health Promotion Practice*, a journal of the Society for Public Health Education (SOPHE).[14] It described, in depth, the role that formative research played in developing strategies to influence HIV/AIDS-preventive behaviors among teens and young adults (ages 15–30) living in Ethiopia. This research was theoretically grounded in a fear appeal theory called the extended parallel process model.[15] Thus, the variables studied were not selected at random but were purposely chosen. Once the researchers discovered what people believed regarding these variables, then they would have specific guidance from the theory about how to influence the beliefs in the direction that promoted the most behavior change.

Focus groups were conducted first to better understand urban youths' perceptions about HIV/AIDS prevention issues by exploring, among other factors, their current knowledge, attitudes, beliefs, and behaviors regarding HIV/AIDS and condom use. Four focus groups were conducted in the two most populous towns in each of five regions in Ethiopia. Of specific interest were perceptions of consequences associated with HIV/AIDS. Participants in groups identified a variety: dysentery, weight loss, family breakdown, increase in orphans, social stigma, long-term disability, and death. The groups also revealed negative perceptions of condoms, including embarrassment, reduction of sexual pleasure, breakage during sexual intercourse, reduction of faithfulness between partners, and a perception among some that condoms actually spread HIV/AIDS. Of interest as well were perceptions of whom participants viewed as most at risk of HIV infection: commercial sex workers, drivers, soldiers, youth in and out of school, government employees, and sexually active young adults.

Most important, "Participants expressed that condom promotion campaigns were either absent or ineffective in most of their localities," and some totally ignored the HIV/AIDS prevention messages.[16]

Quantitative research refers to research that is conducted in order to reliably profile markets, predict cause and effect, and project findings. This reliability is created as a result of large sample sizes, rigorous sampling procedures, and surveys that are conducted in a controlled and organized environment.

For the study in Ethiopia related to HIV/AIDS prevention, a quantitative effort followed the qualitative focus group phase. The study plan included a sample of 160 households per region, for a total of 800 households, drawn from a representative sample. A total of 792 household participants aged 15 to 30 years were interviewed from the 10 towns of priority regions. Of interest was to measure and analyze agreement on a 5-point scale (strongly agree, agree, neutral, disagree, and strongly disagree) with statements related to four beliefs often considered to be predictive of behavior change:

- *Perceived susceptibility*: "I am at risk for getting infected with HIV/AIDS."
- *Perceived severity*: "Getting infected with HIV/AIDS would be the worst thing that could happen to me."
- *Perceived response efficacy*: "Condoms work in preventing HIV/AIDS infection."
- *Perceived self-efficacy*: "I am able to use condoms to prevent HIV/AIDS infection."

Next, the data were analyzed within the theoretical framework. Based on previous research, the researchers knew that they needed high levels of each of the four variables above to promote behavior change. If just one of the variables was at low levels, then they knew that they had to focus on that variable in a subsequent campaign. The authors of the article embarked on five steps to analyze the data:

1. Examine the frequency distribution of each variable (agreement levels for each of the four variables).

2. Compare the mean scores for each variable (average levels of agreement) to assess whether the average beliefs were all at high levels (i.e., 4 or 5).

3. Categorize the four variables into weak, moderate, and strong belief categories. Perceived severity was strong, and thus there was no need to address it in a campaign. However, perceived susceptibility was weak and response and self-efficacy were moderate and thus needed to be strengthened in the subsequent campaign.

4. Strengthen targeted beliefs by examining the psychological, social, cultural, and structural bases of these beliefs in order to determine what caused low perceived susceptibility and only moderate levels of self- and response efficacy. For example, the researchers found that simply talking with partners about condom use was one of the key things that increased perceived self-efficacy.

Table 4.3 Chart of Beliefs to Change, Introduce, Reinforce for HIV/AIDS Prevention

Theoretical Variables	Beliefs to Introduce	Beliefs to Change	Beliefs to Reinforce
Susceptibility	Talk with partner(s) about HIV/AIDS and prevention methods.	HIV/AIDS prevention services are easy to get.	Talk with partner(s) about HIV/AIDS and prevention methods.
Severity	Partner(s) believes HIV/AIDS is serious problem.		Partner(s) believes HIV/AIDS is serious problem
Response Efficacy	Using condoms is good, positive, safe, accepted idea.	Quality of HIV/AIDS prevention services is good.	Using condoms is good, positive, safe, accepted idea.
Self-Efficacy	Talk with partner(s) about HIV/AIDS and prevention methods. Generate positive, nonjudgmental talk in community about HIV/AIDS and prevention methods. Best friends are supportive of HIV/AIDS prevention methods.	Generate positive, nonjudgmental talk in community about HIV/AIDS and prevention methods. Generate approval of condoms as a prevention method. Quality of HIV/AIDS prevention services is good.	Using condoms is good, positive, safe, accepted idea.

SOURCE: Cho, H., & Witte, K. (2005). "Managing Fear in Public Health Campaigns."

5. Then, put the research into a chart of key beliefs to introduce, change, and reinforce. This chart guided writers and program planners in the development and production of a 26-week radio soap opera (see Table 4.3).[17]

WHEN RESEARCH IS USED IN THE PLANNING PROCESS

Research is used to help make decisions and is therefore applicable in each of the planning steps. In fact, multiple decisions will need to be made with each step, and some form of research activity is likely to address the planner's questions and provide input for decision making. Table 4.4 presents a partial list of research questions that might be addressed in each of the 10 steps in the planning process. Answers to questions identified in each step may be found by reviewing existing research, literature, data sources,

Table 4.4   Partial List of Decisions and Questions Addressed by Research

Steps in the Planning Process	Typical Decisions and Questions
1. Describe Background, Purpose, Focus	What social issue will this plan address and why? What approach to the social issue at hand should we focus on?
2. Conduct a Situation Analysis and Review Prior and Similar Campaigns	Should we use materials (e.g., slogans, ads) from similar campaigns elsewhere? Which ones? Do they need to be altered for our market?
3. Select Target Markets	What segmentation variables should we use to create the most meaningful segments for targeting? Which segments should we focus the majority of our resources on?
4. Set Objectives and Goals	What specific behavior should we promote? What knowledge and attitudes do we need to change? What level of change is realistic to create with this campaign?
5. Identify Target Market Barriers, Benefits, and the Competition	Relative to the desired behavior: What are perceived benefits? What are perceived barriers? What major alternative behaviors and competitors do we position against?
6. Craft a Desired Positioning	How do we want our offer to be seen by our target markets?
7. Develop a Strategic Marketing Mix	What tangible products and services are needed to support behavior change? Does the market need a monetary incentive to act or would a nonmonetary one do? What should we do to make access more convenient? What messages will be the most motivating? Clear? Memorable? Who would be the most credible messenger or sponsor of the message? What communication channels will be most cost effective?
8. Outline a Plan for Monitoring and Evaluation	What are the benchmarks that will tell us how we are doing and whether we need to make any changes? How will we know if we reached our goal and what we should do differently next time?
9. Establish Budgets and Find Funding Sources	How much needs to be spent to reach our goal and have the desired impact? What potential corporate sponsors are the best matches for this effort?
10. Complete an Implementation Plan	What prompts in the environment can be built in to sustain campaign messages and desired behaviors?

colleague interviews, and findings from prior similar campaigns. New, additional research is undertaken after existing sources are explored, most often needed for understanding your specific target audience's barriers and benefits and getting their ideas for marketing strategies that will work for them.

STEPS IN DEVELOPING A RESEARCH PLAN

Andreasen recommends that we begin our research journey with the end in mind. He calls this "backward research" and states: "The secret here is to start with the decisions to be made and to make certain that the research helps management reach those decisions."[18]

Eight traditional steps to take when planning a research project are described in the following section, beginning with this critical purpose statement. We'll use a case example to illustrate this process from an article by Simons-Morton, Haynie, Crump, Eitel, and Saylor that appeared in February 2001 in *Health Education & Behavior*.[19] The authors presented a comprehensive research study they conducted for the National Institutes of Health, assessing the "Peer and Parent Influences on Smoking and Drinking Among Early Adolescents."

1. *Purpose*: What decisions will this research help inform? What questions do you have that you need this research to help answer?

Existing research indicated for the study team that less than 10% of 6th graders reported smoking or drinking in the past 30 days, and yet 19.1% of 8th graders and 33.5% of 12th graders reported smoking, and 24.6% of 8th graders and 51.3% of 12th graders reported drinking in the past 30 days.[20] The purpose of this new research effort was to help determine what interventions would be most effective in reducing this prevalence and with what audiences. Key to this decision was data answering the question, to what extent do peers and parents influence smoking and drinking among middle school students?

2. *Informational objectives:* What specific information do you need to make this decision and/or answer these questions?

Major topics to be explored included those related to dependent variables (e.g., incidence of smoking and drinking among the middle school students) and independent variables (e.g., peer and parent-related factors). Relative to dependent variables, factors identified to be queried included demographics (gender, race, school attended, mother's education, family structure) and whether any adults living at the student's home smoke cigarettes. Relative to their peers, topics of interest included levels of direct peer influence (e.g., peer pressure) and indirect influence (e.g., how many of the respondent's five closest friends smoke and how many drink alcohol). Relative to their parents, insights were needed regarding perceived parent awareness, expectations, monitoring, support, involvement, and conflict—primarily related to drinking and smoking behaviors.

3. *Audience*: Who do you need the information from? Whose opinion matters?

Sixth-, seventh-, and eight-grade students in all seven middle schools in a Maryland school district located in a suburb of Washington, D.C., would be recruited for the study. The county was predominantly white but included a relatively large minority of African Americans. Student and parent consent would be needed, as well as review and approval of the study protocol by the Institutional Review Board of the National Institute of Child Health and Human Development, and authorization would be needed from the school district.

4. *Technique:* What is the most efficient and effective way to gather this information?

An anonymous self-administered questionnaire would be used for data collection.

5. *Sample size, source, and selection:* How many respondents should you survey, given your desired statistical confidence levels? Where will you get names of potential respondents? How do you select (draw) your sample from this population to ensure your data are representative of your target audience for the research?

A total of 4,668 students were selected, after 417 special education students with reading difficulties were excluded. (In the end, the parents of 302 students refused to allow their children to participate, and 103 students were absent on both the initial and makeup dates for taking the survey. In total, 4,268, or 91.3% of the students, completed the survey with the following demographic profile: 49.1% boys, 50.9% girls, 67.1% white, 23.5% African American, and 7.2% another race.)

6. *Pretest and Fielding:* Who will pretest the survey instrument (e.g., questionnaire, focus group discussion guide), conduct the research and when?

Extensive pretesting of the measures and the questionnaire were done with repeated samples of volunteer students in the same schools the year prior to the initiation of the study. These assessments included small group sessions where students were asked about the meaning of certain words, phrases, and statements being considered for use in the survey. For the final survey, students were to complete the questionnaire in class or during a makeup session, and two trained proctors were to oversee the data collection in each class of 20 to 30 students. Classroom teachers were to remain in the classroom and were responsible for student discipline but were instructed not to circulate around the room or otherwise be involved while students completed surveys.

7. *Analysis:* How will data be analyzed, and by whom, to meet the planners' needs? A variety of statistical procedures will be considered and applied. This chapter's third primer on basic statistical terminology is presented in Table 4.5.

The prevalence of drinking and smoking behaviors within the past 30 days was to serve as dependent variables for all analyses. Advanced statistical techniques would be used to determine the impact of each of the independent variables on these behaviors.

Table 4.5   A Statistical Primer

Statistics are numbers that help make sense of data. Statistical procedures are tools that are used to organize and analyze the data in order to determine this meaning. The following terms are described very briefly and are only a few among those used in the field.[c]

Terms Describing the Distribution of the Data

Mode: The response or score that occurs with the greatest frequency among findings

Median: The value (score) halfway through the ordered data set, below and above which lies an equal number of values

Mean: The simple average of a group of numbers, often thought of as the one number that best describes the distribution of all other numbers/scores

Range: Determined by subtracting the lowest score from the highest score

Terms Describing Measures of Variability

Margin of Error: A measure indicating how close you can expect your sample results to represent the entire population (e.g., plus or minus 3.5%).

Confidence Interval: A statistic plus or minus a margin of error (e.g., 40% plus or minus 3.5%)

Confidence Level: The confidence level is the probability associated with a confidence interval. Expressed as a percentage, usually 95%, it represents how often the true percentage of the population lies within the confidence interval.

Standard Deviation: A measure of the spread of dispersion of a set of data. It gives you an indication of whether all the data (scores) are close to the average or whether the data are spread out over a wide range. The smaller the standard deviation, the more "alike" the scores are.

Terms Describing Analytical Techniques

Cross-Tabs: Used to understand and compare subsets of survey respondents, providing two-way tables of data with rows and columns allowing you to see two variables at once (e.g., the percentage of men who exercise five times a week compared to the percentage of women who exercise five times a week)

Factor Analysis: Used to help determine what variables (factors) contribute (the most) to results (scores). This analysis, for example, might be used to help determine the characteristics of people who vote (or don't) in every election.

Cluster Analysis: Used to help identify and describe homogeneous groups within a heterogeneous population, relative to attitudes and behaviors used to identify market segments

Conjoint Analysis: Used to explore how various combinations of options (alternatives features, prices, distribution channels, etc.) affect preferences and behavior intent

Discriminant Analysis: Used to find the variables that help differentiate between two or more groups

Terms Describing Samples

Population: A set that includes all units (people) being studied, usually from which a sample is drawn

(Continued)

Table 4.5 (Continued)

Sample: A subset of the population being studied

Probability Sample: Based on some form of random selection. Each population member has a known chance of being included in the sample. This chance measure helps determine the confidence level to be used when interpreting data.

Nonprobability Sample: A sample that was not selected in a random fashion. As a result, results are not representative of the population, and a confidence level cannot then be determined and used when interpreting data.

---

8. *Report:* What information should be included n the report, and what format should be used for reporting?

Final reports and discussions of findings were to include tables displaying results for each of the dependent variables (e.g., friends' problem behavior), cross-referenced by each of the independent variables (e.g., smoking in the past 30 days), and the "odds" that these variables would influence the youth's behavior. Discussions would include a description of prevalence of drinking and smoking, relative to national data. There would be discussions on the degree to which the findings supported (or not) that direct and indirect peer pressure was positively associated with smoking and drinking.

RESEARCH "THAT WON'T BREAK THE BANK"

Alan Andreasen's book *Marketing Research That Won't Break the Bank* has more than 250 pages of suggestions for reducing research costs, a few of which are described in the following section.[21]

• **Use available data,** because it is almost always cheaper than gathering new data and is often "simply lying about as archives waiting to be milked for their marketing and management insights."[22] One place to look is at prior primary research projects that were conducted for your organization but not analyzed thoroughly or with your new research questions in mind. There may also be existing internal records or documents such as attendance levels at events, tallies of zip codes and ages of clients, and anecdotal comments captured by telephone customer service staff. Externally, there are commercial enterprises that sell major marketing research data (e.g., *American Demographics* magazine), and there are also free options, often easily found on the Web (e.g., CDC's BRFSS).

- **Conduct systematic observations,** as they represent "the ultimate in cheap but good research."[23] And just because it might be "free," it doesn't dismiss the need for using a systematic and objective process to collect and interpret the data. As an example, a state drowning coalition may decide they want to measure increases in life vest usage among children as a result of their campaign by observing toddlers on beaches in public parks. A standardized form for volunteers to use and a designated time and day of the week to conduct the research will be important to ensure reliability of the data when comparing pre- and postcampaign measures.

- **Try low-cost experimentation,** a technique often used in the private sector and referred to as "test marketing." In the social sector, it may be more familiar as a "pilot." In either case, the objective is to try things out before rolling them out. There are several advantages, including the ability to control the intervention so that it closely matches the strategic options under consideration. If designed carefully, you can control for extraneous variables and findings can be used to confirm (or not) cause and effect. And they are also "often speedier and more efficient than many other approaches."[24]

- **Use quota sampling** instead of the more costly probability sampling method by developing a profile of the population to be studied and then setting quotas for interviewers so that the final sample matches the major profile of the broader population. For example, a researcher who wanted a projectable sample of opinions of mental health care providers regarding various recovery models might control interviews to match the types of health care organizations in the state (e.g., clinical settings versus hospital settings versus school-based programs). Some maintain these results can still be projectable to the larger similar population "if the quotas are complex enough and interviewers are directed not to interview just easy or convenient cases."[25]

Additional options to consider include *participating in shared cost studies,* sometimes called omnibus surveys. With these studies, you can pay to add a few additional questions to a survey that is being conducted by a research firm for a variety of other organizations, targeting an audience you are interested in. A county department of natural resources, for example, may want to estimate the percentage of households who might be willing to drop off unused prescription drugs at local pharmacies (market demand). They might then take advantage of a marketing research firm's offer to add that question to their monthly countywide survey that queries households on a variety of questions for similar clients. Another option is to *ask professors and students* at universities and colleges to volunteer their assistance. They may find your research proposal of interest and benefit to their current projects and publication goals.

Chapter Summary

It may be easiest for you to remember (even understand) familiar research terms by recognizing the criteria used to categorize them:

- *By research objective*: exploratory, descriptive, causal
- *By stage in planning process*: formative, pretest, monitoring, evaluation
- *By source of information*: secondary, primary
- *By approaches to collecting primary data*: key informant, focus groups, surveys, experimental research, observational research, ethnographic research, mystery shoppers
- *By technique*: qualitative, quantitative

There are eight steps for you to take when developing a research plan, beginning "with the end in mind":

1. Get clear on the purpose of the research.

2. Identify informational objectives.

3. Determine the audience for the research.

4. Find the best technique, given the above.

5. Establish sample size, source, and how it will be drawn.

6. Arrange for pretesting and fielding.

7. Create an analytical approach.

8. Outline contents and format for reporting, helping to ensure methodologies will provide desired management information.

CHAPTER 5

Mapping the Internal and External Environments

Influencing today's teens about clear, consistent, credible anti-drug messages requires full understanding of youth, their wants and needs, and how to counter the ubiquitous pro-drug messages in teens' social and technological environments. Our research and careful crafting of messages is beginning to pay off—teen drug use is down 23 percent over the past five years, and we have reason to believe our campaign has played a significant role.

—Robert Denniston
Director
National Youth Anti-Drug Media Campaign
Office of National Drug Control Policy

With this chapter, the strategic marketing planning process begins, following the 10-step model presented in Chapter 2. Whether you are a student developing a plan for a course assignment or a practitioner working on a project for your organization, this practical approach is intended to guide you in creating a final product destined to "do good." (In Appendix A, you will also find worksheets that follow this planning outline and a resource to receive an electronic copy.) For those among you who are reading this "just for fun," the process is illustrated with a variety of examples to make it come to life for you too.

Step 1, Describing the Plan Background, Purpose, and Focus for your plan, and *Step 2, Conducting a Situation Analysis,* are both relatively brief and will be covered together in this chapter. As mentioned earlier, this model begins "with the end in mind," inspiring your decision-making audiences with the problem your plan will address and the possibility it intends to realize. With this background, you then paint a vivid picture of the marketplace where you will be operating and are honest about the challenges you face and what you will need to address and prepare for in order to be successful.

In our opening case story, you will read how a vivid (though daunting) picture of the marketplace inspired and guided this program to "rise to the occasion."

MARKETING HIGHLIGHT

Above the Influence

National Youth Anti-Drug Media Campaign (2002–2006)

ROBERT W. DENNISTON, MA

Office of National Drug Control Policy

Background

In 1998, the U.S. Congress created the National Youth Anti-Drug Media Campaign with the goal of preventing and reducing youth drug use. Unprecedented in size and scope, the campaign is the most visible symbol of the federal government's commitment to youth drug prevention. A strategically integrated communications effort, the award-winning campaign combines advertising with public communications outreach to deliver clear, consistent, and credible anti-drug messages to America's youth.

Since 2002 the campaign has focused predominantly on marijuana, a policy decision based on the fact that a key public health goal is to delay onset of use of the first drugs of abuse—marijuana, tobacco, and alcohol—which results in fewer drug problems of any kind both in the teen years and for a lifetime. In fact, marijuana constitutes 88% of all teen illegal drug use, and more teens are in drug treatment for marijuana dependence than for all other illegal drugs combined. Today's marijuana is more potent and easily available, and teens are using it at a younger age than a generation ago, which makes them more vulnerable to addiction and related problems.

Situational Analysis

The campaign has spent much effort to assess both its micro-level and macro-level environments, especially factors that help understand the teen target audience.

At the micro-level, the campaign leverages several internal resources and partnerships:

- A solid scientific and behavioral research base to serve as the campaign's foundation, including formative, process, and outcome evaluation
- Rigorous ongoing analysis of teen target beliefs, wants, and needs
- Pro bono advertising partners created in conjunction with the Partnership for a Drug-Free America, involving some of America's top advertising agencies
- Participation by leading media corporations as well as civic, volunteer, youth-serving, education, prevention, public health, and multicultural organizations

Macro-level influences are significant, involving culture, demography, and technology:

- Many teens perceive marijuana to be harmless, despite evidence that use impairs judgment, delays reaction time, and harms brain development and social skills. Some begin use of marijuana to "fit in" with their peers, on the mistaken belief that most are using. Others begin because they have a need for sensation or novelty—the "sensation-seeking" personality. Still others begin use to self-medicate. In popular culture, teen drug use is often normalized and seen as a natural act of youthful rebellion. There is general convergence in drug use patterns among teens: girls have caught up with boys (in part due to the fact that at puberty their self-esteem tends to plummet and they look for more ways to fit in); urban, suburban, and rural rates are more similar than different; and ethnic group use varies more by drug type than across drugs generally.

- Today's technology exposes them to pro-drug messages through the Internet, including pro-drug Web sites, spam, and social networking sites such as MySpace and Facebook. Teens report high prevalence of pro-drug messages in popular media, including movies, video games, television, music, and the Internet, as well as on clothing and other items. When teens kept diaries on drug depiction in the media, they reported that slightly more than half (53%) of the messages they encountered were explicitly pro-drug, with only a little over one third (37%) judged as anti-drug. Moreover, a pulse-check of buzz on the Internet reveals that pro-marijuana messages outnumber anti-marijuana messages 2 to 1.

- While there has always been a generation gap, advances in technology make it even more challenging for parents. One third of 13- to 17-year-olds and half of 16- to 17-year-olds report that their parents know "very little or nothing" about what they do on the Internet, and 65% of parents believe they could do a better job supervising their teen's media use.

- Teens are the most marketed-to segment of society, making it a challenge to break through heavy advertising and teens' media sophistication—and often cynicism.

- Teens' parents are more likely to want to be their teen's friend, thus often giving mixed messages about drug use, in part because their generation was more likely to have used, so they may be uncomfortable asking their own kids not to do something they have done for fear of appearing hypocritical. Many parents believe they are virtually powerless to influence their teen due to the influence of popular culture and peer pressure, so avoid parental responsibilities. Too, they underestimate how easy it is to get alcohol and marijuana.

Audience and Behavioral Objectives

The campaign targets teens, specifically youth aged 12 to 18, their parents, and caregivers. The campaign has segmented its audience to the vast majority of teens who are as yet uncommitted to either use or nonuse, based on the understanding that, like teen sex, just because you did it once does not mean you have to do it again. Parents are considered a key audience because, despite popular belief, they remain the strongest influence on their teens. Goals for the campaign are focused on the overall drug strategy of reducing teen use by 25% within 5 years. To contribute to that bold goal, the campaign has set forth specific objectives to increase teen perception of risk and peer disapproval of drug use, as well as process goals such as advertising reach and frequency. For parents, objectives include increasing the proportion of parents who discuss drugs with their teens frequently and who monitor their teens.

Campaign Strategy

The campaign recognizes that much teen drug use is based on the belief that marijuana is relatively harmless, and that top-down, agenda-driven anti-drug messages have limited credibility and relevance to today's teens. As a result, the campaign has focused for nearly 2 years on the "Above the Influence" brand, which asks teens to remain above the influence of drugs and those who promote drug use as a means of fitting in, demonstrating independence, or just having a good time. A five-phase research process was conducted to explore this concept and develop and test messages before this brand was launched.

This strategy better fits today's teens, who increasingly want to make decisions for themselves and who value relationships. Thus, the message strategy increasingly focuses on aspirational messages, with the key negative consequence being harm to relationships—letting down a friend due to being under the influence or disappointing parents due to drug use—and missing out on opportunities to have fun and enjoy life. Such social consequences tend to be more powerful drivers of behavior than negative consequences that focus on physical harm.

In addition, the campaign aims to reduce the belief that marijuana use is widespread among teens, thus reducing the intent to use the drug to fit in. While today's teens are less likely to disapprove of a peer's drug use—and are generally more accepting of differences in culture and lifestyle—drug use that results in problems for the user or friends is more likely to be actively disapproved of.

The campaign employs various media to deliver its messages to teens:

Advertising: Paid and donated campaign advertising on television, radio, print, and the Internet delivers anti-drug information to target audiences through more than 1,800 media outlets across the country. The ads go through qualitative and quantitative copy testing to ensure messages will be effective when they reach their audiences. About 75% of campaign funds are allocated to the purchase of advertising time and space, which enables high reach and frequency (see Box 5.1).

Box 5.1
Radio Script for Above the Influence
Pete's Couch/Paid Spot: 60 Seconds

VO: I smoked weed and nobody died. I didn't get into a car accident, I didn't drown in some swimming pool, I didn't OD on heroin the next day. Nothing happened. We just sat on Pete's couch for 11 hours. Now you tell me, what's going to happen on Pete's couch? Might be the safest thing in the world, just sitting on Pete's couch for 11 hours—no way you're gonna die. Fact, you wanna keep yourself alive, go over to Pete's and sit on his couch till you're 86. Keep yourself protected from the truly scary things out in the real world—like playing hoops on a concrete court or asking a girl out to the movies. You wanna play it safe, sit on Pete's couch all day every day. Just sit there. Nice and still. Yeah, so I smoked weed and I didn't die. The problem is, I missed driving hard to the basket and I missed a good movie with a nice girl. So even though I didn't die, it's like a different kind of dying. I figure I'll take my chances out there in the real world. I don't know, call me reckless.

ANNCR: Check out abovetheinfluence.com.

Legal: Sponsored by Office of National Drug Control Policy and Partnership for a Drug-Free America.

News Media: Research shows that mass media are a primary source of information about drugs and related issues for both teens and those who influence them, especially parents. The media campaign reaches out to news sources by hosting local/regional media briefings with drug experts; conducting national news conferences with leaders in the areas of public health, education, and youth; and involving youth and parents themselves as authentic voices.

The Internet: The campaign has been a leader in social marketing on the Internet. The campaign's family of Web sites for teens and parents receive approximately 5 million page views and almost 2 million visitors per month. Traffic is driven to the sites through online and traditional advertising and publicity, Web links through Internet sites that support the campaign messages (e.g., news, health, or target-age-related), Internet search engines, and direct access (see Figure 5.1).

Materials: With input from behavioral science experts, the campaign develops a wide range of materials for distribution to its audiences of youth and parents, including a general market booklet, *Navigating the Teen Years: A Parent's Handbook for Raising Healthy Teens*, as well as an interactive CD-ROM for parents. The campaign also produced three parent guides for the general market, African American, and Hispanic (bilingual) parent, and teen postcards encouraging youth to live above the influence of drugs and other pressures.

Entertainment Industry Outreach: The campaign provides information and resources to entertainment industry writers and producers to increase accurate depictions of drug use in entertainment programming. The campaign holds regular media roundtable events for entertainment industry writers and reporters on hot topics such

as methamphetamines, ecstasy, steroids, and early intervention, always involving youth as authentic sources.

Partnerships: Partners distribute anti-drug information, materials, and messages to their members and communities through a number of different channels, including localized Open Letter print ads and events and highly visible meetings attended by young people and their parents. Campaign partners include the National PTA, American Academy of Pediatrics,

Figure 5.1 An Interactive Web Site for Above the Influence Featuring Pete's Couch

American Medical Association, American Academy of Child and Adolescent Psychiatry, Students Against Destructive Decisions, and many ethnic organizations, whose involvement adds credibility and reach to the campaign messages.

Results

In late 2006, the annual Monitoring the Future study, conducted by the University of Michigan, reported a 23% decline in current use of illicit drugs by youth over the past 5 years and a 25% drop in marijuana use (the focus of the campaign). The survey measured past month use of illicit drugs, including marijuana, LSD, other hallucinogens, crack, other cocaine, or heroin, or any use of other drugs among a sample of approximately 50,000 8th, 10th, and 12th graders in public and private secondary schools. The only category of drugs that showed an increase was prescription and over-the-counter products, especially pain relievers such as Vicodin.

While it is difficult to attribute such good news to any particular influence, the campaign interprets these declines as solid signs of success, in part based on tracking data gathered monthly from more than 500 teen interviews to monitor campaign performance in real time. In addition, the campaign has documented a variety of process and output measures through ongoing reports on its results.

For further information about the National Youth Anti-Drug Media Campaign, visit

www.mediacampaign.org

www.abovetheinfluence.com (for youth)

www.freevibe.com (for youth)

www.theantidrug.com (for parents)

MAPPING THE INTERNAL AND EXTERNAL ENVIRONMENTS: STEP #1 AND STEP #2

To illustrate the first two steps in planning, we have chosen, for the most part, scenes and scenarios from China, ones representing social marketing opportunities to address a variety of social issues. Our intention is for you to capture the worldwide applicability for this very portable model.

Step #1: Describing the Plan Background, Purpose, and Focus

Background

Begin the first section of your social marketing plan by briefly identifying the social issue your plan will be addressing—most likely a public health problem, safety concern, environmental threat, or community need. You then move on to present information and facts that led your organization to take on the development of this plan. What's the problem? How bad is it? What happened? What is contributing to the problem? How do you know? It may include epidemiological, scientific, or other research data from credible sources—data that substantiates and quantifies the problem for the reader. The development of the plan might have been precipitated by an unusual event such as a school shooting or it might simply be fulfilling one of your organization's mandates. In either case, this section should leave the reader understanding why you have developed the plan and wanting to read on to find out what you are proposing to do to address the social issue.

It wouldn't be surprising, for example, to find the following paragraphs in the background information of a social marketing plan developed to reduce air pollution in Hong Kong.

In June 2006, a front page article in the *South China Morning Post* reported that according to a major study released the day before, air pollution was costing Hong Kong over 1,600 lives and at least $1.5 billion a year in direct health care costs and $504 million in lost productivity. The research had been conducted and analyzed by experts from three Hong Kong universities and a public policy think tank. The study also found that the city could each year save up to 64,000 bed days in hospitals and 6.8 million visits to family doctors if it improved its air quality from "average" to "good." Hong Kong's air-quality standards were further reported to be below those of Paris, New York, London, and Los Angeles, and the city's concentration of air pollutants exceeded World Health Organization standards by 200%.[1]

Some believe a decade of passive approaches to tackling air pollution is to blame. The good news is that other cities are "recovering," and there are many options and solutions to consider that a social marketing effort could support, including increasing use of public transportation, providing incentives for energy-efficient appliances, fixtures and electric bikes, and replacing old vehicles more quickly.

Purpose

Given this background, you now craft a broad purpose statement for the campaign. It answers the questions, What is the potential impact of a successful campaign? and What difference will it make? This statement is sometimes confused with objective or goal statements. In this planning model, it is different from each of these. An *objective* in a social marketing campaign is what we want our target audience to do (behavior objective) and what they may need to know (knowledge objective) or believe (belief objective) in order to be persuaded. Our *goals* establish a desired level of behavior change as a result of program and campaign efforts. They are quantifiable and measurable. The campaign purpose, by contrast, is the ultimate impact (benefit) that will be realized if your target audience performs the desired behaviors at the intended levels. Typical purpose statements, like the background information, should inspire support for the plan. They don't need to be long or elaborate at this point. The following are a few examples:

- Decrease the spread of HIV/AIDS among African Americans.
- Reduce the amount of time it takes to get through airport security.
- Improve water quality in Lake Sammamish.
- Increase the number of pets in the county that are spayed and neutered.
- Eliminate the stigma surrounding mental illness.

A plausible social marketing plan addressing pedestrian injuries in China illustrates this sequential thought process.

The background section of this plan would have likely included statistics describing pedestrian-related injury rates, locations where injuries occurred, and populations most affected—ones such as the estimate that traffic injuries claim the lives of more than 18,500 children aged 14 and under in China each year. And that further analysis of motor vehicle collisions typically show two main reasons for child traffic injuries: children (1) suddenly running into driveways and (2) crossing a street behind or just in front of a car. Surveys also indicate that 65% of children aged 8 to 10 walk to school, but only 15% are accompanied by adults. And among the 40% of children surveyed who had problems crossing roads, lack of traffic signs and crosswalks were the major problems.[2]

Several related purpose statements might then have been considered, including *increasing proper use of crosswalks by students* and *decreasing accidents among children in driveways*. As you can probably tell, each of these purpose statements will lead you in a different strategic direction, with the crosswalk problem more likely solved by products such as pedestrian flags and fluorescent vests, and the driveway problem addressed by adults walking with children to school and teaching them about navigating driveways. In the end, one would be chosen for the plan (as a start).

Focus

Now a focus is selected to narrow the scope of the plan, choosing from the vast number of potential options to contribute to the plan's purpose (e.g., decrease accidents among children in driveways) one the plan will address (e.g., adults walking with children to school). This decision-making process can begin with brainstorming several major potential approaches (focuses) that might contribute to the plan's purpose. These may be approaches that the agency has discussed or undertaken in the past; they may be new for the organization, recently identified as areas of greatest opportunity or emerging need; or they may be ones that other organizations have focused on and should be considered for your organization. Table 5.1 lists different social issues and possible focuses of each. The areas of potential focus may be behavior-related, population-based (though not yet a target market segment), or product-related strategies, but they are broad at this point. They will get narrowed further in the subsequent planning process.

Several criteria can be used for choosing the most appropriate focus from your initial list of options:

- *Behavior Change Potential:* Is there a clear behavior that can be promoted to address the issue?
- *Market Supply*: Is this issue already being addressed adequately in this way by other organizations and campaigns?
- *Organizational Match:* Is this a good match for the sponsoring organization? Is it consistent with its mission and culture? Can its infrastructure support promoting and accommodating the behavior change? Does it have staff expertise to develop and manage the effort?
- *Funding Sources and Appeal:* Which approach has the greatest funding potential?
- *Impact:* Which approach has the greatest potential to contribute to the social issue?

Table 5.1 **Identifying Potential Focuses for Campaign**

Social Issue (& Hypothetical Sponsoring Organization)	Campaign Purpose	Options for Campaign Focus
Family Planning (Nonprofit Organization)	Decrease teen pregnancies	• Birth control • Abstinence • Sexual assault prevention • Talking to your child about sex • Abortion counseling
Traffic Injuries (State Traffic Safety Commission)	Decrease drinking and driving	• Designated drivers • Underage drinking and driving • Promoting tougher new laws • Military personnel • Repeat offenders
Air Pollution (Regional Air Quality Council)	Reduce fuel emissions	• Carpooling • Mass transit • Walking to work • Telecommuting • Not topping off gas tanks • Gas blowers
Senior Wellness (City Department of Neighborhoods)	Increase opportunities for community senior gatherings	• Tai chi classes in parks • Singing groups in pedestrian malls • Disco dancing under overpasses • Neighborhood watch programs

The best focus for a social marketing campaign would then have a high potential for a behavior change strategy, fill a significant need and void in the marketplace, match the organization's capabilities, and have a high funding potential (see Table 5.2).

Step #2: Conducting a Situation Analysis

Now that you have a purpose and focus for your plan, your next step is to conduct a quick audit of internal factors and external forces that are anticipated to have some impact on or relevance for subsequent planning decisions. As may be apparent, it was critical for you to have selected a purpose and focus for your plan first, as they provide the context for this exercise. Without it, you would be scanning all aspects of the environment versus just the strengths, weaknesses, opportunities, and threats (SWOT) relevant to your specific plan. It would be overwhelming indeed.

Table 5.2   Potential Rationale for Choosing Campaign Focus

Campaign Purpose	Campaign Focus	Rationale for Focus
Decrease teen pregnancies (Nonprofit Organization)	Abstinence	Recent governmental funding for campaigns promoting abstinence in middle schools and high schools Controversial nature of "safe sex" campaigns in school environments
Decrease drinking and driving (State Traffic Safety Commission)	Designated drivers	Opportunities to work with restaurants and bars Familiarity with brand, though little recent promotion in past several years
Reduce fuel emissions (Regional Air Quality Council)	Not topping off gas tanks	Consumer research in other regions revealed a high level of willingness to stop topping off gas tanks after hearing the (low) costs and potential benefits Ease of getting the message out in partnership with gas stations
Increase opportunities for community senior gatherings (City Department of Neighborhoods)	Tai chi classes in parks for seniors	Availability of space at parks and existing roster of tai chi instructors Increasing popularity of this form of exercise and camaraderie for seniors

Figure 5.2 presents a graphic overview of these factors and forces anticipated to have some impact on your target market and therefore your efforts. As indicated, picture your target market at the center of your planning process. (A specific segment of the population you will be targeting will be selected in Step 3, in part based on this analysis.) In the first concentric circle are the 4Ps, the variables that you as a marketer have the most control over. Next, a little farther away from the target, are factors associated with the sponsoring organization for the campaign, ones thought of as the *microenvironment*. The outer concentric circle depicts the *macroenvironment*, forces the marketer has little or no control over but ones that have influence on your target market and therefore your effort.

The Microenvironment: Internal Factors

The microenvironment consists of factors related to the organization sponsoring or managing the social marketing effort—ones therefore considered internal:

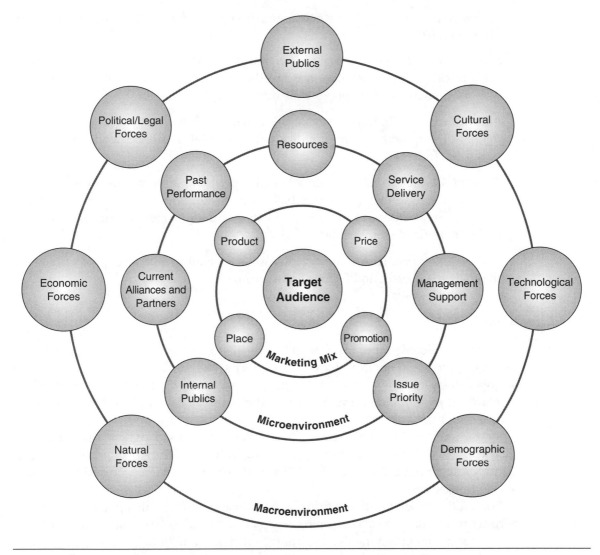

Figure 5.2 Factors and Forces Influencing Your Target Market and Your Efforts

Resources: How are your levels of funding for the project? Is there adequate staff time available? Do you have access to expertise related to the social issue or target populations that you can easily tap?

Service Delivery Capabilities: Does the organization have distribution channels available for current products and services or ones you might develop? Are there any concerns with the current or potential quality of this service delivery?

Management Support: Does management support this project? Have they been briefed on it?

Issue Priority: Within the organization, is the social issue your plan will be addressing a priority for the organization? Are there other issues you will be competing with for resources and support, or is this one high on the list?

Internal Publics: Within the organization, who is likely to support this effort? Who might not? Are there groups or individuals whose buy-in will be needed in order to be successful?

Current Alliances and Partners: What alliances and partners does the sponsoring organization have that could potentially provide additional resources such as funding, expertise, access to target populations, endorsements, message delivery, and/or material dissemination?

Past Performance: How is the organization's reputation relative to projects such as this? What successes and failures are relevant?

Strengths

Make a (bulleted) list of major organizational strengths relative to this plan, based at least in part on an audit of these seven internal factors. These points will be ones your plan will want to *maximize*. You may not have something to note for each of the factors. What you should be aware of is that this list will guide you in many subsequent decisions such as which target markets you can best reach and serve, what products (programs and services) you have the resources and support to develop, prices you will (need to) charge, incentives you will be able to afford to offer, and existing alliances you might be able to tap for delivery of products, services, promotional materials, and messages.

For another brief illustration from China, consider a plan with a purpose to reduce energy consumption and a focus on reducing commercial electrical use, a plan spurred by recent statistics indicating that the energy-efficiency rate of China stood (in 2005) at 33%, 10 percentage points lower than the average advanced world level.[3] One could imagine that a national group charged with responsibility for developing this plan would begin fully aware of one of their major strengths—that as a result of blackouts experienced in dozens of provincial-level power grids, energy saving had topped the government agenda. (In the end, this may have led to changes in infrastructure found today in China—ones such as self-activated escalators in hotel lobbies and hotel rooms that require room keys to be inserted in order for lights to go on. And of course lights then go off as guests leave the room with the key they will need when they return.)

Weaknesses

On the flip side, a similar list is made of factors that don't look as positive for your effort, ones you may need a few action items, even strategies, to *minimize*. This bulleted list is also constructed by reviewing each of the same seven internal factors, noting ones that stand out as a potential concern for developing and implementing a successful plan. Most frequently for governmental agencies and nonprofit organizations (the likely sponsors of a social marketing effort), concerns are in the area of resource availability and issue priority, as in the following example.

Consider internal factors challenging those charged with developing a plan to reduce teen smoking in China, where there are more than 100 million smokers under the age of 18.[4] According to an article in the *China Daily* in May 2006, a nongovernmental organization, China Tobacco Control Association, wants to educate the public about the dangers of teen smoking, "but without money, what can we do?"[5] The article cites a lack of government funds (resources) for antismoking education and a historical lack of priority for this issue. In Beijing, for example, a regulation was issued 10 years ago banning smoking in public areas, but enforcement is apparently weak (an issue priority for a key partner organization in this case) and "smoking is still rampant in these places."[6]

The Macroenvironment: External Forces

The macroenvironment is the set of forces typically outside the influence of the social marketer but must be taken into account, as they may either currently have an impact on your target market or are likely to in the near future. In each of the following seven categories, you will be noting any major trends or events you may want to take advantage of (*opportunities*) or prepare for (*threats*). Remember, you are interested in those related to the purpose and focus for your plan:

Cultural Forces: Trends and happenings related to values, lifestyles, preferences, and behaviors often influenced by factors such as advertising, entertainment, media, consumer goods, corporate policies, fashion, religious movements, health concerns, environmental concerns, and racial issues

Technological Forces: Introduction or potential introduction of new technologies and products that may support or hinder your effort

Demographic Forces: Trends and changes in population characteristics, including age, ethnicity, household composition, employment status, occupation, income, and education

Natural Forces: Forces of "nature," including ones such as famine, fires, drought, hurricanes, energy supply, water supply, endangered species, and floods

Economic Forces: Trends affecting buying power, spending, and perceptions of economic well-being

Political/Legal Forces: Potential laws and actions of governmental agencies that could affect campaign efforts or your target audience

External Publics: Groups outside the organization other than current partners and alliances that could have some impact on your efforts (good or bad) and/or your target audience, including new potential partners

It is important to note, as was discussed in Chapter 1, that social marketing experts are now recommending that you also consider the role you can play to influence decision makers who can impact these upstream forces (e.g., focusing on school district administrators to increase formal physical activity programs in elementary schools).

Opportunities

A major purpose for scanning the external environment is to discover opportunities that you can take advantage of and build into your plan. Your activities can be leveraged by benefiting from the visibility and resources that other groups may be bringing to your issue or the increased awareness and concern that you find is already out there in the general public, as it was in the following example.

According to another article in the *China Daily* in May 2006, the number of pet owners in China has been soaring, as are the associated social problems—ones related to owners not cleaning up pet waste on sidewalks, increases in rabies, and abandonment of pets when an owner turned out to be ill prepared for the responsibility. Several organizations were picking up the challenge, including the country's Ministry of Health and the International Fund for Animal Welfare. An environmental scan on their part would likely identify several macroenvironmental factors impacting their target populations, ones they would consider as they prepare their approach to influencing public behaviors. Most cities in China had removed the ban on dog-rearing in the urban area in the 1980s after food rationing was scrapped (*political/legal*); 2006 was the Year of the Dog on the Chinese calendar (*cultural*); having a pet was now a symbol of prosperity, where in the past it was once looked upon as a bourgeois way of life (*economic*); and some attributed the popularity of pets to a growing sense of loneliness common among city dwellers, particularly the elderly living alone and single white-collar workers (*demographics*).[7]

Threats

On the other hand, some of these forces will represent potential threats to your project and will be something your plan will want to address or prepare for in the event it happens. Understanding the influences on your target population can provide insight, as shown in the following example.

Referring again to the problem with tobacco use in China and the interest in reducing teen smoking, numerous external factors threaten success as well as the internal weaknesses noted earlier. Imagine the following powerful and entrenched cultural, economic, and legal forces operating in the marketplace for those tackling this social issue—ones also mentioned in the May 2006 *China Daily* article:[8]

- People begin smoking at an early age, especially in tobacco-planting areas.
- Parents and teachers smoke in front of children.
- China is the world's largest tobacco producer and consumer, so smoking is accepted, even supported, given the close relationship between the production and consumption of tobacco and the national economy.
- Cigarette companies are still allowed to advertise their brands.
- There are no national laws or regulations in China to forbid selling cigarettes to youngsters.

Review of Past or Similar Efforts

One of the principles for success mentioned in Chapter 3 is to begin your social marketing planning with a search and review of prior efforts undertaken by your agency and similar campaigns planned and launched by others. When reviewing past efforts, you are looking for lessons learned. What worked well? What didn't? What did evaluators think should have been done differently? What was missing? One of the benefits of working in the public and nonprofit sectors is that your peers and colleagues around the world often can and will help you. They can share research, plans, campaign materials, outcomes, and war stories. Finding these resources (and people) can be as simple as joining social marketing Listservs, ones mentioned in Appendix B of this book, that have thousands of members around the world. It can also be as simple as watching what others have done, as illustrated in this next example from China.

Nations and communities around the world interested in increasing bicycling (especially as a commute mode) could benefit from observing what China has done over the decades to make bicycling a social norm. They provide bike lanes, not just paths, ones protected from cars that might be opening a door (see Figure 5.3). At many intersections, there's a traffic signal—just for bikers—one that gives them their own time and space (see Figure 5.4). In Beijing, there are sports coliseums, adding to the excitement

Figure 5.3 Bicycle Lanes Help Create a Social Norm

(and status) of bikers. For those concerned about "overexertion," electric bicycles costing about the same as a cell phone and getting the equivalent of 1,362 miles per gallon of gas are common and certainly not a "sign of weakness." For those concerned about costs, the government makes the competition (cars) very unattractive through escalating gas prices and high fees for vehicle licensing, such as the $5,000 licensing fee in Shanghai that doubles the cost of the cheapest cars.[9] And to those concerned about rain, they've thought of everything, including form-fitted heavy-duty ponchos that protect legs, heads, packages—even two riders (see Figure 5.5).

ETHICAL CONSIDERATIONS WHEN CHOOSING A FOCUS FOR YOUR PLAN

Conscientious social marketers will no doubt face ethical dilemmas and challenges throughout the planning and implementation process. Though ethical considerations are varied, several themes are common: social equity, unintended consequences, competing priorities, full disclosure, responsible stewardship, conflicts of interest, and whether the end justifies (any) means.

Figure 5.4 Traffic Signal Helps Prevent Accidents as Well as "Rewards" Bikers

For each of the planning steps covered in this text, major potential ethical questions and concerns will be highlighted at the completion of most chapters, beginning with this one. We present more questions than answers, with an intention to increase awareness of "ethical moments" and the chances that your decisions will be based on a social conscience that leads all of us to "higher ground."

When you brainstormed potential focuses and then picked one for your current plan, your first ethical question and challenge probably popped up. "What will happen to the ones that you didn't pick?" For decreasing drunk driving, potential focuses mentioned included choosing designated drivers; promoting a new tougher law; and focusing on specific populations, including military personnel or repeat offenders. Since each of these choices would lead to a different marketing strategy, you can only (effectively) deal with one at a time. One potential way to address this challenge is to present a comprehensive organizational plan for the social issue, indicating when important areas of focus will be handled and why they have been prioritized as such.

An additional common question and challenge regarding your focus may also come up, often from a colleague or peer. "If you push your desired behavior, won't you make it tougher for me to accomplish mine?" Some have and will argue, for example, that if you focus on a campaign to increase the number of teens who choose a designated driver, won't you increase the number of teens who drink? Won't it look like "the government" approves of teens drinking? Good questions. And to answer, you will want to be prepared with your background and SWOT data as well as outcomes from prior similar efforts conducted by other agencies in other markets.

Figure 5.5 Removing Another Barrier to Bicycling—Ponchos Made to Fit!

Chapter Summary

This chapter has introduced the first 2 of the 10 steps in the social marketing planning model.

Step #1 is intended to help you (and others) be clear why you are embarking on this project and, in broad and brief terms, what you want to accomplish and where you will focus your efforts. This will include:

- Gathering and presenting background information relative to the social issue your plan will address
- Choosing a campaign purpose
- Brainstorming and then selecting a focus for this plan

Step #2 provides rich descriptions of the marketplace where you will be vying for your customers and creates a common understanding of the internal and external challenges you will face by conducting an analysis of:

- *Internal factors* that impact your readiness for the task, identifying strengths to maximize and weaknesses to minimize related to organizational resources, service delivery, management support, issue priority, internal publics, current alliances and partners, and past performance
- *External forces* that will impact your success, identifying external opportunities to take advantage of and threats to prepare for related to cultural, technological, demographic, natural, economic, and political/legal forces, as well as external publics other than current partners and alliances
- *Prior similar campaigns*, with an interest in lessons learned as well as opportunities for using existing research, plans, and materials developed by others

Part III

ESTABLISHING TARGET AUDIENCES, OBJECTIVES, AND GOALS

CHAPTER 6

Selecting Target Markets

If marketing is a "capitalist tool," then social marketing is a "social capital-
ist" tool. Social marketing can not only make a difference to healthy lifestyle
behaviors like tobacco, physical activity, and nutrition, but it can and should
be used to tackle more complex issues such as violence against women, child
protection, and racial and other forms of discrimination that have enor-
mous implications for people's physical and mental health, community well-
being, and trust between peoples. However, these areas require far more
attention to identifying and communicating with target audiences than do
less complex issues.

—Rob Donovan
Curtin University, Western Australia

Targeted marketing probably makes sense to you by now and sounds good in
theory. It's the practice that creates the greatest angst for many, reflected in
these common musings:

- We're a governmental agency and expected to treat everyone the same. How can
  we justify allocating a disproportionate share of our resources to a few population
  segments? Even worse, how can we justify eliminating some segments altogether?
- I keep hearing about "the low-hanging fruit" that we should go after first. In my
  community clinic, I interpret that to mean that we focus our resources on clients
  who are ready to lose weight, ready to exercise. I don't get it. Don't the ones
  who aren't ready need us the most to convince them they should?
- If a marketing plan is built around and for a particular segment of the population, does that mean we'll have to have separate and multiple marketing plans
  for every audience we are trying to influence? That seems over the top.
- Sometimes this just sounds like fancy language for nothing that really happens
  in reality. When we do a billboard for organ donation, everyone in town sees it.
  How is that target marketing?

We believe this inspiring opening case addressing domestic violence in Australia
will begin to answer these questions and address these concerns.

Freedom From Fear

Targeting Male Perpetrators of Intimate Partner Violence (1998–2005)

ROBERT DONOVAN, PHD

MARK FRANCAS, MA

DONNA PATERSON, MPH

Background

Violence against women is a major public health problem in both developing and developed countries around the globe. The total costs of violence against women—including medical and counseling costs, lost productivity, women's refuges, and justice system costs—run into the billions of dollars.[1] The emotional, psychological, and quality of life costs for women and children exposed to such violence are immeasurable.

Most campaigns in this area have targeted women victims to "break the silence": to report the violence to legal authorities and to seek support for themselves and their children. These campaigns have been supported by changes to judicial systems and public education campaigns that emphasize that domestic violence is as much a crime as any other form of assault and that the police will take prompt action against perpetrators, who will face charges and severe penalties if convicted. These social marketing campaigns are assumed to have some deterrent effects on perpetrators.[2]

Western Australia's Freedom From Fear campaign is one of the first government-funded, population-wide, nonpunitive campaigns to target men who use violence against their female partners to urge the men to voluntarily seek help to stop their violence. Although the campaign explicitly targeted perpetrators and potential perpetrators, the campaign's targeted beneficiaries were the female victims and their children. The core product benefit for women whose partners sought help was freedom from fear.

Target Audience

Men who use violence against women are a diverse group but appear to share common attitudes and beliefs about masculinity and power relationships to women.[3] They are represented in all social classes and demographic groupings, although prevalence appears higher in lower socioeconomic and disadvantaged groups, no doubt due to additional stressors that exacerbate tensions in the relationships. Violence by men against intimate partners is more frequent among men who were exposed to violence against their mother (or themselves) in the home as a child and is exacerbated by alcohol and drug abuse and economic and psychological stressors such as job loss. The roots of men's violence against women may also lie in the far greater propensity to violence in general exhibited by men relative to that exhibited by women.

Given this diversity and the range of predisposing factors among the target audience, our primary segmentation framework was the individual's "readiness" to do something about their violence. The primary target audience consisted of male perpetrators and potential perpetrators in Prochaska and DiClemente's contemplation and ready-for-action stages of change.[4] Precontemplator perpetrators who were unaware of any problem or who denied the problem and "blamed" the woman for the violence were not a primary target audience.

Secondary target audiences were intermediaries who may come into contact with men who used violence (e.g., police, counselors, welfare workers, health professionals).

Given the mass media nature of the campaign, the campaign messages were designed to have a positive impact on men but not cause unnecessary distress to female victims and their children.

Behavior Objectives

The behavior objective for the primary target audience was to seek help—primarily by calling the Men's Domestic Violence Help Line (MDVHL). This was a new service specifically set up for this campaign. Telephone counselors were trained to encourage callers to enroll in behavior change programs provided by nongovernmental partner organizations. Alternatively, callers were asked if they could be sent self-help literature or audiotapes or to stay on the line for counseling (see Figure 6.1).

The behavior objective for intermediaries was to distribute cards and other materials

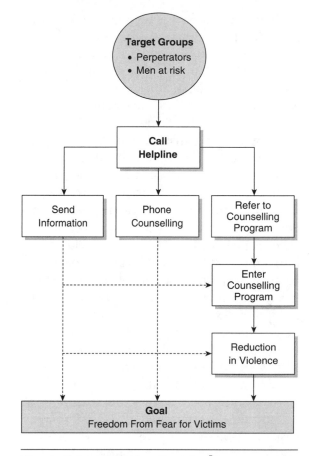

Figure 6.1 Campaign Overview[5]

with the MDVHL number to primary target audience members.

Strategy

Given the covert (and illegal) nature of intimate partner violence, it was decided that paid mass media advertising (a "pull" strategy) was the most viable means to reach the primary target audience in sufficient numbers to achieve a significant response. Extensive qualitative research was then undertaken with potential perpetrators to assess whether a sufficiently sized segment of contemplators existed; what, if any, messages might motivate them to seek help; and whether the men would respond to those messages delivered via mass media advertising.

It was found that men in the "ready to change" stage of change responded positively to messages about the negative consequences of their violence for any children in the household and to the offer of formal help via a men's domestic violence help line. Primary target audience members who did not have children still responded to this message, many of them recalling their own experience of violence as children. It was also found that the "consequences to children" message had the potential to move precontemplators toward contemplation, as they could accept that domestic violence, even if they were not responsible, could impact negatively on any children in the household.

The messages were then executed in various ways and pretested against primary target audiences to ensure the messages were understood, believable, and motivating while at the same time not appearing to condemn or condone violent behavior against women. It was also crucial to ensure that the message executions did not lead to any increased violence against women. The message executions were tested against female victims and their children to ensure there were no undesirable unintended effects on these audiences. The messages were also exposed to other stakeholders for feedback.[6] Ethical issues were of paramount importance in message development.[7] It was crucial that the ads did not aggravate the men and result in increased violence against their partners. Also, even though the ads were only screened outside children's programming times, it was crucial that children exposed to the ads did not misinterpret the ads.

The final television ads were quite graphic and showed verbal threats but no actual physical violence, cutting alternately from scenes of a male directing anger toward a woman and close-ups of children's faces listening to the violence. One scene depicted a young boy tossing and turning in bed with the words "This little boy is not having a nightmare. He is living one" appearing on the screen. All TV ads ended with a call for men to call the help line with the tag "Only you can stop domestic violence. Call the Men's Domestic Violence Help Line . . ."

Television was used in 2- or 3-month-long bursts during each year, supported by radio between these bursts. The campaign received substantial government support from 1998 until 2001 and continues, but with far less funding since 2004. The media budget for the first 2 years was approximately A$450,000 ($384,388 USD) per year, dropping to A$270,000 ($230,633 USD) in the third year, to A$150,000 ($128,129 USD) in 2005.

Men's counselors were recruited and trained for the MDVHL. Twelve new counseling programs, six in rural areas and six in the metropolitan area, were commissioned by the state government and provided by nongovernmental agencies. While results vary, such programs have generally been found to be effective in reducing future violence.[8]

Results

The campaign achieved over 85% awareness among men aged 18–40 years within 6 months of the campaign launch. When asked the unprompted question about where men who used violence against their female partner could go for help, 23% nominated a help line after 6 weeks of the campaign, rising to over 50% 6 months into the campaign. Prior to the campaign, none mentioned a help line. After the initial 6-week evaluation, the ads were changed to place more emphasis on the help line.[9]

Since the beginning of the campaign in August 1998 to January 2005, the help line received 21,000 calls. Of these, approximately 5,000 were identified as potential perpetrators and 8,000 self-identified as perpetrators. Nearly half of the perpetrators accepted a referral for counseling. While we have no data from partners, self-report evaluation instruments indicate that men who complete the programs say they are now less likely to use physical violence.[10] Similar responses were obtained from a small

sample of callers to the help line interviewed early in the campaign.[11] It is estimated that the cost per completion of these programs is around A$3,500 ($2,990 USD) per man, compared with estimated costs for treating a victim of domestic violence at around A$60,000 ($51,252 USD) per annum.

Concluding Comment

Target audience identification and understanding were essential for the success of this campaign. The research was crucial in gaining an understanding of not just the primary target audience but also other stakeholders and those exposed to the campaign, especially female victims and children.

STEP #3: SELECTING TARGET MARKETS

At this point in the planning process, you would have established the following components of your plan, illustrated with a hypothetical example for a city utility:

- *Purpose* (e.g., decrease landfill and hauling costs)
- *Focus* (e.g., backyard composting of food waste)
- *Strengths* to maximize (e.g., as a utility, access to the customer base)
- *Weaknesses* to minimize (e.g., the utility's curbside yard waste collection service just started accepting food waste, an internal, friendly competitor for the food waste)
- *Opportunities* to capture (e.g., continued community interest in natural gardening)
- *Threats* to prepare for (e.g., potential to increase rodent populations)
- Possible discovery of *existing campaigns* that will be useful for your efforts

You are now ready to select one or more target markets for your campaign, defined as *"a set of buyers sharing common needs or characteristics that the company decides to serve."*[12] They are subsets of the larger group (population) that may also be exposed to your efforts. In the utility example, residential households are the implied population of focus for the backyard composting campaign. Your marketing strategy will be crafted, however, to be particularly effective with one or more subsets of these diverse residents.

STEPS INVOLVED IN SELECTING TARGET MARKETS

Determining these targets for your campaign is a three-step process involving *segmentation*, *evaluation,* and then *selection*. Each of these steps is described briefly in the following section and elaborated upon in remaining sections of the chapter.

1. *Segment the Market*

First, the most relevant (larger) population for the campaign is divided into smaller groups that will likely require unique but similar strategies in order to be persuaded to change their behavior. The groups you end up with should have something in common (needs, wants, motivations, values, behavior, lifestyles, etc.)—something that makes them likely to respond similarly to your offer. Based on background information about attitudes toward composting indicating that avid gardeners were the most interested in composting, this city utility might identify four market segments to consider. As you will see, their segmentation is based initially on a combination of lifestyle and behavior variables:

- Avid gardeners putting most of their food waste in their *yard waste container*
- Avid gardeners putting most of their food waste in the *garbage* or *down the drain*
- Avid gardeners putting most of their food waste in a *backyard composter*
- Remaining households without avid gardeners

2. *Evaluate Segments*

Each segment is then evaluated based on a variety of factors described later in the chapter, ones that will assist you in prioritizing (perhaps even eliminating some) segments. For the food waste composting scenario, planners should be very eager to know more about each of these segments, beginning with *size* (number of households in this group) as a way to understand the impact the segment is having on the solid waste stream. They would also consider their *ability to reach* each identified segment and *how receptive* they might be to the idea of composting food waste in their backyard. Avid gardeners, for example, are likely to be the most interested in taking on this new practice, as they would likely see the value in the compost for their gardens.

3. *Choose One or More Segments for Targeting*

Ideally, you are able to select only one or a few segments as target markets for the campaign and then develop a rich profile of their unique characteristics, one that will inspire strategies that will appeal uniquely and effectively to your chosen segment. Keep in mind that if you select more than one market, it is likely you will need a different marketing mix strategy for each one. A campaign to influence the avid gardeners who are currently putting their food waste in their yard waste to switch to putting it in a composter would have different incentives and messages, perhaps even communication channels, than one intending to persuade those who aren't avid gardeners to start composting their food waste. In fact, it is likely the utility would make this segment its last priority, given the challenges they would face in creating and delivering value to this segment in exchange for their effort.

This segmentation and targeting process, though sometimes tedious and complex, provides numerous benefits—ones long familiar to corporate sector marketers who "know that they cannot appeal to all buyers in their markets, or at least not all buyers in the same way":[13]

- *Increased effectiveness:* Outcomes (numbers of behaviors successfully influenced) will be greater, as you have designed strategies that address your target market's unique wants and preferences and have therefore "worked." (It's like fishing. If you use the bait that the fish you want like, you're more likely to catch the ones you want—and more of them!)
- *Increased efficiencies:* Outcomes relative to outputs (resources expended) are also likely to be greater, again as a result of targeting your efforts and resources to market segments with a higher likelihood of responding to your offer. (And back to the fish analogy, you are also likely to catch all these fish in a shorter period of time and with less bait.)
- *Input for resource allocation:* As a result of evaluating each of the segments, you have objective information that will assist you in distributing your resources and providing this rationale to others.
- *Input for developing strategies:* This process will leave you with detailed profiles of a segment that then provides critical insights into what will influence an audience to buy your behavior.

Even if, for a variety of purposes, programs are developed for all markets, segmentation at least organizes and provides a framework for developing strategies that are more likely to be successful with each of the markets.

VARIABLES USED TO SEGMENT MARKETS

Potential variables and models for segmenting a market are vast, and still expanding. Traditional approaches used by commercial sector marketers for decades are described in this section, as well as unique models successfully applied by social marketing theorists and practitioners.

Keep in mind that during this initial segmentation process, before you have actually chosen a target market, your objective is to create several attractive potential segments for consideration. You will select variables that are the most meaningful predictors of market behavior to characterize each group, ending up with groups that are likely to respond similarly to your offer (desired behavior).

Traditional Variables

Segmentation variables typically used to categorize and describe consumer markets are outlined in Table 6.1. Each is applicable to a social marketing environment (marketplace) as well.[14]

Demographic segmentation divides the market into groups on the basis of variables common to census forms: age, gender, marital status, family size, income, occupation (including the media, legislators, physicians, etc.), education, religion, race, and nationality. Sometimes referred to as sociodemographic or socioeconomic factors, these are the most popular bases for grouping markets, for several reasons. First, these are some of the *best predictors* of needs, wants, barriers, and behaviors. Second, this type of information about a market is *more readily available* than it is for other variables, such as personality characteristics or attitudes. Finally, these are often the easiest ways to *describe and find a targeted segment* and to share with others working to develop and implement program strategies.

Example: A demographic basis for segmentation could be quite appropriate in planning an immunization campaign, because immunization schedules vary considerably according to age. Planners might understandably create unique strategies for each of the following population segments in their local community:

- Birth to 2 years (3%)
- 3 to 6 years (5%)
- 7 to 17 years (20%)
- Adults, 18 to 64 years (52%)
- Seniors, 65 years and over (20%)

Geographic segmentation divides a market according to geographical areas, such as continents, countries, states, regions, counties, cities, and neighborhoods, as well as related elements, such as commute patterns, places of work, and proximity to relevant landmarks.

Example: An organization focused on reducing the number of employees driving to work in single-occupant vehicles might find it most useful to develop strategies based on *where employees live* relative to the worksite, current van pools, current car pools, and each other. The planner might then decide that the first four groups represent the greatest opportunity for hooking up employees with attractive alternative and/or existing forms of transportation:

- Employees living on current van pool routes (10%)
- Employees living within 5 miles of current car pools (5%)
- Employees living within 5 miles of each other (15%)
- Employees living within walking or biking distance of the workplace (2%)
- All other employees (68%)

Table 6.1   Major Segmentation Variables for Consumer Markets

Variable	*Sample Classifications*
Geographic	
World, region, or country	North America, Western Europe, Middle East, Pacific Rim, China, India, Canada, Mexico
Country or region	Pacific, Mountain, West North Central, West South Central, East North Central, East South Central, South Atlantic, Middle Atlantic, New England
City or metro size	Under 5,000; 5,000–20,000; 20,000–50,000; 50,000–100,000; 100,000–250,000; 250,000–500,000; 500,000–1,000,000; 1,000,000–4,000,000; 4,000,000 or over
Density	Urban, suburban, rural
Climate	Northern, southern
Demographic	
Age	Under 6, 6–11, 12–19, 20–34, 35–49, 50–64, 65+
Gender	Male, female
Family size	1–2, 3–4, 5+
Income	Under $10,000; $10,000–$20,000; $20,000–$30,000; $30,000–$50,000; $50,000–$100,000; $100,000 and over
Occupation	Professional and technical; managers, officials, proprietors; clerical, sales; craftspeople; supervisors; operatives; farmers; retired; students; homemakers; unemployed
Education	Grade school or less, some high school, high school graduate, some college, college graduate
Religion	Catholic, Protestant, Jewish, Muslim, Hindu, other
Race	Asian, Hispanic, black, white
Generation	Baby boomer, Generation X, echo boomer
Nationality	North American, South American, British, French, German, Italian, Japanese
Psychographic	
Social class	Lower lower, upper lower, working class, middle class, upper middle, lower upper, upper upper
Lifestyle	Achievers, strivers, strugglers
Personality	Compulsive, gregarious, authoritarian, ambitious
Behavioral	
Occasions	Regular occasion, special occasion
Benefits	Quality, service, economy, convenience, speed
User status	Nonuser, ex-user, potential user, first-time user, regular user
Usage rate	Light user, medium user, heavy user
Loyalty status	None, medium, strong, absolute
Readiness stage	Unaware, aware, informed, interested, desirous, intending to buy
Attitude toward product	Enthusiastic, positive, indifferent, negative, hostile toward product

SOURCE: From *Principles of Marketing,* 9th ed. (p. 252), by P. Kotler and G. Armstrong. Copyright © 2001. Reprinted by permission of Pearson Education, Inc., Upper Saddle River, NJ.

Psychographic segmentation divides the market into different groups on the basis of social class, lifestyle, values, or personality characteristics. You may find that your market varies more by a personal value, such as concern for the environment, than by some demographic characteristic, such as age.

Example: A campaign to reduce domestic violence might find it most important to develop campaign programs based on levels of self-esteem among potential victims:

- High self-esteem (20%)
- Moderate self-esteem (50%)
- Low self-esteem (30%)

Behavior segmentation divides the market on the basis of knowledge, attitudes, and behaviors relative to the product being sold. Several variables can be considered within this approach: segmenting according to *occasion* (when the product is used or decided on), *benefit sought* (what the segment wants from using the product), *usage levels* (frequency of usage), *readiness stage* (relative to buying), and *attitude* (toward the product/offering).

Example: A blood donation center may increase efficiencies by prioritizing resource allocation according to donation history, allocating the most resources to loyal donors, those who have given in the past:

- Gave more than 10 times in past 5 years (10%)
- Gave 2 to 10 times in past 5 years (10%)
- Gave only once, less than 5 years ago (5%)
- Gave only once, more than 5 years ago (5%)
- Never given at this blood center (70%)

In reality, marketers rarely limit their segmentation to the use of only one variable, as we did to illustrate each of these variables. More often, they use a combination of variables that provide a rich profile of a segment or help to create smaller, better defined target groups.[15] Even if, for example, the blood center decided to target the 20% of the market who had given more than once in the past 5 years, they might further refine the segment by blood type if a particular type was in short supply and high demand.

Stages of Change

The *stages of change model,* also referred to as the *transtheoretical model,* was originally developed by Prochaska and DiClemente in the early 1980s[16] and has been tested and refined over the past two decades. In a 1994 publication, *Changing for*

Good, Prochaska, Norcross, and DiClemente describe six stages that people go through to change behavior.[17] As you read about each one, imagine the implications for a specific population you are working with or, if you are a student, one you have chosen for the focus of a class project.

Precontemplation: "People at this stage usually have no intention of changing their behavior, and typically deny having a problem."[18] Relative to the behavior you are "selling" you could think of this market as "sound asleep." They may have woken up and thought about it at some point in the past, but they then went back to sleep. In the case of an effort to convince people to quit smoking, this segment is not thinking about quitting, and they probably don't even consider their tobacco use a problem.

Contemplation: "People acknowledge that they have a problem and begin to think seriously about solving it."[19] Or they may have a want or desire and have been thinking about fulfilling it. They are "awake but haven't moved." This segment of smokers is considering quitting for any number of reasons but haven't definitely decided they will, have numerous considerations and concerns, and haven't taken any steps.

Preparation: "Most people in the Preparation Stage are (now) planning to take action . . . and are making the final adjustments before they begin to change their behavior."[20] Back to our analogy, they are sitting up—maybe even have their feet on the floor. In this segment, smokers have decided to quit and may have told others about their intentions. They probably have decided how they will quit and by when.

Action: "The Action Stage is one in which people most overtly modify their behavior and their surroundings. They stop smoking cigarettes, remove all desserts from the house, pour the last beer down the drain, or confront their fears. In short, they make the move for which they have been preparing."[21] They have "left the bed." This segment has recently stopped smoking cigarettes. It may not be, however, a new habit yet.

Maintenance: "During Maintenance (individuals) work to consolidate the gains attained during the action and other stages and struggle to prevent lapses and relapse."[22] This segment has not had a cigarette for perhaps 6 months or a year and remains committed to not smoking. But they have to work at times to remind themselves of the benefits they are experiencing and distract themselves when "tempted" to relapse.

Termination: "The termination stage is the ultimate goal for all changers. Here, (a) former addiction or problem will no longer present any temptation or threat."[23] This segment is not tempted to return to smoking. They are now "nonsmokers" for life.

One of the attractive features of this model is that the authors have identified a relatively simple way to assess a market's stage. They suggest four questions to ask, and on the basis of responses (decision), respondents are categorized in one of the four stages.[24] Table 6.2 summarizes the groupings by stage of change, on the basis of the four responses.

Table 6.2   Determining Stage of Change

Decision/ Response Taken	Decision/Response Taken By:				
	Precontemplation Segment	Contemplation Segment	Preparation Segment	Action Segment	Maintenance Segment
I solved this problem more than 6 months ago	No	No	No	No	Yes
I have taken action within the past 6 months	No	No	No	Yes	Yes
I intend to take action in the next month	No	No	Yes	Yes	Yes
I intend to take action in the next 6 months	No	Yes	Yes	Yes	Yes

In the model shown in Box 6.1, the "name of the marketer's game" is to move segments to the next stage. The authors (Prochaska, Norcross, and DiClemente) offer cautions:

> Linear progression is a possible but relatively rare phenomenon. In fact, people who initiate change begin by proceeding from contemplation to preparation to action to maintenance. Most, however, slip up at some point, returning to the contemplation, or sometimes even the precontemplation stage, before renewing their efforts.[25]

BOX 6.1
Stages of Change Progression

Precontemplation ⇒ Contemplation ⇒ Preparation ⇒

Action ⇒ Maintenance ⇒ Termination

Figure 6.2 is the authors' graphic representation of the more likely pattern of change, a spiral one.

Diffusion of Innovation

Some consider this model one of the more important ones for people (like you) attempting to segment the market and influence the behavior of large groups of people. Kotler and Roberto describe this concept of diffusion (or spread) of the adoption of new behaviors through a population and its applicability to social marketing, referencing original work by Rogers and Shoemaker:

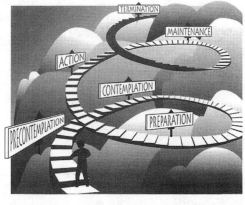

Figure 6.2   The Spiral of Change[26]

The ability of social marketers to plan and manage the diffusion or spread of adoptions to the largest possible target-adopter population requires an understanding of both individual behavior and the mechanisms by which new ideas and practices spread to the larger group or population of target adopters.

Innovation diffusion research suggests that different types of adopters accept an innovation at different points in time. Table 6.3 summarizes the size, timing of adoption, and motivations for adoption of each target-adopter segment. The diffusion process begins with a small (2.5%) segment of innovative-minded adopters. These adopters are drawn to novelty and have a need to be different. They are followed by an early adopter segment (13.5%), who are drawn by the social product's intrinsic value. A third early majority segment (34%) perceive the spread of a product and decide to go along with it, out of their need to match and imitate. The late majority (34%) jump on the bandwagon, and the remaining segment, the laggards (16%), follow suit as the product attains popularity and broad acceptance.[27]

This segmentation model might be applicable, for example, to a campaign influencing citizens to consider renewable energy resources such as solar power, wind power, and biodiesel fuel. Early efforts would be designed to appeal to the Innovators and Early Adopters, a different appeal than to the Late Majority and especially the Laggards.

Healthstyles Segmentation

Another segmentation model used for health-related program planning appears in Table 6.4. This system incorporates several segmentation variables, including demographics, psychographics, and behaviors (knowledge, attitudes, and behaviors related to personal health). Resulting segments provide planners with a rich and memorable picture of each potential target audience, aiding in the development of winning strategies

Table 6.3 **Elements of the Diffusion Innovation Model That Are Useful for Diffusion Planning**

Target-Adopter Segments	Hypothetical Size (%)	Timing Sequence of Adoption	Motivation for Adoption
Innovator segment	2.5	First	Need for novelty and need to be different
Early adopter segment	13.5	Second	Recognition of adoption object's intrinsic/convenience value from contact with innovators
Early majority segment	34.0	Third	Need to imitate/match and deliberateness trait
Late majority segment	34.0	Fourth	Need to join the bandwagon triggered by the majority opinion legitimating the adoption object
Laggard segment	16.0	Last	Need to respect tradition

SOURCE: Adapted with permission of The Free Press, a division of Simon & Schuster, Inc., from *Communications of Innovations: A Cross-Cultural Approach* (2nd ed.), by Everett M. Rogers, with F. Floyd Shoemaker. Copyright @ 1962, 1971 by The Free Press

for that market. For example, a physical activity campaign wanting to influence Decent Dolittles, who may not have confidence in their ability to exercise, might emphasize the benefits of moderate physical activity, how it can fit into everyday life and activities, and the opportunities to "hang out with their friends" while doing it. By contrast, a strategy to influence the Tense but Trying segment would switch the emphasis to the health benefits of exercise, especially for stress-related illnesses.

Cluster Systems: PRIZM® and VALS™

Two well-known commercial models used to group consumer markets into homogeneous segments, often referred to as clusters, are the PRIZM NE and VALS products.

PRIZM NE is a geodemographic classification system offered by the Claritas Corporation that describes every U.S. neighborhood in terms of 66 distinct social group types, called segments.[28] Each zip code is assigned one or several of these 66 clusters, based on the shared socioeconomic characteristics of the area. It is based on the fundamental premise that "birds of a feather flock together," and that when choosing a place to live, people tend to seek out neighborhoods compatible with their lifestyles, where they find others in similar circumstances with similar consumer behavior patterns. Segments are given snappy, memorable names like "God's Country," "Red, White & Blues," "Kids & Cul-de-Sacs," and "Blue Blood Estates." Each segment is then described for the user,

Table 6.4   Healthstyles Segmentation System, American Healthstyles Audience Segmentation Project

Decent Dolittles (24%)

They are one of the less health-oriented groups. Although less likely to smoke or drink, they also are less likely to exercise, eat nutritiously, and work to stay at their ideal weights. Decent Dolittles know that they should be performing these behaviors to improve their health, but they do not feel that they have the ability. Their friends and family tend to avoid these behaviors as well. They describe themselves as "religious," "conservative," and "clean."

Active Attractives (13%)

They place a high emphasis on looking good and partying. Active Attractives are relatively youthful and moderately health oriented. They tend not to smoke and limit their fat intake more than do other groups. They are highly motivated, intending to exercise and keep their weight down, but they do not always succeed at this. Alcohol consumption is an important part of their lifestyle, and Active Attractives often are sensation seekers, constantly looking for adventure. They describe themselves as "romantic," "dynamic," "youthful," and "vain."

Hard-Living Hedonists (6%)

They are not very interested in health and tend to smoke and drink alcohol more heavily and frequently than do other groups. They also enjoy eating high-fat foods and do not care about limiting their fat intake. Despite this, they tend not to be overweight and are moderately physically active. Although they are the group least satisfied with their lives, they have no desire to make any health-related changes. Hard-Living Hedonists also are more likely to use stimulants and illicit drugs than are other segments. They describe themselves as "daring," "moody," "rugged," "independent," and "exciting."

Tense but Trying (10%)

They are similar to the more health-oriented segments except that they tend to smoke cigarettes. They are average in the amount of exercise they get and in their efforts to control their fat intake and weight. They have a moderate desire to exercise more, eat better, and control their weight more effectively as well. The Tense but Trying tend to be more anxious than other groups, with the highest rate of ulcers and use of sedatives and a higher number of visits to mental health counselors. They describe themselves as "tense," "high-strung," "sensitive," and "serious."

Noninterested Nihilists (7%)

They are the least health oriented and do not feel that people should take steps to improve their health. Accordingly, they smoke heavily, actively dislike exercise, eat high-fat diets, and make no efforts to control their weight. Despite this, they tend to drink alcohol only moderately. Of all the groups, Noninterested Nihilists have the highest level of physical impairment, the most sick days in bed, and the most medical care visits related to an illness. They describe themselves as being "depressed," "moody," and "homebodies."

Physical Fantastics (24%)

They are the most health-oriented group, leading a consistently health-promoting lifestyle. They are above average in not smoking or drinking, exercising routinely, eating nutritiously, and making efforts to control their weight. They tend to be in their middle or latter adult years and have a relatively large number of chronic health conditions. Physical Fantastics follow their physicians' advice to modify their diets and routinely discuss health-related topics with others.

Passive Healthy (15%)

They are in excellent health, although they are somewhat indifferent to living healthfully. They do not smoke or drink heavily and are one of the most active segments. Although they eat a high amount of dietary fat, they are the trimmest of all the groups. The Passive Healthy do not place much value on good health and physical fitness and are not motivated to make any changes in their behaviors.

SOURCE: Reprinted by permission of Sage Publications Ltd. from Maibach, E. A., Ladin, E. A. K., Slater, M., "Translating Health Psychology Into Effective Health Communication: The American Healthstyles Audience Segmentation Project," in *Journal of Health Psychology, 1*, pp. 261–277. As appeared in Weinreich, N., *Hands-on social marketing: A step-by-step guide* (p. 55).

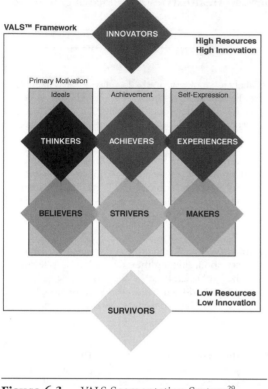

providing demographic as well as lifestyle-related behaviors. A state department of ecology interested in reducing litter, for example, might be interested in having Claritas analyze the addresses and zip codes of citizens receiving tickets for littering, providing information that will help the department with message and communication strategies, such as what bus routes in the city would be best for ads promoting the $1,025 fine for littering lit cigarette butts. (See Appendix B for more information on this resource.)

The well-known VALS segmentation system categorizes U.S. adult consumers into one of eight segments, indicative of personality traits considered to be determinants (drivers) of buying behaviors. The eight primary VALS consumer types are shown graphically in the VALS framework (see Figure 6.3). The horizontal dimension in the figure represents the primary motivations, and the vertical dimension represents resources. Using the primary motivation and resources dimensions, VALS defines eight primary types of adult consumers who have different attitudes and exhibit distinctive behavior and decision-making patterns. How would you use this? If you are a nonprofit organization with a mission to increase voter turnout, this system might be very helpful in

Figure 6.3   VALS Segmentation System[29]

first identifying segments representing the greatest opportunities for increased voting, creating an offer this group would find particularly motivating, and then, by using the GeoVALS system, targeting a direct mail campaign or get-out-to-vote effort in zip codes with high concentrations of these types. (See Appendix B for more information on this resource, including a Web site where you can complete the questionnaire and determine your VALS type.)

Segmenting Target Audiences Upstream

To this point, we have been focusing on consumer market segmentation variables. As you read in Chapter 1, however, real social change strategies often need to focus efforts on influencing markets upstream from the individual—politicians, media figures, community activists, corporations, schools, foundations, and others with influence over your target market and their environments. The segmentation process is the same for these populations; however, the variables are likely to differ. Politicians, for example, might be segmented by what committees they serve on or by political party.

The corporate market will more likely be segmented by industry type, schools by administrative level, foundations by areas of focus, and media figures by type of media. Once segmented, you will still proceed to the next two steps of evaluation and choosing.

Combination of Variables

As noted earlier, it is rare that a market will be segmented using only one variable. However, one base is often used as a primary way to group a market (e.g., age for immunization); then each segment is further profiled, and perhaps narrowed, by using additional important and relevant variables that predict response to strategies (e.g., education and income levels within each of the age segments for immunization).

"The most appropriate segmentation variables are those that best capture differences in the behavior of target adopters."[30] For social marketing planning, we encourage you to consider using behavior-related segmentation variables as the primary base for profiling the market, similar to the ones in the stages of change model described earlier. Segments

Table 6.5   Hypothetical Segmentation Using Stages of Change as Primary Bases

Stage of Change	Precontemplation	Contemplation	Preparation for or in Action	Maintenance
Behavior and intent	Throw cigarette butts out the window and aren't concerned about it.	Throw cigarette butts out the window, feel bad about it, and have been thinking about not doing it.	Sometimes throw cigarette butts out the window and sometimes use ashtray. Trying to increase use of ashtray.	Never throw cigarette butts out the window; use ashtray instead.
Size	20%	30%	30%	20%
Geographics (residence)	Rural (10%) Suburban (40%) Urban (50%)	Rural (8%) Suburban (55%) Urban (37%)	Rural (6%) Suburban (65%) Urban (29%)	Rural (5%) Suburban (70%) Urban (25%)
Demographics (age)	16–21 (60%) 21–34 (25%) 35–50 (10%) 50+ (5%)	16–21 (53%) 21–34 (22%) 35–50 (15%) 50+ (10%)	16–21 (45%) 21–34 (20%) 35–50 (20%) 50+ (15%)	16–21 (30%) 21–34 (18%) 35–50 (27%) 50+ (25%)
Psychographics (environmental ethic)	Environmentally: Concerned (10%) Neutral (30%) Not concerned (60%)	Environmentally; Concerned (15%) Neutral (45%) Not concerned (40%)	Environmentally; Concerned (30%) Neutral (40%) Not concerned (30%)	Environmentally: Concerned (60%) Neutral (30%) Not concerned (10%)

are then profiled using other meaningful variables. Table 6.5 illustrates a hypothetical profile of market segments that a planner might compile at this stage in the planning process. It uses Andreasen's version of the stages of change model, which collapses the six stages to four, a model more manageable for some programs. The issue is litter on roadways. The market is people who smoke in cars.[31]

CRITERIA FOR EVALUATING SEGMENTS

Once the marketplace has been grouped into meaningful population segments, the next task is to evaluate each segment in preparation for decisions regarding selecting target markets.

For social marketers, Andreasen cites nine factors for evaluating segments relative to each other.[32] A list of these factors follows, with typical questions that might be asked to establish each measure. To further illustrate each factor, a situation is described in which a state health agency is deciding whether middle school–aged students would be the most attractive segment for promoting abstinence and safe sex.

1. *Segment Size*: How many people are in this segment? What percentage of the population do they represent? (How many middle school youth are in the state?)

2. *Problem Incidence*: How many people in this segment are either engaged in the "problem-related behavior" or not engaged in the "desired behavior?" (What percentage of middle school youth are sexually active?)

3. *Problem Severity*: What are levels of consequences of the problem behavior in this segment? (What is the incidence of sexually transmitted diseases and pregnancy among middle school youth?)

4. *Defenselessness*: To what extent can this segment "take care of themselves" versus needing help from others? (What percentage of middle school youth have access to condoms and report they are using them?)

5. *Reachability*: Is this an audience that can be easily identified and reached? (Are there media channels and other venues that we can use for abstinence and safe sex messages specifically targeting middle school youth?)

6. *General Responsiveness*: How "ready, willing, and able" to respond are those in this segment? (How concerned are middle school youth with sexually transmitted diseases and pregnancy? How does this compare with high school students or college students? Which group has been most responsive to similar campaign messages in the past?)

7. *Incremental Costs*: How do estimated costs to reach and influence this segment compare with those for other segments? (Are there free or inexpensive distribution channels for condoms for middle school youth? How does this compare with those for high school and college students? Are there campaigns from

other states that have been proven to work well with middle school youth, or will we need to start from scratch?)

8. *Responsiveness to Marketing Mix*: How responsive is this market likely to be to social marketing strategies (product, price, place, and promotion)? (What are the greatest influences on middle school youths' decisions relative to their sexual activity? Will the parents of middle school youth, more so than high school or college, be concerned with potential programs and messages?)

9. *Organizational Capabilities*: How extensive is our staff expertise or availability to outside resources to assist in the development and implementation of activities for this market? (Is our experience and expertise with middle school youth as strong as it is with high school and college students?)

One potential evaluation methodology would use these nine factors to quantitatively score each segment, creating a rational way to rank and prioritize them. Two major steps are involved, the first calculating a *potential for effectiveness* score, and the second, a *potential for efficiency* score.

1. *Effectiveness scores* are determined from statistics and incidence data on four of the factors: segment size, problem incidence, problem severity, and defenselessness. The segment's population size is multiplied by percentages for incidence, severity, and defenselessness (i.e., size × incidence × severity × defenselessness). The resulting number becomes the segment's "true" market size relative to potential effectiveness.

2. *Efficiency scores* are determined from assessments of segments on the next five factors: reachability, responsiveness, incremental costs, responsiveness to marketing mix elements, and organizational capabilities. This process would require assigning some quantitative value or score for each segment relative to each factor.

HOW TARGET MARKETS ARE SELECTED

Market segmentation has identified and described relevant market segments. Evaluation activities provide information on each segment that will help you take the next step, deciding which and how many segments will be target markets for the campaign or program being planned.

Three approaches are "typical" for commercial sector marketers and are useful concepts for the social marketer to consider:[33]

Undifferentiated Marketing: The organization decides to use the same strategy for all segments, focusing on what is "common in the needs of consumers rather than on what is different."[34] This approach is also sometimes referred to as *mass marketing* and is trying to reach and influence the most people at one time. Undifferentiated campaigns include those promoting issues of concern to a large cross section of the population: drinking eight glasses of water a day, wearing seatbelts, not drinking and driving, flossing teeth, sun protection, water conservation, learning CPR, voting, organ donation.

Differentiated Marketing: The organization develops different strategies for different audiences. This approach often includes allocating more resources to priority segments. Campaigns that would benefit from a differentiated strategy are those in which segments have clear and distinguishable wants and needs, as well as recommended behaviors. This approach might be used for campaigns promoting water safety, physical activity, breast cancer screening, and commute trip reduction.

Concentrated Marketing: In this approach, some segments are eliminated altogether, and resources and efforts often concentrate on developing the ideal strategy for one or only a few key segments. Campaigns with narrow and concentrated focuses might include promoting folic acid to women in childbearing years, encouraging horse farmers to cover manure piles to avoid contamination of streams, developing AIDS prevention outreach programs to drug abusers, or recruiting young single men as volunteers for mentoring youth at risk.

As introduced in the prior section, segments could be prioritized and ranked at this point using effectiveness and efficiency scores. This would be especially useful for campaigns using a differentiated or concentrated approach in which the most efficient and effective segments will be targeted.

WHAT APPROACH SHOULD BE CHOSEN?

Most organizations involved in social marketing (public sector agencies and nonprofit organizations) are faced with limited budgets. Segments will need to be prioritized, with a disproportionate amount of resources allocated to those deemed to be the most effective and efficient. Some segments will need to be eliminated from the plan.

Target markets (markets of greatest opportunity) emerge as those with the greatest need and are the most ready for action, easiest to reach, and best match for the organization. Measures used to assess each of these are as follows:

- *Greatest need*: size, incidence, severity, and defenselessness
- *Most ready for action:* ready, willing, and able to respond
- *Easiest to reach:* identifiable, venues for distribution channels and communication
- *Best match:* organizational mission, expertise, and resources

Targeting markets of *greatest opportunity* may run counter to a social marketer's natural desire and inclination (or mandate) to either (a) ensure that all constituent groups are reached and served (markets are treated equally) or to (b) focus resources on segments in which the incidence and severity of the problem is the gravest (markets of greatest need). Concerns can be addressed by emphasizing that this is the most effective and efficient use of scarce resources, reassuring others that segmentation enables plans to be developed that are likely to succeed with individual segments, and explaining that additional segments can be addressed over time. You are simply prioritizing resources and efforts in an objective, systematic, and cost-effective way.

ETHICAL CONSIDERATIONS WHEN SELECTING TARGET MARKETS

The musing at the beginning of the chapter expressing concern with resource allocation represents well the ethical dilemma at this phase in the planning process. In campaigns in which a majority of resources have been allocated to one or a few market segments, how do you address concerns with social inequity? Or what about reverse situations in which resources are allocated equally, when in fact only one or a few market segments have the greatest need? For example, a state water conservation effort may send messages to all residents in the state to voluntarily reduce water usage by a goal of 10% over the next 6 months. Take shorter showers. Flush one less time. But what if water levels and resources are actually adequate in half the state? Should residents on one side of the mountain where it rains "all the time" be asked to make these sacrifices as well? What is fair?

Our recommendation, as it was when selecting a focus for your campaign, is that you present, or at least mention, a long-range plan that will eventually address groups you are not addressing in this phase. In addition, as you will read in the Research Highlight at the end of this chapter, be prepared to present your rational criteria and evaluation that led to decisions to focus resources on the target market you have selected.

Chapter Summary

Selecting target markets is a three-step process: (1) segment the market, (2) evaluate segments, and (3) choose one or more segments for targeting. Traditional variables used to describe consumer markets include demographics, geographics, psychographics, and behavior variables. Three additional models frequently used by social marketing practitioners include the stages of change model, diffusion of innovation, and the healthstyles segmentation system.

Target markets are evaluated based on efficiency and effectiveness measures, using nine variables outlined by Andreasen and presented in this text: segment size, problem incidence, problem severity, defenselessness, reachability, general responsiveness, incremental costs, responsiveness to marketing mix, and organizational capabilities.

Three common targeting approaches include undifferentiated marketing (same strategy for all segments), differentiated marketing (different strategies for different audiences), and concentrated marketing (only a few key segments are targeted and with unique strategies).

It was recommended that the markets of "greatest opportunity" are those with the greatest need, most ready for action, easiest to reach, *and* the best match for the organization.

RESEARCH HIGHLIGHT: USING SECONDARY RESEARCH DATA

This first of nine research highlights illustrates the use of secondary research as a methodology, in this case to help select target markets. This write-up contains excerpts from a more in-depth article that appeared in the *Social Marketing Quarterly,* Volume 12, Number 3, Fall 2006, pp. 16–28.

Encouraging African American Women to "Take Charge. Take the Test"

The Audience Segmentation Process for CDC's HIV Testing Social Marketing Campaign (2006)

NANCY R. LEE, SHELLY SPOETH, KINETRA SMITH,

LAURA MCELROY, JAMI L. FRAZE, AYANNA ROBINSON, AND MELISSA KRAVS TAYLOR

HIV/AIDS remains a formidable public health problem in the United States: in 2005, the Centers for Disease Control and Prevention (CDC) estimated that more than 1 million persons were living with HIV/AIDS[35] and approximately 40,000 persons become infected with HIV each year.[36] Although new infections among the general population are remaining stable, a new at-risk population is emerging—African American women. This population now accounts for 67% of new AIDS cases among all women.[37]

For this campaign, CDC focused on a specific behavior to help decrease the spread of HIV: increasing timely HIV testing among populations at highest risk for HIV infection. Of an estimated 1,039,000 to 1,185,000 persons living with HIV, approximately 24%–27% are unaware of their serostatus.[38] In 2003, as many as two thirds of new cases arose from persons unaware of their infection, who then transmitted the disease to partners unaware of their personal risk.[39]

Segmenting the Market

An analysis was conducted of relevant U.S. Census data, geographic information systems data, public health data, and syndicated market research data. Demographic and behavioral variables created five segments:

1. African American men ages 18–34 who have sex with men only
2. African American men ages 18–34 who have sex with men and women
3. African American men ages 18–34 who have sex with women only
4. African American single women ages 18–34 who have sex with men only (one or more partners)
5. African American married women ages 18–34 who have sex with men only

Evaluating Each Segment

Each segment was then evaluated on several factors, including size, incidence, risk, current behavior, ability to reach, ability to influence, and potential to influence others.

A review of existing literature was then conducted, including relevant journal articles and books, CDC's Behavioral Risk Factor Surveillance System (BRFSS), database–published surveys from groups such as the Kaiser Family Foundation, and findings from research conducted for prior campaigns, including CDC's *KNOW NOW!* campaign.[40] In addition to this secondary research, primary research was also conducted using focus groups and in-depth interviews with members of potential target markets; interviews with key informants, including those with special expertise regarding the African American audience and HIV testing, and social marketing professionals; and consultation meetings, including forums with representatives from advocacy groups, health institutions, and faith-based organizations.

Choosing a Target Audience

After we evaluated all available target audience data, *single African American women ages 18–34* emerged as the clear choice for the campaign target audience.

Size: This audience segment was substantive in size. The 2000 census data indicated there were 3.7 million single African American women ages 18–34 in the United States, and this segment of single women represented more than one third (42%) of the total population under consideration (African Americans ages 18–34). By contrast, there were only 1.1 million married African American women ages 18–34.[41]

Incidence: The incidence of HIV/AIDS within this segment was high, and rates were increasing. By 2003, African American women represented an estimated 67% of AIDS diagnoses among all women in the United States.[42]

Risk: Many in this segment were engaged in risk behaviors at high levels: according to BRFSS data, an estimated 44% of these single women were not using protection when having sex.[43]

Current Behavior: BRFSS data also indicated that approximately 40% of this segment had not been tested for HIV/AIDS in the past year.[44] By contrast, one key study showed that 88% of men who have sex with men only (MSM) had been tested for HIV, and most had been tested more than once.[45]

Ability to Reach: Single African American women ages 18–34 could be easily reached through media buys and community outreach. Existing mechanisms and community structures, such as churches, public and private health institutions, and child care institutions, created accessible networks for interfacing with African American women in this audience segment. In contrast, trying to reach the segment of African American MSM and African American men having sex with men and women was a more daunting task.

Ability to Influence: Significant barriers to influencing African American male audiences included extreme denial of risk behavior. BRFSS data also indicated this segment of African American women believed it was important to know their HIV status, with 99% rating it as very important to them.[46]

Potential to Influence Others: This audience segment was also more likely than the three African American male segments to be willing to spread the word—to discuss the importance of testing, even results of their own test, with partners, families, and friends—a reflection of the strong role women play in the

African American community. In addition, women, as a whole, are often the disseminators of health information and influencers of health behavior to others in their family and communities.[47]

Within this audience segment of single African American women ages 18–34 having unprotected sex, we further defined the primary target audience by cross-referencing the PRIZM segmentation system by Claritas—a national syndicated research database that defines markets based on distinct demographic, psychographic, lifestyle, and regional characteristics. PRIZM's *Inner Cities* and *Southside City* clusters most closely matched the target market profile and mirrored populations in which HIV infections were continuing to rise. By reviewing the characteristics of these two clusters, we were able to define further the audience as those who make less than $30,000 per year, have some college education or less, and live in specific regions of the United States.

Post Note

Creative executions targeting this audience were based on a "look out for yourself" theme, with an emphasis on the risky behavior for getting HIV and the empowerment that comes with getting tested (see Figure 6.4).

Figure 6.4 A Billboard Posted in Philadelphia Encouraging HIV Testing in Young African American Women

Setting Objectives and Goals

When considering a problem as vast as global warming, it's easy to feel over-whelmed and powerless—skeptical that individual efforts can actually have an impact. But we need to resist that response, because this crisis will get resolved only if we as individuals take responsibility for it. By educating our-selves and others, by doing our part to minimize our use and waste of resources, by becoming more politically active and demanding change—in these ways and many others, each of us can make a difference.

—Al Gore
An Inconvenient Truth[1]

e recognize the challenges, even resistance, some of you may have with this section in the planning process—that of setting campaign objectives (desired behaviors) and goals. Do any of these sound familiar?

- I always have trouble choosing among the numerous optional good behaviors we want to promote. Why do we need to (once more) narrow our focus, as we did with target audiences? It seems to me the more we can get them to do, the better.
- When I look at this model and the use of the terms *objective* and *goal,* I get con-fused, even discouraged. We were taught in public health programs that goals were what we were trying to accomplish, like decrease obesity. This model says that goals are the quantifiable measure of your objective. Does it matter?
- This goal setting is nice in theory but near to impossible, in my experience. If we haven't done this particular behavior change campaign before, how could we possibly know what kind of a target goal or milestone to set?

In this opening case story, we have organized information and activities related to former Vice President Al Gore's effort to stop global warming into our social marketing model. We consider it an important and challenging social marketing effort, one that captures the fundamental assignment that social marketers accept—to move people from knowledge to belief to action. You be the judge on how you think it's working.

MARKETING HIGHLIGHT

An Inconvenient Truth and a Social Marketing Story (2007)

Figure 7.1   An Inconvenient Truth[2]

Background and Situation

In a description of the film *An Inconvenient Truth* on the climate crisis Web site (http://www.climatecrisis.net), evidence of global warming is presented and summarized as follows:[3]

Carbon dioxide and other gases that warm the surface of the planet naturally by trapping solar heat in the atmosphere keep our planet habitable. However, by burning fossil fuels such as coal, gas, and oil at the rate we are, and by clearing forests, we have dramatically increased the amount of carbon dioxide in the earth's atmosphere. As a result, temperatures are rising, and we are seeing dramatic changes. The number of severe hurricanes is increasing, glaciers are melting, and hundreds of species of plants and animals are moving closer to the poles.

If the warming continues, catastrophic consequences are anticipated, including these mentioned in both the movie and the book:

- Deaths from global warming will double in just 25 years—to 300,000 people a year.
- Global sea levels could rise by more than 20 feet with the loss of shelf ice in Greenland and Antarctica, devastating coastal areas worldwide.
- Heat waves will be more frequent and more intense.
- Droughts and wildfires will occur more often.
- The Arctic Ocean could be ice-free in summer by 2050.
- More than a million species worldwide could be driven to extinction by 2050.[4]

Authors of the book and Web site believe it is not too late to solve this problem and that "small changes to our daily routine can add up to big differences in helping to stop global warming."[5]

Target Audiences

Although all citizens in the world are of interest and important to influence, the initial bull's-eye target markets for this effort appear to be adults 18+ years old in the United States who are concerned about the environment but need more (believable) facts to make significant changes.

Desired Behaviors

Among the more than 30 specific desired behaviors promoted at the end of the book *An Inconvenient Truth,* 10 were selected for a handout titled *tenthingstodo*:[6]

- *Change a light*: If you replace just one regular light bulb with a compact fluorescent light bulb, you will save 150 pounds of carbon dioxide a year.
- *Drive less*: When you walk, bike, carpool, or take mass transit, you will save one pound of carbon dioxide for every mile you don't drive!
- *Recycle more*. If you recycle just half of your household waste, you can save 2,400 pounds of carbon dioxide per year.
- *Check your tires*. Many of us are not aware that if we keep our tires inflated properly, it can improve gas mileage by more than 3%, and for every gallon of gasoline saved, we keep 20 pounds of carbon dioxide out of the atmosphere.
- *Use less hot water*. By installing a low-flow showerhead, you will reduce 350 pounds of carbon dioxide per year, and by washing your clothes in cold or warm water, you'll reduce 500 pounds per year.

- *Avoid products with a lot of packaging*. If you cut down your garbage by 20%, you can save 1,200 pounds of carbon dioxide.
- *Adjust your thermostat*. By moving your thermostat just two degrees in winter and up two degrees in summer, you could save about 2,000 pounds of carbon dioxide a year with this simple adjustment.
- *Plant a tree*. Over its lifetime, a single tree absorbs 1 ton of carbon dioxide.
- *Turn off electronic devices*. Thousands of pounds of carbon dioxide can be saved each year by simply turning off your television, DVD player, stereo, and computer when you're not using them.
- *Spread the word!* Encourage your friends to see the movie and buy the book *An Inconvenient Truth.*

Strategies

All four tools in the marketing toolbox are apparently being used:

Product: The *core product* is a healthier planet through reduced carbon dioxide emissions; the *actual products* are the 30+ desired behaviors that will reduce carbon dioxide emissions; and the *augmented products,* which are more than promotional materials, include the film, DVD, book, educational guides for teachers, and Web site that provides a way to calculate your personal impact.

Price: The *Inconvenient Truth* DVD is available in most venues for under $20 and the book for as little as $15. The Alliance for Climate Protection receives 100% of proceeds from the DVD and the companion book.

Place: The DVD and book can be purchased on several Web sites, including Amazon.com. In 2006 and 2007, the film could be seen in movie theaters, and rented and downloaded beyond those years for in-home viewing.

Promotional Messages: Messages were crafted to increase knowledge, alter beliefs, and inspire action. Knowledge-focused messages present facts regarding concentrations of carbon dioxide, such as the one comparing preindustrial concentrations (280 parts per million) with those in 2005 (381 parts per million). The campaign points out that in Antarctica, measurements of carbon dioxide go back 650,000 years and indicate that where we were in 2005 is significantly above anything measured in the prior 650,000-year record. Messages are intended to influence audience beliefs regarding global warming and include photos of receding glaciers in Glacier National Park, Peru, Switzerland, Italy, and Tibet. A scientific note accompanies each, such as one for Mount Kilimanjaro that quotes one scientist as predicting that within 10 years, there will be no more "snows of Kilimanjaro."

Promotional Communication Channels: Strategies rely heavily on publicity (e.g., appearances on *Oprah* and *The Daily Show*), special events, international speaking tours, grassroots activities such as home parties to view and discuss the film, and training for 1,000 community volunteers to prepare them to give presentations on global warming to community groups throughout the United States. Internet blogs, links, and special mentions on partner sites also expand the reach, as John Kerry did on December 13, 2006, when he sent e-mail messages encouraging communities to "join the Sierra Club, the League of Conservation Voters and others in sponsoring nationwide house parties" to discuss the film and actions to take—ones "crucial to our environmental future."[7]

Results

Citizen response to many of these campaign elements can be measured fairly easily by counting the number of hits to the Web sites, purchases of the book and DVD, and attendees at movie theaters, special events, house parties, and grassroots trainings. Of most interest and more difficult will be correlated changes in behaviors, with a focus on the number of people adopting the 30+ behaviors promoted in the book and on Web sites, ones that can have an impact on reducing carbon dioxide emissions and someday halting or reversing global warming.

STEP #4: SETTING OBJECTIVES AND GOALS

Once target markets for a campaign have been selected, your next step is to establish *campaign objectives,* with the primary objective always being the very specific *behaviors* you want to influence your audience to accept, modify, abandon, or reject. As you will read, the key to success is to select single, doable objectives—and then explain them in simple, clear terms.

This chapter presents examples of the three types of objectives associated with a social marketing campaign:

1. *Behavior objectives (*something you want your audience to do*)*
2. *Knowledge objectives (*something you want your audience to know*)*
3. *Belief objectives (*something you want your audience to believe or feel*)*

A social marketing campaign always has a behavior objective. When and if you determine there is something your audience needs to know or believe in order to "act," these objectives are identified and incorporated as well. As will become clear, campaign objectives are different from campaign purpose, defined earlier in this model as the ultimate impact of a successful campaign on the social issue being addressed.

After determining campaign objectives, campaign *goals* are established, ones that are specific, measurable, attainable, relevant, and time sensitive (S.M.A.R.T.).[8] Ideally, they specify targeted rates of change in behaviors such as the increase in numbers of those in the target audience who will be performing the desired behavior after the campaign. They may also establish desired changes in knowledge and belief, especially in cases where behavior change may be a long-term effort. We recognize that in some models, such as ones used in public health, goals are the nonquantifiable components of a campaign and objectives are then the quantifiable ones. This social marketing model is based on commercial marketing models, where goals are expressed as "sales goals." We recommend, however, that you feel free to reverse these labels to match your organization's language and culture.

Remember the comment in the second chapter that this planning model should be considered spiral in nature? Objectives and goals established at this point should be considered *draft objectives and goals.* You may learn in Step 5, for example, when you "talk" with your target market about these desired behaviors, that your objectives and goals are not realistic, clear, and/or appropriate for them and that they should be revised. Or you might find when developing preliminary budgets that you will need to reduce your goals due to funding realities.

As a final overview of this step, keep in mind that objectives and goals will affect your campaign evaluation strategy. Given the fact that campaign goals represent the foundation for campaign evaluation, it is crucial that goals are relevant to campaign efforts and are feasible to measure.

Table 7.1 illustrates key concepts that will be presented in this chapter, using an example of an effort that might be undertaken by a state department of transportation to reduce traffic injuries and deaths caused by driver distractions while using cell phones.

BEHAVIOR OBJECTIVES

All social marketing campaigns should be designed and planned with a specific behavior objective in mind. Even if the planner discovers that the campaign needs to include additional knowledge and belief objectives, a behavior objective will need to be identified that these additional elements will support. As you develop and consider potential behavior objectives for your efforts, the following five criteria should help you choose one(s) with the greatest potential for meaningful change, or at least assist you in prioritizing them:

1. *Impact:* If your audience adopts the behavior, will it make a difference relative to the purpose of your campaign, in comparison to others being considered?

Table 7.1   Example of a Campaign Purpose

Campaign Purpose	*Reduce traffic injuries and deaths*
Focus	*Cell phone usage while driving*
Campaign Objectives:	
Behavior Objective	To wait until you arrive at your destination to use your cell phone
Knowledge Objective	To know the percentage of traffic accidents involving someone talking on a cell phone
Belief Objective	To believe that talking on a cell phone, even a hands-free model, can be a distraction
Campaign Goal	Increase the number of people who wait to use their cell phones by 25%

2. *Doable:* The behavior should be a simple, clear, doable act, even though it may not be perceived as easy (e.g., quitting smoking). A theory of interest and applicability here is the foot-in-the-door theory, which posits that people are more likely to agree to a large request later if they are approached with a small request first.[9] The reason this may work may be related to the self-perception theory, which says that we learn about our internal states (attitudes, beliefs, preferences, etc.) by observing our own behavior.[10] Then, after people say yes to the response to a small request, they are more likely to accept the second request because they are "that" kind of person. The basic principle of this theory, then, is that people want, even need, to maintain psychological consistency in their thoughts, actions, and feelings.

3. *Measurable:* Can the behavior be measured, either through observation, record keeping, or self-reporting? You should be able to "picture" your target audience performing the behavior (e.g., removing the plastic insert from the cereal box before sorting for recycling). And your target audience should be able to determine that they have performed the behavior (e.g., placing infants in cribs on their backs to reduce the risk of infant death).

4. *Market Demand:* How many people are not currently doing the behavior? How many seem receptive to the idea? Have they heard of doing this behavior before? Do they perceive it will solve some problem or concern they have or will it satisfy some unfulfilled need?

5. *Market Supply:* Does the behavior need more support? If some other organization is already "doing all that can be done" to influence this behavior, perhaps a different behavior would be more beneficial to the social issue.

The 10 recommendations from our opening case story on ways that citizens can reduce carbon dioxide emissions would make an interesting prioritization exercise and could be approached using a grid like the one in Table 7.2. Assume that once launched, efforts would then focus on highlighting two behaviors each year and that they would prioritize them based on scores for each of the five criteria just mentioned. To keep it simple, each behavior could be rated on each criterion as a High (3), Medium (2), or Low (1), as illustrated in the first row. Ideally, these would be determined using objective information (e.g., citizen surveys, scientific data). In reality, it might be more subjective in nature—still better than prioritizing them based on less rigorous ways, such as informal conversations or hunches.

To increase the rigor (and value) of the exercise, you could also weight the criteria. For example, you could understandably decide that "Impact" was more important than other criteria and decide to double the score (2 × 2 = 4). That way, something that was low impact (1) but had the highest scores on other criteria would not automatically surface as the number one priority.

Table 7.2   Process for Prioritizing Behavior Objectives: High (3) Medium (2) Low (1)

Behaviors	Impact	Doable	Measurable	Demand	Supply	Average
Change a light	2	3	3	3	1	2.4
Drive less						
Recycle more						
Check your tires						
Use less hot water						
Avoid products with a lot of packaging						
Adjust your thermostat						
Plant a tree						
Turn off electronic devices						
Spread the word						

A behavior objective should be distinguished from several other planning components. It is not the same as a campaign slogan or campaign message, although it is used to develop both (e.g., "Eat five or more fruits and vegetables a day" became "5 A Day The Color Way™"). It is not quantifiable as we are defining it. The goal is the quantifiable, measurable component that provides the ability to measure and track the impact of efforts (e.g., a blood bank's goal may be to increase the number of donors by 10% in the next fiscal year).

If you are familiar with logic models, you may be curious where social marketing objectives fit in the model. Most likely, they will be mentioned among program "Outcomes" in the traditional model, reflecting the result of program "Outputs."

For those not familiar with logic models, these are visual schematics that show links between program processes (inputs, activities, and outputs) and program impact (outcomes and long-term impact). This tool will be discussed in more depth in Chapter 15, which covers evaluation.

Although a campaign may promote more than one behavior, it should be recognized that different tactics or strategies might be necessary to promote each one (e.g., getting people to use a litterbag will take different strategies than getting people to cover their loads in pickup trucks). Table 7.3 presents examples of potential behavior objectives in our familiar arenas of health, injury prevention, the environment, and community well-being.

KNOWLEDGE AND BELIEF OBJECTIVES

When gathering background data and conducting the strengths, weaknesses, opportunities, and threats (SWOT) analysis, you probably learned from existing secondary research or from prior similar campaigns that typical audiences need a little help before they are willing, sometimes even able, to act. They may need to have some *knowledge* (information or facts) and/or *belief* (values, opinions, or attitudes) before they are convinced that the action is doable and/or worth the effort. Those in the precontemplation stage, for example, typically don't believe they have a problem. Those in the contemplation stage may not have made up their mind that the effort (cost) is worth the gain (benefit). Even those in the action stage may not be aware of their accomplishments and are therefore vulnerable to relapses.

Knowledge objectives are those relating to statistics, facts, and other information and skills your target audience would find motivating or important. Typically, the information has simply been unavailable to the audience or unnoticed. Here are examples:

- Statistics on *risks* associated with current behavior (e.g., percentage of obese women who have heart attacks versus those not medically obese)
- Statistics on *benefits* of proposed behavior (e.g., percentage of men over the age of 50 with prostate cancer and the survival rates associated with early detection through annual exams)
- Facts on *attractive alternatives* (e.g., lists of flowering native plants that are drought and disease resistant)

Table 7.3   Examples of Potential Behavior Objectives

	Examples of Potential Behavior Objectives for Specific Audiences
Improved Health	
Tobacco use	Don't start smoking.
Heavy/binge drinking	Drink less than five drinks at one sitting.
Alcohol and drug use during pregnancy	Don't drink alcoholic beverages if you are pregnant.
Physical inactivity	Exercise moderately 30 minutes a day, 5 days a week, at least 10 minutes at a time.
Teen pregnancy	Choose abstinence.
Sexually transmitted diseases	Use a condom.
Fat gram intake	Make sure total fat grams consumed are below 30% of total daily calories.
Water intake	Drink eight glasses of water a day.
Fruit and vegetable intake	Eat five servings of fruits and vegetables a day.
Obesity	Have your body mass index measured by a health care professional.
Breast cancer	Learn the proper procedure for examining your breasts.
Prostate cancer	Talk with your health care provider about an annual prostate exam if you are 50 years of age or older.
Oral health	Use a cup to give an infant juice instead of a bottle.
Osteoporosis	Get 1000 to 1200 milligrams a day of calcium.
Avian flu	Limit sources of food for wild and free-flying birds.
Early learning	Read aloud with your child 20 minutes every day.
Injury Prevention	
Drinking and driving	Keep your blood alcohol level below .08% if you are drinking and driving.
Seatbelts	Buckle your seatbelt before you put your vehicle in gear.
Domestic violence	Have a plan that includes a packed bag and a safe place to go.
Gun storage	Store handguns in a lockbox or safe or use a reliable trigger lock.
Fires	Check smoke alarm batteries every month.
Falls	Include some form of strength building in your exercise routine.
Household poisons	Place recognizable stickers on all poisonous products in the kitchen, bathroom, bedroom, basement, and garage.

(Continued)

Table 7.3 (Continued)

	Examples of Potential Behavior Objectives for Specific Audiences
Protecting the Environment	
Waste reduction	Buy bulk and unpackaged goods rather than packaged items.
Wildlife habitat protection	Stay on established paths when walking through forests.
Forest destruction	Use materials made from recycled tires and glass for garden steps and paths.
Toxic fertilizers and pesticides	Follow instructions on labels and measure precisely.
Water conservation	Replace old toilets with new low-flow models.
Air pollution from automobiles	Don't top off the gas tank when refueling your car.
Air pollution from other sources	Use an electric or push mower instead of a gas-powered model.
Forest fires	Chip wood debris that can be used for composting instead of burning it.
Conserving electricity	Turn off computer monitors when leaving work at the end of the day.
Litter	Clean out litter that might blow out of the open back of your pickup truck.
Community Involvement	
Volunteering	Give 5 hours a week to a volunteer effort.
Mentoring	Encourage and support caring relationships between your child and a nonparent adult.

- Facts that *correct misconceptions* (e.g., cigarette butts are not biodegradable and can take more than 10 years to disintegrate completely)
- Facts that might be *motivating* (e.g., learning that moderate physical activity has been proven to have some of the same important medical benefits as vigorous physical activity)
- Information on *how to perform* the behavior (e.g., prepare a home for an earthquake)
- *Resources* available for assistance (e.g., phone numbers where battered women can call to find temporary shelter)
- *Locations* for purchase of goods or services (e.g., locations where handgun lockboxes can be purchased)
- Current *laws and fines* that may not be known or understood (e.g., a fine of $1,025 can be imposed for tossing a lit cigarette)

Belief objectives are those relating to attitudes, opinions, feelings, or values held by the target audience. The target audience may have current beliefs that the marketer may need to alter in order for them to act, or you may find that an important belief is missing, ones such as the following:

- They will personally *experience the benefits* from adopting the desired behavior (e.g., increased physical activity will help them sleep better).
- They are *at risk* (i.e., they currently believe they are capable of driving safely with a blood alcohol level of over 0.08).
- They will be *able to successfully perform* the desired behavior (e.g., talk to their teenager about thoughts of suicide).
- Their individual behavior *can make a difference* (e.g., taking mass transit to work).
- They *will not be viewed negatively* by others if they adopt the behavior (e.g., not accepting another drink).
- The costs of the behavior will be *worth it* (e.g., replacing an old but functioning toilet with a newer water-efficient one).
- There will *be minimal negative consequences* (e.g., worrying that organ donation information might be shared with third parties).

These knowledge and belief objectives provide direction for developing subsequent strategies (positioning and the marketing mix). They have important implications *especially for developing a brand identity and key messages* that provide the information and arguments that will be most motivating. Advertising copywriters, for example, will reference these objectives when developing communication slogans, script, and copy. There are also opportunities for other elements of the marketing mix to support these additional objectives: an immunization product strategy that incorporates a wallet-sized card to ensure that parents know the recommended schedule; an incentive offered by a utility for trading in gas mowers for mulch mowers as a way to convince homeowners of their harm to the environment; or a special Web site dedicated to purchasing booster seats, sponsored by a children's hospital, as a testimonial to the safety concern.

Table 7.4 provides examples of each of the objectives described. It should be noted that even though each campaign illustrated has a knowledge and belief objective, this is neither typical nor required. As stated earlier, the behavior objective is the primary focus.

THE NATURE OF SOCIAL MARKETING GOALS

Ideally, social marketing goals establish a desired level of behavior *change* as a result of program efforts (from 10% of homeowners who check for leaky toilets on an annual basis to 20% in 1 year). To establish this target for the amount or percentage of change, you would, of course, need to know current levels of behavior among your target audience. This is similar to commercial sector marketers, who establish sales goals for their products when developing annual marketing plans and then

Table 7.4   Purpose, Audience, and Objectives

Campaign Purpose	Target Audience	Behavior Objective	Knowledge Objective	Belief Objective
Reduced birth defects	Women in child-bearing years	Get 400 micrograms of folic acid every day.	For it to help, you must take it before you become pregnant and during the early weeks of pregnancy.	Without enough folic acid, the baby is at risk for serious birth defects.
Reduced child injuries from automobile accidents	Parents with children aged 4 to 8	Put children who are aged 4 to 8 and weigh less than 80 pounds in booster seats.	Traffic accidents are the leading cause of death for children aged 4 to 8.	Children aged 4 to 8 weighing less than 80 pounds are not adequately protected by adult seat belts.
Improved water quality	Small horse farmers within 5 miles of streams, lakes, or rivers	Cover and protect manure piles from rain.	Storm water runoff from piles can pollute water resources.	Even though your manure pile is small, it does contribute to the problem.
Increased number of registered organ donors	People renewing driver's licenses	Register to be an organ donor when you renew your driver's license.	Your family may still be asked to sign a consent from for your donation to occur.	Information will be kept private and can only be accessed by authorized officials.

develop strategies and resource allocations consistent with these goals. Consider how the specificity and time-bound nature of the following goals would inspire and guide your planning and eventually help justify your resource expenditures:

- Increase by 25% in a 24-month period the percentage of women over the age of 50 who get annual mammograms.
- Increase the percentage of people wearing seatbelts at checkpoints from 82% in 2003 to 95% by 2006.
- Decrease the amount of glass, paper, aluminum, and plastic litter on roadways by 4 million pounds in 2 years.
- Increase the average number of caring adults in the lives of middle school youth from 1.5 to 3.0 over a period of 3 years.

Goals may also be set for Knowledge and Belief objectives, as illustrated in Table 7.5. Although the goals are hypothetical for the purposes of this illustration, the effort to

Table 7.5   Hypothetical Objectives and Goals

Purpose	Behavior	Knowledge	Belief
Reduce birth defects	What we want them to do	What they may need to know before they will act	What they may need to believe before they will act
Objective	Get 400 micrograms of folic acid every day	For it to help, you need to take it before you become pregnant, during the early weeks of pregnancy (see Figure 7.2).	Without enough folic acid, the baby is at risk for serious birth defects.
Goal[a]	Increase the percentage of women aged 18 to 45 who take a daily vitamin containing folic acid from 25% in 1995 to 40% in 2001.	Increase the percentage of women aged 18 to 45 who know folic acid should be taken before pregnancy from 2% in 1995 to 20% in 2001.	Increase the percentage of women aged 18 to 45 who believe folic acid prevents birth defects from 4% in 1995 to 30% in 2001.

increase the intake of folic acid as a way to prevent birth defects is real. The U.S. Public Service and the March of Dimes recommend that all women of childbearing age consume 400 micrograms of folic acid per day in a multivitamin in addition to eating a healthy diet (see Figure 7.2).

In reality, this process is difficult or impractical for many social marketing programs. Baseline data on current levels of behavior for a target market may not be known or may not be available in a timely or economically feasible way. Projecting future desired levels (goal setting) often depends on data and experience from years of tracking and analyzing the impact of prior efforts. Many social marketing efforts are conducted for the first time, and historic data may not have been recorded or retained.

There are several excellent resources in the public health arena you can explore, however, that may provide data that guide efforts to establish baselines as well as goals.

- *Behavioral Risk Factor Surveillance System (BRFSS)* was developed by the Centers for Disease Control and Prevention (CDC), headquartered in Atlanta, Georgia. It is used throughout the United States to measure and track the prevalence of major risk behaviors among Americans, including tobacco use, sexual behavior, injury prevention, physical activity, nutrition, and prevention behaviors, such as breast, cervical, and colorectal cancer screening. Details on this system are

Figure 7.2 Promoting Daily Use of a Vitamin Before Pregnancy[11]

included in the Research Highlight at the end of this chapter. Data are available over the Internet and, for many of the behaviors, provide statistics by state.

- *Healthy People 2010* is managed by the Office of Disease Prevention and Health Promotion and the U.S. Department of Health and Human Services. It is a set of health objectives for the United States to achieve by the year 2010 and is used by states, communities, professional organizations, and others to develop programs to improve health. Nearly all states have developed their own Healthy People plans, building on national objectives and tailoring them to their specific needs. Box 7.1 presents information from the Healthy People 2010 Web site on leading health indicators, the 10 high-priority areas for the nation's health. Each indicator has specific objectives, as illustrated in Box 7.2.[12]
- Explore availability of data from *peers in other agencies* who may have conducted similar campaigns.
- Often, *nonprofit organizations and foundations* with a related mission (e.g., the American Cancer Society) may have excellent data helpful to establishing meaningful campaign goals.

BOX 7.1
Healthy People 2010: Leading Health Indicators

What are the Leading Health Indicators?

The Leading Health Indicators will be used to measure the health of the Nation over the next 10 years. Each of the 10 Leading Health Indicators has one or more objectives from Healthy People 2010 associated with it. As a group, the Leading Health Indicators reflect the major health concerns in the United States at the beginning of the 21st century. The Leading Health Indicators were selected on the basis of their ability to motivate action, the availability of data to measure progress, and their importance as public health issues.

The Leading Health Indicators are—

Physical Activity	Mental Health
Overweight and Obesity	Injury and Violence
Tobacco Use	Environmental Quality
Substance Abuse	Immunization
Responsible Sexual Behavior	Access to Health Care

SOURCE: U.S. Department of Health and Human Services (2000, November). *Healthy People 2010: Understanding and Improving Health* (2nd ed.). Washington, DC: U.S. Government Printing Office.

BOX 7.2
Healthy People 2010:
Details on Specific Targets for Substance Abuse

Alcohol and illicit drug use are associated with many of this country's most serious problems, including violence, injury, and HIV infection. The annual economic costs to the United States from alcohol abuse were estimated to be $167 billion in 1995, and the costs from drug abuse were estimated to be $110 billion.

In 1998, 79% of adolescents aged 12 to 17 years reported that they did not use alcohol or illicit drugs in the past month. In the same year, 6% of adults aged 18 years and older reported using illicit drugs in the past month; 17% reported binge drinking in the past month, which is defined as consuming five or more drinks on one occasion.

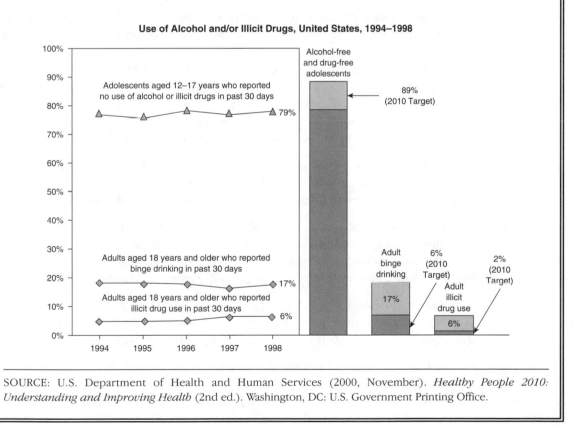

Use of Alcohol and/or Illicit Drugs, United States, 1994–1998

SOURCE: U.S. Department of Health and Human Services (2000, November). *Healthy People 2010: Understanding and Improving Health* (2nd ed.). Washington, DC: U.S. Government Printing Office.

(Continued)

(Continued)

The objectives selected to measure progress among adolescents and adults for this Leading Health Indicator are presented below. These are only indicators and do not represent all the substance abuse objectives in Healthy People 2010.

- Increase the proportion of adolescents not using alchol or any illicit drugs during the past 30 days.

- Reduce the proportion of adults using any illicit drug during the past 30 days.

- Reduce the proportion of adults engaging in binge drinking of alcoholic beverages during the past month.

Alternatives for Goal Setting

If baseline data are not available and setting goals relative to behavior change is not practical or feasible at the time, the following alternatives might be considered for goal setting:

Establish goals for campaign awareness and recall: A statewide tobacco prevention program establishes a goal for the first 3 months of an advertising campaign for 75% of the target audience (adults who smoke) to correctly recall the campaign slogan and two of the four television ads on an unaided basis. Results will then be presented to the state legislature to support continued funding of the campaign.

Establish goals for levels of knowledge: A program for improved nutrition among low-income families sets a goal that 50% of women participating in a pilot project correctly identify and describe the recommended daily servings of fruits and vegetables.

Establish goals for acceptance of a belief: A chain of gas stations is conducting a pilot project to influence customers not to top off their gas tanks and establishes a goal that 80% of customers report they believe topping off a gas tank can be harmful to the environment versus 25% prior to the campaign launch.

Establish goals for a response to a campaign component: A water utility will consider a campaign a success if 25% of residential customers call a well-publicized toll-free number or visit a Web site for a listing of drought-resistant plants.

Establish goals for intent to change behavior: A state coalition promoting moderate physical activity is eager to know if a brief 6-week pilot program increased interest in physical activity. They establish a goal that states their "reported intention to increase physical activity in the next 6 months from 20% to 30%, a 50% increase in behavior intent."

Establish goals for the campaign process: A school-based program promoting abstinence has a goal that 40 abstinence campaigns be developed and implemented by youth in middle schools and high schools around the state during the upcoming school calendar year.

In situations such as these, in which campaign goals are not specifically related to behavior change, it should be reemphasized that campaign objectives should still include a behavior objective. These alternative goals will relate to some activity that supports and promotes the desired behavior.

OBJECTIVES AND GOALS ARE
ONLY A DRAFT AT THIS STEP

In Step 5 of this planning process, you will deepen your understanding of your target audience. You will learn more about their knowledge, beliefs, and current behavior related to objectives and goals established at this point. It is often necessary to then revise and finalize objectives and goals that are more realistic, clear, and appropriate.

OBJECTIVES AND GOALS WILL
BE USED FOR CAMPAIGN EVALUATION

One of the last steps (Step 8) in developing a social marketing plan will be to develop an evaluation plan, a process covered in Chapter 15. It is important to emphasize at this point, however, that the planner will return to this step of the plan, campaign objectives and goals, and will need to select methodologies and develop plans to measure these stated goals. For the examples presented in this chapter, the following items would need to be measured:

- Number of mammograms among women in the pilot community
- Number of people wearing seatbelts stopped at checkpoints
- Pounds of specific types of litter on roadways
- Number of caring adult relationships that middle school youth have
- Number of women in childbearing years taking folic acid

The message is simple. Establish a goal that is meaningful to campaign efforts and that will be feasible to measure.

ETHICAL CONSIDERATIONS WHEN
SETTING OBJECTIVES AND GOALS

What if trends indicate that a behavior objective you are planning to support (e.g., putting food waste in curbside pickup containers) is in conflict with the desired behaviors for other agency programs (e.g., backyard composting)? Or what if your research reveals that the goals that your funders or sponsors would like to support are not realistic or attainable for your target audience? For example, a community clinic may know they are to encourage and support pregnant women to quit smoking—completely. But what if research has shown that cutting down to 9 cigarettes a day would have significant benefits for those not able to quit? Can they consider their efforts a success if they persuade pregnant women in their clinic to decrease from 24 cigarettes a day to 9? Do they suggest a more attainable behavior (maybe using the foot-in-the-door technique) for this segment instead of just sending a "quit" message?

Chapter Summary

The primary objective of a social marketing campaign is behavior change. All social marketing campaigns should be designed and planned with a specific behavior objective in mind, something we want our target audience to do. Behavior objectives should be clear, simple, doable acts—ones the target audience will know they have completed.

Occasionally, the social marketer will also need to establish one or two additional objectives. *Knowledge objectives* (something you want your target audience to know) are those relating to statistics, facts, and other information your target audience would find motivating or important. *Belief objectives* (something you want your target audience to believe) are those relating to attitudes, opinions, or values held by the target audience. The target audience may have current beliefs that the marketer may need to alter in order for them to act, or we may find that an important belief is missing.

Goals are quantifiable, measurable, and relate to the specific campaign focus, target audience, and time frame. Ideally, they establish a desired level of behavior change as a result of program and campaign efforts. When establishing and measuring behavior change is not practical or economically feasible, alternatives can be considered, including ones that measure campaign awareness, response, process, and/or increase in knowledge, beliefs, and intention.

Given the fact that campaign goals represent the foundation for campaign evaluation, it is critical that goals are relevant to campaign efforts and feasible to be measured.

RESEARCH HIGHLIGHT: TRACKING STUDIES FOR GOAL SETTING

Since the early 1980s, the CDC has tracked major health risk behaviors, using standardized telephone surveys with citizens around the United States conducted in conjunction with state health departments. Included in this overview are (a) a summary of the system and (b) a list of topics covered in the telephone survey.[14]

Surveillance is the essential underpinning for all efforts by CDC and the states to promote health and prevent disease. Surveillance is the tool that provides the necessary data to define the disease burden, identify populations at highest risk, determine the prevalence of health risks, and guide and evaluate disease prevention efforts at the national, state, and local levels.

Unlike at the beginning of this century, chronic diseases are now our nation's leading killers. T wo chronic diseases, cardiovascular disease and cancer, account for almost two thirds of all deaths among Americans. In many cases, the roots of chronic diseases are grounded in a limited number of health-damaging behaviors practiced by people every day for much of their lives. These behaviors include

- Lack of physical activity
- Poor nutrition (e.g., high-fat, low-fiber diets)
- Tobacco use
- Underuse of known prevention strategies, such as breast, cervical, and colorectal cancer screening

Reducing the prevalence of these and other behaviors that endanger the health of Americans demands strategies such as public and provider education, prevention research, and policy and environmental changes that facilitate healthy living. To be effective, however, these strategies must be supported by ongoing surveillance of health risks.

CDC's Unique State-Based Surveillance

In the early 1980s, CDC worked with the states to develop the Behavioral Risk Factor Surveillance System (BRFSS). This state-based system, the first of its kind, made available information on the prevalence of risk behaviors among Americans and their perceptions of a variety of health issues (see Figure 7.3).

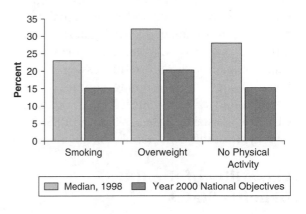

Figure 7.3 Prevalence of Behavioral Risk Factors Among Adults for Cardiovascular Disease

Now active in all 50 states, the BRFSS continues to be the primary source of information on major health risk behaviors among Americans. State and local health departments rely heavily on BRFSS data to

- Determine priority health issues and identify populations at highest risk
- Develop strategic plans and target prevention programs
- Monitor the effectiveness of intervention strategies and progress toward achieving prevention goals
- Educate the public, the health community, and policymakers about disease prevention
- Support community policies that promote health and prevent disease

In addition, BRFSS data enable public health professionals to monitor progress toward achieving the nation's health objectives outlined in Healthy People 2000: National Health Promotion and Disease Prevention Objectives. BRFSS information is also used by researchers, volunteer and professional organizations, and managed care organizations to target prevention efforts. Recognizing the value of such a system in addressing priority health issues in the coming century, China, Canada, and other countries have looked to CDC for assistance in establishing BRFSS-like systems for their own populations.

Versatility of the BRFSS Benefits States

Unlike many surveillance systems, the BRFSS is flexible enough to satisfy individual state needs while also meeting information needs at the national level.

The benefits of the BRFSS for states include the following:

- **Data can be analyzed in a variety of ways.** BRFSS data can be analyzed by a variety of demographic variables, including age, education, income, and racial and ethnic background. The ability to determine populations at highest risk is essential in effectively targeting scarce prevention resources.
- **The BRFSS is designed to identify trends over time.** For example, state-based data from the BRFSS have revealed a national epidemic of obesity.
- **States can add questions of special local interest.** For example, following the bomb explosion at the Alfred P. Murrah Federal Building in Oklahoma City, the Oklahoma BRFSS included questions on such issues as stress, nightmares, and feelings of hopelessness so that health department personnel could better address the psychological impact of the disaster.
- **States can readily address urgent and emerging health issues.** Questions may be added for a wide range of important health issues, including diabetes, oral health, arthritis, tobacco use, folic acid consumption, use of preventive services, and health care coverage. In 1993, when flooding ravaged states along the Mississippi River, Missouri added questions to assess the impact of the flooding on people's health and to evaluate the capability of communities to respond to the disaster.

Although the BRFSS is flexible and allows for timely additions, standard core questions enable health professionals to make comparisons between states and derive national-level conclusions. BRFSS data have highlighted wide disparities between states on key health issues. In 1998, for example, the prevalence of current smoking among U.S. adults ranged from a low of 14% in Utah to a high of 31% in Kentucky. These data have also been useful for assessing tobacco control efforts. For instance, BRFSS data revealed that the annual prevalence of cigarette smoking among adults in Massachusetts declined after an excise tax increase and anti-smoking campaign were implemented.

The BRFSS is the perfect instrument for adding state-specific questions. What else do we have for surveying the behavior of the general adult population?

—Epidemiologist, Connecticut
Department of Public Health

Deepening Your Understanding of the Target Market and the Competition

To be effective in the field of social marketing and influence behavior change, marketers must understand what their target audiences perceive to be the barriers to change. Marketers focus on removing barriers to an activity while simultaneously enhancing the benefits. There is a tendency for individuals to respond positively to actions that are highly beneficial and have few barriers. Social marketers conduct research to discover the key barriers and potential benefits and then develop strategies and tactics that address them.

—Jim Mintz
Director
Centre of Excellence for Public Sector Marketing

By the time you reach this stage in the planning process, you may (understandably) just want to "get going." You will probably be eager to design the product, brainstorm incentives, search for convenient locations, dream up clever slogans, and envision beautiful billboards. After all, you have analyzed the environment, selected a target market, and you know what you want them to do. And you may think you know what they need to know or believe in order to act. The problem is, unless you are the target market, you probably don't know how they really feel about what you have in mind for them, or what they may be thinking when approached to "behave" in ways such as these:

- Put all your liquids in a quart-size ziplock bag before reaching security checkpoints.
- Reduce your lawn in half.
- Eat five or more fruits and vegetables a day, the color way.
- Take one of these flags and wave it at cars when you cross the crosswalk.

You may not know what's really in the way of taking you up on your offer, what they want in exchange for your proposed behavior, and who or what you are competing with. This is the time to find out, and by conducting this investigation well, the rest of your planning process will be grounded in reality and guided by the customer's hand, as it was in this opening case.

Is Your Family Prepared?

Public Safety Canada (2006–2007)

JIM H. MINTZ, DIRECTOR
Centre of Excellence for Public Sector Marketing

THERESA WOOLRIDGE, COMMUNICATIONS ADVISOR
Marketing and Outreach, Public Safety Canada

Background and Situation Analysis

Canadians view public safety and security as a priority and expect their governments to reduce the impact of emergencies. Events such as Hurricane Juan (2003) in Nova Scotia, floods in Alberta and Newfoundland (2005), and winter storms in British Columbia (2006–2007) demonstrate that hazards can occur with little notice and lasting consequences. It is too soon to tally the total financial impact of these events, but the Saguenay floods (1996), the Red River flood (1997), and the Quebec/Ontario ice storms (1998) have so far amounted to an estimated $7.8 billion in costs to government, private, and voluntary sectors—to say nothing of the human hardship and suffering.[1]

Public Safety Canada is the focal point of the government of Canada's efforts to foster safer, more secure communities. In an effort to improve Canada's overall readiness to prepare for and respond to an emergency, Public Safety launched "Is Your Family Prepared?" in November 2006, a national social marketing initiative with three purposes and an estimated cost of $3.5 million for the first year:

- Raise awareness of the threat/risk environment ("all hazards" approach)
- Increase the number of Canadians who have a family emergency plan
- Increase the number of Canadians who have a 72-hour emergency kit

Research conducted prior to the campaign indicated that the level of personal emergency preparedness among Canadians ranged from moderate to low.[2] At the same time, Canada's national emergency response strategies may require individuals to attend to their own needs for a minimum of 72 hours during a major disaster. And yet, only about one quarter of Canadians (28%) had sought information on what to do in case of an emergency, and only slightly more had prepared a family emergency plan (33%) or kit (32%).[3]

Although Canadians are generally aware of a wide variety of potential disasters, only one in five intended to learn more about the types of emergencies that they might have to face, and slightly fewer planned to create an emergency plan (15%) or put together a kit (18%).[4] Furthermore, a large number of those who haven't prepared a kit don't believe they need one, even though 61% of Canadians believed that preparing a kit is an important part of safety.[5]

Target Audience

The primary target audience is parents 35–54, living in urban centers, skewed toward women. In late 2007 the program extended its reach to lower-income families, seniors, and persons with disabilities (mobility, visually, and hearing impaired), the corporate and business sector, first responders, and educators.

Objectives

Behavior objectives seek to increase a percentage of the target audience who obtain information about emergencies, complete an emergency plan, and assemble or purchase an emergency kit.

Knowledge objectives focus on increasing a percentage of the target audience who know more about emergency situations and how to respond.

Belief objectives focus on decreasing a percentage of the target group who believe that there are many emergencies that you simply can't prepare for. In addition, the campaign was designed to increase the number of Canadians who believe there is a sense of urgency about getting prepared and that preparedness is necessary for their own and their family's safety.

Audience Barriers

The challenge to influencing Canadians to be prepared for emergencies includes four main barriers:

1. Psychological beliefs that deter vigilance and preparation[6]

2. Lack of awareness among the public about where to go for security and emergency preparedness information[7]

3. Reliance on government in emergency situations[8]

4. Language barriers among Canadians who speak neither official language (French and English)

Time and money are not significant barriers to becoming prepared. The lowest income group (under $30,000) is just as willing to pay $60 for an emergency kit as those with incomes $100,000 and over.[9]

Strategies

Product

Augmented products include an *emergency-preparedness Web site*, a *toll-free number*, a *family emergency preparedness guide,* and *prepackaged emergency kits.* The workbook-style preparedness guide informs Canadians how to find out more about their local risks, a family emergency plan template, and a checklist of emergency kit items and locations where prepackaged kits can be purchased (see Figure 8.1). *Prepackaged emergency kits* were developed for distribution through collaborative agreements/partnerships between not-for-profit organizations and retail chains across Canada.

Price

The prepackaged emergency kits are made available for approximately $60 CDN ($57 USD). Emergency guides and the Web site with information on regional risks, family plan templates, and kit checklists are available at no cost.

Place

Canadians were asked to list "trusted sources of information" on preparing for

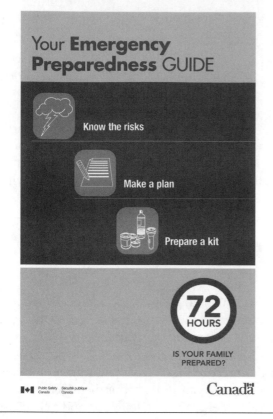

Figure 8.1 Cover of Canada's Emergency Preparedness Guide

emergencies. The list was used to guide decisions regarding distribution channels and included fire and police departments, not-for-profit organizations, friends/neighbors, municipal government, provincial governments, news media, and the federal government.

Public Safety expanded its distribution channels for the emergency preparedness guides and added credibility to its messaging by partnering with trusted organizations and associations such as provincial and territorial emergency management organizations, the Canadian Red Cross, St. John Ambulance, the Salvation Army, the Canadian Association of

Fire Chiefs, the Canadian Association of Chiefs of Police, and the private sector.

Prepackaged kits and campaign promotional material were distributed to retail partners, including hardware stores, grocery stores, department stores, and pharmacies. A total of 25 chains (4,000 stores) participated. A kit checklist and a list of retailers participating in the project are available from the Public Safety Canada Web site (http://www.getprepared.ca). Callers to the toll-free number were told which retailers in their province carried the kits.

Promotion

All campaign products included the Is Your Family Prepared? icon, and all communications products directed Canadians to the dedicated Web site, and a toll-free number was made available for those who don't use the Web (see Figure 8.2). Media channels included the following:

- Advertising included two national television flights, print ads in 16 national women-targeted magazines and newspapers, contests, ads on Web sites matching the magazine buy, and e-marketing programs.
- Public relations included staff seminars and a testimonials program where motivational testimonials were solicited through contests and will be featured in future phases of the campaign.
- Direct marketing: Public Safety worked with partners to create direct marketing programs. Emergency preparedness guides were inserted into emergency kits and training manuals, and retail collateral such as posters and end-of-aisle

displays supported the Is Your Family Prepared? messaging.

- Internal communications: Staff training seminars were developed for 380,700 federal government employees and will be implemented over the next several years.
- Parliamentary engagement plan: elected members of Parliament (307 MPs) were also invited to champion this program, bringing messages and communications products to their constituencies across the country.
- Event marketing and exhibits program: A nationwide program was launched in 2007.

Evaluation

Initial indicators have been positive. For instance, from November 16, 2006, to February 11, 2007, there were

- 242,694 visitors to the http://www.getprepared.ca Web site
- 50,800 downloads of the Emergency Preparedness Guide
- 2,955 people completing the online emergency plan
- 2,728 opt-in e-mail subscribers
- 4,758 calls to the 1-800-O-Canada hotline (80% female)
- 30,793 guides ordered

Figure 8.2 Home Page for Campaign Web Site and Icon "72 Hours. Is Your Family Prepared?"

A tracking survey conducted 1 month into the campaign (December 2006) indicated increases in knowledge, beliefs, and behaviors:[10]

- 10% increase in the general population and 15% increase in the target audience of those who responded that they "completely agree" with the statement that "preparing an emergency kit is a necessary part of ensuring my own and my family's safety."
- 9% increase in the general population and a 6% increase in the target audience of those who responded that they "completely agreed" with the statement "In an emergency, I would know what to do and where to go for help."
- 4% increase in the general population of those who responded that they or a family member had sought information on what to do in an emergency.
- 4% increase in the general population who responded that they or a family member had prepared an emergency plan.
- Intention to act also increased, with a 13% general population and 10% target audience increase among those who responded that it was very likely that they would create a family emergency plan in the next month or so. Along the same lines, there was a 15% and 16% increase among the general population and the target audience, respectively, among those who responded that it was very likely that they would put together an emergency kit in the next month or so.
- About one of five Canadians who saw the program's advertising campaign had taken action as a result, such as preparing an emergency kit, gathering emergency supplies for their car, or buying bottled water.

Media coverage has been positive, and interest has been sustained since the launch of the program. Messaging has highlighted the significance of being prepared for 72 hours, as well as the need for citizens to understand their role in preparing for an emergency. News articles and broadcast segments emphasized the key steps people could take to prepare themselves, and provided examples of what to put in an emergency kit.

STEP #5: IDENTIFY TARGET MARKET BARRIERS, BENEFITS, AND THE COMPETITION

In the marketing game, the winners almost always have one "maneuver" in common—a customer-centered focus. The best have a genuine curiosity, even hunger, to know what the potential customer thinks and feels about their offer. This fifth step in the planning process is designed to do just that—deepen your understanding of your target market.

This chapter will first identify and discuss what current and specific knowledge, beliefs, attitudes, and practices will be helpful for you to know and understand. You then will read about how to gather this information, behavior change theories and models to consider, and finally, how you will use these insights in developing your strategies. First, a word about the exchange theory, another marketing cornerstone— one that helps to envision this "deal-making" process.

The Exchange Theory

The traditional economic exchange theory postulates that, in order for an exchange to take place, target markets must perceive benefits equal to or greater than perceived costs.[11] In other words, they must believe they will get as much or more than they give. In 1972, Philip Kotler published his article in the *Journal of Marketing* asserting that exchange was the core concept of marketing and that free exchange takes place when the target market believes they will get as much or more than they give.[12] And earlier, in 1969, Kotler argued that exchange theory applies to more than the purchase of tangible goods and services, that it can in fact involve intangible or symbolic products (e.g., recycling), and that payments are not limited to financial ones (e.g., time and effort may be the only major perceived costs).[13] In 1974 and 1978, Richard Bagozzi broadened this framework by adding several ideas, including that more than two parties may be involved in the transaction and the primary beneficiary of an exchange may in fact be a third party (e.g., the environment).[14] This is certainly consistent with the definition of social marketing used throughout this text, as it acknowledges that society is always intended to be better off, as well as the target market.

Given this, three target market perspectives are crucial and will be elaborated upon in the remainder of the first section of this chapter:

1. *Barriers:* What do they think they will have to give (up) in order to perform the behavior? What concerns do they have regarding the behavior? Do they think they can do it? Why haven't they done it in the past, or on a regular basis? Why, perhaps, did they quit doing it? These could also be thought of as the "costs" the target audience perceives.

2. *Benefits:* What do they think they will get if they perform the behavior (as suggested)? How likely do they think it is that they will get this? What do they really want to get? These are also sometimes referred to as potential "motivators" for the target audience.

3. *Competition:* What behaviors are they doing instead? Why? What benefits do they perceive in this competing offer? What does it cost and how does that compare with your offer?

WHAT MORE DO YOU NEED TO KNOW ABOUT THE TARGET MARKET?

Barriers

Doug McKenzie-Mohr, an environmental psychologist known and respected for his community-based social marketing approach, notes that barriers may be *internal* to the individual, such as lack of knowledge or skill needed to carry out an activity, or *external*, as in structural changes that need to be made in order for the behavior to be more convenient. He also stresses that these barriers will differ by target market and by behavior. In our planning process, this is why target markets and the desired behavior (activity) are identified up front.[15]

Barriers may be related to a variety of factors, including knowledge, beliefs, skills, abilities, infrastructures, technology, economic status, or cultural influences. They may be *real* (e.g., taking the bus will take longer than driving alone to work) or *perceived* (e.g., people who take the bus can't really afford any other mode of transportation). In either case, they are always from the target market's perspective and often something you can address.

To illustrate both barriers and benefits, we'll use an example of blood donation. Founded in 1962, America's Blood Centers (ABC) is the national network of nonprofit, independent community blood centers, and in 2006, ABC members served more than 180 million people at 600-plus collection sites and more than 4,200 hospitals and health care facilities across North America.[16]

In May 2001, ABC conducted a survey to determine nationwide attitudes toward blood donation. The objective of the survey was to determine effective public messages and program changes that would increase blood donations. Telephone interviews were conducted with 600 adults from May 7 through May 9, 2001. The 95% confidence interval that is associated with a sample of this type produces a margin of error of plus or minus 4.1%.

When nondonors cite their reasons for not giving blood, there is an interesting split. About half the respondents (44%) cite health issues as their reason for not giving blood. However, as seen in Table 8.1, more than half of nondonors (52%) cite other reasons for not donating.

Benefits

Benefits are something your target market wants or needs and therefore values that the behavior you are promoting has the potential to provide.[17] They are what will motivate your target audience to act. Again, these will be benefits in the eye of the customer—not necessarily the same as yours. Bill Smith at the Academy of Educational Development (AED) asserts that these benefits may not always be so obvious. For example, "The whole world uses health as a benefit. [And yet] health, as we think of it

Table 8.1   Major Barrier (Reason) for Not Donating Blood Among Nondonors

Health issues/not qualified	44%
Never thought about it	17%
Too busy	15%
Scared of process	10%
Afraid of infection	4%
Don't know where/how	4%
Don't know anyone in need	2%

in public health, isn't as important to consumers—even high-end consumers—as they claim that it is. What people care about is looking good (tight abdominals and buns). Health is often a synonym for sexy, young, and hot. That's why gym advertising increases before bathing suit time. There is not more disease when the weather heats up, just more personal exposure."[18]

Returning to our blood donation example, as seen in Table 8.2, current and prior blood donors cite humanitarian reasons as their primary reason for giving blood (perceived benefits). Five of the top six responses are altruistic motives, such as helping the community or responding to a blood shortage.

In this same survey, potential messages were tested in terms of their ability to increase intent to give blood in the next 12 months. Before exposure to potential messages, findings indicated that 34% of respondents planned to give blood in the next 12 months. After hearing the potential message series, this increased to 41%, and, not surprisingly, humanitarian reasons tested well both in terms of intensity and in the multiple regression analysis. The most effective messages included "A family member, friend, or child is in need," which 86% said is an "extremely compelling" reason; 56% rated the statement that "4 million Americans would die every year without lifesaving blood transfusions" as extremely

Table 8.2   Major Benefit Perceived in Donating Blood Among Donors

Wanting to help others	34%
Responding to a blood drive	25%
Helping the community	13%
Hearing about a shortage	7%
Because I might need it someday	4%
Helping a local child	2%

Figure 8.3 Highlighting the Beneficiary of the Lifesaving Gift of Blood[20]

compelling.[19] One appeal even focused on saving the lives of emergency response professionals (see Figure 8.3).

The Competition

Identifying the Competition

The third area you'll want to explore with your target audience is the competition. Social marketers have tough competitors, for we define *the competition* as follows:

- Behaviors our target audience would prefer over the ones we are promoting (e.g., condoms may be preferred over abstinence as a way to prevent unwanted pregnancies)
- Behaviors they have been doing "forever" that they would have to give up (e.g., driving alone to work)
- Organizations and individuals who send messages that counter or oppose the desired behavior (e.g., the Marlboro Man)

Table 8.3 illustrates the challenges you (will) face. Consider the pleasures and benefits we are asking our target audience to give up. Consider the economic power of organizations and sponsors that are sending messages countering those you are sending. Consider the persuasiveness and influence of typical key messengers. And consider that the competition may even be your own organization! We call this "friendly" competition, where one program within the organization (e.g., needle exchange programs) may in fact potentially erode the success of another (e.g., reducing drug use).

Table 8.3   **What and Who You May Be Competing With**

Behavior Objective	Competing Behaviors	Competing Messages and Messengers
Drink less than five drinks at one sitting	Getting really "buzzed"	Budweiser
Wear a life vest	Tanning	Fashion ads showing tan shoulders, midriffs, and arms
Compost your food waste and use it in your gardens	City offering free pickup for food waste in yard waste containers	The waste management division of the city utility where you work
Give 5 hours a week to a volunteer effort	Spending time with family	Your kids

Another potential framing (and way to identify the competition) is offered by Sue Peattie and Ken Peattie of Cardiff University in Wales.[21] They suggest that in social marketing, the competition is better thought of as a "battle of ideas" and that these competing ideas can come from four sources that can be considered potential competitors: (1) *commercial counter-marketing* (e.g., cigarette companies), (2) *social discouragement* of your desired behavior (e.g., anti-gun-control activists), (3) *apathy* (e.g., when considering whether to vote), and (4) *involuntary disinclination* (e.g., physical addictions).

Identifying Barriers and Benefits of the Competition

Once competitors are identified, there is more you want to know while you're at it. McKenzie-Mohr and Smith provide a useful framework to capture your research findings—one that will prepare you for developing your product's positioning and 4P marketing mix strategy in Steps 6 and 7. The name of this marketing game is to change the ratio of benefits to barriers so that the target behavior becomes more attractive. They propose four nonmutually exclusive ways (tactics) to accomplish this:

1. Increase the benefits of the target behavior.

2. Decrease the barriers (and/or costs) to the target behavior.

3. Decrease the benefits of the competing behavior(s).

4. Increase the barriers (and/or costs) of the competing behaviors.[22]

Table 8.4 is a simple illustration of what would include in reality a more exhaustive list of benefits and barriers/costs that would be created (ideally) from audience research. Keep in mind there are likely to be more than one preferred or alternative behaviors identified as the competition.

An important component of this research process will include attempting to prioritize these benefits and barriers/costs within each of the quadrants. You are most interested in the "higher values"—the key benefits to be gained or costs that will be avoided by adopting the desired behavior. In the example in Table 8.4, your research won't be complete until you determine how your target audience ranks benefits and barriers in each quadrant (e.g., what is the number one benefit for using a litterbag?).

HOW DO YOU LEARN MORE FROM AND ABOUT THE TARGET?

Research will help you gain insights into audience barriers, benefits, and the competition. Existing behavior change theories and models will then help deepen your understanding of your customer—even develop empathy and compassion.

Table 8.4   Identifying Perceived Barriers and Benefits of the Competition

Audience Perceptions	Desired Behavior Use a Litterbag in the Car	Competing Behavior Tossing Fast-Food Bags Out the Window
Perceived benefits/motivators	It's good role modeling for my kids. I am doing my part for the environment. I help save tax dollars. I don't feel as guilty.	It's easier. I avoid the smell of old food in my car. I avoid the trash all over my car. It gives prisoners a job to do.
Perceived barriers/costs	Having to find one and remember to put it in the car. Having liquid spill out of it. Looking like a nerd with a white plastic bag in my black leather interior car.	I might have to do community service and pick up litter. I could get caught and fined. I'm contributing to the litter on the roadways that looks bad and will have to be picked up.

Research

As usual, you should begin with a review of existing literature and research and discussions with peers and colleagues. If, after this review, informational gaps still exist, it may be important to conduct original research using qualitative methods, such as focus groups and personal interviews, to identify the barriers, benefits, and the competition. Quantitative instruments, such as telephone and self-administered surveys, would be very helpful in prioritizing the benefits and barriers, such as those listed in Table 8.4, for using a litterbag. Consider the implications, for example, of this finding—representing a major barrier to timely cancer screening tests.

Health Information National Trends Survey (HINTS) is a nationally representative telephone survey of the general population that was first conducted in 2002–2003 and repeated in 2005. The National Cancer Institute developed HINTS to evaluate how the general public accesses and uses information about cancer and how this information can be delivered most effectively. A recent analysis of HINTS 2005 data found that while most Americans know that mammograms, pap smears, and colonoscopies are screening exams for cancer, the majority of Americans do not know the appropriate age at which initiation of these tests is recommended. For example, 57% of American women are unaware that they should receive mammograms to screen for breast cancer beginning at age 40, and 40% of respondents could not name even one of the several different tests available to screen for colorectal cancer.[23]

One popular survey model to know about is the knowledge, attitudes, practices, and beliefs (KAPB) survey. As described by Andreasen, "These are comprehensive surveys of a representative sample of the target population designed to secure information about the social behavior in question and on the current status of the target audience's Knowledge, Attitudes, Practices, Beliefs. KAPB studies are relatively common in social marketing environments, especially in the area of health. They are very often carried out routinely by local governments, the World Bank, or the United Nations. For this reason, they are sometimes available to social marketers as part of a secondary database."[24]

As an example, a KAPB-type study was conducted by the Gallup Organization for the March of Dimes in 1995, 1997, 1998, and 2000 and was supported by the Centers for Disease Control and Prevention.[25] Telephone surveys conducted nationwide were designed to track knowledge and behavior related to folic acid among women aged 18 to 45. Consider how these summary findings in the year 2000 would shape campaign strategies and priorities:

- 9 out of 10 women did not know that folic acid should be taken prior to pregnancy.
- More than 8 out of 10 women did not know that folic acid could help prevent birth defects.
- Only 1 in 3 women not pregnant at the time of the survey reported consuming a multivitamin containing folic acid daily.

Behavior Change Models and Theories

Information on target audience barriers, benefits, and the competition will help deepen your understanding, but it may not be enough. Sometimes it helps to understand underlying behavior change theories. One of these theories, stages of change theory, was mentioned in our Chapter 6 on segmentation. Four additional theories and one model of interest include the social norms theory, the health belief model, the theory of planned behavior, and the social cognitive theory. At the end of this section, you will read about themes that reflect all four models.

Social Norms Theory

Linkenbach describes the social norms approach to prevention, with clear potential implications to strategy development:[26]

The social norms approach to prevention emerged from college health settings in the mid-1980s in response to the seemingly intractable issue of high-risk drinking by college students. Wesley Perkins and Alan Berkowitz, social scientists at Hobart, Williams, and Smith Colleges, discovered that a significant disparity existed between actual alcohol use by college students and their perceptions of other students' drinking. Simply put, most college students reported that they believed drinking norms were higher and riskier than they really were.

The major implication of these findings is that if a student believes that heavy alcohol use is the norm and expected by most students, then regardless of the accuracy of the perception, he or she is more likely to become involved in alcohol abuse—despite his or her own personal feelings. Perkins came to call this pattern of misperception the "reign of error" and suggested that it could have detrimental effects on actual student drinking. According to Berkowitz, if students think "everyone is doing it," then heavy drinking rates rise due to influence from "imaginary peers."

This norming theory highlights the potential benefit of understanding perceived versus actual behaviors among target audiences. Results may signal an opportunity to correct the perception.

Health Belief Model

Kelli McCormack Brown describes clearly the model originally developed by social psychologists Hochbaum, Kegels, and Rosenstock, who were greatly influenced by the theories of Kurt Lewin:

The Health Belief Model states that the perception of a personal health behavior threat is itself influenced by at least three factors: general health values, which include interest and concern about health; specific health beliefs about vulnerability to a particular health threat; and beliefs about the consequences of the health problem. Once an individual perceives a threat to his/her health and is simultaneously cued to action, and his/her perceived benefits outweigh his/her perceived costs, then that individual is most likely to undertake the recommended preventive health action. Key descriptors include:

- *Perceived Susceptibility*: Perception of the likelihood of experiencing a condition that would adversely affect one's health
- *Perceived Seriousness*: Beliefs a person holds concerning the effects a given disease or condition would have on one's state of affairs: physical, emotional, financial, and psychological
- *Perceived Benefits of Taking Action*: The extent to which a person believes there will be benefits to recommended actions
- *Perceived Barriers to Taking Action*: The extent to which the treatment or preventive measure may be perceived as inconvenient, expensive, unpleasant, painful, or upsetting
- *Cues to Action*: Types of internal and external strategies/events that might be needed for the desired behavior to occur[27]

This model suggests you would benefit from reviewing or conducting research to determine each of these forces (susceptibility, seriousness, benefits, barriers, and perceptions of effective "cues to action") *before* developing campaign strategies. The National High Blood Pressure Education Program (NHBPEP) understands this well, as illustrated in the following highlight of their social marketing efforts and successes.

Example: More than 65 million American adults (in 2006), one in three, had high blood pressure and less than 30% were controlling their condition.[28] Key to influencing desired behaviors (increasing monitoring and recommended lifestyle and medication plans) is an understanding of perceived susceptibility, seriousness, and barriers—ones such as the following:

- It is hard for me to change my diet and to find the time to exercise.
- My blood pressure is difficult to control.
- My blood pressure varies so much, it's probably not accurate.
- Medications can have undesirable side effects.
- It's too expensive to go to the doctor just to get my blood pressure checked.
- It may be the result of living a full and active life. Not everybody dies from it.

You can see as you read on how messages in the NHBPEP materials and related strategies reflect an understanding of these perceptions:

- "You don't have to make all of the changes immediately. The key is to focus on one or two at a time. Once they become part of your normal routine, you can go on to the next change. Sometimes, one change leads naturally to another. For example, increasing physical activity will help you lose weight."[29]
- "You can keep track of your blood pressure outside of your doctor's office by taking it at home."[30]
- "You don't have to run marathons to benefit from physical activity. Any activity, if done at least 30 minutes a day over the course of most days, can help."[31]

The year the program began in 1972, less than one fourth of the American population knew of the relationship between hypertension, stroke, and heart disease. In 2001, more than three fourths of the population was aware of this connection. As a result, virtually all Americans have had their blood pressure measured at least once, and three fourths of the population has it measured every 6 months.

The Theory of Reasoned Action and the Theory of Planned Behavior

The theory of reasoned action (TRA), developed by Ajzen and Fishbein in 1975 and restated in 1980, suggests that the best predictor of a person's behavior is his or her intention to act. This intention is determined by two major factors: our beliefs about the outcomes associated with the behavior and perceptions of how people we care about will view the behavior in question. Using language from other theories presented throughout this text, our likelihood of adopting the behavior will be greatly influenced by perceived benefits, costs, and social norms. In 1988, Ajzen extended the TRA to include the influence of beliefs and perceptions regarding control—beliefs about our ability to actually perform the behavior (e.g., self-efficacy). This successor is called the theory of planned behavior (TPB).[32]

Social Cognitive Theory/Social Learning

Fishbein summarized Bandura's description of the social cognitive theory, also referred to as the social learning theory:

> The Social Cognitive Theory states that two major factors influence the likelihood that one will take preventive action. First, like the Health Belief Model, a person believes that the benefits of performing the behavior outweigh the costs (i.e., a person should have more positive than negative outcome expectancies). [This should remind you of the exchange theory mentioned frequently throughout this text.] Second, and perhaps most important, the person must have a sense of personal agency or self-efficacy with respect to performing the preventive behavior, . . . must believe that he or she has the skills and abilities necessary for performing the behavior under a variety of circumstances.[33]

Andreasen adds that this self-efficacy comes about at least in part from learning specific skills and from observing social norms, hence the name "social learning." This learning of specific new behaviors, he describes, has three major components: sequential approximation, repetition, and reinforcement. Sequential approximation acknowledges that individuals do not often instantly leap from not doing a behavior to doing it. They may prefer to work their way up to it. One way of teaching smokers, for example, how to adopt a nonsmoking lifestyle is to reduce their consumption step by step, perhaps one cigarette at a time, starting with the easiest behavior to give up and working up to the most difficult. Encouraging repetition (practice) and providing reinforcement strategies will then make it more likely the behavior will become a "part of a permanent behavioral repertoire."[34]

Themes From All Models

Fishbein's summary of behavior change interventions combines themes from most of the models presented in this section and provides a quick reference for gauging whether your target audience is "ready for action" or what might be needed to help them out. Generally speaking, it appears that in order for a person to perform a given behavior, one or more of the following must be true:

1. The person must have formed a strong *positive intention* (or made a commitment) to perform the behavior.

2. There are *no environmental constraints* that make it impossible to perform the behavior.

3. The person has the *skills* necessary to perform the behavior.

4. The person believes that the *advantages* (benefits, anticipated positive outcomes) of performing the behavior *outweigh the disadvantages* (costs, anticipated negative outcomes).

5. The person perceives more *social (normative) pressure* to perform the behavior than not to perform the behavior.

6. The person perceives that performance of the behavior is more consistent than inconsistent with his or her *self-image* or that its performance does not violate personal standards that activate negative self-actions.

7. The person's *emotional reaction* to performing the behavior is more positive than negative.

8. The person perceives that he or she has the *capabilities* to perform the behavior under a number of different circumstances.[35]

HOW WILL THIS HELP DEVELOP YOUR STRATEGY?

If you understand (better yet, empathize with) your target audience's real and perceived barriers, benefits, and competitors relative to your desired behavior, it will be akin to having a guiding hand as you craft your positioning statement and 4P strategies. We'll illustrate this application and process with a brief case.

In 2006, the Washington State Department of Health developed a social marketing plan with a *purpose* to decrease falls among seniors and a *focus* on developing fitness classes that could be offered by a variety of community organizations. The *target audiences* for the pilot (first year) were seniors aged 70–79 living in one county of the state. Formative research with key informants and seniors in the target market identified the following major perceived *benefits, barriers,* and *competition* to joining and attending classes:

- **Benefits:** "It could improve my strength, balance, and fitness, and then perhaps I can live independent longer. I also want it to be fun and a chance to make new friends."
- **Barriers to Joining:** "It depends on how much it will cost, where the class is located, the time of day it is offered, and who will be leading the class. I don't want some young instructor I can't relate to!"

- **Barriers to Attending Regularly:** "I'd probably drop out if it's too strenuous, I hurt myself, or I couldn't keep up. And I'd need to see improvements in my fitness for it to seem worthwhile."
- **Competition:** "I can probably just do my own thing at home for free, at my own pace, by watching an exercise video or going out for a walk. I guess the advantage of the class, though, is that it's a way to make sure I do it!"

A **positioning** statement, as you will read in the next chapter, describes how you want your target audience to see your desired behavior, especially relative to the competition. Planners wanted the fitness classes to be seen by their target audience of 70- to 79-year-olds as "a fitness class for seniors that *works*, as it will improve strength and balance; is *safe*, as it has experienced skilled instructors offering tested exercises; and is *fun,* as it offers an opportunity to meet others and get out of the house. It is an important and worthwhile activity for seniors wanting to stay *independent*, *be active*, and *prevent falls*."

The **product** platform includes a description of the core, actual, and augmented product, all inspired by your benefits, barriers, and competitive research. For the fitness classes, the *core* product (benefits of the class) was subsequently refined to be "staying active, independent, and preventing falls." The *actual* product (features of the classes) included a 1-hour strength and balance fitness class, meeting three times a week, with up to 20 participants. They would include strength exercises with wrist and ankle weights, balance exercises, and moderate aerobics. They could be done standing or sitting, and the instructor would be a certified fitness instructor with special training for strength and balance exercises for seniors. The *augmented* product (extras to add value) would include a fall prevention booklet that included a way to conduct a self-assessment for falls risk, give information on falls prevention, and determine readiness to exercise (see Figure 8.4). External safety effectiveness assessments would be available as well.

Pricing strategies include *costs* for products, *fees* for services, and any *monetary* and *nonmonetary incentives* and *disincentives*. Based on target audience comments, it was determined that the recommended fee per class be $2.00–$2.50, enough to help cover costs of the instructors, add to perceived value, and build commitment. It was also recommended to offer a coupon for a free first class, a punch card that gives 12 classes for the price of 11, and a suggestion to organizers to build in a reward of a free class to participants who attend at least 10 classes in a month.

Place strategies refer to where and when behaviors are performed and tangible objects and services are accessed. For the exercise classes, nine sites were selected, with eight of them at senior centers and one at a senior retirement facility. Suggested ideal start times were at 9 or 10 a.m. or 1, 2, or 3 p.m. There should be free, adjacent parking at each site.

Promotional elements include messages, messengers, and media channels. The recommended name of the program was S.A.I.L. (Stay Active and Independent for

Life), with a tagline of "A Strength and Balance Fitness Class for Seniors." Consistent with the desired positioning, key messages to incorporate in promotional materials included the following:

- It works. You'll be stronger, have better balance, feel better, and this will help you stay independent, active, and prevent falls.
- It's safe. Instructors are experienced and skilled, and exercises have been tested with seniors.
- It's fun. You'll meet other seniors, make new friends, and this will get you out of the house three days a week.

Types of media channels to promote the class would include flyers, posters, articles in newsletters and local newspapers, packets for physicians, Web site information, sandwich board signs at senior centers, and a Q&A fact sheet for senior center staff.[36]

Figure 8.4 Brochure Cover for Senior Fall Prevention Class

POTENTIAL REVISION OF TARGET MARKETS, OBJECTIVES, AND GOALS

This new in-depth understanding of target audiences may signal a need to revise target markets (Step 3) and/or objectives (Step 4) because it may reveal one or more of the following situations:

- One of the target markets has beliefs that you would have a difficult time changing or may not want to: "Moderate physical activity like this is 'wimpy,' and I'd rather increase vigorous activity from 2 to 3 days a week if I do anything more."
- The desired behavior has too many insurmountable barriers for one or more target markets: "I can't get to the farmers' market to use my coupons because they close before I get off work."

- The audience tells us the behavior objective isn't clear: "I don't understand what reducing my BMI means."
- Perceived costs are too high: "Quitting smoking while I'm pregnant looks impossible, but I might be able to cut down to a half a pack a day."
- The behavior objective has already been met: "My child already has five caring adult relationships outside the home, so for you to suggest I go find one caring adult for my child says you're not talking to people like me."
- We learn that a major knowledge objective isn't needed but a belief objective is: "I already know that tobacco kills one out of three users. I just don't believe I'll get addicted."
- The original behavior objective isn't the solution to the problem: "I always cover the load in the back of my pickup truck with a tarp. The problem is, it still doesn't keep stuff from flying out. What we need is a net or cable that holds the tarp down."
- The goal is too high: "This latest survey says that 75% of high school seniors are sexually active, so a goal of 50% choosing abstinence looks impossible with this group!"

ETHICAL CONSIDERATIONS WHEN RESEARCHING YOUR TARGET AUDIENCE

Perhaps the greatest ethical concern when conducting activities to learn more about your target audience is the research process itself. Concerns range from whether questions will make respondents uncomfortable or embarrassed to deceiving respondents regarding purposes of research to assurance of anonymity and confidentiality.

Institutional Review Boards (IRBs) have been formed to help avoid these ethical problems. An IRB is a group formally designated to review and monitor behavioral and biomedical research involving human subjects. The purpose of an IRB review is to ensure that appropriate steps are taken to protect the rights and welfare of humans participating as subjects in a research study. In the United States, IRBs are mandated by the Research Act of 1974, which defines IRBs and requires them for all research that receives funding, directly or indirectly, from the Department of Health and Human Services. These IRBs are themselves regulated by the Office for Human Research Protections within HHS and may be based at academic institutions, medical facilities, or conducted by for-profit organizations.[37]

Chapter Summary

In this important step in the marketing planning process, you take time out to deepen your understanding of your target market. What you are most interested in knowing are perceived *barriers*, *benefits*, and *competitors*. What you are most interested in feeling is compassion and a desire to develop marketing strategies that decrease these barriers, increase benefits, and upstage your competition.

These insights may be gathered through a literature review or other secondary research resources. They are more likely to involve at least some qualitative surveys such as focus groups or personal interviews. Quantitative surveys such as a KAPB (Knowledge, Attitudes, Practices, and Beliefs) survey will help prioritize your findings and provide sharp focus for your positioning and marketing mix strategies.

Several behavior change theories and models may also help explain why your audience thinks and feels the way they do regarding your desired behavior: exchange theory, social norms theory, health belief model, theory of reason, theory of planned behavior, and the social cognitive theory/social learning theory. Fishbein's summary pulling all theories and models together is worth rereading, even keeping close at hand.

RESEARCH HIGHLIGHT

Rete Sanitaria

Formative Research to Introduce an E-Health Network
in the Ticino Canton, Switzerland (2006)

MARZIO DELLA SANTA[38]
Project Manager
Repubblica e Cantone Ticino

FRANÇOIS LAGARDE[39]
Social Marketing Consultant
University of Montreal

In May 2003, the Ticino Grand Council (Switzerland) voted unanimously to grant funding for the experimental phase of an e-health card and network to familiarize citizens, health care providers, and elected officials with modern health information management. After 18 months of preparation, the experimental phase began in November 2004 and continued through 2006 in the Lugano urban area with 2,500 volunteer patients. The purpose of the formative research that will be described in this highlight conducted prior to the experimental phase was to factor in key audiences' receptiveness, motivations, and barriers, as well as to identify possible partners.

Research Objectives

Formative research was conducted prior to the experimental phase to answer the following questions:

What was the level of technological, organizational, cultural, legal, and financial readiness of the various stakeholders?

What was the profile of the segments most ready to participate?

What were the perceived benefits of a future e-health network and participation in the project?

What were the perceived barriers?

How should the project be designed (product, price, place) in order to provide more benefits and reduce barriers?

Who were the key partners that would provide credibility and resources to the project?

Methodology

A variety of research activities were needed to address these informational objectives:

- *Secondary research* through literature searches, as well as reviews of prior surveys and existing data for each category of professionals and the various health institutions involved—not only at the canton level, but at the national level as well. Additional sources reviewed included national and international scientific journals on e-health or journals that have published relevant clinical studies. Demographic data were also analyzed.

- *Personal interviews* were organized with managers of hospitals or other health institutions, physicians, pharmacists, and key politicians with a view to understanding or validating a problem or draft solution. The interviews conducted at the very beginning of the project helped to determine e-health acceptance levels of the various stakeholders.

Interviewees were selected for their opinion leader status and strategic decision making in different professional categories and political groups.

- A first series of *focus groups* followed interviews to assess the level of consensus around given e-health problems and solutions as well as to analyze the cultural, organizational, legal, and financial feasibility of the proposed solutions. These focus groups involved representatives from a variety of professions and political leaders.

- Before the e-health card experiment began, a *second series of six focus groups* was jointly organized with academics in charge of the faculty of medicine's graduate public health program at the University of Geneva. The purpose was to better understand a number of issues raised in the discussion groups to make the offer more user friendly. More specifically, a focus group was organized for each of the following institutions: Lugano Regional Hospital, Association of Pharmacists (district of Lugano), home care and ambulance services, private clinics (two groups), and the Physicians' Association (district of Lugano).

Highlights of Findings

The project team used the formative research to finalize the project design and promote its implementation. The project was modified as follows:

- Doctors were directly involved in the actual design of the card to ensure that all their concerns would be addressed (including identifying some software- and hardware-related barriers) and that colleagues would view the card and network as coming from their own ranks.

- Hardware (new or updated) was made available to those who did not have the basic requirements in place.
- A help desk was set up to respond quickly to any technical problems.
- Ethically acceptable compensation was provided to cover lost income resulting from participation in the project.
- The project was first offered to professionals already involved in quality improvement programs and those working in multidisciplinary care networks.
- All concerns regarding the protection of personal information were addressed.

Two cards were ultimately used in the experimental phase: (1) a patient health card (designed according to international standards) onto which important medical information can be recorded: allergies, vaccinations, list of medications, and main health problems, and (2) a complementary card for medical professionals that enables them to identify the patient's primary health professional, have access to private information (always with the patient's permission), and modify or update it (see Figure 8.5).

Figure 8.5 Sample Patient E-Health Card—*Rete Sanitaria* Project, Ticino Canton, Switzerland

A social marketing strategy was developed to promote e-health among professionals, patients, and politicians so they would adopt it in a way that would improve the quality of services offered and ensure service continuity at a sustainable cost. The commitment of numerous stakeholders was essential: managers of hospitals and other health institutions, physicians, pharmacists, and elected officials.

Post Note

The insight gathered from the formative research had enabled planners to focus on the most receptive segment of doctors while adjusting and adding some project features that addressed key barriers—both perceived and real—expressed by doctors. The formative steps also opened an ongoing dialogue among opinion leaders, managers, physicians, pharmacists, and elected officials. This ongoing dialogue builds equity and consensus into the partnerships fundamental to the future phases of the initiative.

The following outcomes were achieved after the first 2 years of experimentation:

- The number of health institutions (particularly physicians' practices and pharmacies) that participated in Phase I exceeded expectations (37 physicians' practices participated, while the objective was 30; 41 pharmacies participated, while the objective was 30).
- An increasing number of health institutions are integrating e-health into their strategies.
- The Ticino pilot project led to a national debate on e-health.
- The State Council extended the project until the end of 2007.

Part IV

DEVELOPING SOCIAL MARKETING STRATEGIES

CHAPTER 9

Crafting a Desired Positioning

Let's get radical. Let's change the world. Let's become real marketers. If we always do what we've always done, we'll always get what we've always gotten.

—Michael Rothschild

Back in the early 1970s, a couple of advertising executives, Al Ries and Jack Trout, started a small revolution—a marketing revolution, that is. They introduced the concept and art of positioning. It was more than a new approach. It was, as they described it, a creative exercise.

Positioning starts with a product. A piece of merchandise, a service, a company, an institution, or even a person. But positioning is not what you do to a product. Positioning is what you do to the mind of the prospect. That is, you position the product in the mind of the prospect.[1]

Their premise was that our mind, as a defense against the volume of today's communications, screens and rejects much of the information offered it and accepts only that which matches prior knowledge or experience.

The best approach to take in our overcommunicated society, they advocated, is the oversimplified message. "The average mind is already a dripping sponge that can only soak up more information at the expense of what's already there. Yet we continue to pour more information into that supersaturated sponge and are disappointed when our messages fail to get through. . . . In communication, as in architecture, less is more. You have to sharpen your message to cut into the mind. You have to jettison the ambiguities, simplify the message, and then simplify it some more if you want to make a long-lasting impression."[2]

And as you no doubt have discovered, or at least have read so far in this text, different markets have different needs, and your challenge is to position your offer "perfectly" in the mind of your desired prospect. The positioning exercise you will explore in this chapter will help provide that clarity. And in the following opening case story and the closing Research Highlight, you'll experience the power this can have.

MARKETING HIGHLIGHT

Road Crew

Reducing Alcohol Impaired Driving (2007)

MICHAEL ROTHSCHILD

Professor Emeritus
University of Wisconsin

Background

In spring 2000, Martha Florey (assistant to the director) and Carol Karsten (alcohol program manager) of the Wisconsin Department of Transportation were wondering how to move forward in reducing alcohol-related crashes. For several years, the numbers had remained fairly constant, while the department had spent its budget on creating new message campaigns. In addition, laws were not being made more onerous and the budget for law enforcement was not increasing.

They were told that they should try social marketing, so they came to visit me at the University of Wisconsin and I then took them on a journey that led to the development of the Road Crew, which has, by early 2007, given over 65,000 rides to potentially impaired drivers in rural Wisconsin. One of the keys to the success of Road Crew has been its consideration of positioning issues. This is the story of Road Crew, how its positioning evolved, and how it was then translated into a winning service.

Target Audience

Good positioning begins with a clear understanding of the target and the competitive choices. My team first did seven focus groups around the state talking to expert observers of drunk drivers. These experts included law enforcement officials, bar owners and waitstaff, members of the judicial system, ambulance drivers, teachers of courses aimed at convicted drunk drivers, and others.

Most marketers will sell their product to anyone who wishes to buy, but the product, its positioning, and its advertising are generally aimed at the most likely target. Anyone can buy a Coke, but its marketing is aimed at teenagers. Similarly, Road Crew would ultimately be available to anyone who wanted to use it, but it would be designed for the primary target. There was ample prior evidence that the group of people most likely to drink, drive, and crash were 21- to 34-year-old single men living in rural areas. The team next conducted 17 focus groups with this target. All meetings were held in the back of local taverns so that attendees would feel comfortable in discussing the issues.

Strategy

In developing a new product, a marketer would want to learn about the target, current usage patterns, and why existing competitive brands were succeeding. To that end, the research focused on the following issues, interested in describing the target audience beyond demographics:

- What are they looking for out of life?
- Why do they drink?
- Why do they drive after drinking?
- Why don't they drive after drinking?
- What are the processes of life they go through so that they end up at a tavern at 1:00 a.m., drunk, and with their car in the parking lot?
- What might be done to change that behavior?

It was immediately clear that the target knew that drunk driving was not the right thing to do. Virtually everybody has seen messages telling them not to drive drunk. People know not to do this, and most feel that drunk driving is a bad thing, yet it continues. There is a disconnect between awareness, attitude, and motivation, and later behavior. The research would try to uncover ways to overcome this disconnect so that the target could easily behave as society desired.

When people can freely choose what to do, there is competition among the choices. Here the competition was a brand called "I can drive myself home, no matter how drunk I am." This brand had a dominant share in most communities and was often a monopoly brand, because there was no other way to get home at the end of an evening. In order to change driving behavior, the community needed to develop a ride program that would be perceived as providing greater benefit to the target than the brand they currently bought. The new brand also needed to be easily accessible.

By asking the target why they drive after drinking, the team could learn the benefits of the competitive brand and also the barriers that would keep people from buying a new brand. Reasons for driving drunk included the following:

- To get home.
- To avoid the hassle of coming back in the morning to get the vehicle.
- Everybody does it.
- At 1:00 a.m. the target is fearless.
- There is a low risk of getting caught.

When they were asked to help design a ride program that they would use, they asked for

- Vehicles that were at least as nice as their own (they wouldn't ride in old school buses)
- A ride from home to the bar, between bars, and then home again (if they drove to the bars, they said, they'd drive home, so they needed to leave their vehicles at home at the beginning of the evening)
- The right to smoke and drink in the vehicles (they already smoked and drank in their own vehicles)

This research allowed the program to be developed in general, and then each community repeated the exercise with their own target members. This local research focused on routing, time and days of operation, and pricing so that the product would serve the target needs as best as possible and would be perceived to be more appealing than driving drunk.

Results

The resulting service uses utilizes limousines and other luxury vehicles to pick people up at their home, business, or hotel, take them to the bar of their choice, take them between bars, and then take them home at the end of the evening. As allowed by local ordinances, passengers may smoke and drink in the vehicles. The cost to the passenger is $15–$20 for the evening.

The program now operates in 32 small communities in rural Wisconsin. The communities have been using Road Crew from 1 to 4 years, and over 65,000 rides have been taken. Research shows that while driving behavior has been changed dramatically, people are not drinking more as a result of getting rides. After receiving seed money to begin the program, communities are able to self-sustain from ride fares and tavern contributions. Cost benefit analysis shows that it is less expensive to run the program than to clean up after crashes take place, with an estimated $15,300 cost per crash avoided and a savings to all those impacted by a crash of $610,000.[3]

Figure 9.1 shows the initial poster that was used to raise awareness. It doesn't tell people not to drive drunk; it focuses on Road Crew's position. That is, it tells people that they can have more fun if they use Road Crew than if they drive themselves. Research had shown that the target wanted to have fun and that drinking was a part of having fun. The target didn't feel that driving drunk was fun, but it was necessary in order to have fun earlier in the evening.

Summary

Road Crew has succeeded because it is well positioned relative to its competition. In the early research, the target told us that they saw driving as scary, dangerous, and the chance to get an expensive penalty. The Road Crew, though, is seen as a cool way to get

Figure 9.1 Positioning Road Crew as a Cool Way to Get Around and Have Fun

around and have fun; the evening's fun continues until the person is home.

Rather than telling people that drunk driving is bad, they are told that using Road Crew is more fun than the competitive choice. Road Crew offers more benefits than driving. In the past, driving was often the only choice available; anyone who admitted to not being able to drive home was seen as a weak person, but now, choosing the Road Crew is a sign of being cool rather than a sign of being weak.

Social marketing is most relevant in situations where people have easy and appealing choices. In a free-choice society, we rarely have the power to force a decision, so people tend to choose what they see to be in their own immediate self-interest. When the competitive choice is appealing, we need to make the desired behavior even more appealing. Positioning our choice becomes an important part of strategy. In the Road Crew case, the competitive brand, "I can drive myself home, no matter how drunk I am," had a large and loyal share of the market, so it was important to understand what it would take to develop a more appealing choice. The new-product development research that was done led to an understanding of how to position Road Crew, and the ride service was then developed to be consistent with the positioning. (For more insights on Road Crew, go to www.roadcrewonline.org and click through to a 5-minute video to see what people in one community thought about Road Crew.)

POSITIONING DEFINED

Positioning is the act of designing the organization's actual and perceived offering in such a way that it lands on and occupies a distinctive place in the mind of the target market—where you want it to be.[4]

Think of your target audience as having a perceptual map, one they will use to locate your offer. Consider further that they have a different map for different product categories (e.g., one for cars, airlines, fast food, beverages, and, more relevant for social marketers perhaps, one for exercise, workplace safety, recycling, and organ donation). Figure 9.2 illustrates a simplified version of a perceptual map, showing which brands are perceived as being similar and competing against each other. Most perceptual maps for products use data from consumer surveys evaluating products/services on specific attributes.

There is a good reason we present and recommend you take this step *after* you have selected and researched your target audience and *prior* to developing your marketing mix strategy. Since offers are positioned differently for different markets (e.g., exercise for tweens versus seniors), this decision, of course, comes first. And since your product, price, place, and promotion will determine (to a great extent) where you land, it makes sense to know your desired destination. This will help guide your marketing strategy by clarifying the brand's essence, what goals it helps the consumer achieve, and how it does so in a unique way.

As you may recall, our definition of social marketing describes this discipline as a process that applies marketing principles and techniques to create, communicate, and deliver value in order to influence target audience behaviors. The result of positioning is the successful creation of a customer-focused value proposition, a cogent reason why the target market should buy the product—from you![5]

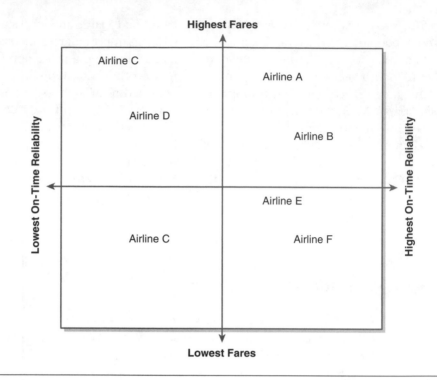

Figure 9.2 A Simple, Hypothetical Illustration of a Perceptual Map, Placing Two Attributes of a Product on a Map, as They Are Perceived Relative to Competitors

Positioning in the Commercial Sector

Perhaps because this sector has embraced this positioning concept for decades, great examples of clear positioning and the value proposition are easy to find, as suggested in Table 9.1. In the Focus column, we have linked these value propositions to social marketing theories and models we have discussed in prior chapters: benefits, barriers, and competition. One new option, now that we have introduced the positioning concept, would be a focus on repositioning—where a brand manager is interested in moving a product from its current location in the mind of target markets to a new, more desirable one (see Figure 9.3).

Commercial marketers also often consider and establish what is referred to as *Points-of-Difference* and *Points-of-Parity* and are described by Kotler and Keller.

Points-of-difference are attributes or benefits consumers strongly associate with a brand and believe they could not find the same positive benefits with a competitive brand. Examples include FedEx *(guaranteed overnight delivery)*, Nike *(performance)*, and Lexus *(quality)*. Points-of-parity, by contrast, are associations that are not necessarily

Table 9.1   Commercial Sector Brand Positioning Examples

Category	Brand	Focus	Value Proposition
Car	Volvo	Benefits	Safety
Fast food	Subway	Barriers	Fresh, healthy options
Airlines	Southwest	Competition	No frills. Lower costs
Beverages	Milk	Repositioning	From boring to cool

unique to the brand but may be considered essential to be a legitimate offering within a certain product or service category (e.g., a bank needs to at least offer access to ATM machines, online banking services, and checking accounts in order to be considered a bank). Competitive points-of-difference positioning might instead or also work to negate the competitors' points of difference. One good example they highlight is a Miller Lite beer advertising strategy that ends with the tagline "Everything You've Always Wanted in a Beer . . . And Less."[6]

STEP #6: DEVELOPING A POSITIONING STATEMENT FOR SOCIAL MARKETING PRODUCTS

Positioning principles and processes are similar for social marketing products. With the profile of your target market in mind, including any unique demographic, geographic, psychographic, and behavior-related characteristics and the findings from your research on perceived barriers, benefits, and competitors, you will now "simply" craft a positioning statement for Step 6.

Figure 9.3   Repositioning Milk as "Cool"

SOURCE: Courtesy of National Dairy Council®

One way to develop a positioning statement is to fill in the blanks to this phrase, or one similar to it:

"We want [TARGET AUDIENCE] to see [DESIRED BEHAVIOR] as [DESCRIPTIVE PHRASE] and as more important and beneficial than [COMPETITION]."

Keep in mind this positioning statement is "for internal use only." It is not your ultimate message to your target audiences. It will, however, be shared with others working with you on your effort to develop your marketing mix strategy, helping to unify and strengthen decision making. Consider how agreement on the following statements would guide these teams:

- "We want pregnant women to see breastfeeding exclusively for the first 6 months as a way to bond with their child and contribute to their health and as more important than concerns with nursing in public."
- "We want the media to see using nonstigmatizing mental health labels (e.g., this person has schizophrenia versus this person is schizophrenic) as a way to help those with mental illnesses as well as to be a respected and leading role model in the profession."
- "We want homeowners who love gardening to see composting food waste as an easy way to contribute to the environment and create great compost for their garden at the same time and better than putting it in the garbage, which then goes to the landfill or down the drain and then has to be treated."
- "We want people shopping for a puppy to visit the Humane Society's Web site first to see if the pet they have in mind is just waiting for someone to adopt it, and that this is likely to be a less expensive and more convenient option than going to the classified ads."

Inspiration for your descriptive phrase will come from the lists of barriers and benefits identified in your research. As you may recall, the ideal research will have included a prioritization of barriers and benefits, giving you a sense of what factors would be most important to highlight. You are searching for the "higher value," the key benefits to be gained or costs that will be avoided by adopting the desired behavior.

To leverage prior steps in the planning model, you may find it advantageous to consider a focus for your positioning statements, choosing from among those that drive home specific *behaviors*, highlight *benefits*, overcome *barriers*, upstage the *competition,* or *reposition* an "old brand." More detail on each of these options is presented in the next five sections, with a couple of brief examples and one longer illustration.

BEHAVIOR-FOCUSED POSITIONING

For some social marketing programs, especially those with a new and/or very specific desired behavior in mind, you may benefit from a behavior-focused positioning. In these cases, a description of your behavior will be highlighted, as shown in these examples:

- 3DAYS3WAYS, a campaign sponsored by King County (Washington) Emergency Management, encourages citizens to be prepared for emergencies and disasters in three ways: Make a Plan, Build a Kit, and Get Involved.[7]
- 3-1-1, Transportation Security Administration's travel tip effort, was developed in 2006 to support travelers in knowing what liquids and gels they could carry on and how many (see Figure 9.4).

In these cases, making sure target audiences know the specifics of the desired behavior are key to successful outcomes, as illustrated in the following example.

Figure 9.4 A Behavior-Focused Positioning From the Transportation Security Administration on a Wallet Card for Travelers[8]

Example: 5 A Day

In 1991, the National Cancer Institute (NCI), in cooperation with the Produce for Better Health Foundation, created "5 A Day for Better Health," a national program that approaches Americans with a simple, positive message: "Eat five or more servings of vegetables and fruit daily for better health" (see Figure 9.5).

This key message has been repeated using a well-integrated strategy and a multitude of venues over the years: plastic produce bags, grocery bags, in-store signage and displays, produce packaging labels, supermarket tours, recipe cards, brochures, grocery store flyer ads, magazine articles, newspaper ads, news stories, the Internet, radio news inserts, television news inserts (cooking/recipe spots), radio public service announcements (PSAs), television PSAs, billboards, CD-ROMs in elementary schools, nutrition newsletters, patient nutrition education materials, pay stubs, school curricula, preschool programs, food assistance program

Figure 9.5 The Produce for Better Health Foundation's Behavior-Focused Positioning[9]

materials, church bulletins and newsletters, posters, restaurant menus, Girl/Boy Scout badges, 4-H materials, food bank program materials, health fairs, county fairs, cookbooks, children's coloring books, and videotapes. In 2006 a new slogan, "The Color Way," was added to influence more variety in the 5 A Day mix we choose.

A press release from the Produce for Better Health Foundation in November 2005 reported good outcome news. According to the ACNielsen study of nearly 2,600 households, the number of Americans claiming to eat five or more daily servings was 18% in 2004, up 50% from 2003. The study also finds a clear link between awareness and consumption, with a jump in consumption of five or more daily servings reported by those claiming awareness of the foundation's Color Way messages. More than 30% of those who were most aware of the Color Way message reported consuming five or more servings of fruits and vegetables a day compared to less than 10% of those who were not aware of the campaign. This is further backed up by purchasing data, which show that those most aware of the Color Way message spent $111 more annually on fruits and vegetables than those not aware of the campaign.[10]

BARRIERS-FOCUSED POSITIONING

With this type of focus, you want your offer's positioning to help overcome or at least minimize perceived barriers, ones such as a concern with self-efficacy, fear, or perceived high costs associated with performing the behavior:

- For tobacco users who want to quit, quitlines are often positioned as hopeful and encouraging, as in the following poem (perhaps more like a rap) that appeared on the Washington State Department of Health's Web site in 2007:

  In the New Year, make smoking a thing of the past,
  Put yourself first and your habit last.
  Start the year right; start out on top,
  And make '07 the year that you stop.

  Tobacco products will harm your health.
  They'll deplete your energy as well as your wealth.
  Although smoking is a hard habit to break,
  With determination and support it's a change you can make.

  Call the Washington State Tobacco Quit Line to learn how.
  A quit coach will assist you at 1-800-QUIT-NOW.
  A customized plan and one-on-one counseling you'll get
  To help make '07 smoke-free, and your best year yet.

  The call is confidential, the service is free
  And can double your chance of quitting successfully.
  More than 80,000 Washingtonians have made the call
  For free counseling and quit kits available for all.

  Don't hesitate; call the quit line today,
  And in the New Year, you'll be well on your way![11]

- Some women avoid or postpone having mammograms when they are afraid to get bad news. This explains why many organizations have positioned mammograms as "early detection," a way to get treatment before it spreads.

In the following illustration, the positioning must have a concern with belonging or rejection in mind.

Example: Positioning Condoms as "OK"

In the late 1980s, the Swiss AIDS Foundation, in cooperation with the Swiss government, introduced the first-ever Swiss AIDS campaign. The foundation created its own brand of condoms, "Hot Rubber," and its own distribution channels, focusing on intravenous drug users, males with homosexual contacts, and adolescents. The campaign was titled "STOP AIDS," with the *O* of the word *STOP* in the form of a pink, rolled-up condom. This symbolic graphic approach was also used in a variety of campaign executions (see Figure 9.6). Sales of the condoms reached more than 75,000 per month, with condom sales rising from 7.6 million to 15 million units between 1986 and 1992. Approximately 50% of those aged 17–30 involved in occasional sexual contacts reported use of condoms (always) in 1990, compared with the previous 8% in 1987. Condom use among individuals between the ages of 31 and 45 also increased from 22% in 1989 to 52% in 1992.[12]

Interestingly, and from a positioning standpoint, similarly, on January 8, 2007, an article in the *New York Post* announced that New York Mayor Bloomberg was about to unveil the city's own "NYC" brand of free condoms—in foil packets with a variety of colors representing the different subway lines. New York City is the country's HIV/AIDS capital, as this disease is the third leading cause of death among citizens under 65, behind cancer and heart disease. In 2005, 1,400 city residents died of AIDS. This effort appears to position these condoms as a norm—perhaps just like taking the subway.[14]

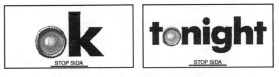

Figure 9.6 Promoting Condom Use, a Core Strategy for the Swiss Campaign[13]

BENEFIT-FOCUSED POSITIONING

When the best hook seems to be one related to the WIFM factor (What's in It for Me), perceived benefits become the focus of the positioning:

- Natural yard care practices such as pulling weeds versus spraying them are positioned as ways to *ensure the health of your children and pets.*

- Moderate physical activity such as raking leaves and taking the stairs instead of the elevator is positioned as *something you can fit into your daily routine.*
- Reading to your child for 20 minutes each night is positioned as a way to help *ensure they will do well in school.*

You will be reminded, as you read the following illustration of a benefit-focused positioning, that once more the focus is on benefits your target market wants and believes they can get.

Example: ENERGY STAR®

In 1992, the U.S. Environmental Protection Agency (EPA) established the ENERGY STAR program to increase the nationwide use of energy-efficient products and practices. Computers and monitors were the first labeled products. Today, the program encompasses more than 40 product categories for the home and workplace and promises real consumer benefits: By purchasing ENERGY STAR products you can save money and help protect the environment at the same time. "Change a Light, Change the World" is an annual campaign of the EPA, cosponsored by the Department of Energy and Department of Housing and Urban Development, that encourages Americans to replace a conventional bulb or fixture in the home or workplace with ENERGY STAR–qualified bulbs and fixtures, ones that use one quarter the energy of traditional models and last up to 10 times longer. Each light can save $30 or more in utility costs over its lifetime and keep more than 400 pounds of greenhouse gases out of our atmosphere. This annual campaign encourages citizens to make a pledge to replace at least one light bulb with an energy-saving one. By Earth Day 2007, more than half a million Americans had pledged to change more than 1 million lights to ENERGY STAR–qualified ones. This will save enough energy to light nearly 145,000 homes for an entire year, save close to $30 million in energy costs, and prevent greenhouse gases equivalent to the emissions from more than 35,000 cars. Americans are invited to visit the ENERGY STAR Web site to join individuals in all 50 states who have pledged to replace at least one light at home and see how even small energy-saving actions at home can add up to a world of difference (see Figure 9.7).

COMPETITION-FOCUSED POSITIONING

A fourth option for focus is the competition, one quite appropriate when your target market finds "their offer" quite appealing or your offer "a pain":

- Youth abstinence advocates have tough competitors, including the media, entertainment, peer pressure, and raging hormones. Positioning abstinence as postponing sex, versus "no sex," has become an easier sell for many.

- Consequences of tobacco use are often positioned as *gross, realistic,* and *shocking* (see Figure 9.8).

An additional model for developing competitive advantages is focused on creating *competitive superiority*, a more rigorous objective. The same four tactics mentioned in Chapter 8 are used in tandem, as illustrated in Table 9.2. A *benefit-to-benefit superiority* tactic appeals to values higher than those perceived for the competition (e.g., a child who wants and needs a parent is compared to the short-term pleasures from smoking). A *cost-to-benefit superiority* tactic places an emphasis on decreasing costs/barriers to adopting the desired behavior and, at the same time, decreasing perceived benefits of the competition (e.g., success stories from cessation classes include testimonials from a spouse talking about how nice it is to have clean air in the house). A *benefit-to-cost superiority* tactic places an emphasis on the benefits of the desired behavior and the costs of the competing behavior(s) (e.g., abilities of teen athletes who don't smoke as compared with those who do). A *cost-to-cost superiority* tactic relies on a favorable comparison of costs of the desired behavior relative to the competition (e.g., short-term nicotine withdrawal symptoms are compared with living with emphysema).

Figure 9.7 ENERGY STAR's Web Site Encouraging Citizens to Take a Pledge to Replace at Least One Light in the Home With an Energy Star–Qualified One[15]

Example: Dial 311 for Routine Information

In 2003, New York City announced a convenient and cost-saving alternative to dialing 911—dialing 311 instead. With a vast majority of the more than 8 million annual calls

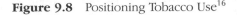

Figure 9.8 Positioning Tobacco Use[16]

Table 9.2   Creating Competitive Superiority

Competing Behavior	Desired Behavior	
	Increase Benefits	Decrease Costs/Barriers
Decrease benefits:	Tactic A: Benefit-to-benefit superiority tactic	Tactic B: Cost-to-benefit superiority tactic
Increase costs/barriers:	Tactic C: Benefit-to-cost superiority tactic	Tactic D: Cost-to-cost superiority tactic

to 911 representing nonemergency situations, the service is anticipated to delight citizens and decrease operating costs. Before 311, the city operated more than 40 separate call centers and hotlines, along with hundreds of agencies, programs, and offices, making it very difficult for citizens to know who to call for what and when. Most citizens were obviously confused about which agency to contact for services, so they were dialing 911 for concerns with noises, blocked driveways, garbage pickup, potholes, and burned-out streetlights.

All calls are answered by a live operator, 24 hours a day, 7 days a week, and can be translated into 170 languages. In 2004, colorful posters appeared in New York City as a result of a joint effort between the city and Sun Microsystems to help build awareness for the new 311 hotline.[17]

REPOSITIONING-FOCUSED

What happens when your program has a current positioning that you feel is in the way of achieving your behavior change goals? Several factors may have contributed to this wake-up call and sense that you need to "relocate":

- You might need to attract *new markets* in order to sustain your growth, and these new markets may not find your current position appealing. For example, adults over 50 not engaged in regular physical activity may have tuned out messages regarding exercise long ago, as they only could hear the "vigorous aerobic" recommendation. Planners turned to moderate physical activity.
- You may be suffering from an *image problem*. When bike helmets were first promoted to youth, they balked. Making the behavior **Fun, Easy, and Popular** for the audience is Bill Smith's recommendation and could well describe the strategy in Figure 9.9. These three words focus program managers on how to change behavior by giving people what they want, along with what we feel they need.

○ FUN in this context means to provide your audience with some perceived benefits they care about.

○ EASY means to remove all the possible barriers to action and make the behavior as simple and accessible as possible.

○ POPULAR means to help the audience feel that this is something others are doing, particularly others who the audience believes are important to them.[18]

Or you may have just received (as do lots of others usually) the results of an *evaluation* research project indicating disappointing outcomes as a result of your current positioning strategy, as was the case in the following example.

Example: The New D.A.R.E. Program

The Drug Abuse Resistance Education (D.A.R.E.) program was considered a pioneer prevention effort when it was founded in Los Angeles in 1993. But the old-style approach where an officer stands behind a podium and lectures students in straight rows is gone. The New D.A.R.E., revitalized as a result of a national research effort funded by a $13.7 million grant from the Robert Wood Johnson Foundation in 2001, has gone high tech, incorporates inter-

Figure 9.9 Positioning of Wearing Protective Gear as Fun, Easy, and Popular[19]

active exercises, and is using a decision-based model. Now D.A.R.E. officers are trained and positioned as "coaches," supporting kids who are using research-based refusal strategies in high-stakes peer-pressure environments. As described on the program's Web site, "students are getting to see for themselves—via stunning brain imagery—tangible proof of how substances diminish mental activity, emotions, coordination, and movement. Mock courtroom exercises are bringing home the social and legal consequences of drug use and violence."[20] (See Figure 9.10.)

According to Charlie Parsons, president and chief executive director of D.A.R.E. America, "New D.A.R.E. is setting the gold standard for the future. Prevention inside the 21st century school house will need to be effective, diverse, accountable, and mean more things to more people, particularly with the safety issues that have emerged since Columbine and terrorist alerts."[21]

HOW POSITIONING RELATES TO BRANDING

Although the concept of the brand and the branding process will be covered in the next chapter focusing on product, you may have immediate questions regarding

Figure 9.10 Repositioning D.A.R.E. for the 21st Century

positioning and how it relates to branding that we will address briefly at this point. It helps to distinguish the two by referring to a few basic definitions:

- **Brand** is a name, term, sign, symbol, and/or design that identifies the maker or seller of a product (e.g., ENERGY STAR is a term that identifies products that are energy efficient, according to the EPA).[22]
- **Brand identity** is how you (the maker) want your target audience to think, feel, and act with respect to your brand (e.g., EPA wants citizens to see products with the ENERGY STAR label as a way to help the environment and save on electrical power bills).
- **Brand image** is how your target audience actually ends up thinking, feeling, and acting relative to your brand (e.g., what citizens know about the ENERGY STAR label and whether they associate it with energy and cost savings).
- **Branding** is the process of developing an intended brand identity (e.g., activities that EPA has undertaken to determine and ensure this desired brand identity).

Your positioning statement is something you and others can count on to provide parameters and inspiration for developing your desired brand identity—how you want the desired behavior to be seen by the target audience. It will provide strong and steady guidance for your decision making regarding your marketing mix, as it is the 4Ps that will determine where your offer lands in the minds of your target audience. And when your brand image doesn't align with your desired positioning (brand identity), you'll look to your 4Ps for "help" in repositioning the brand.

ETHICAL CONSIDERATIONS WHEN DEVELOPING A POSITIONING

When developing your positioning statement, several ethical questions may (actually should) come to your mind. You will notice many of these relate to the familiar "truth in advertising" code.

If your positioning statement is *behavior-focused*, ensure your recommendations are accurate. For the 5 A Day the Color Way, detailed information on the Web site clarifies why these specific behaviors are important. "Blue/purple fruits and vegetables contain varying amounts of health-promoting phytochemicals such as anthocyanins and phenolics, currently being studied for their antioxidant and anti-aging benefits."[23]

If your positioning statement focuses on *benefits* for the target audience, you will want to be certain that you can really deliver these benefits. A campaign promoting moderate physical activity should make it clear to potential "buyers" what levels and types of physical activity are needed in order to achieve any health gains promised, and at what levels.

If your positioning statement focuses on how the target audience will be able to overcome their *barriers*, you will want to be certain you paint a realistic picture. Communications promoting quitlines as a way to quit smoking should be certain to include rates of success and the fact that not all those who call will be able to quit. Note that if you reread the poem on the Washington State Department of Health's Web site, the quitline delivers on its positioning as "hopeful and encouraging" but doesn't mention any guarantees.

If your positioning statement focuses on the *competition*, be certain what you say about them is really true, and not exaggerated. As you read, New York City promises better and "seamless" service when you call 311 for a missing car. It wouldn't take many citizens not getting quick help to spread the word that 911 will get you better service faster.

And if your positioning statement focuses on *repositioning* the brand, be sure your offer is really "new and improved." The New D.A.R.E program will need to be obviously distinct from the prior program.

Chapter Summary

Positioning is the act of designing the organization's offering in such a way that it lands on and occupies a distinctive place in the mind of the target market—where you want it to be. Step 6 in the marketing planning process recommends that you develop a positioning statement at this point. The research on your target audience's barriers, benefits, and competitors in Step 5 will provide the inspiration you need. It will also help build consensus among your colleagues and partners, ensuring fewer surprises and disappointments as you move forward to developing your strategies.

Positioning statements may be focused on behaviors, barriers, benefits, the competition, and/or on repositioning. Your decisions will reflect your value proposition, a reason why the target market should buy the product—from you!

Take time and care to develop this statement, as you will refer to it frequently when developing each of the 4Ps. This will help ensure that "proper landing" you have in mind.

RESEARCH HIGHLIGHT

American Legacy Foundation—truth® Campaign

Evaluation Survey (2005)

PATRICIA MCLAUGHLIN, MA

Senior Director of Communications
American Legacy Foundation

Background

About 80% of smokers begin using tobacco before the age of 18. Each day, about 3,900 kids in the United States try smoking for the first time. For many, it becomes an addiction that can lead to a life of disease and tobacco-related death.[24]

Launched in February 2000, truth® is a national youth smoking prevention campaign directed and funded by the American Legacy Foundation®, a national public health foundation based in Washington, D.C., devoted to tobacco use prevention and cessation. The largest national youth smoking prevention campaign truth® is the only national campaign in the United States not directed by the tobacco industry. The objective of the campaign is to change social norms and reduce youth smoking. Youth aged 12 to 17 years are the primary focus of the campaign.

The truth® campaign directly counters messages from the tobacco company brands, which spent more than $15.1 billion in 2003 to market their products in the United States alone. The campaign exposes the tactics of the tobacco industry, the truth about addiction, and the health effects and social consequences of smoking, allowing teens to make informed choices about tobacco use by giving them the facts about the industry and its products. It is designed to engage teens by exposing Big Tobacco's marketing and manufacturing practices, as well as highlighting the toll of tobacco in relevant and innovative ways.

The campaign uses research with teen audiences, marketing and social science research, and evidence from the most successful antitobacco campaigns to inform its strategies.

The truth® campaign also uses actual tobacco industry documents that were made public after the Master Settlement Agreement. The documents are used to find the facts teens see in truth® ads and on the truth® Web site. The truth® campaign has an integrated communications strategy, utilizing multiple communication channels, including the following:

- Television, radio, and print advertising
- A Web site and interactive communications
- Grassroots outreach through a summer tour
- Gear, including wearable and cool products like T-shirts, iPod socks, and other items reflecting the brand and subtly raising attention to the tobacco issue

- Earned media, supported by an extensive media relations effort to place related stories in youth media and raise attention in adult media to the issue and to the campaign's award-winning work

Ads like truth® are known for being "in your face," hard hitting, and even humorous, because teens respond to up-front and powerful messages that display courage and honesty in a forceful way (see Figure 9.11). In addition, teens are involved in testing all truth® advertising concepts and provide suggestions and feedback through the truth® Web site.

Purpose of Research

In March 2005, the campaign evaluation was featured in an article appearing in the

American Journal of Public Health, "Evidence of a Dose-Response Relationship Between 'truth' Antismoking Ads and Youth Smoking Prevalence." The study was the first to evaluate the behavioral outcomes of the truth® campaign, with two major purposes:

- To study the impact of the truth® campaign on national smoking rates among U.S. youth
- To assess whether there is a dose-response relationship between the level of exposure to the campaign and changes in youth smoking during the first 2 years of the campaign

Audience for Research

Major audiences for the research included public health professionals, tobacco

Figure 9.11 You Too Can Be an Independent, Rugged, Macho-Looking Dead Guy[25]

control leaders, and policymakers. It was assumed that many in the general public, including youth, would also be interested in the findings.

Methodology

The study examined changes in youth smoking as they related to varying rates of exposure to the ads over time and across media markets in the United States, controlling for national and state trends in tobacco control measures and other risk behaviors. Individual factors such as grade, race/ethnicity, gender, parental education, and weekly income were also controlled factors in the study.

The Monitoring the Future survey is designed to monitor youth alcohol, tobacco, and illicit drug use in the United States and is conducted by the University of Michigan's Institute for Social Research. Data from the Monitoring the Future survey were used to provide a nationally representative sample of approximately 50,000 students in Grades 8, 10, and 12 who were surveyed each spring from 1997 to 2002. It utilizes an anonymous, self-administered survey completed in a monitored classroom setting.

Highlights of Findings

The decline in current smoking accelerated after the launch of the national truth® campaign between 2000 and 2002. Before the launch (1997–1999), the annual percentage decline in youth smoking was 3.2%. After the launch (2000–2002), the annual percentage decline was 6.8%. During this time, youth smoking prevalence fell from 25.8% to 18.0%. Youth smoking prevalence measures the percentage of youth who are currently smoking. The type of question we might ask to assess this information is, "During the last 30 days, did you smoke cigarettes, even just a puff?"

Findings show a significant dose-response relationship between truth® campaign exposure and current smoking among youth. Twenty-two percent of the overall decline in youth smoking between 2000 and 2002 was attributable to the truth® campaign.

Most important, it was estimated that because of the campaign, there were 300,000 fewer youth smokers in 2002.

Post Note

The campaign truth® is adopting new ways to reach teens by integrating truth® messaging and imagery into digital technologies that are very present in teens' lives. The campaign has added some distinctive interactive elements through its Web site (http://www.thetruth.com), where teens can use downloads, minisites, screen savers, do-it-yourself print tools, and games to spread the truth® message virally throughout the online teen community. In addition, truth® "profile pages" are on popular social networking sites such as MySpace, Hi5, Bebo, Piczo, and Xanga.

CHAPTER 10

Product

Creating a Product Platform

Problems worthy of attack prove their worth by attacking back.

—Bill Novelli
Chief Executive Officer, AARP

Y ou are (finally) ready to develop your marketing strategy.

- You have identified a target market and developed rich descriptions using relevant demographic, geographic, psychographic, and behavioral variables.
- You know what you want your audience to do and what they may need to know and/or believe in order to act, and you've come to some agreement on levels of desired behavior change you will develop a plan to achieve.
- You know what benefits and barriers they perceive relative to the desired behavior you have in mind.
- You know how this stacks up against the competition—most often their current or preferred behavior or those programs and organizations sponsoring them.
- You have a positioning statement that will align and guide your team's decision making.

It is time to decide how you will influence your target audience to accept the desired behavior. You have four tools (product, price, place, and promotion) to help make this happen. And you'll probably need all of them to create and deliver the value your target market expects in exchange for a new behavior.

This chapter will focus on developing your product strategy and determining how to present the desired behavior so that it is most motivating to your audience, with an emphasis on exploring opportunities for tangible objects and services that will support behavior change. We begin with a case story, with a powerful product platform for a powerful audience!

AARP's "Don't Vote" Campaign (2007)

BILL NOVELLI

Chief Executive Officer, AARP

Situation

AARP is a nonprofit, nonpartisan organization that neither endorses nor contributes to any candidates for public office. We work with elected officials from across the political spectrum to address issues important to people over 50 and their families. We also work to educate the candidates and the voters on these issues so that they become part of the election debate and so that voters can choose the candidates that best represent them.

We've been doing this for many years, and our focus is always the same: to serve as a resource for educating our 38 million members and everyone else on important public issues. We're always learning, and we try to build on our previous efforts to make sure our members know where the candidates stand. Likewise, we strive to make sure that issues of importance to our members and their families, such as the long-term strength and solvency of Social Security and making health care affordable for all Americans, are addressed by the candidates.

Voters aged 55 and older lead all other age groups both in percentage of those registered to vote and those who do vote. In the November 2004 election, nearly 70% of voters aged 55 to 64 went to the polls, as did over 70% of those 65 to 74. By contrast, only 19% of 18- to 24-year-olds and 32% of 25- to 34-year-olds voted. As such, we viewed the federal and state elections in 2006 as an excellent opportunity to advance our issue agenda by encouraging our members (and others 50+) to vote and to help them make informed voting decisions based on the candidates' positions.

Target Audience

Our target audience was the members of AARP and all other people 50+. So the focus of this case study will be on what we did to influence this target audience. At the same time, we also wanted candidates to adopt our positions and campaign on them. So in that sense, we were also targeting the candidates themselves.

Behavior Objectives

The primary behavioral objective of our campaign was for our members and other people 50+ to take time to be informed on the issues and the candidates' positions and then vote in the 2006 federal and state elections.

Strategy

Product Strategy

Core Product: Candidates elected to office who are aligned with the issues you care about.

Actual Product: Know where candidates stand on the issues you care about and then vote.

Augmented Product: Voter guides by congressional district and state that inform voters on where candidates stand on AARP issues and Don't Vote Web site.

Promotional Strategy

Our 2006 election strategy was designed to frame issues with a clarity that creates real distinctions between candidates and to take full advantage of our credibility with the public. We accomplished this through expanded grassroots activity and a multichannel communications program using paid and earned media, as well as traditional and nontraditional media, to ensure that AARP's issues were deciding factors in voters' candidate choices. Two key components of this were our "Don't Vote" national advertising campaign and our "Frontrunner Race" strategy.

Key Messages. The "Don't Vote" ad campaign was conceived as a fresh, intrusive way of conveying AARP's perennial election message: that candidate choices should be based on where the candidates stand on the issues, not on personalities. In this case it translates to *"Don't vote until you know where the candidates stand on the issues"* (see Figure 10.1). That was the theme of the campaign, and it got to the heart of why we get involved. We ran full-page ads in newspapers, had a billboard truck winding through the streets of Washington, and ran television ads telling people, "DON'T VOTE . . . until you know where the candidates stand on the issues." Our most effective TV spot was our "Song 'n Dance" ad that featured an attractive candidate with the perfect image at a community event singing about why voters should vote for him. After

running off a litany of superficial reasons, he says, "You can vote for me with assurity, just don't ask about Social Security." This approach not only made our point effectively, it broke through the cluttered landscape of political ads and captured people's attention.

Key Messengers. AARP has staffed offices in every state, the District of Columbia, the Virgin Islands, and Puerto Rico, and they, along with a network

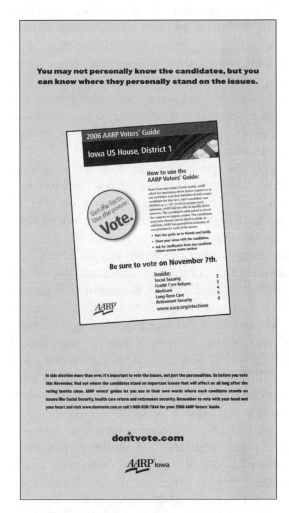

Figure 10.1 Print Ad for AARP's "DON'T VOTE . . . Until You Know Where the Candidates Stand on the Issues" Campaign

of thousands of AARP volunteers, all work to educate voters in their own communities, neighbor to neighbor, about where candidates stand on the issues that matter to them by hosting candidate forums, distributing information, and conducting other election-related outreach.

Key Media Channels. Everything we did was aimed at getting voters to focus on the issues that were most important to them personally and helping them learn where candidates stood on those issues. In addition to our national Don't Vote advertising campaign, our elections Web site, http://www.dontvote.com, gave voters across the country access to the information and resources they needed to cast an informed ballot on the elections in their state and district, including AARP voters' guides, links to candidate Web sites, and information on voting.

At the same time, in 2006 we sought to have a higher level of outreach activity to reach our target audience in a smaller number of races. Thus, we initiated our Frontrunner Race strategy as part of our continuing effort to find new ways to get the issues our members care about in front of the candidates and the voters.

We selected six races to test our Frontrunner Race strategy—two gubernatorial races (Arkansas and Colorado) and four federal races (Colorado Congressional District 7, Iowa Congressional District 1, Ohio Congressional District 6, and the Tennessee Senate contest). The races were selected based on a number of criteria, including how competitive the races were projected to be, the fact that they were open seats in swing states and districts, and whether there had been a history of bipartisan cooperation in the states involved. The key media channels we utilized to reach AARP members and 50+ voters in these races included candidate forums, voter guides, issue brochures, direct mail, targeted advertising in select media, absentee voter outreach, phone banks, expanded distribution of our *State Member Update* publication, and a van tour.

Results

Some 52% of all voters in the 2006 national elections were aged 50 and over, and about 25% of all those who voted were AARP members. An analysis of the campaign (conducted through pre- and postelection surveys, opinion leader surveys, media evaluation and tracking in Frontrunner races, and an omnibus survey of baseline races) produced the following results:

- In five of the six races, the candidate most closely aligned with AARP's policy positions in our voters' guides was elected.
- Despite an environment in which Iraq dominated much of the debate, AARP issues were central to the campaign debate in five of the six races.
- AARP's campaign encouraged voters to focus on issues rather than personalities in making candidate decisions. Pre- and postelection surveys showed that the percentage of members reporting that candidates' issue positions were the key factor in their voting decisions increased from 29% to 42% over the course of the campaign.
- The percentage of AARP members who reported turning to AARP for information to help them make voting decisions increased from 9% to 16% over the course of the campaign.
- The percentage of members who viewed AARP as the most trusted source of information to make voting decisions increased from 6% to 13%, making AARP *the most trusted source* for voting information of all sources, including

churches or religious organizations, unions, fraternal organizations, universities or alumni associations, professional organizations, and political parties.

- A majority of members believe that the information AARP provided about political candidates was important in helping them understand where candidates stand on issues of interest to them and say that information from AARP was important in helping them make distinctions between political candidates' positions.

- Awareness of AARP voters' guides among members increased 20 percentage points over the course of the campaign, from 30% to 51%.
- TV ads (61%), newspaper ads (54%), and voters' guides (51%) generated the highest awareness.
- The three most informative tactics— candidate forums (62%), van tours (59%), and the voters' guide (54%)— were also the three most helpful (56%, 47%, and 42%, respectively).

PRODUCT: THE FIRST "P"

A product is anything that can be offered to a market to satisfy a want or need.[1] It isn't, as many typically think, just a tangible offering like soap, tires, or hamburgers. It can be one of several types: a physical good, a service, an experience, an event, a person, a place, a property, an organization, information, or an idea.[2]

In social marketing, you are selling a desired behavior (e.g., exercise, recycle, vote), one that "most neatly" falls in the *idea* category above. Your social marketing campaign, however, may also include the creation, distribution, and/or promotion of a physical good (e.g., dye tabs to test for leaky toilets), a service (e.g., a tobacco quitline), an experience (e.g., reading 20 minutes to a child at night), an event (e.g., natural gardening demonstration), a person (e.g., a New York City firefighter urging us to be prepared for emergencies), a property (e.g., walking trails), and/or an organization (e.g., community health clinic). These additional product types, as you will read, can often be key to your success, as they may be critical to assisting your target market's behavior adoption. Additional relevant terms often associated with product strategy in the commercial sector are presented in Table 10.1.

STEP #7: DEVELOPING THE SOCIAL MARKETING PRODUCT PLATFORM

Traditional marketing theory propounds that from the customer's perspective, a product is more than its features, quality, name, and style and identifies three product levels you should consider when developing your product: *core product, actual product,*

Table 10.1   A Product Primer

Product Type includes physical goods, services, experiences, an event, a person, a place, a property, an organization, information, or an idea.

Product Line refers to a group of closely related products offered by an organization, ones that perform similar functions but are different in terms of features, style, or some other variable.[a]

Product Mix refers to the product items that an organization offers, often reflecting a variety of product types.

Product Features describe product components (e.g., number of days or hours it takes for results from an HIV/AIDS test).

Product Platform includes decisions regarding the core product (benefit), actual product (specific desired behavior), and augmented product (additional product types included to support the desired behavior).

Product Quality refers to the performance of the product and includes such valued attributes as durability, reliability, precision, and ease of operation.[b]

Product Development is the systematic approach that guides the development and launch of a new product that is managed by a product manager, sometimes called a brand manager.

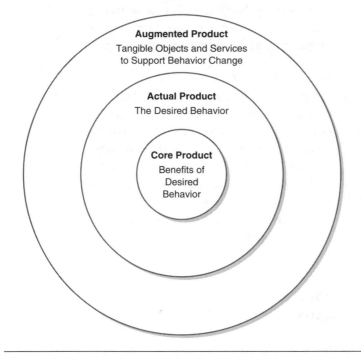

and *augmented product*.[3] This platform is illustrated in Figure 10.2, and each of these levels will be described in detail in the next three sections of this chapter. It will be helpful to you when conceptualizing and designing your product strategy.

Briefly, your *core product* is the benefit the target audience wants and expects in exchange for performing the behavior. The *actual product* is the specific behavior you will be influencing your target audience to "buy." And the *augmented product* includes any additional goods (tangible objects) and services that you may develop, distribute, sell, or just promote. Examples are presented in Table 10.2.

Figure 10.2   Three Levels of the Social Marketing Product

Table 10.2   Examples of Three Product Levels

Core Product (Benefits)	Actual Product (Desired Behavior)	Augmented Product (Tangible Objects and Services)
For Improved Health		
Prevention of alcohol poisoning	Drink less than five drinks at one sitting.	Breathalyzers in bars
Early detection and treatment of breast cancers	Conduct a monthly breast self-exam.	Laminated instruction card for placement on shower nozzle
Protection from preventable diseases	Immunize children on time.	Wallet-size immunization card
Natural immunities for infants and mother-child bonding	Breastfeed exclusively for the first 6 months.	In-home nurse consultation
For Injury Prevention		
Prevention of suicide	Know when to intervene and what to say.	Gatekeeper training for teachers, counselors, and youth group leaders
Protection from physical abuse	Call for help if you are being abused.	Help line for domestic abuse
Prevention of injury for self and others	Don't drink and drive.	Free taxi rides on New Year's Eve
Drowning prevention	Wear a life vest.	Life vests available for loan at beaches
To Protect the Environment		
Improved water quality	Plant native plants.	Natural gardening workshops
Prevention of forest fires	Dispose of cigarettes properly.	Disposable cigarette pouches
Reduced levels of carbon dioxide in the air	Conserve electricity.	Lightbulbs with the ENERGY STAR label
Avoidance of costly fines and penalties	Use a litterbag.	Litterbags that are leak-proof and that seal
For Community Involvement		
Saving someone's life	Become an organ donor.	National Organ Donor Card
Helping members of your community	Volunteer 5 hours a week.	Training for crisis line
Voicing your opinions	Vote.	Voter's guide
Saving an animal from being euthanized	Adopt a dog or cat.	Web site with pictures and description of animals currently at a shelter

Core Product

The core product, the center of the product platform, answers the questions, What's in it for the customer to buy your product? What benefits will they receive? What needs will the desired behavior satisfy? What problems will it solve? The core product is not the behaviors or accompanying tangible objects and services you will be promoting. It is the benefits your audience wants and expects to experience when they perform the behavior—benefits *they say* are the most valuable to them (e.g., moderate physical activity will make me feel better, look better, and live longer). The great Harvard marketing professor Theodore Levitt was known to have told his students, "People don't want to buy a quarter-inch drill. They want a quarter-inch hole!" And Charles Revson, of Revlon, also provided a memorable quote illustrating the difference between product features (our actual product) and product benefits (our core product): "In the factory we make cosmetics; in the store, we sell hope."[4]

Decisions about the core product focus primarily on what potential benefits should be stressed. This process will include reviewing (from Step 5) audience perceptions of (a) benefits from the desired behavior and (b) perceived costs of the competing behaviors that the desired behavior can help the target audience avoid. You may have even identified this core product when constructing your positioning statement (in Step 6). Decisions are then made on which of these should be emphasized in a campaign. And keep in mind, the key benefit you should highlight is the benefit the target audience perceives for performing the behavior—not the benefit to your organization or agency.

Example: Interviews with teens often reveal several perceived benefits that youth associate with not smoking: doing better in school, doing better in sports, being seen as smart, and looking and feeling good. They may also have revealed the following perceived costs: You could get addicted and not be able to quit, you might die, you'll stink, and you won't be as good in sports. Further discussions may indicate that one of these (e.g., fear of addiction) is the most concerning and should be highlighted in the campaign (see Figure 10.3). In this case, the core product for the campaign becomes "By not smoking, you don't risk addiction."

Figure 10.3 A Testimonial Used to Persuade Youth That Tobacco Is Addictive[5]

Actual Product

Surrounding the core product is the *specific behavior* we are promoting (e.g., eat five to nine fruits and vegetables a day). It is more specific than the core idea (healthy eating). It is what is required in order to achieve the benefits identified as the core product. Additional components at this level may include any brand names developed for the behavior (e.g., 5 A Day), the *campaign's sponsoring organization* (e.g., Produce for Better Health Foundation), and any *endorsements and sponsors* (e.g., National Cancer Institute and Centers for Disease Control and Prevention). Sponsor and endorsement decisions are important, as they can significantly affect the credibility as well as the appeal of a campaign. Research indicates that credibility is a function of expertise, trustworthiness, and likability, so perceptions of target audiences may need to be explored.[6]

Example: Telephone surveys could ask litterers to rank the impact on their littering of a variety of potential endorsements of an antilitter campaign: Department of Ecology, State Patrol, Department of Transportation, Department of Licensing, Department of Fish and Wildlife, Department of Natural Resources, and the state Traffic Safety Commission. It might not be surprising to find that responses indicate that the best (visible) sponsoring organizations for the campaign would be the department of licensing and/or the state patrol, because these organizations are perceived as having the most impact on potential penalties and driving privileges, important personal benefits to these drivers.

Since decisions regarding the actual product (the desired behaviors) to be promoted were made in Step 4 when behavior objectives were established, major tasks at this phase of planning are to consider other major actual product factors such as features and brand name (a topic covered in more detail later in this chapter).

Example: The City of Seattle and Seattle Public Utilities engage in numerous programs to influence residential gardeners' contribution toward salmon survival. They named (branded) their program Salmon Friendly Gardening and promote the adoption of six key behaviors: (1) build healthy soil with compost, (2) choose the right plant for the right place, (3) use water wisely, (4) use natural fertilizers and pest controls, (5) direct rainwater appropriately, and (6) protect shoreline habitats. Campaign materials emphasize the real threat to salmon extinction; how gardening affects salmon; and how Salmon Friendly Gardens can be beautiful, healthy, and easy to maintain. Residents are assured that Salmon Friendly Gardens work with natural processes to grow healthy plants with minimal irrigation, fertilizer, and pesticides. In addition to keeping the water clean and protecting habitat, Salmon Friendly Gardens can save time and money (see Figure 10.4).

Figure 10.4 Salmon Friendly Gardening Logo[7]

Augmented Product

This level of the product platform includes any *tangible objects and services* you will be promoting along with the desired behavior. Although they may be considered optional, they are sometimes exactly what is needed to provide encouragement (e.g., a walking buddy), remove barriers (e.g., a detailed resource guide and map of local walking trails and organized walking programs), or sustain behavior (e.g., a journal for tracking exercise levels). They may also provide opportunities to brand and to "tangibilize" the campaign, creating more attention, appeal, and memorability for target audiences.[8]

In 1952, G. D. Wiebe raised the question, "Why can't you sell brotherhood like you sell soap?" and then embarked on a research journey to find the answer.[9] Dr. Wiebe, at the time a research psychologist for the CBS Radio Network and lecturer in psychology at the City College of New York, concluded after examining four social campaigns that "the more the conditions of a social campaign resemble those of a product campaign, the more successful the campaign will be."[10] One of the specific factors he felt was critical was the presence of a "Mechanism," one that would enable the target audience to translate their motivation (wants, needs, awakened desires) into action. These tangible objects and services may well be providing this critical mechanism. You will face several decisions in regard to developing tangible objects.

Should you develop or encourage the development at some cost of a new product that would greatly support the behavior change? For example, many adults wih diabetes conduct finger-prick blood tests to monitor their blood sugar levels. A painless, needle-free mechanism that would provide reliable readings would be a welcome innovation and might result in more regular monitoring of blood sugar levels. Not all new products will require retooling or significant research and development costs, as illustrated in the following example:

Example: In November 2006, a study published in the journal *Science* warned that the world's wild-caught seafood fisheries could collapse by 2050. Dr. Steven Palumbi of Stanford University, a coauthor of the *Science* paper, warned that "unless we fundamentally change the way we manage all the oceans species together, as working ecosystems, then this is the last century of wild seafood."[11] Monterey Bay Aquarium's Seafood Watch program responded with a news release confirming the concern. "Much of the seafood on the market today is caught or farmed in ways that are not sustainable over the long term. The only way we can keep seafood in our diet is by making choices that preserve the abundance of wild fish populations, protect the habitats that support productive fishing grounds, and encourage environmentally responsible fish farming."[12]

And the Seafood Watch program has a fairly simple product (tangible object) to help influence these desired behaviors. In 1999 they developed and began distributing consumer pocket guides to help consumers choose seafood that is caught or farmed in sustainable ways (see Figure 10.5). Since that date, they have distributed more than 21 million pocket guides nationwide, including 6 regional guides, 1 national guide, and 3 pocket guides in Spanish (a West Coast regional guide, Southwest guide, and national guide). They collaborate with more than 100 partners nationwide to distribute these pocket guides and promote sustainable seafood. They also work with a team of fisheries researchers who evaluate the most popular seafood items on the market and make consumer recommendations that each item is either a "Best Choice," "Good Alternative," or a species to "Avoid" based on whether it is caught or farmed in a sustainable manner.

Does a current product need to be improved or enhanced? For example, typical compost bins require the gardener to use a pitchfork to regularly turn the yard waste to enhance compost development. New and improved models that a social marketing campaign might make known to target audiences are suspended on a bracket that only requires a regular "tumble." And relative to product enhancement, until recent years, most users (and especially nonusers) have perceived life vests as bulky and uncomfortable. For teens, concerns with tan lines and the "ugly" orange color were also raised. New options are vastly improved, with a look similar to suspenders and a feature for automatic inflation using a pull tab. Consider the incredible positive impact of the following new product:

Example: In the rural areas of many developing countries, the only access to water is from boreholes, using hand pumps. The chore of fetching the water is usually the responsibility of women and children, who walk long distances to collect sufficient water for their family's daily requirements. It is estimated that the minimum amount of water a human needs each day is 6 liters, which can be a huge physical burden for the women and children pumping the water. In 2000, a South African company came up with a device, however, to reduce this toil. It looks more like child's play. The Play Pump™ water system is a type of merry-go-round that pumps groundwater from boreholes into a storage tank. With the children spinning the merry-go-round about 16 times a minute, it is capable of producing approximately 1,400 liters of water per hour into an overhead storage tank. The 2,500-liter storage tank is a prominent landmark in communities. It is fitted with four outdoor advertising signs, two for product advertising and two for public service messages, resulting in a unique messaging opportunity. Product advertising includes soap, sugar, bread, and mobile phones, while public service messaging ranges from hand washing and other hygiene messages to HIV/AIDS awareness to malaria-reducing bed nets (see Figure 10.6). Revenue from the advertising pays for system maintenance for 10 years. And there's more good news here. Roundabout Outdoor, the company that created the pump, has developed a partnership with Play Pumps International, as well as others, to donate the systems to rural and periurban communities in sub-Saharan Africa.

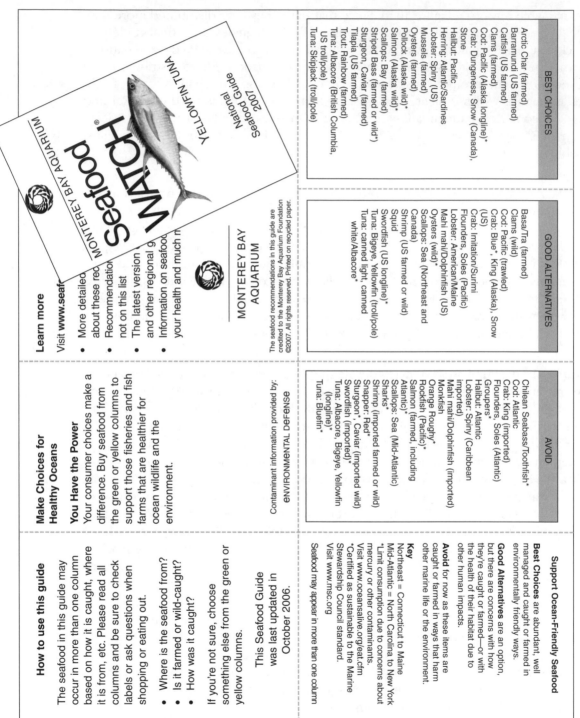

How to use this guide

The seafood in this guide may occur in more than one column based on how it is caught, where it is from, etc. Please read all columns and be sure to check labels or ask questions when shopping or eating out.

- Where is the seafood from?
- Is it farmed or wild-caught?
- How was it caught?

If you're not sure, choose something else from the green or yellow columns.

This Seafood Guide was last updated in October 2006.

Make Choices for Healthy Oceans

You Have the Power

Your consumer choices make a difference. Buy seafood from the green or yellow columns to support those fisheries and fish farms that are healthier for ocean wildlife and the environment.

Learn more

Visit www.seaf...

- More detailed ... about these rec...
- Recommendatio... not on this list
- The latest version ... and other regional g...
- Information on seafood... your health and much m...

MONTEREY BAY AQUARIUM

National Seafood Guide 2007

MONTEREY BAY AQUARIUM
Seafood WATCH®

YELLOWFIN TUNA

BEST CHOICES

Arctic Char (farmed)
Barramundi (US farmed)
Catfish (US farmed)
Clams (farmed)
Cod: Pacific (Alaska longline)*
Crab: Dungeness, Snow (Canada), Stone
Halibut: Pacific
Herring: Atlantic/Sardines
Lobster: Spiny (US)
Mussels (farmed)
Oysters (farmed)
Pollock (Alaska wild)*
Salmon (Alaska wild)*
Scallops: Bay (farmed)
Striped Bass (farmed or wild*)
Sturgeon, Caviar (farmed)
Tilapia (US farmed)
Trout: Rainbow (farmed)
Tuna: Albacore (British Columbia, US troll/pole)
Tuna: Skipjack (troll/pole)

GOOD ALTERNATIVES

Basa/Tra (farmed)
Clams (wild)
Cod: Atlantic
Cod: Pacific (trawled)
Crab: Blue*, King (Alaska), Snow (US)
Crab: Imitation/Surimi
Flounders, Soles (Pacific)
Lobster: American/Maine
Mahi mahi/Dolphinfish (US)
Oysters (wild)*
Scallops: Sea (Northeast and Canada)
Shrimp (US farmed or wild)
Squid
Swordfish (US longline)*
Tuna: Bigeye, Yellowfin (troll/pole)
Tuna: canned light, canned white/Albacore*

AVOID

Chilean Seabass/Toothfish*
Cod: Atlantic
Crab: King (imported)
Flounders, Soles (Atlantic)
Groupers*
Halibut: Atlantic
Lobster: Spiny (Caribbean imported)
Mahi mahi/Dolphinfish (imported)
Monkfish
Orange Roughy*
Rockfish (Pacific)*
Salmon (farmed, including Atlantic)*
Scallops: Sea (Mid-Atlantic)
Sharks*
Shrimp (imported farmed or wild)
Snapper: Red*
Sturgeon*, Caviar (imported wild)
Swordfish (imported)*
Tuna: Albacore, Bigeye, Yellowfin (longline)*
Tuna: Bluefin*

Support Ocean-Friendly Seafood

Best Choices are abundant, well managed and caught or farmed in environmentally friendly ways.

Good Alternatives are an option, but there are concerns with how they're caught or farmed—or with the health of their habitat due to other human impacts.

Avoid for now as these items are caught or farmed in ways that harm other marine life or the environment.

Key
Northeast = Connecticut to Maine
Mid-Atlantic = North Carolina to New York
*Limit consumption due to concerns about mercury or other contaminants.
Visit www.oceansalive.org/eat.cfm
*Certified as sustainable to the Marine Stewardship Council standard.
Visit www.msc.org

Seafood may appear in more than one column

Figure 10.5 Seafood Watch Distributes Free Pocket Guides to Help Consumers Choose Seafood That Is Caught or Farmed in

Is there a need or opportunity for a substitute product?[14] A substitute product is one that offers the target audience a "healthier and safer" way to satisfy a want, fulfill a need, or solve a problem. The key is to understand the real benefit (core product) of the *competing* behavior and to then develop and/or promote products offering the same or at least some of the same benefits. These include, for example, food and beverages such as nonalcoholic beers, garden burgers, fat-free dairy products, and decaffeinated coffee; natural fertilizers, natural pesticides, and ground covers to replace lawns; an older sibling (versus a parent) taking a younger

Figure 10.6 Advertising Around the Tank Helps Pay for the Upkeep of This Roundabout Play Pump[13]

teen to a community clinic for STD screening; and a package containing a can of chicken soup, tissues, and aspirin "prescribed" to patients suffering from colds, in an effort to reduce the overuse of antibiotics.

Chakravorty defines substitute products as "a product offered to a market that is thought of and used by those in the market as a replacement for some other product."[15] She further surmises:

> An acceptable and accessible substitute product may promote desirable behaviors by enhancing the user's perceived self-efficacy. Self-efficacy is expected to be strengthened to the extent that many of the behaviors required in using a substitute are similar to behaviors associated with reference product use.[16]

> For example, a heavy coffee drinker may come to believe that eliminating coffee will lead to improved cardiac health. The prospective former coffee drinker may decide that she is very likely to quit coffee if she replaces it with decaffeinated coffee. A variety of factors may have contributed to this perception. First, she may feel that as a result of her coffee drinking behavior, she "knows how" to execute the behaviors required in drinking decaf. The beverage will be consumed in the same container, at the same temperature, and she will not have to make great adjustments to the flavor of the substitute. If she is able to consume decaf in all the same situations where she usually drinks coffee (i.e.,

at home, work, or a favorite restaurant), her efficacy for "decaf-drinking" behavior may raise as she estimates that she will be able to perform the new behavior across a wide variety of settings. [17]

Services are often distinguished as offerings that are intangible and do not result in the ownership of anything.[18] In the social marketing environment, examples of services that support the desired behavior change might include *education-related services* (e.g., parenting workshops on how to talk to your kids about sex), *personal services* (e.g., escorts for students back to their dorms at night), *counseling services* (e.g., a crisis line for people considering suicide), *clinical services* (e.g., community clinics for free immunizations, and *community services* (e.g., hazardous waste mobiles for disposal of toxic waste products). It should be noted that services that are more sales oriented in nature (e.g., demonstrations on the efficiency of low-flow toilets) fall into the promotional category and will be discussed in Chapter 14. You will also face several decisions regarding any services you offer.

Should a new service be developed and offered? For example, given the apparent success and popularity of toll-free tobacco quitlines to support smoking cessation in other states, a community without one might want to develop and launch a line to accompany mass media campaigns encouraging adults to quit smoking.

Does an existing service need to be improved or enhanced? For example, what if customer surveys indicate that an estimated 50% of callers to the state's 800 number for questions about recycling hang up because they typically have to wait more than 5 minutes on hold? Relative to enhanced services, what if customer feedback also indicates that residents would be interested in (and would pay for) recycling of yard waste in addition to glass, paper, and aluminum?

BRANDING

Branding in the commercial sector is pervasive and fairly easy to understand and recognize. A brand, as mentioned earlier, is a name, term, sign, symbol, or design (or a combination of these) that identifies the maker or seller of a product (see Table 10.3).[19] You have contact with brands when you start your day with a Starbucks, drive your Volvo, listen to music on your lPod, use Microsoft Word, run in your Nikes, and TiVo the CBS News.

Branding in social marketing is not as common, although we would like to encourage more of it, as it helps create visibility and ensure memorability. The following list includes a few of the stronger brands, in these cases names that have

Table 10.3   A Branding Primer

Brand is a name, term, sign, symbol, or design (or a combination of these) that identifies the maker or seller of a product or service.

Brand Identity is how you (the maker) want consumers to think, feel, and act with respect to your brand.

Brand Image is the core idea that you want the brand to evoke in the target audience.

Branding is the process of developing an intended brand identity.

Brand Awareness is the extent to which consumers recognize a brand.

Brand Promise is the marketer's vision of what the brand must be and do for consumers.

Brand Loyalty refers to the degree to which a consumer consistently purchases the same brand within a product class.

Brand Equity is the value of a brand, based on the extent to which it has high brand loyalty, name awareness, perceived quality, strong brand associations, and other assets such as patents, trademarks, and channel relationships. It is an important, although intangible, asset that has psychological and financial value to a firm.

Brand Elements are those trademarkable devices that serve to identify and differentiate the brand.

Brand Mix or **Portfolio** is the set of all brands and brand lines a particular firm offers for sale to a buyer in a particular category.

Brand Contact can be defined as any information-bearing experience a customer of prospect has with the brand.

Brand Performance relates to how well the product or service meets customers' functional needs.

Brand Extension is using a successful brand name to launch a new or modified product in a new category.

Cobranding is the practice of using the established brand names of more than one company on the same product or are marketing them together in the same fashion.

SOURCE: From Kotler, P., & Lee, N. (2006). *Marketing in the Public Sector: A Roadmap to Improved Performance.* Upper Saddle River, NJ: Wharton School. Reprinted with permission.

been used to identify programs and products and are used consistently in an integrated way:

- Wildfire prevention: **Smokey Bear**
- Nutrition: **5 A Day**
- Physical activity: **VERB**
- Crime protection: **McGruff the Crime Dog**
- Safe produce: **USDA Organic**
- Sustainable seafood: **Seafood Watch**
- Drinking and driving: **RoadCrew**
- Tobacco prevention: **truth®**
- Litter prevention: **Don't Mess With Texas**
- Pet waste: **Scoop the Poop**
- Youth drug prevention: **Parents: The Anti-Drug**
- Schoolchildren: **Walking School Bus**
- Voting: **Rock The Vote**
- SIDS: **Back to Sleep**
- Water conservation: **Water—Use It Wisely**
- Water quality: **Chesapeake Club**
- Energy conservation: **ENERGY STAR**

Figure 10.7 EPA's New Label to Help Consumers Choose Water-Efficient Products and Services

In June 2006, the Environmental Protection Agency launched a new water efficiency program intended to influence American consumers to look for and purchase water-efficient products. Similar to ENERGY STAR, the WaterSense^{SM} label will be easily identified on products and services that perform at least 20% more efficiently than market counterparts (see Figure 10.7). Many of us are not aware, for example, that in the average American home, more water is used for flushing the toilet than running the shower, a family of four can save more than 16,000 gallons of water every year just by replacing a traditional toilet with a WaterSense-labeled high-efficiency model, and up to 50% of water used for landscape irrigation is lost due to overwatering, evaporation, or bad irrigation system design or maintenance.[20]

ETHICAL CONSIDERATIONS RELATED TO CREATING A PRODUCT PLATFORM

One way to highlight ethical considerations relative to product decisions is to revisit each component of the product platform.

The *core product* promises the target audience a benefit they will receive (or cost they will avoid) if they perform the behavior. Can you be sure? How much should you disclose about the probabilities of success? Tobacco prevention specialists emphasize the health costs of smoking cigarettes, and yet how many times have you seen or read the research that claims that much of the physiological damage done by smoking during the first 10 to 20 years will be repaired by the body if and when you quit? Should this information be prominently displayed?

For the *actual product,* decisions are made relative to a specific behavior you will be promoting and any name and sponsors that will be associated with the behavior. Perhaps one major ethical consideration here is whether you make the actual sponsor/funder of the project very visible or not. For example, should who the campaign is funded by be visible on a teen pregnancy prevention campaign poster? Did it bother you that the letter to litterers came in an envelope with the return address of the state patrol, even though it was managed by the department of ecology? This may be where the rule of thumb "Do more good than harm" can help you decide.

For the *augmented product,* decisions regarding tangible goods and services are similar to those in the private sector, although in this case you are often dealing with taxpayer-funded programs, a different constituent group with different agendas than shareholders. Does your product "perform as promised"? If you distribute condoms in high school, do those concerned with sending a "sex is okay" message have a good point? In terms of services, can you deliver and provide good service if you are successful in generating demand?

Chapter Summary

The product in a social marketing effort is what you are selling: *the desired behavior and the associated benefits of that behavior.* It also includes any tangible objects and services developed to support and facilitate the target audience's behavior change.

The *product* platform has three levels: the core product (the benefit of the behavior), the actual product (the specific behavior being promoted), and the augmented product (any tangible objects and services associated with the program).

Decisions are faced at each level. At the core product level, decisions will need to be made regarding what potential benefits should be stressed. Although major decisions regarding the actual product were made in Step 3 when the behavior objective was established, additional decisions may need to be made, including choosing a name (brand) and identification of sponsors and endorsements for campaign communications. At the third level, you will make decisions related to whether to develop new products and services, as well as needs for improving existing ones.

RESEARCH HIGHLIGHT

USDA Food Stamp Media Campaign (2004)

An Audience Assessment From a Social Marketing Perspective[21]

BEVERLY SCHWARTZ

JIM LINDENBERGER

Background and Purpose of Research

The Food Stamp Program (FSP) is managed by the U.S. Department of Agriculture/ Food and Nutrition Service (USDA/FNS) and provides food support, nutrition education, and referrals to economically disadvantaged citizens. In 2004, at the time of this assessment, over 21 million people received benefits from FSP, and it was determined that more than 11 million *eligible* individuals were not enrolled in the program.

The amount of eligible nonparticipants caused great concern to FSP officials. Proper nutrition plays a significant role in maintaining good health. Five of the 10 leading causes of death in the United States—heart disease, certain types of cancer, stroke, diabetes mellitus, and atherosclerosis—are linked to dietary practices. Eating habits also play a role in obesity, hypertension, gastrointestinal disorders, osteoporosis, and neural tube defects.[22] That nearly 34% of the eligible population was not enrolled in FSP had significant implications for the health of many at-risk families.

The project team decided to examine this problem from a social marketing perspective and assumed that reluctance to enroll would likely involve reasons outside the influences of communications alone. Therefore, we felt there was a real need to determine the multiple influences that might affect lack of program participation, beyond message influence, and to do so strategically, embedded within the required framework of a focus group methodology.

Two tiers of inquiry were included in the investigation for cost and time efficiency:

- Comparative testing of the current FSP brand "Food Stamps Make America Stronger" with two new concepts
- Formative research regarding the perceptions and understanding of the FSP and "life aspirations research" that would underscore the goals that participants and eligible nonparticipants have for themselves and their families. Results would be helpful in providing context for future FSP communications approaches and for *non*communications/ program elements.

Research was designed to address the following informational objectives:

- Familiarity with existing FSP materials among eligible nonparticipants
- Perceptions of existing FSP messages among eligible nonparticipants

- Attitudes, perceptions, and experiences with the FSP among eligible nonparticipants
- Concepts and messages that position the FSP as a nutrition assistance and work support program
- Message preferences among eligible nonparticipants

Audience for Research

Specific target audiences within this eligible population were determined to be senior citizens, the working poor, nonworking economically disadvantaged, and Spanish-speaking immigrants. The desired behavior for these groups was simple: The USDA wanted more eligible citizens to enroll in the program.

Methodology

Fleishman-Hillard International Communications (Project Director Beverly Schwartz) with research support from Best Start Inc. (Executive Director Jim Lindenberger, Research Director Maria Cabrera) was selected by the USDA to determine if current FSP communications strategies were effective in encouraging nonparticipating eligibles to enroll, and if not, how they could be improved.

Data were collected in four sites: San Antonio, Texas; Philadelphia, Pennsylvania; San Diego, California; and Chicago, Illinois.

The items and concepts tested ranged from radio and television advertising to print, educational, and promotional items. Items that were intended to target each of the respective audience segments in the study, including English- and Spanish-speaking populations, were included.

In addition, new message/brand identifiers were tested and compared with Food Stamps Make America Stronger, the current FSP brand identifier:

- Food Stamps: Feed Your Future (Cupones Para Alimentos: Alimenta Su Futuro)
- Food Stamps: Help Yourself to a Healthier Life (Cupones Para Alimentos: Ayúdate a Tener Una Vida Más Saludable)

Highlights of Findings

All audience segments expressed self-determination and independence to "handle their own affairs." They shared common life aspirations of improved lives for their children, economic security, and being contributors to the well-being of their communities. Many, particularly senior citizens, were active in volunteer work or community service. They seemed to be resourceful and understood how to manage even in difficult times. Only in dire need (loss of employment, debilitating injury or illness, risk to the health/well-being of children) did they feel comfortable seeking government assistance. Even then, they would first look to known community organizations or work independently to resolve their respective crises before seeking government assistance as a last resort.

Respondents also believe that FSP should, as a matter of most critical importance, provide short-term, temporary assistance, primarily for families with children. However, even in these situations, there are barriers to participation that can outweigh the value of FSP and prevent enrollment, such as rude treatment by FSP office staff, long waits for interview appointments in FSP offices, and perceived nominal financial benefits. While Spanish-speaking participants share similar experiences with the FSP, they also reported concerns about issues related to citizenship status. Fear of deportation dissuades illegal residents from applying for foods stamps for their eligible children.

What became most clear to all of us was that most participants had a deep desire to retain their sense of dignity, a need to be self-determined, and a highly integrated value system in which they saw family well-being as their own responsibility. As a reflection of their independence, all audience groups seemed to be more interested in how to enhance employment opportunities, learn new job skills, or develop entrepreneurial initiatives than receive food assistance from the government. These factors, *not communications messages*, became the more significant dynamics in their decisions not to seek help from government or nongovernmental organizations.

However, when pressed about communications, all groups believed that FSP should utilize messages and communication strategies that are representative of the intended audience, are positive and direct, and make realistic offers/promises of FSP services. The dominant response to Food Stamps Make America Stronger was negative. This suggested a need for additional message development, creative treatments, and audience-testing research to develop an alternative message/brand approach.

Implications of Findings

The project team then developed a list of multiple message elements to guide the repositioning of FSP outreach and promotional efforts (see Figure 10.8):

- Emphasize that the FSP is for temporary assistance intended to ensure long-term independence.

- Focus on how FSP can help participants stay on course with their life goals and aspirations if they hit a bumpy patch in the road.
- Emphasize how FSP is community based and partnered with other community resources.
- Provide clear, easy-to-understand eligibility information in all repositioning, advertising, and outreach materials.
- Use visual and auditory imagery that is clearly representative of the target audience.
- Make accurate declarations about what FSP offers; don't overpromise the capacity of the FSP.
- Emphasize that everyone needs a helping hand at one time or another. Using FSP during those brief, difficult times demonstrates strong parenting and caregiving.
- Depict participants as strong, knowledgeable, and savvy people who know how to navigate difficult times with dignity.
- Conduct methodologically appropriate testing of all new creative approaches, message concepts, and materials using one-on-one interviews rather than focus groups.

More valuable, however, was the set of concerns regarding aspects of eligible nonparticipation that went beyond the purview of the promotion "P" of the social marketing model. These suggested considering the following:

- Exploring issues that arose concerning customer service and service delivery in order to provide organizational structures that support the communications strategies being employed to increase enrollment and reposition the program.

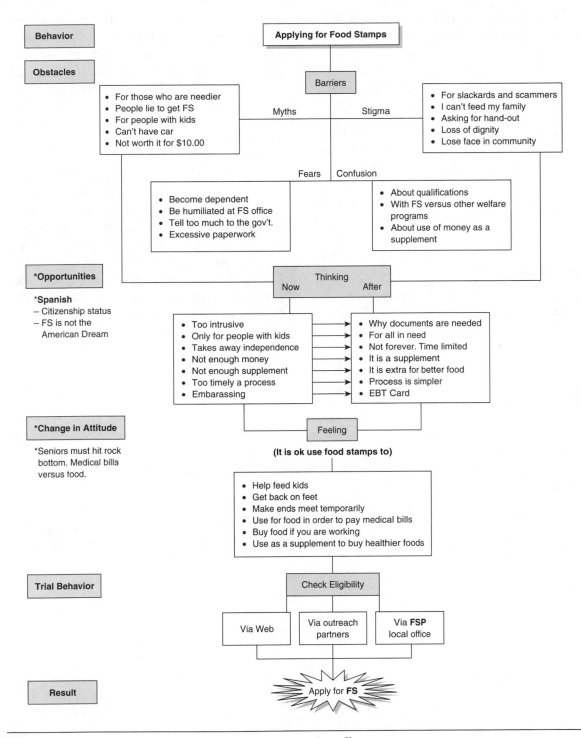

Figure 10.8 Behavioral Goal Map for Food Stamp Campaign[23]

- Exploring means by which the FSP can enhance existing involvement with work support initiatives in order to strengthen its status as a program that helps recipients to help themselves.

And possibly, of most importance:

- Given the nonexistence of (food) "stamps" and the stigma of exchanging "coupons" at the cash register, explore new name/descriptor/for the FSP and new mechanisms to deliver benefits, for example, an electronic benefits transfer card.[24]

Post Note

Our research and findings suggested that a media campaign alone, without additional strategies to improve customer service, benefits, benefit delivery, and cross-programmatic outreach, cannot singularly reframe these well-established negatively perceived values toward and attitudes about the current FSP. For communications to work in repositioning FSP as a nutritional support for families who are temporarily in need of help, it must be combined with actual shifts in the product offering and by providing services in a mutually respectful environment in which recipients are treated as valued customers. As a further illustration of this point, we created the behavioral map shown in Figure 10.8 to visually demonstrate the research findings as well as the "behavioral" recommendations.

CHAPTER 11

Determining Monetary and Nonmonetary Incentives and Disincentives

Pricing has traditionally been strongly associated with commercial marketing, where setting the right or wrong price has a very direct impact on the potential profit and revenue stream for a product launch. In Singapore, we often use the pricing tool to motivate behavior change and have found recognition incentives that reward desired behaviors particularly powerful.

—Dr. K. Vijayalakshmi
Health Promotion Board
Singapore

On March 19, 2007, a Canadian news network announced that the new federal budget would include several environmental protection-related strategies, ones that appear to be using, as Michael Rothschild would describe them, carrots as well as sticks: "Gas guzzlers will be dinged with a new tax of up to $4,000, fuel-efficient cars will get a rebate worth up to $2,000 and old wrecks will be offered a short-cut to the junkyard."[1]

This chapter introduces this second tool in your marketing toolbox, one you may find especially helpful in overcoming financial-related barriers associated with adopting your behavior. You will find it useful in "sweetening the pot," and not necessarily with just monetary-related incentives that could add significant costs to your program budget. You may also find it effective in reducing the appeal of the competition's offer. You'll read how others have used creative monetary and nonmonetary incentives to add value, sometimes just enough to tip the exchange in their favor:

- How China uses pill pals and bonuses to increase the numbers of tuberculosis patients who complete their full regimen of antibiotics
- How coupons helped increase the use of bike helmets from 1% to 57% in one community
- How a state Department of Fish and Wildlife increases the likelihood of natural yard care by awarding "simple" plaques designating a backyard as a Wildlife Sanctuary
- How Ireland decreased use of plastic bags by more than 80% in 3 months
- How a group of teens convince their peers to postpone having sex by sharing the pain of pubic lice (crabs)

MARKETING HIGHLIGHT

Recognition and Rewards Program

For Healthier Eating Establishments in Singapore (2007)

DR. KARUPPIAH VIJAYALAKSHMI, DIRECTOR

Corporate Marketing & Communications Division
Health Promotion Board, Singapore

JOHNSON SEAH, DEPUTY DIRECTOR

Corporate Marketing Department
Health Promotion Board, Singapore

Background and Situation

The Singapore Health Promotion Board (HPB) was established in 2001. The vision of the board is to build a nation of fit and healthy Singaporeans. Although Singaporeans today enjoy good health with high life expectancy and low mortality rates, HPB aims to further improve the health status of Singaporeans and encourage them to continue to adopt healthy lifestyles.

To achieve this, HPB assumes the role as the main driver for national health promotion and disease prevention programs. The board strives to empower Singaporeans to achieve optimal health throughout life by ensuring accessibility to health information and preventive health services and collaborations with public, private, and community organizations in health promotion. HPB also aims to create a conducive environment for leading a healthy lifestyle. One such example is the board's collaboration with eating establishments nationwide to promote healthier eating.

Close to half of all Singaporeans have at least one meal outside their homes six or more times a week.[2] In recognition of this lifestyle profile, the board has launched a series of initiatives to promote the availability of healthier options when eating out.

In 1998, the board launched the Ask for Healthier Food program to provide patrons dining at hawker centers (informal outdoor food courts) and food courts the option to ask for healthier food choices at these food outlets. These healthier choices include asking for more vegetables, less oil, less sugar/syrup, less sauce/gravy, for skin to be removed from poultry dishes, and for fruit to be included at every meal. Food vendors were encouraged to participate in the program by offering one appropriate healthier choice to their customers (see Figure 11.1).

Following the success of the healthy hawker program and the increased number of restaurant goers, HPB extended the program to include restaurants. This extension marks a two-pronged strategy by the board to not just stimulate consumer demand but to enhance and increase supply side so that there are sufficient healthier eating options for consumers.

The Healthier Restaurants Programme was introduced to provide an array of healthier

Figure 11.1 "Ask for" Labels Used in Food Courts to Prompt Healthy Choices

dishes that are lower in fat, salt, and sugar and enhanced with added vegetables and fruit to diners. Though the dishes with healthier modifications are not necessarily less expensive than dishes on the regular menu, the pricing tactic used by the board aims to lower the barriers to the adoption of the prescribed behavior by increasing the ease of choosing healthier options. Diners no longer need to request the chef to prepare dishes with less fat, less salt and sugar, and to add more vegetables and fruit. Diners simply have to select the healthier dishes that are available in every category of the menus of participating restaurants. To date, over 150 restaurants are participating in the Healthier Restaurant Programme, thereby ensuring that there are sufficient avenues for healthier eating.

Target Audiences and Behavior Objectives

Although promotions are likely to reach most residents in Singapore, the strategies developed were designed to most influence those who dine out frequently. We want them to choose healthier options at participating restaurants. Critical to success is the key secondary audience, the restaurants themselves. We want the restaurants to provide a wide range of healthy food selections for their dining patrons.

Strategies

One of the key distinguishing features of the Healthier Restaurant Programme is the focus on supply side economics. The key was to work on supply so as to reduce pricing and increase places for conversion to the desired behavior—healthier eating.

The board engages in industry outreach to restaurant chefs and managers through a series of dialogue sessions and workshops. Nutritionists from the board will provide advice on technical and professional matters relating to food and nutrition, national nutrition, and dietary guidelines as well as food and nutrition policies. Restaurants are encouraged to customize their menu to serve healthier food options for patrons. To create awareness and branding for the program, the Healthier Restaurant Programme logo is also displayed on the menu boards of the participating restaurants (see Figure 11.2).

Figure 11.2 Healthier Choice Seal

Once a crucial mass of 150 restaurants had signed on for the Healthier Restaurant Programme, HPB embarked on a marketing communications campaign to create public awareness and drive consumer demand to these restaurants. The advertising campaign also aimed to recognize and reward participating restaurants and thereby increase the number of new restaurant sign-ups that recognize the positive publicity value of association with the program and hence the importance of "keeping up with the Joneses" in this highly competitive market.

The communications strategy for the Healthier Restaurants Programme comprises a

television and print advertisement campaign, supported by promotional collaterals such as posters and tent cards at all participating restaurants. All promotional materials highlight that the list of the 150 healthier restaurants could be found on the board's Web site. Selected healthier restaurants were also featured in newspapers and magazines, and a promotion was organized with selected publications for diners at the restaurants to win a free 1-year magazine subscription if they had visited any of these restaurants and ordered at least two healthier choice dishes during a fixed time period. An on-site promotion offered diners the chance to dine for free if they had ordered at least one healthier choice dish and their names were selected from a lucky draw (see Figure 11.3).

To sustain continuous awareness of the program among Singaporeans, HPB worked with food critics from various radio stations to promote restaurants offering healthier choices. These restaurants were reviewed over a 6-week period, and the participating radio stations also offered contests and incentives for listeners.

Results

The board's Research and Evaluation Department conducted a survey in early 2006 to evaluate the program. Survey findings revealed that two out of five respondents (42.6%) asked for healthier modifications when buying food at hawker centers and food courts and 45% of table orders comprised a healthier dish among participating healthier restaurants. The key to the effective marketing strategy undertaken by HPB is the recognition that in order to alter beliefs and change the behavior of consumers, it is necessary to provide facilitating mechanisms to make it easier

Figure 11.3 Restaurant Promotion in Print Publications—Simply Health-Ilicious

Programmes by eating establishments ensured that there is a wide distribution network where behavior modification could take place. In addition, an aggressive marketing communications campaign actively promoted the key products of the campaign—the Ask for Healthier Food and Healthier Restaurants Programmes—to drive consumer traffic to these products. The availability of a healthy food supply and healthier menu choices, together with the immense publicity efforts, aimed to create awareness and alter beliefs and behavior among consumers to accept the norming proposition that it is convenient to choose to eat healthy when eating out. At the same time, the campaign also addressed supply side by ensuring more restaurants come on board to provide healthier food.

for consumers to make healthier food choices and adopt healthy dietary habits when eating out. The Ask for Healthier Food and Healthier Restaurants Programmes were products developed by the board to reduce barriers and increase benefits for both consumers and participating restaurants.

The widespread adoption of the Ask for Healthier Food and Healthier Restaurants

As such, the key strategy of pricing was effective in the promotion of healthier eating, as it was able to increase benefits and decrease nonmonetary costs (e.g., time, effort, energy) for the desired behavior among consumers.

PRICE: THE SECOND "P"

Price is the cost that the target market associates with adopting the desired behavior. Traditional marketing theory has a similar definition: "The amount of money charged for a product or service, or the sum of the values that consumers exchange for the benefits of having or using the product or service."[3]

Adoption costs may be *monetary* or *nonmonetary* in nature. Monetary costs in a social marketing environment are most often related to *tangible objects and services* associated with adopting the behavior (e.g., buying a life vest or paying for a swim class for toddlers). Nonmonetary costs are more intangible but are just as real for your audience and often even more significant for social marketing products. They include costs associated with *time, effort, and energy* to perform the behavior, *psychological risks and losses* that might be perceived or experienced, and any *physical discomforts* that may be related to the behavior. Most of these nonmonetary ones were probably discovered when you conducted barriers research, identifying concerns your target audience had with adopting the desired behavior. There may be more to add to the list at this point, however, as you may have decided, you want to include tangible objects and services such as those listed in Table 11.1. This is the time to do that.

If your organization is actually the maker or provider for these tangible objects (e.g., rain barrels) or services (e.g., home energy audits), you will want to be involved in establishing the price your customer will be asked to pay. This is the time to do that as well, prior to developing the incentives that are the emphasis of this chapter. A section at the end of this chapter presents a few tips on price setting.

STEP #7: DETERMINING MONETARY AND NONMONETARY INCENTIVES AND DISINCENTIVES

Your objective and opportunity with this second marketing tool is to develop and provide *incentives* that will increase benefits or decrease costs, incentives that can be used to do one or more of the following. The first four of the six tactics focus on the desired behavior and the last two on the competing one(s).

1. Increase monetary benefits for *the desired behavior.*
2. Decrease monetary costs for *the desired behavior.*
3. Increase nonmonetary benefits for *the desired behavior.*
4. Decrease nonmonetary costs for *the desired behavior.*
5. Increase monetary costs for *the competing behavior.*
6. Increase nonmonetary costs for *the competing behavior.*

The next six sections of this chapter explain each of these in more detail and provide an illustration for each.

#1: Increase Monetary Benefits for the Desired Behavior

Monetary rewards and incentives can take many forms familiar to you as a consumer and include *rebates, allowances, cash incentives,* and *price adjustments* that reward

Table 11.1   Potential Costs for Performing the Desired Behavior

Type of cost	*Examples*
Monetary: Tangible Objects	• Nicotine patches • Blood pressure monitoring equipment • Condoms • Bike helmets, life vests, and booster seats • Breathalyzers • Earthquake preparedness kits • Smoke alarm batteries • Food waste compost tumblers • Natural fertilizers (versus regular fertilizers) • Recycled paper (versus regular paper) • Energy-saving lightbulbs • Electric mulch mowers
Monetary: Services	• Fees for family planning classes • Smoking cessation classes • Athletic club fees • Suicide prevention workshop • Taxi rides home from a bar
Nonmonetary: Time, Effort	• Cooking a balanced meal • Pulling over to use the cell phone • Driving to a car wash versus washing at home • Taking the food waste outside to a composter
Nonmonetary: Psychological	• Finding out whether a lump is cancerous • Wondering about whether to believe the warning about eating too much fish when pregnant • Having a cup of coffee without a cigarette • Feeling "dorky" carrying a flag across a crosswalk • Listening to the chatter of others in a car pool • Asking your son whether he is considering suicide • Telling your husband you think he drinks too much • Using sunscreen and coming back from Hawaii "pale" • Letting your lawn go brown in the summer
Nonmonetary: Physical Discomfort	• Exercising • Pricking a finger to monitor blood glucose • Having a mammogram • Lowering the thermostat • Taking shorter showers

customers for adopting the proposed behavior. Some have been rather "tame" in nature (e.g., 3.5-cent credit for reusing grocery bags), others a little more aggressive (e.g., quit and win contests that offer a chance to win a $1,000 prize for successfully stopping smoking for a least 1 month,[4] a $20 annual license fee for a neutered dog versus $60 for an unaltered one), and a few quite bold (e.g., offering drug-addicted women a $200 incentive for voluntary sterilization, offering voters a chance at a $1 million lottery just for showing up at the polls). Where would you place the following example on that continuum?

Example: Paying People to Be Tuberculosis Pill Pals

Tuberculosis is curable. And as an article in the *New York Times* in November 2006 lays out, this is because a simple course of four antibiotics, which can cost as little as $11, can usually vanquish this dreaded killer. And yet, nearly 2 million people a year are still dying from it.[5]

Why? "Because these antibiotics must be taken daily for six to nine months. That means that the local health clinic must have a steady supply. Patients must continue to take the full course even though they stop coughing, and the medicine causes nasty side effects. TB strikes mostly the poor, especially those living in crowded conditions. Many of them are migrants, who may be lost to the health system when they move. If they don't finish the course, terrible things can happen."[6]

The solution many countries have discovered includes a monetary as well as social contact incentive. Directly Observed Treatment Short-Course (DOTS) is a strategy developed in Tanzania in the 1970s and is now used to manage about 60% of the world's diagnosed TB cases. At its core is a "pill pal," someone who commits to watching the patient actually swallow the medicines. It can be a community health worker or even a family member, friend, or neighbor.

Then China found a way to make DOTS even more effective, adding monetary incentives to up the numbers. With financial assistance from the World Bank, China's government started giving village health workers *bonuses* to find TB patients, get them to the lab for checkups, and observe them until they completed their full course of antibiotics. And the numbers were encouraging, with China's TB cure rate then rising from 52% to 95%, preventing 30,000 TB deaths per year.[7] Many believe DOTS is one of the most cost-effective health programs available, with each cure costing an estimated $100 and bringing a return of $60 for every dollar spent.[8]

#2: Decrease Monetary Costs for the Desired Behavior

Methods to decrease monetary costs are also familiar to most consumers: discount coupons, cash discounts, quantity discounts, seasonal discounts, promotional pricing (e.g., a temporary price reduction), and segment pricing (e.g., price based on geographic locations). Many of these tactics are also available to you as a social marketer to increase sales. You yourself may have used a discount coupon from a utility for compost, taken advantage of a weekend sales event for water-efficient toilets, or received a discount on parking at work because you are part of a car pool. The social marketing organization may be involved in subsidizing the incentive, distributing coupons, and/or getting the word out, as illustrated in the following example.

Example: Bike Helmet Coupons[9]

Harborview Injury Prevention and Research Center's (HIPRC) Web site reported in February 2000 that "more bicyclists in Seattle wear helmets than bicyclists in any other major city in the country where laws do not require it." The Washington Children's Helmet Bicycle Campaign was launched in 1986 by physicians at Harborview Medical Center in Seattle who were alarmed at the nearly 200 children they were treating each year with bicycle-related head injuries.

"Although bicycle helmets were available in 1985, just one child in 100 wears one." HIPRC physicians conducted a study to understand why parents don't buy bike helmets for their children and what factors influenced whether children actually wore them. "The results, from a survey of more than 2,500 fourth graders and their parents, shaped the eventual campaign. More than two thirds of the parents said that they had never thought of providing a helmet and *another third cited cost as a factor.*"

A campaign was designed around "four key objectives: increasing public awareness of the importance of helmets, educating parents about helmet use, overcoming peer pressure among children against wearing helmets, and lowering helmet prices."

The HIPRC formed a coalition of health, bicycling, helmet industry, and community organizations to design and manage a variety of promotions. As a result, parents and children heard about helmets on television, on the radio, in the newspapers, in their doctors' offices, at school, and at youth groups. These advertised discount coupons cut helmet prices by half, to $20. Nearly 5,000 helmets were distributed at no or low cost to needy families.

By September 1993 (7 years later), helmet use had jumped from 1% to 57% among children in the greater Seattle area and adult use increased to 70%. Five years into the campaign, an HIPRC evaluation revealed its ultimate impact: Admissions at five Seattle-area hospitals for bicycle-related head injuries dropped by approximately two thirds for children 5 to 14 years old.

#3: Increase Nonmonetary Benefits for the Desired Behavior

There are also ways to encourage changes in behavior that don't involve cash or free goods and services with significant monetary value. Instead, they provide a different type of value. In the social marketing environment, they are often ones that deliver some form of *recognition* and/or *appreciation* acknowledging the adoption of a desired behavior. In most cases, the benefit is psychological and personal in nature. It can be as simple as an e-mail from a supervisor thanking an employee for signing up for a car pool, or as formal and public as an annual awards program for a dry cleaner who has adopted the most significant green behaviors in the past year. These nonmonetary benefits are distinct from tangible objects and services (e.g., safe bike storage) that are offered to actually help the target audience adopt the behavior. They are also distinct from sales promotion tactics that are more similar in nature to gifts or prizes (e.g., T-shirts and coffee mugs).

Example: Backyard Wildlife Sanctuary Recognition Programs

Some state and local agencies, such as the Washington State Department of Fish and Wildlife, recognize good environmental stewardship by providing homeowners with impressive weatherproof plaques for the yard and frameable certificates for inside the home (see Figure 11.4). Programs typically include filling out a habitat inventory application that ensures the presence of numerous trees and shrubs, birdbaths or some other source of water, bird feeders, and birdhouses or shelters. Applicants "promise" (in writing) to minimize their use of dangerous chemicals in fertilizers and pesticides.

This recognition program not only increases perceived benefits of being a habitat manager but also makes it more likely that homeowners will know and practice the desired environmental behaviors that protect wildlife. Packets of information sent to the homeowner along with the plaque and certificate include the following:

- Lists of plants to attract butterflies
- How to best feed birds
- Types of natural fertilizers and pesticides
- How to design a small wildlife pond
- Tips for attracting hummingbirds
- References for landscaping
- Instructions on building a songbird nest box

Figure 11.4 Plaque Given to Homeowners Completing Application and Agreeing to Practices

#4: Decrease Nonmonetary Costs for the Desired Behavior

Tactics are also available for decreasing *time, effort, physical,* or *psychological* costs. Fox suggests reducing usage time by "embedding" a new behavior into present activities.[10] Thus, people might be encouraged to floss their teeth while they watch television. People can also be encouraged to "anchor" a new behavior to an established habit.[11] To encourage physical activity, for example, you can recommend that people climb the stairs to their third-floor office instead of taking the elevator.

Gemunden proposed several potential tactics for reducing other nonmonetary costs in this model:

1. Against a perceived psychological risk, provide social products in ways that deliver *psychological rewards.*

2. Against a perceived social risk, gather *endorsements from credible sources* that reduce the potential stigma or embarrassment of adopting a product.

3. Against a perceived usage risk, provide target adopters with *reassuring information* on the product or with a free trial of the product so they can experience how the product does what it promises to do.

4. Against perceived physical risk, solicit *seals of approval* from authoritative institutions, such as the American Dental Association, the American Medical Association, or other highly respected organizations.[12]

Example: Redeeming Farmers' Market Checks

Women, Infants, and Children (WIC) program offices often distribute checks to qualified families to purchase fresh fruits and vegetables at local farmers' markets. Yet clients often face significant nonmonetary costs that lead to lower redemption rates than many WIC offices would like to see. Many experience increased *effort* to find the market and parking, *embarrassment* around other shoppers when using coupons, *difficulty* in identifying qualified produce when signs are inconsistently displayed or difficult to see, *concern* with not getting change back from checks, *frustration* with misplacing checks that are often stored or forgotten in drawers or strollers, and *fear* of what the WIC counselor will think if they decline the checks, even though their chances of using them are minimal, given work schedules that conflict with market hours.

These costs could be overcome with a variety of tactics:

- Detailed maps to the market and for parking printed on the back of checks
- Electronic debit cards in place of the checks
- Signs on poles above the stands that display some recognizable logo that doesn't "brand" the client, such as the 5 A Day logo
- Printing checks in lower amounts, such as $1 denominations
- Packaging checks in sturdy check folders
- Offering hesitant clients fewer checks, and more if they use them all

#5: Increase Monetary Costs for the Competing Behavior

In the social marketing environment, this tactic is likely to involve influencing policymakers, as often the most effective monetary strategies against the competition include ones requiring *increasing taxes* (e.g., on gas-guzzling cars), *imposing fines* (e.g., for not recycling), and/or *decreasing funding* (e.g., if a school doesn't offer an hour of physical education classes). As Alan Andreasen lays out in his book *Social Marketing in the 21st Century*, these policy changes may be critical to significant social change, and the social marketer can play a role in making this happen. "Our models and frameworks are flexible enough to guide efforts aimed at this kind of upstream behavior, especially for the many smaller organizations, especially at the local level, that cannot afford lobbyists."[13]

He proposes you use familiar components of the social marketing model. You can segment the potential audience using the stages of change model, where in the legislative environment this may get translated to those who are opponents, undecideds, or supporters. You will then, he recommends, benefit from identifying and understanding your target audience's BCOS factors: benefits (motivators), costs (demotivators), others in the target audience's environment and their influence, and self-assurance (perceptions of opportunity and ability).[14] These should sound familiar as well.

In the following example, this increasing monetary cost strategy produced impressive results.

Example: Discouraging Use of Plastic Bags in Ireland

Every year, an estimated 500 billion to 1 trillion plastic bags are "consumed" worldwide. That amounts to over 1 million per minute, with billions ending up as litter each year.[15] In March 2002, the Republic of Ireland became the first country to do something about it. At that time, the Environment Ministry of Ireland estimated that about 1.2 billion free plastic bags were handed out each year to shoppers, with so many ending up littering Irish streets and flapping from trees and hedgerows across the countryside that some had dubbed it the Emerald Isle's "national flag."[16] The new tax required shoppers to pay 15 euro cents per bag.

In the first 3 months after the tax was introduced, shops handed out only about 23 million bags, a decrease of more than 80% (from 1.2 billion to 23 million per year). And as of February 2007, use has been cut by 95%, and the tax has raised 75 million euros, funds that will be used to support environmental projects.[17] The Environment Minister in 2002 was jubilant with the results. "Over one billion plastic bags will be removed from circulation while raising funding for future environmentally friendly initiatives. . . . It is clear that the levy has not only changed consumer behaviour in relation to disposable plastic bags, it has also raised national consciousness about the role each one of us can, and must play if we are to tackle collectively the problems of litter and waste management."[18]

#6: Increase Nonmonetary Costs for the Competing Behavior

Nonmonetary tactics can also be used to increase actual or perceived nonmonetary costs associated with choosing the competing behavior. In this case, you may be creating or emphasizing negative public recognition. Tacoma, Washington, for example, created a Web site that features properties not in full compliance with municipal codes. They call it "The Filthy 15," and although property owners' names do not appear on the Web site, it does includes photos of the building, specific reasons the property is on the list, and what is next in the cleanup process, including something a neighbor or other concerned citizen could track.[19]

In a different scenario, you might be highlighting the downsides of the competition, as illustrated in the following example, one where research was key to understanding what costs should be highlighted.

Example: Encouraging Teen Abstinence

The Teen Aware Project is part of a statewide effort to reduce teen pregnancy and is sponsored by the Washington State Office of Superintendent of Public Instruction. Funds are allocated through a competitive grant process to public middle/junior and senior high schools for the development of media campaigns to promote sexual abstinence and the importance of delaying sexual activity, pregnancy, and childbearing. These campaigns are substantially designed and produced by students. Student media products include video and radio productions, posters, theater productions, print advertising, multimedia, T-shirts, buttons, and Web sites. Campaign messages are distributed in local project schools and communities.

This particular research effort was conducted by teens at Mercer Island High School, a grant recipient. A team of nine students from marketing, health, and communication classes volunteered to develop the campaign, from start to finish. Several teachers and outside consultants served as coaches on the project. At the time this research effort was undertaken, the team had chosen their campaign focus (abstinence), purpose (reducing teen pregnancies), target audience (eighth graders), and their campaign objective (to persuade students to "pause and think in a heated moment"). Information from existing student surveys indicated that about 75% of eighth graders—but only 25% of seniors—were abstinent. It was decided that the campaign bull's-eye would be eighth graders, who were seen as being the most vulnerable for making choices regarding sexual activity.

The team of juniors and seniors wanted to refresh their memories about middle school years. As one student expressed, "It's been a long time since I was an eighth grader, and I don't have a clue what they know and think about sex these days." The primary purposes of their research were to (a) help decisions regarding which benefits of abstinence and costs related to sexual activity should be highlighted in the campaign and (b) provide input for selecting a slogan for the campaign. More specifically, the study was designed to determine major perceived benefits of abstinence, costs associated with being sexually active, and what messages (and tone) would be most effective in influencing an eighth grader to consider abstinence.

Each of the nine students agreed to conduct casual interviews with at least five eighth graders over a 1-week period. They used an informal script that explained the project and assured respondents that their comments would be anonymous. They recorded and summarized responses to the following three open-ended questions:

1. What's the most important reason you can think of for delaying having intercourse until you are older?

2. What are the worst things you can think of that can happen to you if you have intercourse before you are ready?

3. What would you say to your best friend if she or he told you that they thought they were going to have sex for the first time tonight?

Interviews were conducted with district permission, before and after classes at the middle schools, as well as in informal settings such as sports events, after-school programs, and in friends' homes. Students returned to class the following week, shared summary findings, and were guided to identify the following themes for each of the informational areas:

- Major Reasons for Delaying Sex:
  You won't get sexually transmitted diseases (STDs).
  You can save it for someone special.
  You won't get pregnant.

- The Worst Things That Can Happen: They could drop you later for someone else. You could get pregnant, and childbirth really hurts. You can get really bad STDs, like crabs.

- Words for a Friend: You should wait until you are older. Are you sure he really loves you? Do you have protection? Are you ready for all the things that could happen?

The team used this input to develop a campaign centered around emphasis on three "gross" consequences of having sex before you're ready. They developed the campaign slogan "Are you ready?" and followed the question with each of the three consequences. Graphic, in-your-face images were reflected on the posters and depicted in radio scripts (see Figures 11.5, 11.6, and 11.7).

Radio spots that were played on the high school radio station followed the three gross consequence themes. In one, a male voice says,

I remember the day I learned what an STD really was. I had seen little things crawling around in my . . . hair. I woke up in the middle of the night, my . . . you know . . . was burning from an itch. My entire crotch was swarming with miniature crabs. Finally, I had to get help. If you think you're going to have sex, ask yourself: Are you ready for that?" (See Figure 11.5.)

In another approach, a girl graphically recounts the pain of giving birth (see Figure 11.6). And in the third spot, a girl sadly yet frankly relates how the guy she slept with immediately told everyone at school and found a new girlfriend. It took her years to trust a guy again[23] (see Figure 11.7).

SETTING PRICES FOR TANGIBLE OBJECTS AND SERVICES

Prices for tangible objects and services involved in social marketing campaigns are typically set by manufacturers, retailers, and service providers. Social marketers are more often involved in helping to decide what tangible objects and services would be beneficial in facilitating behavior change, recommending discount coupons and related incentives, and then promoting their use.

When a social marketer gets involved in the price setting, however, several principles can guide decision making. The first task is to reach agreement on your pricing objectives. Kotler and Roberto[24] outline several potential objectives:

- *Maximizing retained earnings* where the primary consideration is money making (e.g., charging advertisers for space on the billboards above the Play Pumps in Africa)
- *Recovering costs* where revenue is expected to offset a portion of costs (e.g., charging customers $32 for a rain barrel that cost the utility $45)
- *Maximizing the number of target adopters* where the primary purpose is to influence as many people as possible to use the service and/or buy the product (e.g., providing free condoms to farm workers)
- *Social equity* where reaching underprivileged or high-risk segments is a priority and different prices might be charged according to ability to pay (e.g., sliding scale fee for bike helmets)
- *Demarketing* where pricing strategies are used to discourage people from adopting a particular social product (e.g., taxes on cigarettes)

Figure 11.5 Abstinence Campaign Poster[20]

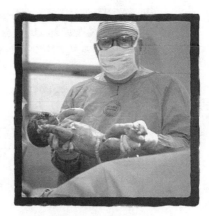

Figure 11.6 Abstinence Campaign Poster[21]

Mercer Island Teens For Delaying Sex

Figure 11.7 Abstinence Campaign Poster[22]

Once the pricing objective is agreed upon, setting specific prices gets easier. Three options to consider include the following:

1. *Cost-based pricing,* where prices are based on a desired or established profit margin or rate of return on investment (e.g., condoms are sold at community clinics at prices to cover purchase costs)

2. *Competitive-based pricing,* where prices are more driven by the prices for competing (similar) products and services (e.g., a life vest manufacturer partnering on a drowning prevention campaign offers discount coupons to make pricing similar to less expensive vests that are not Coast Guard approved)

3. *Value-based pricing,* where prices are based on an analysis of the target adopters' "price sensitivity," evaluating demand at varying price points (e.g., food waste composters that require simple spinning are priced higher than those requiring manual tossing)

ETHICAL CONSIDERATIONS RELATED TO PRICING STRATEGIES

Ethical considerations related to pricing strategies include issues of *social equity* (e.g., fixed versus sliding scale fees), *potential exploitation* (e.g., offering monetary incentives to drug-addicted women for voluntary sterilization), impact and fairness of *public shame* tactics (e.g., what if owners of one of The Filthy 15 buildings had lost their job, and this explains why they hadn't repaired their dilapidated building), and *full disclosure* of costs (e.g., requirements to toss food composters daily in order to receive stated benefits). In the case of promoting farmers' markets to WIC clients, each of these issues might apply. Should clients receive additional coupons if they use all of their first set, making it necessary to give some clients only half a pack? What do we do about the fact that many items at the market are less than the $2 coupon denomination, and yet change cannot be given? Are we consistent about telling our clients that they will probably need to pay $3 for parking while at the markets?

Chapter Summary

The price of a social marketing product is *the cost that the target audience associates with adopting the new behavior.* Costs may be monetary or nonmonetary in nature. Your task is to use this second tool to ensure that what you offer the market (benefits) is equal to or greater than what they will have to give up (costs).

Your objective (and opportunity) is to develop and provide *incentives* that will increase benefits or decrease costs, incentives that can be used to do one or more of the following. The first four tactics focus on the desired behavior and the last two on the competing one(s).

1. Increase monetary benefits for *the desired behavior.*

2. Decrease monetary costs for *the desired behavior.*

3. Increase nonmonetary benefits for *the desired behavior.*

4. Decrease nonmonetary costs for *the desired behavior.*

5. Increase monetary costs for *the competing behavior.*

6. Increase nonmonetary costs for *the competing behavior.*

Although most prices for tangible objects and services are established by manufacturers, retailers, and service providers, several principles can guide a social marketer faced with price-setting decisions, beginning with establishing pricing objectives. What do you want the price to accomplish for you? Once defined, you will then likely decide to establish your price based on cost, the competition, or the perceived value that your target audience holds.

RESEARCH HIGHLIGHT

Click It or Ticket

Observation Research (2006)

Background

Click It or Ticket (CIOT) is a high-publicity law enforcement effort that gives people more of a reason to buckle up—the increased threat of a ticket and a fine. Most people buckle up for safety, but for others it seems to take this threat of a ticket to spur them to put on a safety belt. In Click It or Ticket programs, law enforcement agencies mobilize to focus on safety belt violations and publicize the stepped-up effort through news media and advertising. Most agree it is this two-pronged approach that makes these campaigns powerful.

Click It or Ticket campaigns and similar efforts have increased safety belt use in cities, states, and even entire regions of the country. These efforts have helped to increase U.S. national seatbelt use rate to a record high, at 81% in 2006.[25] Rates are calculated scientifically using trained spotters who count the number of motorists in a given area wearing seatbelts. This research highlight from Alabama presents more detail on the probability-based observational surveys used to determine these rates. Surveys are designed and conducted in accordance with criteria established by the National Highway Traffic Safety Administration (NHTSA) to ensure reliable results. The information for this highlight appeared in a report prepared in September 2006 by *CARE* Research & Development Laboratory for the Law Enforcement/Traffic Safety Division of the Alabama Department of Economic and Community Affairs.[26]

Research Objectives

In 2006, Alabama elected for the seventh consecutive year to participate in NHTSA's Click It or Ticket program. As in the past, field observation surveys were performed as one way to evaluate the impact of the effort, measuring shoulder safety belt use rates among drivers and front seat passengers in passenger motor vehicles. (Other methodologies to measure campaign awareness and changes in citizen attitudes included self-administered and telephone surveys.)

Methodology

Statewide surveys of vehicle safety belt usage were coordinated by the Injury Prevention Division of the Alabama Department of Public Health (ADPH). A precampaign survey was conducted in April 2006 to establish a baseline usage rate, and a second measurement was taken in June 2006. Surveys included results from 15 counties throughout the state. The survey, following NHTSA guidelines, included a sampling plan that was probability-based, multistaged, and stratified for both rural and urban roadways. The sample included the 4 counties with the largest metropolitan areas plus 11 additional counties selected at random from a pool of 37 large counties. In the end, at least 85% of the state's population was represented by the study sample.

For both the pre- and postsurveys, 23 sites were selected at random in each selected county from three traffic volume categories: low (0–4,999 vehicles per day), medium (5,000–10,499) and high (10,500–75,000). For each of these selected counties, the number of sites selected in each volume category reflected the total number of miles in that volume class. At least one site was selected from each volume category for each county chosen for the survey sample.

Each site was observed for 1 hour, using the curbside lane as a reference position. The observer determined drivers' and front seat passengers' use or nonuse of safety belts. Additional data were captured to help categorize the gender and race of observed occupants and the type of vehicle.

Highlights of Findings

The ADPH survey team observed a total of 57,214 front seat occupants in 23 randomly selected sites in the 15 selected counties during the pre-CIOT period. An additional 46,218 were observed during the post-CIOT period. The total number of observations, 103,423, represented about 2.27% of Alabama's population.

Using these procedures, ADPH established the Alabama safety belt use rates at 78.6% for baseline and 82.9% for the postperiod. Variance and standard error were calculated and considered acceptable. The estimated usage rates for the statewide observations in 2006 are reflected in Table 11.2 along with results from similar surveys for the 4 prior years. As indicated, the belt use in the postperiod reached a new high of 82.90%. This was an increase from the 81.85% seen in the postperiod in 2005. The 82.90% is a new record for the state.

In addition to establishing the basic safety belt use rates, the observation studies also gathered demographic data on belt use, and results were reported by county. Table 11.3 reflects belt use by gender, race, and vehicle type. Clearly, women in Alabama are more prone to wear safety belts than men (89.9% versus 78.7%). However, CIOT appears to have a slightly greater effect on the male portion of the population. Among the men observed in the pre- and postperiods, there was a growth of 4.1% over the course of the CIOT campaign. Conversely, there was only a growth of 2.9% seen among women during this same time frame. By race, data indicate that safety belt compliance was lowest among non-whites and highest among whites and that usage increased the most among whites during this effort.

Post Note

These observation data were combined with findings from the self-administered and telephone surveys to provide more clues as to why some motorists wore seatbelts and others "refused." In the long term, these findings will assist the state in developing methodologies that can "push belt use to its ultimate position—100%."

Table 11.2 Five-Year Pre- and Postbelt Usage Levels

Statewide	Pre "Click It" April 11–16	Post "Click It" June 5–11
2006	**78.60%**	**82.90%**
2005	78.72%	81.85%
2004	73.50%	80.00%
2003	74.39%	77.41%
2002	70.30%	78.70%

SOURCE: Alabama Department of Public Health, 2006 Observational Surveys

Table 11.3   Safety Belt Use by Gender, Race, and Vehicle Type, 2006

	Presurvey	*Postsurvey*
Gender		
Male	74.6%	78.7%
Female	87.0%	89.9%
Race		
Non-White	78.9%	76.6%
Hispanic	81.3%	80.4%
White	79.5%	84.8%
Vehicle Type		
Truck	71.0%	77.3%
Car	82.0%	84.6%
Van	81.4%	86.3%
SUV	83.6%	88.2%

12

Place

Making Access Convenient and Pleasant

Private sector marketing strategies are likely the most overlooked opportunity today for creating large-scale health impact in the developing world. The adoption of private sector methodologies has the potential to save millions of lives in developing countries in this decade.

—Steven W. Honeyman
Country Representative—Nepal
Population Services International 2007

Store-based retailers say that the three most important things in the success of their business are "location, location, location!" You may find this true for many social marketing efforts as well. Consider how much lower the following scores would be without the convenient access component of these programs, as well as those in the opening case story:

- *Recycling:* Nationwide, 48% of all paper was recycled in 2000, 71% of old newspapers, 75% of old corrugated boxes, and 41% of all office paper.[1] Though certainly not as much as we would like to see, imagine how grim the statistics would be without curbside recycling and recycle containers in office buildings and most public places.
- *Pet Waste Pickup:* Although an estimated 40% of dog owners in the United States do not pick up their dog's waste, at least 60% do, and without "Mutt Mitts" available in parks and public places around the country, we can imagine that number would be even smaller.[2]
- *Tobacco Quitlines:* The prevalence of smoking among adults in the United States has declined from about 25% in 1990 to 22.5% in 2002. At least 33 states now have quitlines, providing convenient access to telephone counseling to help tobacco users quit, and in some cases these lines provide limited access to medication.[3] Quitlines overcome many of the barriers to traditional smoking cessation classes, as they require no transportation and are available at the smoker's convenience.
- *Organ Donations:* Many initiatives in the United States aim to increase the number of organs from deceased donors. Convenience of registering as an organ donor is one important strategy, with at least 21 states now linking registration through driver's license bureaus or departments of motor vehicles, where individuals can designate their wish to be an organ donor on their license.[4]

Social Franchising of Family Planning Service Delivery

A Rising Sun in Nepal (2007)

STEVEN W. HONEYMAN

Country Representative—Nepal
Population Services International

Background

Nepal, a landlocked nation famous for Mount Everest and the Himalaya mountain range, is an unlikely location to showcase a family planning program. Ranked as one of the poorest nations in the world, Nepal's social indicators remain well under global averages, with 40% of the population living below the poverty line. Access to family planning services has been one of the tremendous challenges faced by the Nepal government since it began family planning programming in the 1960s. Distribution or "place" has traditionally been the most difficult marketing "P" to deliver in the country. Modern family planning products have been available in Nepal for more than four decades and offered free in government outlets. Promotion of family planning through mass media has meant that family planning knowledge is high. But access to these products and services remains low, with 28% of family planning needs still unmet, driving an endless cycle of poverty.

Some 85% of Nepalis live in remote areas of the country known for its high mountains, plunging river valleys, and thousands of villages perched atop steep ridges often far from government health posts. Access to health posts often requires several hours of walking in each direction over arduous terrain. Mothers burdened with the dual responsibility of contributing to subsistence farming and raising many small children have difficulty simply finding the time and energy to make the journey. When they do, they often arrive at health posts that are underresourced, understaffed, or simply closed. Villagers then need to travel even farther afar to adjacent villages or district headquarters in order to receive services or simply do without.

Strategy: PLACE: The Key to Service Delivery in Nepal

This was the challenge facing Population Services International (PSI), a nonprofit organization headquartered in Washington, D.C., in 2002. How can family planning products and services be better delivered in rural areas of Nepal? It was first decided that a new service delivery mechanism would be needed. The idea of consumers traveling great distances was abandoned, and instead the idea of bringing high-quality services to the consumer was explored. A social franchise model of service delivery was adopted as the best way to bring services to remote villages of Nepal. This social franchise was called the Sun Quality Health network (see Figure 12.1).

A social franchise is a group of private sector providers who all provide standardized service delivery for social good. The difference between a social franchise in health and a commercial franchise (like McDonald's restaurants) is that in social franchising the franchisor is only interested in the health impact achieved—not profits. The social franchising model consists of the franchisor (in this case PSI), who provides the products and processes of the franchise, and the franchisee (an existing private sector provider), who is required to meet defined quality standards by following standardized service delivery protocols and procedures. The social franchise then subsidizes high-quality health products and services, brands them, ensures they are widely available through the franchised outlets, monitors the quality of service provision, and promotes the services offered through the franchise using mass media, interpersonal communications, and tailored community-level marketing activities.

As with all franchisees around the world, the motivation to join Sun Quality Health was profit.

> *It must be remembered that Sun Quality Health franchisees are businesspeople that are primarily motivated by profit. Our franchisees understand that if they meet or exceed our defined service delivery standards they will get more clients, meaning greater profit for their businesses. This motivates private providers to carry product offerings consumers demand at affordable price points and to ensure those products and services are available when and where consumers demand them.*
>
> —Steven W. Honeyman

Establishing the Sun Quality Health Franchise Network

The Sun Quality Health network in Nepal was established by first identifying the geographic locations that would best serve the rural poor and vulnerable. Then an extensive set of franchise protocols for service delivery were developed that included minimum standards of everything from cleanliness of the provider's premises to counseling techniques for family planning services. Then 230 private sector franchisees were identified, trained, and contracted. The Sun Quality Health product portfolio included a wide range of "OK" branded family planning products, such as modern temporary methods of contraception

Figure 12.1   Family in Front of a Mobile Operating Theatre

(condoms, pills, injectable, and the IUCD), as well as permanent family planning methods, such as voluntary surgical contraception (vasectomies for men and minilaps for women) that were completed in mobile operating theatres (vans and tents) brought into each community.

After the closure of the transport factory where he worked, Krishna Tamang was despondent; he didn't know how he would care for his family and was worried about what would happen if his wife, Laxmi, had any more children. Krishna had three sons whom he loved dearly, but he knew that he couldn't afford to look after any more children. After hearing a radio advertisement about quality family planning services offered through Sun Quality Health, he decided to pay a visit to his local Sun Quality Health clinic. Krishna and Laxmi's experience with Sun Quality Health had a huge impact on their lives. After receiving counseling on all the family planning methods available, they decided that Krishna should have a vasectomy. This was successfully conducted at a mobile operating clinic that regularly supports each outlet. The couple no longer worries about having additional children and both have become strong advocates in their community for the quality family planning services they received through Sun Quality Health.

Implementation: Launching the Sun Quality Health Franchise Network

The Sun Quality Health network was launched in each targeted community with an exciting 2-day health fair. The goal of the health fairs was to provide the Sun Quality Health

providers with a link to consumers in their community. At each fair, magicians were seen magically producing family planning oral contraceptives out of a hat; crowds jostled each other to see the family planning theater play; parents packed the cinema room to watch an entertaining family health video; and kids fought for the chance to win small gifts by playing ring toss and other fun games (see Figure 12.2).

Figure 12.2 Sun Quality Fair Showing Magician Pulling Oral Contraceptives Out of a Hat

Sun Quality Health providers counseled clients on family planning and sold products. Referrals were made to the on-site voluntary surgical contraception teams, and after proper screening, clients underwent surgery on the spot. Hundreds of community members attended each fair, with many commenting that this was the first time services had been brought to their community.

After working nearly 18 months on the development of the Sun Quality Health franchise, we were finally ready for launch. We were a little nervous about whether we had the right marketing mix, launch plan, and communications strategy. During launch I discovered that my fears were unfounded and I knew we had hit the right mix when at our first Health Fair a fistfight broke out in the lineup for surgical vasectomies. Apparently, one distraught consumer, worried he might not be able to receive his operation before the end of the day, tried to jump the queue and was accosted by others in the line. Our doctors had to jump into the fray to separate the combatants and assure them they would all be receiving their Sun Quality Health vasectomies before they closed up the operating theatre for the day.

—David Valentine
Sun Quality Health Program Director

Results: The Impact of Private Sector-Related Solutions to Place

Significant new uptake of family planning products and services was accomplished, with the Sun Quality Health network providing a new channel of access. Tens of thousands of Nepalis who had limited or no access to family planning received service delivery right in their own community. Social franchising has provided at least one piece of the complex puzzle of place in marketing to the rural poor and vulnerable in Nepal. Indeed, in the near future, PSI hopes to leverage the franchise platform to address an array of health issues, including access to prevention and treatment for sexually transmitted infections, unsafe water, diarrheal disease, malaria, malnutrition, and tuberculosis.

PLACE: THE THIRD "P"

Place is where and when the target market will perform the desired behavior, acquire any related tangible objects, and receive any associated services.

We live in a convenience-oriented world in which many of us place an extremely high value on our time, trying to save some of it for our families, friends, and favorite leisure activities. As a social marketer, you'll want to be keenly aware that your target audience will evaluate the convenience of your offer relative to other exchanges in their lives. And the convenience bar has been raised over the past decades for all marketers by companies such as Starbucks, McDonald's Federal Express, amazon.com, 1-800-Flowers, Netflix for online movie rentals, and of course, the Internet.

In commercial sector marketing, place is often referred to as the distribution channel, with options and examples for social marketing pervasive:

- **Physical Locations:** Walking trails
- **Phone:** Domestic violence help line
- **Mail:** Immunization wallet card to keep track of a child's immunizations
- **Fax:** Signed patient agreement with physician to quit is faxed to a quitline
- **Internet:** Rideshare matching
- **Mobile Unit:** For hazardous waste

- **Where People Shop:** Mammograms in a department store
- **Where People Hang Out:** HIV/AIDS tests at gay bars
- **Drive-Throughs:** For flu shots at medical centers
- **Home Delivery/House Calls:** Home energy audits
- **Kiosks:** For determining your body mass index (BMI)
- **Vending Machines:** Condoms

It is important to clarify that place is *not the same as communication channel,* which is where your communications will appear (e.g., brochures, radio ads, news stories, and personal presentations). Chapter 14 presents a detailed discussion of communication channels.

STEP #7: DEVELOPING THE PLACE STRATEGY

Your objective with the place marketing tool is to develop strategies that will make it as convenient and pleasant as possible for your target audience to perform the behavior, acquire any tangible objects, and receive any services. It is especially helpful in reducing access-related barriers (e.g., lack of transportation) and time-related barriers (e.g., at work all day). You will also want to do anything possible and within reason to make the competing behavior (seem) less convenient. The next sections of this chapter will elaborate on 10 successful strategies for you to consider.

#1: Make the Location Closer

Example: A Dental Office on Wheels

Many children don't get the regular dental care they need. They may be struggling with language barriers, poverty, rural isolation, or homelessness. A mobile clinic called the SmileMobile travels to communities all across Washington State. This modern dental office on wheels brings dental services directly to children aged 13 and younger who don't otherwise have access to care. Children enrolled in Medicaid have no out-of-pocket expenses, and other children are charged on a sliding fee schedule. Families may even enroll in Medicaid at the SmileMobile.

The brightly painted clinic features three state-of-the-art dental operatories and includes X-ray facilities. A full-time dentist and teams of local volunteer dentists and their staffs provide a range of dental services, including diagnostic services (e.g., exams and X-rays), prevention services (e.g., cleaning and sealants), acute and emergent relief of pain (e.g., extractions and minor surgical procedures), and routine restorative services (e.g., fillings and crowns).

The SmileMobile was developed by Washington Dental Service, the Washington State Dental Association, and the Washington Dental Service Foundation (see Figure 12.3). Staff work closely with local health departments and community, charitable, and

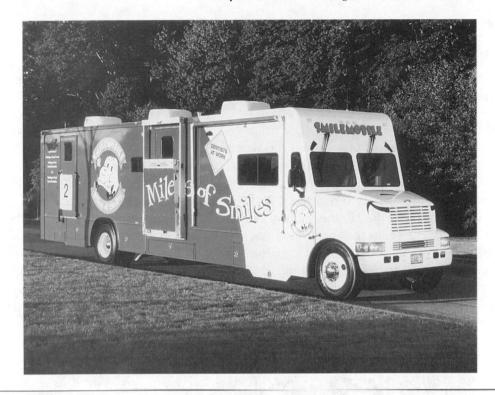

Figure 12.3 Making Dental Care for Children More Accessible[6]

business organizations to coordinate visits to cities and towns throughout the state. Every effort is made to reach the neediest children and provide translators for non-English-speaking patients and their families. Since it first hit the road in 1995, the mobile clinic has treated more than 15,000 children throughout the state.[5]

Additional examples illustrating ways to save your target audience a little time and travel include the following:

- Exercise facilities at work sites
- Flu shots at grocery stores
- Needle exchange tables on street corners
- Breastfeeding consultation provided during home visits
- Print cartridges recycled at office supply stores
- Litter receptacles that make it easy to drive by and deposit litterbags
- Dental floss kept in the TV room or, better yet, attached to the remote control
- Xmas tree recycling drop-off at the local high school

#2: Extend Hours

Example: Vote by Mail

Oregon has one of the highest voter turnouts in the nation—at 74% for the 2004 presidential election compared with 64% nationwide.[7] Perhaps this is because it is so convenient, with Oregonians *voting only by mail*. There are no polling places, and election day is just a deadline to turn in your ballot and has been that way since 1998, when nearly 70% of Oregonians approved the Vote by Mail initiative. Some believe it is the most "effective, efficient and fraud-free way to conduct an election."[8]

Oregon's Vote by Mail system is simple, straightforward, and most of all, convenient. Ballots are mailed to registered voters 14 to 18 days before an election. Voters can complete the ballot "in the comfort of their own home" and on their own schedule. They have 2 weeks to return the ballot through the mail, or they can drop it off at one of many official conveniently located sites, including ones in a downtown park (see Figure 12.4). And there are additional advantages as well, including reduced election costs (since there are no polling places) and the fact that some feel voters give more thought to how they mark their ballots, having access to campaign materials at their fingertips.

Figure 12.4   One of Oregon's Conveniently Located Ballot Boxes in a Park in Downtown Portland

As one editorial opinion expressed: "While the idea of the polling place at your local elementary school is something that provokes nostalgia in many of us, the realities of modern life as well as the demands on election officials outstrip any nostalgia we may feel for voting at a polling place. . . . Isn't the true definition of 'democracy in action' one where the mechanism for casting ballots advantages the voter, not the system set up to count the ballots?"[9]

Additional examples of strategies that offer target audiences more options in terms of time and day of the week include the following:

- Licensed child care searches online (versus calling a telephone center during normal business hours)
- 24-hour help lines for counseling and information
- Recycling centers open on Sundays
- Natural yard care workshops offered weekday evenings

#3: Be There at the Point of Decision Making

Example: Ecstasy Pill Testing at Nightclubs

DanceSafe is a nonprofit organization promoting health and safety within the rave and nightclub community. They report that they neither condone nor condemn the use of any drug. Rather, they engage in efforts to reduce drug-related harm by providing health and safety information and on-site pill testing to those who use.[10] In 2006, they had more than a dozen chapters throughout the United States.

Among other programs and services, volunteers in communities with chapters offer *on-site pill testing* to ecstasy users at raves, nightclubs, and other public events where ecstasy is being used socially. Users who are unsure of the authenticity of a pill they possess can bring it to a booth or table where trained harm reduction volunteers will test it for use. DanceSafe reports on their Web site that volunteers staff booths at raves, nightclubs, and other dance events, where they also provide information on drugs, safe sex, and other health and safety issues concerning the dance community (such as driving home safely and protecting one's hearing).[11]

They cite two fundamental operating principles: *harm reduction and popular education.* They believe that "combining these two philosophies enables them to create successful, peer-based educational programs to reduce drug abuse and empower young people to make healthy, informed lifestyle choices."[12] They believe that "while abstinence is the only way to avoid all the harms associated with drug use, harm reduction programs provide non-abstentionist health and safety information under the recognition that many people are going to choose to experiment with drugs despite all the risks involved. Harm reduction information and services help people use as safely as possible as long as they continue to use."[13]

Other creative solutions to influence "just in time" decision making include the following:

- Place a glass bowl of fruits and vegetables at eye level in the refrigerator versus in closed drawers on the bottom shelf.
- Negotiate with retailers to place natural fertilizers in a prominent display at the end of the aisle.
- Place a small, inexpensive plastic magnifier on fertilizer jugs so that gardeners can read the small print, including instructions for safe usage.

#4: Make the Location More Appealing

Example: Bicycle Paths and Lanes in Los Angeles

One of the major barriers a potential bicyclist will give for not commuting by bike to work is the lack of safe, pleasant, and interconnected bike paths and lanes. In 1994, the City of Los Angeles, led by its Department of City Planning, developed its first-ever comprehensive Bicycle Plan. It was adopted by the city council in 1996 and then provided the Department of Transportation a template for bicycle paths, lanes, and a myriad of bicycle amenities and policies to be implemented throughout the city.

And the plan has a goal, one of increasing bicycle travel in the city to *5% of all utilitarian trips taken* by 2025, the year the plan is expected to be fully implemented. Public input for the plan was provided primarily through the city's Bicycle Advisory Committee (no bicycle advocacy group existed in Los Angeles at the time). The public learned about potential bike routes by visiting the committee's "war room," which posted the city's arterial roadway system maps and provided an opportunity for citizen reactions and recommendations.

To date (2007) the city has installed 47 miles of bicycle paths, 130 miles of bicycle lanes, and 156 miles of bicycle routes (see Figure 12.5). In addition, the Los Angeles Department of Transportation has installed over 2,500 inverted-U bicycle racks, developed and distributed over 250,000 comprehensive city bicycle maps, and is working on a myriad of funded bicycle path, lane, and parking projects to be put on the ground in the next 5 years. And data from the 2004 census show progress, with bicycle mode-share (percentage of trips) at 1.8%.[14]

Figure 12.5 Making Bicycling More Appealing and Safer in Los Angeles, With the Orange Line Bike Path Built in Conjunction With a Metro Bus Rapid Transit Project

Additional examples of enhanced locations include the following:

- Conveniently located teen clinics that have reading materials and décor to which the market can relate
- Stairways in office buildings that employees would want to take, ones that are well lit, carpeted, and have art exhibits on the walls that get changed out once a month
- Organized walking groups for seniors in shopping malls

#5: Overcome Psychological Barriers Associated With Place

Example: Pets on the Net

It is estimated that close to 10 million dogs end up in shelters across America every year and only about 25% get adopted.[15] Potential pet owners have several considerations (barriers) associated with visiting animal shelters to see what pets are available. In addition to the time it takes to travel to a center, some describe the psychological risk, a concern that they might take home a pet that isn't what they are really looking for. They worry they won't be able to say no. Viewing pets available for adoption on the Internet can help reduce both of these costs.

Many humane societies across the country have created Web sites where all or some of the pets currently available for adoption are featured, 24 hours a day, 7 days a week. As illustrated in the photo on Sacramento's Pets on the Net Web site, detailed information on the pet includes a personality profile based on information provided by the previous owner (see Figure 12.6). Web site visitors are told that adoptions are on a first-come, first-serve basis, and directions to the facility are provided.[16] Some Web sites include features such as daily updates, an opportunity to put a temporary hold on an animal, information on how to choose the right shelter pet, and reasons the pet was given up for adoption. A few national sites offer the ability to search nationwide for a pet by providing criteria such as desired breed, gender, age, size, and geographic locales.

Additional examples of strategies that reduce psychological barriers of "the place" include the following:

Name: **Jake**

Sex: Neutered Male

Age: 3 yrs

Breed: German Shepherd/Boxer

Color: Brown/Black, Bicolor

Personality Profile:
Hey there! I'm Jake. I'm a friendly and playful young dog in need of a good home, and a little love and guidance from someone special like you! I walk well on a leash and I like to ride in the car, so maybe we could run errands together! Please come and adopt me and give me the chance I deserve.

CASE: 47862A

Figure 12.6 Pets on the Net: Reduces a Concern With Not Being Able to Say No[17]

- Needle exchange services provided by a health clinic on a street corner or from a mobile van versus at the facility of a community clinic
- Offering a Web site to help youth quit smoking, with an option to e-mail a counselor instead of calling—an option some research with youth indicates just "isn't going to happen"

#6: Be More Accessible Than the Competition

Example: School Vending Machine Reform

Fifty-four million students attend nearly 123,000 elementary, middle, and high schools across America, making schools a natural "place" to influence food choice and to make healthy options the most accessible ones.[18] And yet, a survey in 2000 for the Centers for Disease Control and Prevention's School Health Policies and Programs Study concluded that 43% of elementary schools, 89.4% of middle/junior high, and 98.2% of senior high schools had either a vending machine or a school store, canteen, or snack bar where students could purchase competitive foods or beverages, ones other than meals served through the U.S. Department of Agriculture (USDA) school breakfast, school lunch, and after-school snack programs.[19] And unfortunately, children tend to choose food and beverages from among these competitive ones that are higher in calories and lower in nutritional value.[20]

Debates have heated up regarding soda and food vending machines in elementary, middle/junior, and high schools. And many of these are taking place "upstream," with a focus on influencing policies. According to the USDA, competitive food policies exist in many states and include laws that restrict access to food and beverage vending machines, school canteens, and stores at certain times during the school day or limit access to foods with minimum nutritional value.[21] As of 2005, state legislatures in at least 39 states have considered or enacted legislation related to the nutritional quality of school foods and beverages. This includes 20 states in which school nutrition legislation was considered in 2005, 17 states in which such legislation was enacted, 1 state in which a legislative resolution was sent to the lieutenant governor, and 1 state in which such legislation was vetoed.[22] And this is not just a state issue, with some cities and local school districts having taken the lead and enacted policies to ban or replace certain foods and beverages in vending machines or restrict student access to the machines.

Other examples in which the desired behavior is made more accessible relative to the competition include the following:

- Family-friendly lanes in grocery stores where candy, gum, and adult magazines have been removed from the checkout stand
- High-occupant vehicle lanes that reward high-occupant vehicles with less traffic congestion (most of the time)

#7: Make Access to the Competition More Difficult or Unpleasant

Example: Tobacco's "25-Foot Rule"

On December 8, 2005, Washington became the fifth state to implement a comprehensive statewide law prohibiting smoking in all indoor public places and workplaces, including restaurants, bars, taverns, bowling alleys, skating rinks, and nontribal casinos. But this law went further than any state had to that point in time. Unlike Washington's measure, most other statewide bans exempt some businesses, such as bars, private clubs, card rooms, and cigar lounges. And no state has a deeper no-smoking buffer than Washington's 25-foot rule that prohibits smoking within 25 feet of entrances, exits, windows that open, and ventilation intakes that serve indoor public places or places of employment.

This (upstream) measure, supported by the American Cancer Society and the American Lung Association, created a heated and emotional debate for months before the election on local talk shows and editorial pages. Opponents argued that bars would be put out of business, people would lose their jobs, all the patrons (and revenues) would just move to tribal casinos that would be exempt from the law, and outside dining would decline. And since people can simply choose to work at or frequent a nonsmoking restaurant or bar, why remove their choice? More than a year after the measure went into effect, some are still angry and advocating with legislators to amend at least the "draconian" 25-foot rule: "It's overly harsh. It's turning my servers into cops. They are working for tips and to take care of customers—not to be authority figures."[23]

But research shows that state tobacco prevention programs must be broad-based and comprehensive to be effective and that requiring smokers to "step out in the rain" would be a significant deterrent. With one of the lowest smoking rates in the country (17.6% of adults in 2005), Washington's Tobacco Prevention and Control Program also provides services to help people, restricts the ability of kids to get tobacco, conducts public awareness and media campaigns, supports programs in communities and schools, and evaluates the effectiveness of its activities.[24]

Other examples limiting access to competitive behaviors include the following:

- Campaigns offering coupons for lockboxes for safe gun storage and distributing brochures listing convenient retail locations for purchase
- Distributing padlocks for home liquor cabinets to reduce alcohol access for minors—better yet, advocating with home builders to make these standard in new homes
- Pruning bushes in city parks so that youth are not able to gather in private and share their cigarettes and beer

#8: Be Where Your Target Audience Shops

Example: Mammograms in the Mall

The following excerpt from an article in the *Detroit Free Press* provides an example of reducing barriers through improving access and location appeal.[25]

> Many women already pick up birthday gifts, grab dinner, and get their hair cut at the malls, so why not schedule their annual mammograms there, as well? With a concept that screams "no more excuses," the Barbara Ann Karmanos Cancer Institute will open a cancer prevention center at the Somerset Collection South in Troy in September. A first for Michigan and the Detroit Institute, the mall-located screening center will provide a comfortable, spalike atmosphere for patients in a less intimidating setting than a traditional doctor's office or hospital.
>
> Targeting shoppers, mall workers—including about 3,000 women—and the 100,000 employees near the mall, Karmanos is renovating a 2,000-square-foot space in the lower level of the mall. The center initially will focus on breast cancer prevention, with clinical breast exams and mammography available. However, services could expand to prostate, lung, and gastrointestinal cancer screenings and bone density testing, said Yvette Monet, a Karmanos spokeswoman. Taking its cues from the spas, the Karmanos Prevention Center will pamper patients with privacy, peace and quiet, and warm terry cloth robes.
>
> The center is expected to encourage regular mammograms and breast exams. Nearly 44,000 women in the United States died last year from breast cancer—including 1,500 in Michigan—even though American Cancer Society studies show early diagnosis can mean a 97% survival rate. The Karmanos Center is expected to reach women who think they are too busy to get mammograms or are afraid to do so. "This is intended to be a nonclinical-type setting that will feature soothing shades of blue and comfy couches," Monet said.

Other examples of similar opportunities to provide services and tangible objects where your target market is already shopping include the following:

- Distributing sustainable seafood guides at the fish counter of fish markets
- Providing litterbags at gas pumps, similar to pet waste bags in parks
- Giving demonstrations on how to select a proper life vest at sporting goods stores
- Offering beauty salon clients laminated cards to hang on a shower nozzle with instructions and reminders to conduct a monthly breast self-exam

#9: Be Where Your Target Audience Hangs Out

Example: HIV/AIDS Tests in Gay Bathhouses

A headline in the *Chicago Tribune* on January 2, 2004, exemplifies this ninth-place strategy: "Rapid HIV tests offered where those at risk gather: Seattle health officials get aggressive in AIDS battle by heading into gay clubs, taking a drop of blood and providing answers in 20 minutes." The article described a new and aggressive effort for Public Health-Seattle & King County, one that included administering rapid result HIV tests in bathhouses and gay sex clubs.[26]

To this point in time it had been common for health counselors to visit bathhouses to administer standard HIV testing. Although this certainly made taking the test more convenient, it didn't address the place barrier associated with getting the results. They would still need to then make an appointment at a medical clinic and then wait at least a week to hear the results, a critical step in the prevention and early treatment process that was not always taken. With this new effort, counselors would be with clients to present their results within about 20 minutes of taking the test. To address concerns with whether people carousing in a nightclub could handle the sudden news if it turned out they were HIV positive, counselors would refuse to test people who were high, drunk, or appeared emotionally unstable.

Initially, apparently the bathhouse and sex club owners expressed concern with health officials about whether this effort might offend customers, even drive them away. Perhaps the fact that one of the clubs a year and a half later touted the availability of free and anonymous rapid HIV tests every Friday night from 10 p.m. to 2 a.m. on its Web site is an indication of how things actually turned out.[27] Between July 2003 and February 2007, 1,559 rapid HIV tests were administered to gay male patrons of these bathhouses, identifying 33 new cases, a rate of 2.1%. In general, new case-finding rates of greater than or equal to 1% are considered cost effective, and screening in the baths has substantially exceeded that threshold.[28]

To further explore this strategy, imagine places where these target audiences hang out that you might consider a distribution channel for your services or tangible objects associated with your campaign:

- Where could you find groups of seniors so you can give them small, portable pedestrian flags to wave when entering crosswalks?
- What would be a good place to distribute condoms to Hispanic farmworkers who are having unprotected sex with prostitutes while away from home?
- In an effort to increase voting among college students, where could you distribute voter registration packets?
- Where could you efficiently provide dog owners a mail-in pet licensing form?

#10: Work With Existing Distribution Channels

Example: Influencing the Return of Unwanted Drugs to Pharmacies

In 2006, Washington State launched a pilot program to influence households to properly dispose of unwanted pharmaceuticals. Their story provides an inspirational illustration of leveraging existing distribution channels (as well as formative research).

Background: This social marketing effort is intended to impact four environmental and health concerns: (1) water pollution: Pharmaceuticals are being detected at low levels in wastewater systems, streams, rivers, and the Puget Sound environment. Improper disposal of unwanted pharmaceuticals, whether over-the-counter medicines or controlled substances, contributes to this pollution; (2) long-term exposure: There is increasing concern regarding the disposal of pharmaceuticals in landfills. Captured leachate from landfills is typically discharged to water bodies via treatment facilities that don't extract pharmaceuticals. There is also concern about the long-term leaking from landfill liners, resulting in discharge of pharmaceutical contaminants to groundwater; (3) poisoning: Medications account for the most common poison exposure category in the United States. The massive number of medications available presents a substantial accidental poisoning risk if they are not properly stored or disposed; (4) diversion to other users: Prescription drugs, over-the-counter medications, and controlled substances are targets of drug users and abusers. Unsecured disposal to the garbage or using improper facilities may result in increased drug abuse.

Target Audience, Desired Behavior, and Audience Research: The concept was simple. Program planners wanted to test a collection system that would be able to safely sweep out significant amounts of unused, expired, or otherwise unwanted medications from households but were not sure what option would be most appealing to target audiences. A telephone survey of 400 households in King County helped gain a greater understanding of current attitudes, practices, and preferences regarding disposal of unused or expired medicines.[29] The following highlights provided strategic guidance and buy-in:

- About a half (52%) of the respondents said that their household typically disposes of unwanted medicines in the garbage, while 20% flush them down the toilet or sink.
- More than a third (39%) said that they have 10 or more medicine containers in their household. Only 1% said that they have no medicine containers.
- Only a third (33%) said that they are currently using or planning to use all of the medicines in their household in the next 6 months. The majority (57%) are using or planning to use some portion of their medicines, and 10% don't plan to use any of it.
- Three quarters (74%) of respondents reported that they are willing to properly dispose of their unwanted medicines if a convenient location is offered.

- A considerable majority (84%) indicated that a local pharmacy would be the most convenient place to dispose of their unwanted medicines. Only a small portion preferred the idea of a special community collection event (5%), a police or sheriff's office (4%), or a household hazardous waste site (2%).
- Four in five (80%) respondents said they'd likely return their unwanted medicines to a secure drop box set up at their pharmacy.
- More than half of respondents (53%) agreed that manufacturers of medicines should be responsible for funding a safe and convenient disposal solution.

Strategy: Based on survey results, a take-back, drop-box approach at clinical and retail pharmacies was determined to be the best option to test. Pharmacists will be able to accept pharmaceuticals during open hours via a secure, mail box–style container near the pharmacy counter. Pharmacists will not handle or inventory the pharmaceuticals being returned, and customers will be given an opportunity to remove or mark out all identifying information.

The collection bucket will be serviced by the same distributor who delivered pharmaceutical products to the pharmacy. Each secured bucket will have tracking technology to identify and track the shipment of the material, for both security and accountability. The distributor will then ship the filled and tagged buckets to a secure consolidation point and subsequently arrange for final disposal following procedures approved by the Washington State Board of Pharmacy and the Washington State Department of Ecology. (Note: At the time this went to press, more than a ton of pharmaceutical products had been dropped off, and the pilot project team was in negotiations with the federal Drug Enforcement Administration for a licensure, or exemption, from the Controlled Substances Act while conducting this tightly monitored test in order to be able to accept all types of pharmaceuticals legally.)

Group Health Cooperative and Bartell Drugs Company volunteered to serve as locations for collection during the 2-year-long pilot program. This will include approximately 70 locations statewide.

Evaluation and Budget Plan: During the pilot, volumes of pharmaceuticals returned will be measured and a survey will assess consumer behaviors, attitudes, and knowledge. Program operational problems and success will be documented and a sampling protocol will be implemented in order to characterize what and how many pharmaceuticals are turned in. The set-up costs for the pilot would be jointly financed by public agencies and participating private companies. Costs will include those associated with purchasing secure containers, advertising, collection, transportation, and disposal.[30]

MANAGING DISTRIBUTION CHANNELS

In situations in which tangible objects and services are included in your campaign or program, a network of intermediaries may be needed to reach target audiences through the distribution channel.

Kotler and Roberto describe four types of distribution levels to be considered, illustrated in Figure 12.7.[31] In a *zero-level channel*, there is direct distribution from the social marketer to the target audience. Tangible objects and services are distributed by mail, over the Internet, door-to-door, or through outlets managed by the social marketing organization (e.g., the health department providing immunizations at community clinics). In a *one-level channel*, there is one distribution intermediary, most commonly a retailer (e.g., grocery stores where health care officials set up tables for flu shots). In a *two-level channel*, you would be dealing with the local distributor as well as the retailer (e.g., working with distributors of life vests to include safety tips attached to the product). In a *three-level channel*, a national distributor finds local distributors.

Choices regarding distribution channels and levels are made on the basis of variables such as the number of potential target adopters, storage facilities, retail outlet opportunities, and transportation costs, with a focus on choosing the most efficient and cost-effective option for achieving program goals and reaching target audiences. This process can be guided by several principles offered by Coughlan and Stern:[32]

- The purpose of channel marketing is to satisfy end users, which makes it critical that all channel members have their attention on this focus and that channels are selected on the basis of the unique characteristic of each market segment.
- Marketing channels "play a role of strategic importance in the overall presence and success a company enjoys in the marketplace."[33] They contribute to the

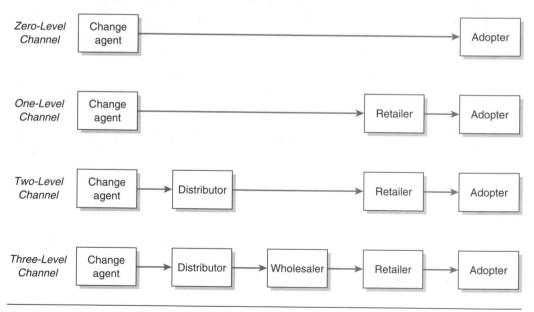

Figure 12.7 Distribution Channels of Various Levels

product's positioning and the organization's image, along with the product's features, pricing, and promotional strategies.

- Marketing channels are more than just a way to deliver the product to the customer. They can also be an effective means to add value to the core product, evidenced, for example, by the fact that employees are often willing to pay a slightly higher price for the convenience of bottled water at a vending machine at a work site than they would in a retail location.
- Issues currently challenging channel managers include increasingly demanding consumers, management of multiple channels, and the globalization of markets.

ETHICAL CONSIDERATIONS WHEN SELECTING DISTRIBUTION CHANNELS

Issues of equity and unintended consequences are common when planning access strategies. How do working mothers get their children to the free immunization clinic if it is only open on weekday mornings? How do drug addicts get clean needles if they don't have transportation to the exchange site? In these cases, "more" of this place tool may be just the answer, with mobile units, for example, traveling to villages and neighborhoods to reach more of the target population.

Do critics of the ecstasy-testing volunteers at dance clubs have legitimate and higher priority concerns that this will increase use of the drug? What about those who argue that restricting access (e.g., alcohol to teens) leads to more serious consequences (e.g., driving home drunk)? And does a safe gun storage campaign that distributes coupons for lockboxes send a message that having guns is a norm and might thereby increase ownership? One strategy to consider when addressing the potential for unintended consequences is to conduct a pilot and measure actual behavior changes, both intended and unintended. This data can then be used to conduct a cost-benefit analysis and help guide decision making for future efforts and potentially a quantifiable rationale for a sustainable effort and expanded markets.

Chapter Summary

Place, the third "P," is where and when the target market will perform the desired behavior, acquire any related tangible objects, and receive any associated services.

Distribution channels, as they are often referred to in the commercial sector, include more than physical locations, with other alternatives that may be more convenient for your target audience, including phone, mail, fax, Internet, mobile units, drive-throughs, home delivery, kiosks, and vending machines.

Your objective with the *place marketing tool* is to develop strategies that will make it as convenient and pleasant as possible for your target audience to perform the behavior, acquire any tangible objects, and receive any services. You were encouraged to consider the following winning strategies:

1. Make the location closer.
2. Extend hours.
3. Be there at the point of decision making.
4. Make the location more appealing.
5. Overcome psychological barriers related to "the place."
6. Be more accessible than the competition.
7. Make accessing the competition more difficult.
8. Be where your target audience shops or dines.
9. Be where your target audience hangs out.
10. Work with existing distribution channels.

And, finally, since this tool is often misunderstood, it is worth repeating that place is *not the same as communication channel,* which is where your communications will appear (e.g., brochures, radio ads, news stories, and personal presentations).

RESEARCH HIGHLIGHT

Observation

Research for Needle Exchange Programs

From The Tipping Point[34]

MALCOLM GLADWELL

In Baltimore, as in many communities with a lot of drug addicts, the city sends out a van stocked with thousands of clean syringes to certain street corners in its inner-city neighborhoods at certain times in the week. The idea is that for every dirty, used needle that addicts hand over, they can get a free clean needle in return. In principle, needle exchange sounds like a good way to fight AIDS, since the reuse of old HIV-infected needles is responsible for so much of the virus's spread. But, at least on first examination, it seems to have some obvious limitations. Addicts, for one, aren't the most organized and reliable of people. So what guarantee is there that they are going to be able to regularly meet up with the needle van? Second, most heroin addicts go through about one needle a day, shooting up at least five or six times—if not more—until the tip of the syringe becomes so blunt that it is useless. That's a lot of needles. How can a van, coming by once a week, serve the needs of addicts who are shooting up around the clock? What if the van comes by on Tuesday, and by Saturday night an addict has run out?

To analyze how well the needle program was working, researchers at Johns Hopkins University began, in the mid-1990s, to ride along with the vans in order to talk to the people handing in needles. What they found surprised them. They had assumed that addicts brought in their own dirty needles for exchange, that IV drug users got new needles the way that you or I buy milk: going to the store when it is open and picking up enough for the week. But what they found was that a handful of addicts were coming by each week with knapsacks bulging with 300 or 400 dirty needles at a time, which is obviously far more than they were using themselves. These men were then going back to the street and selling the clean needles for $1 each. The van, in other words, was a kind of syringe wholesaler. The real retailers were these handfuls of men—these *superexchangers*—who were prowling around the streets and shooting galleries, picking up dirty needles, and then making a modest living on the clean needles they received in exchange.

At first some of the program's coordinators had second thoughts. Did they really want taxpayer-funded needles financing the habits of addicts? But then they realized that they had stumbled inadvertently into a solution to the limitations of needle exchange programs. "It's a much, much better system," says Tom Valente, who teaches in the Johns Hopkins School of Public Health. "A lot of people shoot on Friday and Saturday night, and they don't

necessarily think in a rational way that they need to have clean tools before they go out. The needle exchange program isn't going to be available at that time—and certainly not in the shooting galleries. But these (super-exchangers) can be there at times when people are doing drugs and when they need clean syringes. The provide twenty-four seven service, and it doesn't cost us anything."

One of the researchers who rode with the needle vans was an epidemiologist by the name of Tom Junge. He would flag down the superexchangers and interview them. His conclusion is that they represent a very distinct and special group. "They are all very well connected people," Junge says. "They know Baltimore inside and out. They know where to go to get any kind of drug and any kind of needles. They have street savvy. I would say that they are unusually socially connected. They have a lot of contacts. . . . I would have to say the underlying motive is financial or economic. But there is definitely an interest in helping people out."

Does that sound familiar? The superexchangers are the Connectors of Baltimore's drug world. What people at Johns Hopkins would like to do is use the superexchangers to start a counter-drug epidemic. What if they took those same savvy, socially connected, altruistic people and gave them condoms to hand out, or educated them in the kinds of health information that drug addicts desperately need to know? Those superexchangers sound as though they have the skills to bridge the chasm between the medical community and the majority of drug users, who are hopelessly isolated from the information and institutions that could save their lives. They sound as if they have the ability to translate the language and ideas of health promotion into a form that other addicts could understand.

CHAPTER 13

Promotion

Deciding on Messages, Messengers, and Creative Strategies

Say the right thing/In the right way/to the right person/In the right places/Enough times.

—Lynne Doner Lotenberg

Consider for a moment the fact that this chapter on promotion is the 13th of 17 chapters in this book. Twelve chapters precede it. It is placed more than two thirds of the way into the journey to complete a social marketing plan. Those who started this book thinking, as many do, that marketing *is* promotion are probably the most surprised. We imagine and hope, however, after reading the first 12 chapters, you understand that you wouldn't have been ready before now to explore or use this final tool in the marketing mix.

Many of you who are following the planning process are probably eager for the more creative, often fun-filled exercises associated with brainstorming slogans, sketching out logos, picking out colors, even screening potential actors. Others find this the most intimidating, even dreaded, process of all, having experienced in the past that it can be fraught with internal battles over words, colors, and shapes, and in the end, experienced disappointment and frustration with their final materials or radio and television spots.

This time will be different. You have help. You know your target audience and a lot about them. You have clear behavior objectives in mind and understand what your potential customers really want out of performing the behavior and the barriers that could stop them in their tracks. You know now this understanding is your inspiration, a gift—one that has already helped you craft a powerful positioning statement, build a product platform, find incentives, and select distribution channels.

We predict your promotional efforts will go a lot better this time. And we think you'll be inspired by this opening story, one using storytelling in Rwanda to influence safe and responsible sexual behaviors.

Using Storytelling to Deliver Health Messages in Rwanda[1] (2007)

LYNNE DONER LOTENBERG, MA, SOCIAL MARKETING CONSULTANT

MICHAEL SIEGEL, MD, MPH, BOSTON UNIVERSITY

Health Unlimited Rwanda

Background

Rwanda is a small country in central Africa where about 90% of the population lives in rural areas. Women comprise more than half the population, with disproportionately high levels of widow-headed households.[2] Fifty percent of the population is under the age of 18, and over 30% of the children are orphans due to civil war and genocide in the 1990s and a high prevalence of HIV/AIDS.[3] The civil war also destroyed much of Rwanda's health infrastructure and resulted in the deaths or exile of many health professionals.

To increase public awareness and discussion of women's sexual and reproductive health issues leading to positive changes in knowledge, belief, attitude, and behavior in the target group, Health Unlimited (a British nongovernmental organization) established the Well Women Media Project-Africa Great Lakes Region. Communicating about women's sexual and reproductive health issues is a very challenging task in Rwanda, where most sexual and reproductive health issues—including sexuality, condom use, and family planning—are considered taboo.

Target Audience

The primary audiences are rural Rwandan women of reproductive age and youth. These groups are the most vulnerable part of the population; they live in extreme poverty and desperately need sexual and reproductive health information to avoid unwanted pregnancies, HIV/AIDS, and other sexually transmitted diseases. Men are a secondary audience, as they are the main partners in behavior change.

Desired Behavior

Discussions of sexual and reproductive health issues are the primary desired behavior. Such discussions are taboo in traditional Rwandan society; these topics are to be discussed only by adults and only in their bedroom or other private place. As a result, misinformation is common, and youth, in particular, lack knowledge critical to successfully avoiding HIV and other STDs as well as unplanned pregnancies.

Strategies

In Rwanda, radio reaches a wider audience than any other medium. Only 61% of the population is literate, and only 0.1% owns television sets.[4] About 42% own radios, but people in rural areas come together to listen to their favorite radio programs either at home, in the local bar, at the workplace, or on the bus.

Drama ranks among the three most popular types of programs.[5]

Because radio has such a wide audience and drama was popular, program managers developed a radio soap opera set in a fictional Rwandan village. The soap opera, titled *Urunana* (meaning "hand in hand" in Kinyarwanda, Rwanda's national language), is broadcast each Tuesday and Thursday evening. The soap opera format allows writers to connect with the audience through familiar characters, story lines, and humor to deliver relevant and accurate information, model behaviors, and encourage discussions on sexual and reproductive health issues.

Prior to developing the program, Health Unlimited Rwanda conducted a quantitative knowledge, attitudes, practices, and beliefs (KAPB) survey to identify knowledge gaps and misinformation to be addressed. They then conducted focus groups and interviews with key informants, which helped them develop ideas for the characters and settings. The name *Urunana* was drawn from the aspirations expressed by research participants.

The soap opera is set in Nyarurembo, a fictional but typical rural village with schools, a church, banana plantations, a river, houses, and roads in bad condition. Writers take great care to choose settings within the village that are appropriate for the characters and the scene and to include traditional practices around life cycle events (births, weddings, burials) that are not harmful (harmful traditions are addressed in a respectful way). The language used is what would be used in villages, with proverbs and idioms appropriate to the rural population. Three types of characters are used:

1. Positive role models, who deliver information on how disease is transmitted and uphold and reflect the values promoted in *Urunana*. For example, married couple Munyakazi and Mariana are used to show that anyone can get HIV (even though Munyakazi was a role model in his village, one day he cheated on his wife). These characters are also used to deliver messages on stigma and discrimination, as Munyakazi developed AIDS and Mariana cared for him until death.

2. Negative role models, who reject the values promoted in the program and get penalized for their actions. One example is Stefano, an irresponsible man in his late 40s who does not take care of his family, beats his wife, and takes a mistress. He contracts gonorrhea, gets his mistress pregnant, and is forced to flee the village. When he returns, his wife accepts him back in the home but refuses sex, recalling the health adviser's advice regarding what to do if one suspects a partner has had other sexual partners and therefore may have contracted HIV or another STD.

3. Doubters, who are unsure which side to take and are easily manipulated by both sides. As the plot develops, they realize they need to belong to the group that best serves their interests. They are rewarded or punished depending on the side they choose. Bushombe, *Urunana's* funniest character, is a doubter. After long years of a childless relationship with his wife, he tries to "prove his manhood" in an extramarital relationship. When it also proves fruitless, he must accept that he, rather than his wife, may have the fertility problem. Subsequently, he and his wife seek medical counsel at a hospital, Bushombe's fertility problem is treated, and they have a baby.

To further ensure that the *Urunana* stories are authentic and acceptable to the target audiences, each month a team of writers and producers visit various provinces in Rwanda to discuss reactions to past story lines, acting, and language and gather input on proposed story lines and message points, including what actions the characters would be likely to take and how they would discuss the various topics. In addition, for 4 days each year, the team of writers immerse themselves in rural village life by spending days and nights in peoples' homes to observe what they do and how they live rather than relying on what they say they do.

Outcomes

Urunana was the most popular radio program in Rwanda in 2005, with up to 74% of the population listening.[6] Listeners largely find the health messages relevant (91%), practical (76%), and acceptable (94%), but rates of understanding are somewhat lower (54%). Large proportions of listeners report that they engage in discussions of the sexual and reproductive health messages (55%–81%) and that they advise others on sexual reproductive health messages they have learned from the program (59%–81%).[7]

In addition, indirect and anecdotal evidence suggests that *Urunana*'s approach has made substantial impact not only on the target audience but also on policymaking and sexual and reproductive health in Rwanda.

PROMOTION: THE FOURTH "P"

Promotions are persuasive communications designed and delivered to inspire your target audience to action.

You will be highlighting your product's benefits, features, and any associated tangible objects and services. You will be touting any monetary and nonmonetary incentives as well. And you will be letting target adopters know where and when they can access any tangible objects and services included in your program's effort and/or where you are encouraging them to perform the desired behavior (e.g., recycle motor oil). In this step, you create the voice of your brand and decide how you will establish a dialogue and build relationships with your customer.[8]

Developing this communication strategy is the last component of Step 7: the Marketing Mix. Your planning process includes four major decisions:

1. *Messages:* What you want to communicate, inspired by what you want your target audience to do, know, and believe

2. *Messengers:* Who will deliver your messages or be perceived to be sponsoring or supporting your offer

3. *Creative Strategy:* What you will actually say and show and how you want to say it

4. *Communication Channels:* Where and when your messages will appear, distinct, of course, from distribution channels

This chapter discusses strategies for developing messages and choosing messengers and presents nine tips for developing creative strategies (how to say it). Chapter 14 covers communication channels.

A WORD ABOUT THE CREATIVE BRIEF

One of the most effective ways to establish clear messages, choose credible messengers, inspire winning creative strategies, and select effective communication channels is to develop a document called a creative brief, usually one to two pages in length.[9] It helps ensure that communications will be meaningful (pointing out benefits that make the product desirable), believable (the product will deliver on the promised benefits), and distinctive (how it is a better choice than competing behaviors).[10] Its greatest contribution is that it helps ensure that all team members, especially those in advertising and public relations firms working on the campaign, are in agreement with communication objectives and strategies prior to more costly development and production of communication materials. Typical elements of a creative brief are illustrated in the following section, with a sample creative brief featured in Table 13.1.

Key Message: This is a brief statement that summarizes the bottom-line message. This is not the actual slogan, tagline, or ultimate headline. In a social marketing campaign, at a minimum it includes the behavior you are trying to influence.

Target Audience: This section presents a brief description of the target audience in terms of key variables determined in Step 3. Most commonly, it will include a demographic and geographic profile of the target audience. It is helpful to include what you know about your audience's current knowledge, beliefs, and behaviors relative to the desired behavior, as well as to competing ones. Ideally, it describes the target's current stage of change and anything else that you think is special about them.

Communication Objectives: This section specifies what you want your target audience to *know* (think), *believe* (feel), and/or *do,* based on exposure to your communications. This can be taken directly from decisions made in Step 4. (Individual campaigns may or may not have all three types of objectives.)

Positioning Statement: The product positioning established earlier in Step 6 is presented here. This provides guidance to those selecting images and graphics and developing script and copy points.

Benefits to Promise: Key benefits the audience hopes they will receive from adopting the behavior were identified as the *core product* when developing the product platform in Step 7. The primary benefit may be expressed in terms of a cost that the audience can avoid by adopting the desired behavior (e.g., stiff penalties for drinking and driving).

Support for the Promise: This section refers to a brief list of additional benefits and highlights from product, price, and place, strategies established earlier in Step 7. The ones to be highlighted are those that would most help convince the target audience that they can perform the desired behavior, that the benefits are likely, and that they exceed perceived costs.

Openings: This final important section will be helpful to those selecting and planning communication channels. Siegel and Doner describe openings as "the times, places, and situations when the audience will be most attentive to, and able to act on, the message."[11] Input for this section will come from profiles and audience behaviors explored in Step 5 (barriers and benefits). Additional input may come from secondary and expert resources on the target market's lifestyle and media habits.

MESSAGE STRATEGY

At this point, you are focused on the content of your communications, not the ultimate slogans, scripts, or headlines. That comes later. What those developing your creative strategies need to know first is what responses you want from your target audience. In our social marketing model, you've already done the hard work here and can simply fill in the blanks to the following by refining and elaborating on campaign objectives established earlier in Step 4 and referencing barriers, benefits, and your competition from Step 5. Bullet points are usually adequate.

What do you want your target audience to do? What the specific desired behavior is your campaign is focused on (e.g., get an HIV/AIDS test 3 to 6 months after having had unprotected sex). It will also include any more immediate calls to action (e.g., call this toll-free number for locations in your area for free, rapid HIV/AIDS tests). If your behavior objective was stated in fairly broad terms (e.g., practice natural yard care techniques), this will be the time you break these down into more single, simple doable messages (e.g., leave grass clippings on the lawn).

What do you want them to know? Select key facts and information regarding your offer that should be included in campaign messages. If you are offering tangible objects or services related to your campaign (e.g., free quart-size ziplock bags at security checkpoints), you will want messages that inform target audiences *where and when they can be accessed*. There may be key points you want to make on *how to perform* the behavior (e.g., the limit for carry-on liquids is 3 ounces, and they must fit in a ziplocked 1-quart-sized bag). To highlight benefits of your offer, you may decide a key point you want them to know relates to *statistics on risks* associated with competing behaviors (e.g., makeup and other liquids not in these bags will be taken and discarded) and *benefits you promise* (e.g., having this ahead of time can save you and fellow passengers up to 20 minutes in lines).

Table 13.1   Creative Brief for a Youth Tobacco Prevention Campaign

Key Message:

Don't start to smoke or chew tobacco.

Target Audience:

Middle school and high school youth who don't currently smoke or chew tobacco, although they may have experimented with it in the past. They are vulnerable, however, to using tobacco because they have family members and friends who smoke or chew. They know many of the facts about the consequences of using tobacco. They've been exposed to them in health classes and may even have experienced the reality with family members who have smoking-related illnesses or who have died from smoking. The problem is, they don't believe it will happen to them. They don't really believe they will get addicted. There are many peer pressures to fit in by smoking. They also have heard that smoking is a great stress relief and is appealing to pass the time. Some think kids who smoke look older and cool.

Communication Objectives:

To Know: Addiction is real and probable.
To Believe: Smoking-related illnesses are shocking, "gross," and painful.
To Do: Refuse to try cigarettes or chew.

Benefits to Promise:

You will have a longer, healthier, and happier life, free of tobacco addiction.

Supports to Promise

- Real stories from real people who started smoking at a young age
- Stories of personal loss about having a family member die or about living with or dying from a smoking-related illness
- Graphic visuals depicting real, shocking, and "gross" consequences to the body
- Real facts from the American Cancer Society and Surgeon General

Openings:

- Listening to the radio
- Watching television
- Surfing the Internet
- Talking with friends

Postitioning:

People who smoke are risking their health and hurting their future families and friends. It's not worth it.

What do you want them to believe? This is a different question than what you want your target audience to know. This is about what you want your target audience to believe and/or feel as a result of your key messages. Your best inspiration for these points will be your barriers and benefits research. What did they say when asked why they weren't planning to vote (e.g., "My vote won't make a difference"); why they thought they were safe to drive home after drinking (e.g., "I've done it before and was perfectly fine"); or why they were hesitant to talk with their teen about suicide (e.g., "I might make him more likely to do it"). These are points you will want your communications to counter. And what was their response when you asked what would motivate them to exercise 5 days a week (e.g., "believing I would sleep better"), fix a leaky toilet (e.g., saving 200 gallons of water a day), or take the bus to work (e.g., having Wi-Fi available for the duration). These are points you'll want to put front and center.

Example: Booster Seats as a Better Alternative

While great strides have been made to protect infants and toddlers in a motor vehicle crash, preschoolers and young children remain at high risk of injury. Most of the nation's 20 million children aged 4–8 ride in motor vehicles either unprotected or use adult seatbelts that do not fit them properly. Seatbelts alone can cause serious internal injuries and even death (see Figure 13.1). Booster seats raise the child up so that the lap and shoulder belts fit the child. A booster seat provides a safe transition from child seats that have their own harness systems to adult lap and shoulder belts.

One-Sided Versus Two-Sided Messages

A one-sided message usually just praises the product, while a two-sided one also points out its shortcomings. In this spirit, for example, Heinz ran the message "Heinz Ketchup is slow good," and Listerine ran the message "Listerine tastes bad twice a day."[13]

Figure 13.1 Wanting Parents to See Booster Seats as Less Costly Than the Competition[12]

Intuitively, you might think that the one-sided presentations would be more effective (e.g., "Three out of four students drink less than four drinks at one sitting"). But research suggests that one-sided messages tend to work better with audiences that are initially favorably predisposed to your product. If your audience is currently "opposed" to your idea or has suspicions or negative associations, a two-sided argument might work better (e.g., "Although 25% of students drink more than four drinks at one sitting, most of us don't"). Furthermore, an organization launching a new brand whose other products are well accepted might think of favorably mentioning the existing products and then going on to praise the new one (e.g., "Click It or Ticket has saved lives, and now Drive Hammered, Get Nailed will too"). Research also indicates that two-sided messages tend to be more effective with better-educated audiences and/or those who are likely to be exposed to counterpropaganda. By mentioning a minor shortcoming in the product, it can take the edge off this mention when it comes from a competitor, much as a small discomforting inoculation now prevents a greater sickness later. But you must take care to inoculate only enough negative vaccine to make the buyer resistant to counterpropaganda, not to your own product.[14]

Messages Relative to Stages of Change

Messages will also be guided by your target audience's current stage of change. As mentioned in Chapter 6 on target markets, the marketer's role is to move target adopters to the next stage, influencing precontemplators to become contemplators, contemplators to take action, and those in action to make it a habit (maintenance). Most important, there are different recommended message strategies for each stage.[15]

For *precontemplators*, your major emphasis is on making sure your target audience is aware of the costs of competing behaviors and benefits of the new one. These are often stated using statistics and facts, especially ones that your target audience was not aware of—ones that serve as a wake-up call. When these facts are big news, they can often move some target audience members very quickly through subsequent stages— all the way to maintenance in some cases (e.g., when it was discovered that aspirin given to children for flu is related to a potentially fatal disease called Reye's syndrome).

For *contemplators* (now that they are "awake"), your message options include encouraging them to at least try the new behavior and/or restructure their environment to make adoption easier (e.g., put a recycle container under the kitchen sink). You'll want to dispel any myths (e.g., air bags are as good as seatbelts) and potentially address any concerns they have with their ability to successfully perform and maintain the behavior.

For those *in action*, you'll want them to start to see the benefits for having "gotten out of bed." Perhaps you will be acknowledging that they reached targeted milestones (e.g., 30 days without a cigarette) or persuading them to use prompts to ensure sustainability (e.g., put the laminated card to track monthly breast self-exams in the shower), and to sign pledges or commitments to "keep up the good work." Your messages will target a tendency to return to old habits and at the same time prepare them to create a new one.

For those in *maintenance,* you still have a role to play, for as you learned earlier, behavior change is spiral in nature, and we can easily regress back to any of the stages— even go "back to sleep." This is the group whose behavior you want to recognize, congratulate, feature, and reward. You want to be sure they are realizing the promised benefits, and you may want to occasionally remind them of the long-term gains they are bound to receive or contribute (e.g., a statement message on a utility bill that selectively thanks residents for helping to reduce peak hour electrical consumption by 6%).

MESSENGER STRATEGY

Who your target audience perceives to be delivering your message and what they think of this particular messenger can make or break the deal. And this is the right time to be choosing this messenger, as this decision will have important implications when developing the creative strategy as well as selecting media channels. You have three major options, described next, followed by considerations for choosing.

The sponsoring organization can be the *sole sponsor*, with campaign communications highlighting the organization's name (somewhere). A quick audit of social marketing campaigns is likely to indicate a public sector agency sponsor (e.g., EPA promoting energy-efficient appliances) or a nonprofit organization (e.g., American Cancer Society urging colon cancer screenings). Though not as frequent, the sole sponsor might be a for-profit organization (e.g., Safeco Insurance promoting "10 Tips to Wildfire Defense").

For many efforts, there will be *partners*, involved from the beginning in developing, implementing, and perhaps funding the campaign. In this scenario, target audiences may not be certain of the main or actual sponsors. These partners may form a coalition or just a project, one where the target audience may or may not be aware (or clear) what organizations are sponsoring the effort (e.g., a water quality consortium that includes utilities, departments of health, and an environmental advocacy group).

Some organizations and campaigns make effective use of *spokespersons* to deliver the messages, often achieving higher attention and recall, as well as increased credibility. In 2006, for example, Illinois Senator Barack Obama traveled to Kenya and received a public HIV test. He then spoke about his trip on World AIDS Day: "So we need to show people that just as there is no shame in going to the doctor for a blood test or a CAT scan or a mammogram, there is no shame in going for an HIV test. Because while there was once a time when a positive result gave little hope, today the earlier you know, the faster you can get help. My wife Michelle and I were able to take the test on our trip to Africa after the Centers for Disease Control informed us that by getting a simple 15-minute test, we may have encouraged as many as half-a-million Kenyans to get tested as well."[16]

You may want to include *endorsements* from outside organizations, often then seen as one of the messengers. These can range from simply including an organization's name or logo in your communications to more formal testimonials in support of your campaign's facts and recommendations (e.g., the American Lung Association verifying that a public health department's statistics on the dangers of secondhand tobacco smoke are scientifically based).

How do you choose? In the end, what you want is for your target audience to see the messenger, or messengers, as a *credible source* for the message. Three major factors have been identified as key to source credibility: expertise, trustworthiness, and likability.[17]

Expertise is the perceived knowledge the messenger has to back the claim. For a recent campaign encouraging 12-year-olds to receive the new human papillomavirus (HPV) vaccine to help prevent cervical cancer, the American Academy of Pediatrics was an important messenger, in addition to local health care providers. *Trustworthiness* is related to how objective and honest the source is perceived to be. Friends, for example, are more trusted than strangers, and people who are not paid to endorse a product are viewed as more trustworthy than people who are paid.[18] This is why for-profit organizations often need the partnership or at least the endorsement of a public agency or nonprofit organization, with target audiences innately skeptical about the commercial sector's motive (e.g., a pharmaceutical company encouraging childhood immunizations). *Likability* describes the source's attractiveness, with qualities like candor, humor, and naturalness making a source more likable.

The most credible source, of course, would be the option scoring highest on all three dimensions. Perhaps that's what inspired the strategy in the following example, one that will be featured as a research highlight at the end of this chapter as well.

Example: The Meth Project[19] in Montana

The United Nations has identified methamphetamine abuse as a growing global pandemic. Law enforcement departments across the United States rank meth as the #1 crime problem in America. In response to this growing public health crisis, Montana rancher Thomas M. Siebel established the Meth Project to significantly reduce meth use through public service messaging, community action, and public policy initiatives.

The state of Montana, where the Meth Project was first initiated, ranks among the top 10 states nationally in per capita treatment admissions for methamphetamine. The social costs reported on the project's Web site are staggering, and the human costs, incalculable: 52% of children in foster care are there due to meth, costing the state $12 million a year; 50% of adults in prison are there due to meth-related crime, costing the state $43 million a year; and 20% of adults in treatment are there for meth addiction, costing the state $10 million a year.

The Meth Project, launched in 2005, focuses on informing potential meth consumers about the product attributes and risks. The integrated program consists of an ongoing, research-based marketing campaign—supported by community outreach and public policy initiatives—that realistically and graphically communicates the risks of methamphetamine use.

At the core of the Meth Project's effort is research-validated, high-impact advertising with the tagline "Not Even Once" and bold images that communicate the risks of meth use. Television, print, radio, and a documentary feature testimonials from youth meth users (see Figure 13.2). Approaching meth use as a

Figure 13.2 The Primary Messengers for This Successful Effort Are Youth Meth Users

consumer product marketing problem, the Project aims to unsell meth. It organizes a broad range of community outreach programs to mobilize the people of Montana to assist in meth awareness and prevention activities. Through its Paint the State art contest, thousands of teens and their families were prompted to create highly visible public art with a strong anti-meth message. The Meth Project is now being adopted by other states, including Arizona, Illinois, and Idaho.

CREATIVE STRATEGY

Your creative strategy will translate the content of your intended, desired messages to specific communications. This will include everything from logos, typeface, taglines, headlines, copy, visuals, and colors in printed materials to script, actors, scenes, and sounds in broadcast media. You will be faced with choosing between informational appeals that elaborate on behaviors and their benefits and emotional appeals using fear, guilt, shame, love, or surprise. Your goal is to develop (or approve) communications that will capture the attention of your target audience and persuade them to adopt the desired behavior. We present nine tips in these next sections for you to consider and to help you and others decide.

Creative Tip #1: Keep It Simple and Clear[20]

Given the inherent focus of a social marketing campaign on behaviors, try to make your instructions simple and clear. Assume, for a moment, that your target audience is interested, even eager, to adopt the behavior. Perhaps it was something you said or something they were already inclined to do and they are just waiting for clear instructions. Messages like this are probably familiar to you. "Eat five or more fruits and vegetables a day." "Wash your hands long enough to sing the Happy Birthday song twice." "Move right for sirens and lights." "Check your fire alarm batteries when you reset your clocks in the fall and spring." Consider how easy these make it for you to know if you had performed the desired behavior and can therefore count on receiving the promised benefits. Often visual instructions can help make the behavior seem simple and clear. You have, no doubt, seen many versions of messages in hotel rooms asking us to let staff know if we are happy to sleep on our sheets another night and to reuse our towels. Notice how quickly you know what to do in a hotel with a sign such as the one in Figure 13.3.

Figure 13.3 Visual Graphics Make It Easy and Quick to Know What to Do

Creative Tip #2: Focus on Audience Benefits

Since, as Roman and Maas suggest, people don't buy products but instead buy expectations of benefits,[21] creative strategies should consider highlighting benefits your target audience wants (most) and expects in return for costs associated with performing the behavior. This would be especially effective when the perceived benefits already outweigh perceived costs. The target audience just needs to be prompted and reminded of this, as they were in the following example.

Example: "Be Under Your Own Influence"

In an article in the *Social Marketing Quarterly* in the summer of 2006, Kelly, Comello, and Slater describe the development of a school and community-based media campaign that was shown to reduce uptake of substances (including marijuana) by 40%.[22] The campaign was tested in a randomized community trial funded by the National Institute on Drug Abuse. Sixteen communities (eight treatment and eight control) from across the United States participated in the study. The campaign, with the tagline "Be Under Your Own Influence," emphasized personal autonomy and future aspirations. Based on findings from the literature and focus groups, it was decided that messages should not focus on long-term health risks, preach to kids, or put down any particular group. Instead, messages highlighted youth norms and were seen as unique with their emphasis on the inconsistency of drug use with personal aspirations and valued social relationships. Creative executions encouraged youth to aspire to a bright future and to consider the inconsistency of substance use with attaining that future (see Figure 13.4).[23]

Figure 13.4 Posters With a Focus on Benefits Versus Costs[25]

Creative Tip #3: When Using Fear, Follow Up With Solutions and Use Credible Sources

Social marketers debate frequently about whether or not to use "fear appeals." Some researchers suggest that part of the reason is the lack of distinction between a fear appeal and what might better be called a "threat appeal."[25] They argue that threats simply illustrate undesirable consequences from certain behaviors (e.g., cancer from smoking) and that the emotion triggered may in fact not be one of fear, which some worry can immobilize the audience.

Others focus on scenarios and strategies where fear appeals work best. Kotler and Roberto point to research by Sternthal and Craig suggesting that decisions to execute fear-based messages should take several factors into account:[26]

- A strong fear-based appeal works best when it is accompanied by *solutions* that are both effective and easy to perform. Otherwise, you may be better off with a moderate appeal to fear (see Figure 13.5).

- A strong fear-based appeal may be most persuasive to those who have *previously been unconcerned* about a particular problem. Those who already have some concern may perceive a message of fear as going too far, which will inhibit their change of attitudes or behaviors.

- An appeal to fear may work better when it is directed toward *someone who is close to a potential target adopter rather than to the target adopter*. This may explain some research indicating fear appeals are more effective with older people.[27]

- The more credible the source, the more persuasive the fear-based appeal, with a more *credible source* reducing the chances the audience will discount or underestimate the fear-based appeal (see Figure 13.6).

Creative Tip #4: Try for Messages That Are Vivid, Personal, and Concrete[30]

McKenzie-Mohr and Smith believe one of the most effective ways to ensure attention and memorability is to present information that is vivid, concrete, and personal. They point to a variety of ways to make this happen.

Vivid information, they describe, increases the likelihood that a message will stand out

Figure 13.5 A Fear Appeal From a Credible Source: "The Surgeon General Warns That Smoking Is a Frequent Cause of Wasted Potential and Fatal Regret"[28]

against all the other information that is competing for our attention. Furthermore, because it is vivid, we are more likely to remember it at a later time. In a home energy audit, for example, an assessor was trained to present vivid analogies: "You know, if you were to add up all the cracks around and under these doors here, you'd have the equivalent of a hole the size of a football in your living room wall. Think for a moment about all the heat that would escape from a hole that size."[31]

Information that is *personalized* uniquely addresses your target audience's preferences, wants, and needs, fully informed by their perceived barriers and benefits for the behavior. To influence energy conservation, for example, they have a suggestion for utilities. Show the percentage of home energy by use item. Rather than using bars for the graph, replace them with a picture of the item itself (furnace, water heater, major appliances, lighting, etc.) and the corresponding energy use in the home.[32]

Figure 13.6 A Fear Appeal Followed by a Solution[29]

And they illustrate information that is *concrete* with an example of a more powerful way to depict waste. Instead of stating that Californians each produce 1,300 pounds of waste annually, Shawn Burn at the California Polytechnic State University depicts Californians' annual waste as "enough to fill a two-lane highway, ten feet deep, from Oregon to the Mexican border."[33]

We think the postcard illustrated in Figure 13.7 used for a youth tobacco prevention campaign in Washington State demonstrates that a creative strategy can be vivid, personal and concrete.

Creative Tip #5: Make Messages Easy to Remember

The magic of persuasive communications is to bring your messages to life in the minds of the target audience. And as Kotler and Keller describe, every detail matters. Consider, they suggest, how the legendary private sector ad taglines listed in Table 13.2 were

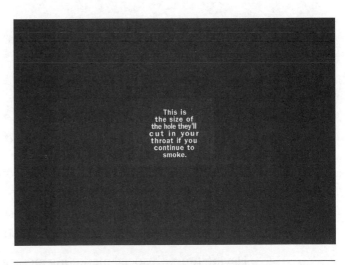

Figure 13.7 A Vivid, Personal, and Concrete Creative Strategy[34]

Table 13.2   Sample Ad Taglines

Brand Theme	Ad Tagline
Our hamburgers are bigger.	Where's the Beef? (Wendy's restaurants)
Our tissue is softer.	Please, Don't Squeeze the Charmin (Charmin bathroom tissue)
No hard sell, just a good car.	Drivers Wanted (Volkswagen automobiles)
We don't rent as many cars, so we have to do more for our customers.	We Try Harder (Avis auto rental)
We provide long-distance phone service.	Reach Out and Touch Someone (AT&T telecommunications)

SOURCE: Kotler, P., & Keller, K. (2005). *Marketing Management* (12th ed., p. 545). Upper Saddle River, NJ: Prentice Hall.

able to bring to life the brand themes listed on the left. Consider, as well, how familiar many or most of them (still) are for you:

A quick audit of familiar, perhaps even "famous," social marketing messages provides a few additional clues as to what seems to help target audiences remember what to do, especially when your communications aren't close at hand:

- *Try rhyming* techniques such as "Click It or Ticket" and "If it's yellow let it mellow, and if it's brown flush it down."
- Those that *surprise* you may be more likely to stick with you, such as "Save the Crabs. Then Eat 'Em."
- Create a simple and memorable mental *picture* like "Drop. Cover. Hold" in case of an earthquake.
- Connect the timing to some other *familiar event* like a birthday with "Get a colonoscopy when you turn 50."
- Leverage the *familiarity of another brand or slogan* as "Just Say No" did with Nike's "Just Do It."

Creative Tip #6: Sometimes Have a Little Fun

Having fun with social marketing messages is often as controversial as using fear-based appeals. We suggest the key here is to know when it is an appropriate and potentially effective solution—and when it isn't. A host of variables will impact your success, including your target audience (e.g., demographics, psychographics, geographics), whether the social issue is one that your target audience can "laugh about," and how a humorous approach contrasts with what has been used in the past to impact this issue.

In general, humorous messages are most effective when they represent a *unique approach* for the social issue. Consider how surprised and perhaps delighted you would be, for example, to read a sign in a subway in New York like the one in Figure 13.8. There are probably opportunities for humor where your target audience gets a kick out of *laughing at themselves or with others*. The Ad Council's Small Steps campaign, launched in 2004 for the U.S. Department of Health and Human Services, is a great example. Campaign elements use humor to inspire overweight adults to incorporate some of the 100 suggested small steps into their hectic lives (see Figure 13.9).[35]

On the other hand, humorous messages are not as effective for *complex messages*. There would be no benefit, and perhaps even a detriment, to a campaign to influence parents to childproof their home, an effort involving multiple, specific instructions. Nor is it appropriate for issues with *strong cultural, moral, or ethical concerns* (e.g., child abuse or domestic violence).

Creative Tip #7: Try for a "Big Idea"

A "big idea" brings the message strategy to life in a distinct and memorable way.[37] In the advertising business, the big idea is thought of by some as the Holy Grail, a creative solution that in just a few words or one image sums up the compelling reason to buy.[38] It takes message strategy statements that tend to be plain, straightforward outlines of benefits and desired positioning and transforms them into a compelling campaign concept.[39] It might be inspired by asking yourself if you only had "one thing" you could say about your product, how would you say it and how would you show it? Others suggest that getting to this is not a linear process, but rather a concept that might emerge while in the shower or in a dream. At Porter Novelli, a global public relations firm, the big idea is described as one that has a head, heart, hands, and legs. "Not only can The Big Idea straddle across a period of time through several campaigns, but at the same time it can stand astride any channel we choose. The Big Idea brings campaigns and channels together, rather than working as disconnected executional elements."[40]

Figure 13.8 A Welcome Approach in a Subway in New York City[36]

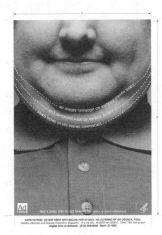

Figure 13.9 A Graphic Print Ad With Copy Reading "Starts Doing Sit-Ups During Commercials. Gets 30 Minutes a Day of Physical Activity. No Longer Dependent on Vertically Striped Shirts." Take A Small Step to Get Healthy. Get Started at www.smallstep.gov

Examples in the commercial sector to model include the well-known "Got milk?" campaign that has been adopted for a variety of celebrities and occasions for product usage. For a social marketing example, in Chapter 3 you read about the U.S. Department of Health and Human Services Office on Women's Health national breastfeeding campaign, with an example of one of the print ads (page 60). The big idea for this campaign will seem more obvious when you see two additional ads that were used in the campaign intended to increase knowledge about the benefits of breastfeeding exclusively for the first 6 months (see Figure 13.10).

Creative Tip #8: Consider a Question Instead of a Nag

Are you going to drink eight glasses of water today? Are you going to vote tomorrow? Some believe the very act of asking these questions can be a force for positive change, a technique referred to as the "self-prophecy effect," or the behavioral influence of a person making a self-prediction. Research conducted by Eric Spangenberg, professor of marketing, and Dave Sprott, assistant professor of marketing, both at Washington State University, believe that having people predict whether they will perform a socially normative behavior increases their probability of performing that target action. They have even demonstrated successful application of self-prophecy through mass-communicated prediction requests.[41] They have also found theoretical support for a dissonance-based explanation for self-prophecy.

Spangenberg and Sprott's studies show that when people predict they will do something, they are more likely to do it. Their analysis of the technique's application showed an average effectiveness rate of 20% immediately following the asking of the question and the fact that sometimes the behavior change would last up to 6 months after people predicted their behavior.[42] Specific studies have shown that self-prophecy has increased voter turnout in elections, improved attendance at health clubs, increased commitment to recycling aluminum cans, and increased the chances a family will eat dinner together. They believe this result can be explained by the phenomena of cognitive dissonance, that uncomfortable feeling we humans sometimes get when we say we'll do something and then we don't. (Some of us would probably call it guilt.) This uncomfortable feeling then drives us to act consistently with our predictions. In other words, the prediction becomes a self-fulfilling prophecy.

Spangenberg stresses that to be successful, the target audience must see the behavior as a social norm, be predisposed to the behavior, or at least not have strong commitments to the other, undesirable one. Asking a group of drug users, for example, "Are you going to stop using today?" is probably not going to work.[43]

Figure 3.10 Part of a Big Campaign Idea

Creative Tip #9: Highlight Relevant Social Norms

Social norms marketing, as mentioned in earlier chapters, is based on the central concept of social norms theory—that much of people's behavior is influenced by their perceptions of what is "normal" or "typical." It was listed by the *New York Times Magazine* as one of the most significant ideas of 2001. Jeff Linkenbach, director of the national MOST of Us® Institute at Montana State University, points out that what we are doing is turning the problem, that we often severely misperceive the typical behaviors or attitudes of our peers, into an opportunity. "For example, if people believe that the majority of their peers smoke, then they are more likely to smoke. Using social norms marketing to inform people that the majority of their peers do not smoke can potentially lead them to avoid smoking. There are many areas in which people's behaviors, attitudes or opinions have been shifted by using strategic marketing to realign their perceptions with reality. Informing people that the majority of their peers are acting in a positive or healthy way can create an environment in which people actively strive to emulate what they believe is typical of their peers."[44]

Highlighting the norms in your messages and creative executions can help correct these misperceptions (see Figure 13.11).

PRETESTING

Appropriate Reasons for Testing

The primary purpose for pretesting potential messages and creative executions is to *assess their ability to deliver on the strategies and objectives developed in Step 4 and highlighted in your creative brief.* When faced with several potential executions, the process can also help *choose the most effective options* or eliminate the least effective. It provides an opportunity to *refine materials* prior to production and distribution.

Figure 13.11 Social Norms Marketing Corrects Misperceptions of the Norm

In addition, it helps identify any red flags, something about the potential ad that might interfere with communications or send the wrong message. This often happens when planners and campaign developers are too close to their work or don't have the same profile and characteristics as the target audience. For example, a potential tobacco prevention ad targeting teens with the fact that "all it takes is 100 cigarettes to become addicted" raised a couple of red flags when several youth commented, "Well, then I'll just have 99," and others expressed the idea that 100 cigarettes (to a nonsmoker) "sounds like a lot!"

Potential Pretesting Techniques

Techniques used for pretesting are typically qualitative in nature and most often include *focus groups* or *personal interviews* and *professional review* of materials for technical accuracy and readability (i.e., literacy levels). When a more quantitative, controlled approach is required, methodologies may include *theater* or *natural exposure testing* (e.g., ads are embedded between other spots or in the middle of programming) and/or a *larger number of focus groups, intercept interviews,* and *self-administered surveys.* This more extensive testing is often warranted when (a) interested parties are divided on their initial assessments of creative executions, (b) there will be significant economic and political implications to choices, and (c) the campaign needs to have a longer-term shelf life (e.g., years versus months).

Often these techniques vary according to stages in the pretest process. At early stages, when concepts and draft executions are being tested, qualitative instruments are usually most appropriate. After concepts have been refined, quantitative techniques may be important to help choose from several potential executions.

Typical topics explored with respondents to assess the ability of potential executions to deliver on the strategy are listed as follows. Responses will then be compared with intentions developed in the creative brief.

1. What is the main message you get from this ad?

2. What else are they trying to say?

3. What do you think they want you to know?

4. What do you think they want you to believe or think?

5. What action do you think they want you to take?

6. If the respondent doesn't mention the desired behavior, say, "Actually, the main purpose of this ad is to persuade you and people like you to . . ."

7. How likely do you think it is that this ad will influence you to take this action?

8. What about this ad works well for that purpose?

9. What doesn't work well for that purpose?

10. How does the ad make you feel about (doing this behavior)?

11. Where is the best place to reach you with this message/ad? Where would you most likely notice it and pay attention to it? Where are you when you make decisions about (this behavior)?

Words of Caution About Pretesting

The idea of pretesting potential messages, concepts, and executions is often dreaded among creative professionals. Many of their concerns are legitimate, grounded in experiences with respondents who typically don't like advertising, don't really want to adopt the desired behavior you're promoting, want to be art directors, want to meet expectations to be an ad critic, can't imagine what the finished ad will really be like, or seize the opportunity to vent about the campaign's sponsor.

Principles and practices that can help to assuage these concerns and produce more effective results from testing efforts include the following:

1. *Inform respondents up front that this testing has nothing to do with whether they like or dislike the ads.* We are trying to find out whether they think the ad will work relative to stated objectives and why or why not. Respondents should be told (at some point) what the intended purpose of the ads are and then be asked to comment relative to that intention. One successful technique is to put the objective on a flipchart or whiteboard and continue to refer to the statement throughout discussions.

2. *Consider testing concept statements* that describe the theme and ad, instead of using storyboards or illustrations, especially when dealing with executions that involve fantasy, humor, or other styles that are difficult to convey with two-dimensional descriptions.

3. *Test conceptual spots in the lineup before finished ads* when evaluating several potential executions at the same time relative to each other.

4. *Ask respondents to write down their comments first before discussing reactions to ads.* They should be instructed that they can ask for points of clarification if needed, but to hold their comments until they have had a chance to capture them in writing.

5. *Thoroughly brief clients and colleagues not familiar with the creative testing process* on the limitations of this type of research and the potential pitfalls. Emphasize the importance of listening for what the ads are communicating and what components work and don't work relative to the intended objectives. Warn them not to be surprised or discouraged if participants don't like an ad and not to celebrate just because they do.

ETHICAL CONSIDERATIONS WHEN DECIDING MESSAGES, MESSENGERS, AND CREATIVE STRATEGIES

Many of the ethical issues regarding communications seem straightforward. Information should be accurate and not misleading. Language and graphics should be clear and appropriate for audiences exposed to communications. Gray areas are hard to avoid, however, and what and whose criteria should be used to decide whether something is appropriate? Is this tagline in a teen sexual assault prevention campaign too risky—"If you force her to have sex, you're screwed"—even though it tested well with the target audience? Should someone blow the whistle on a local television station that promoted the television sitcom *Friends* on an outdoor billboard featuring photos of the three slender stars and the headline "Cute Anorexic Chicks"? In most cases, the funders of the effort will likely be the ones to make the final call.

Chapter Summary

Promotion is persuasive communication and is the tool we count on to ensure that the target audience knows about the offer, believes they will experience the stated benefits, and is inspired to act. There are four major components of a communications strategy:

- *Messages:* What you want to communicate, inspired by what you want your target audience to do, know, and believe
- *Messengers:* Who will deliver your messages or be perceived to be sponsoring or supporting your offer
- *Creative Strategy:* What you will actually say and show and how you want to say it
- *Communication Channels:* Where and when your messages will appear, distinct, of course, from distribution channels

Several tips were suggested to assist you in evaluating and choosing a creative strategy:

#1: Keep It Simple and Clear

#2: Focus on Audience Benefits

#3: When Using Fear, Follow Up With Solutions and Use Credible Sources

#4: Try for Messages That Are Vivid, Personal, and Concrete

#5: Make Messages Easy to Remember

#6: Sometimes Have a Little Fun

#7: Try for a "Big Idea"

#8: Consider a Question Instead of a Nag

#9: Highlight Relevant Social Norms

Prior to producing campaign materials, you are encouraged to pretest messages and creative concepts, even if informally. You will be testing their ability to deliver on the objectives for your campaign, especially those outlined in your creative brief. Potential pitfalls in testing are real and can be minimized with careful construction of questioning and briefing of respondents, as well as colleagues and clients.

RESEARCH HIGHLIGHT

Measuring Campaign Impact of the Meth Project in Montana

Using Multiple Key Indicators (2006)

Background and Purpose of Research

This research highlight presents excerpts from a January 2007 report from the Montana Attorney General titled *Methamphetamine in Montana: A Preliminary Report on Trends and Impact*. It goes beyond reporting on changes in attitudes and behaviors. It also analyzes additional indicators of success, including local law enforcement data, drug task force incident reports, crime lab toxicology reports, hospital discharge and admission information, State Department records, and interviews with participating agencies, as well as comparing survey results with national reports.

Key Indicators

Changes in Attitudes

Two instruments are used in the state to measure how young people view the risks associated with methamphetamine. The Prevention Needs Assessment (PNA) is administered by the Department of Public Health and Human Services and surveys teens in the 8th, 10th, and 12th grades and measures risk and protective factors predictive of drug abuse. A second survey, the Meth Use & Attitudes Survey, is commissioned by the Meth Project in cooperation with the Department of Justice and measures attitudes

and beliefs held by teens, young adults, and parents of teens.

In March 2006, the PNA expanded to include four specific questions regarding methamphetamine. When asked about the risks of taking six different drugs, including alcohol, methamphetamine was perceived as the most dangerous: 93% of all respondents saw meth as having *great risk*. Montana teens' perception of risk is 10% higher than teen perception nationwide. In addition, 73% ranked using meth once or twice as having *great risk,* compared to only 54% of teens nationally.[45]

The 2006 Montana Meth Use & Attitudes Survey found that for teens, perceptions of risk for meth use increased by more than 10% in 8 out of 14 risk factors from 2005 results. In 2007, this survey, which included over 3,000 respondents (teens, young adults, and parents of teens combined), showed that more teens (87%) reported there would be disapproval attached to trying meth and that perceived benefits of meth use had declined since the Meth Project campaign launched, and concern over one's physical appearance due to meth use had increased significantly. A testament to the media campaign's effectiveness in the state, 81% of teens reported that the ads show that meth is dangerous to try even once, with 75% saying that the ads show meth is more destructive than they had originally thought. Virtually all respondents said they had seen an ad in the last month.

Changes in Meth Use

In this 2007 survey, teens and young adults reported having *fewer friends* who use meth than in past surveys, with 10% of teens saying they have close friends who use meth, down by 33% since 1999, and 23% of young adults say they have friends who use meth, down 20% since 2006.

In the *workplace*, according to the semiannual Drug Testing Index, Montana had the greatest decline in the nation in the frequency of workers testing positive for meth, falling by 70% between 2005 and 2006.[46] And changes in *hospital admissions and discharge* data were encouraging as well. From 2005 to 2006, the number of amphetamine/methamphetamine-addicted patients reported by Montana hospitals declined by 67%, and the number of related poisonings dropped by 33%.

Changes in Supply

In July 2005, Montana enacted strict precursor control laws that put cold medicines containing pseudoephedrine behind pharmacy counters. Since that time, law enforcement has seen a steady decline in the number of clandestine meth labs in Montana, with that number dropping from 122 in 2002 to 29 in 2005. Since October 1, 2006, the Drug Enforcement Administration has reported only one meth lab in Montana.

Changes in Crime

In 1 year, meth seizures by law enforcement agencies decreased by 51%. Meth-positive crime toxicology tests in all categories decreased by 45% from 2005 to 2006. Finally, Montana saw a 44% reduction in meth-positive arrests from 2005 to 2006. And meth-related crime had increased by 21% between 2004 and 2005 but declined by 53% between 2005 and 2006. The state crime lab provides scientific and technical support to Montana's law enforcement community. The drug chemistry specialists analyze samples of dangerous drugs discovered at crime scenes. The number of cases in which methamphetamine was found decreased from 70% in 2005 to 47% in 2006, a 36% drop.

Concluding Comments

While the data are preliminary, the evidence available demonstrates that the prevention campaign started in 2005 by the Meth Project has had a positive impact on the state of Montana. Critical indicators point to reductions in meth use, related crime and availability, and to a growing perception of the great risk associated with using this drug. Combined with other enforcement and prevention efforts, the Meth Project's education campaign has had dramatically positive results. Virtually all Montana citizens are aware of the dangers posed by meth, and early results show that drug use has been altered in the short term.

Ongoing efforts on the part of federal, state, and local law enforcement to make the drug less available in Montana will continue to be a priority. However, continuing to execute aggressive prevention and education programs is also critical to eradicating Montana's meth problem. By systematically focusing on demand reduction, the hope is to set the pace for the rest of the nation in addressing this epidemic.

14

Promotion

Selecting Communication Channels

If social marketers wish to create social institutions that think "customer first," social marketers must further develop their role in policy influence and development.

—Jeff French
Director
National Social Marketing Centre, London, 2007

Many social marketers might identify with a famous quote from John Wanamaker: "I know that half the money I spend on advertising is wasted; but I can never find out which half. " You may find the following previews of innovative types of communication strategies featured in this chapter more encouraging.

The TravelSmart program in Portland, Oregon, is an innovative strategy to encourage environmentally friendly ways to travel. The concept, used in more than 300 projects around the world, first identifies individuals who say they want to change the way they travel and then uses personal, individualized contact to help make this happen. In one project in 2004, 5,753 households were contacted by phone regarding interest in alternative transportation modes; 3,418 (60%) indicated they were interested, and 77% of this group returned a service request form, specifying what additional information they wanted. Information was then packed in a bag, and 98% of the packages were delivered by bicycle (of course) within 1 week of the request. One year later, in the spring of 2005, an after-survey was conducted showing that car travel in the TravelSmart target area decreased by 9% over that of the control group area.[1]

And then there's the viral video game Darfur is Dying, developed by college students and sponsored by Reebok and mtvU, the college-oriented TV network. It was launched in April 2006 and is a narrative-based simulation where the gamer, from the perspective of a displaced Darfurian, negotiates forces that threaten the survival of his or her refugee camp. It is intended to offer a glimpse of what it's like for the more than 2.5 million who have been internally displaced by the crisis in Sudan. On the Web site there is a message: "This game can be spread virally, so play the game and pass it on to your friends." By January 2007, it had been played more than 2 million times by over 1 million people.[2]

In the following case, you'll read about how understanding the communication preferences of those engaged in policy development informed the selection of the right media channels appropriate to influence the desired behavior change.

MARKETING HIGHLIGHT

Marketing Social Marketing in England (2007)

Dr. Jeff French, Director
National Social Marketing Centre

This case demonstrates that policy making can be influenced by social marketing and that marketing interventions focused on changing policy are fundamentally the same as those focused on influencing individual or organizational behavior.

Background

In 2004 the U.K. Department of Health, as part of its new national health strategy Choosing Health, decided to undertake a review of social marketing to assess its potential to guide future health promotion efforts at national, regional, and local levels. A project team was recruited, and 18 months later the review, called "It's Our Health," was published in June 2006 (see Figure 14.1). The review concluded that social marketing has a great deal to contribute to improving health if its principles are applied systematically. The review also recommended a number of changes in policy and professional behavior.

The team leading the work developed a marketing strategy to increase the probability that politicians would accept the review's recommendations on utilizing social marketing. A key part of this strategy was to select the right communication and media channels to influence the target market.

Figure 14.1 A National Review of Social Marketing, "It's Our Health," Published in June 2006

Target Audience

The key target audiences for this intervention were *politicians* (20 named individuals including the prime minister and secretary of state for health); *policy advisers* (30 named individuals, including advisers in departments other than health); *senior civil servants* (approximately 100, including permanent secretaries, directors of communication, and senior policy leads); *professional associations* (15, including faculty of Public Health Chartered Institute of Environmental Health and Community Practitioners' and Health Visitors' Association); *influential practitioners* (approximately 2,000, including public health, health promotion, and environmental health).

Each group was subdivided into those predisposed or known to support the principles of social marketing (the Natural Advocates) and those who would oppose it. The objectors (or "competition") were subdivided into those who would oppose because they believed that social marketing could add little to current efforts (Skeptics) and those who had ideological objections to social marketing (Objectors). Competition analysis revealed that the Skeptics and the Objectors would require different approaches to influence their attitudes and behavior. Different tactics and channels were developed to influence the behavior of each group.

Behavior Objectives

The overall *policy influencing objective* was to get the recommendations of the national review of social marketing accepted and implemented and to see the recommendations reflected in a growing number of national policy documents. The *strategy and individual objectives* related to specific tangible behavioral change among the selected individuals and groups.

The behavioral objectives were set for each group. They included the number of times targeted politicians made reference to the need to apply social marketing, the number of policy citations of social marketing, examples of health strategy referencing social marketing, and observable change in the way budgets were allocated.

One of the key reasons for success of this program was the development of a clear exchange that would appeal to each target group. For the Natural Advocates, the exchange that was developed centered on costs and benefits.

The Costs

- Investment in scoping and coordination
- The potential pain of change
- Loss of total control
- Transition costs

The Benefits

- Improved impact
- Better policy and delivery coherence
- Enhanced learning
- Better use of assets

For the Skeptics group, an exchange was crafted that set out tangible benefits of social marketing in the form of evidence reviews and case studies. Communication with this group was framed in terms of the value that social marketing could bring to enhancing current good practice. In this way social marketing was positioned as something all responsible practitioners had a duty to learn about and, when appropriate, apply.

The exchange crafted for the Objectors in each target group used a different approach.

For this group the issues were largely focused on a misunderstanding about the nature of social marketing and its key principles. The approach was one of drawing out the perceived ideological objections and then positively confronting these. Research discovered that one of the key problems was associated with the language of marketing; words such as *customers* and *competition* were a turnoff for this group. They associated this language with the worst excesses of commercial marketing and the ill effects of rampant capitalism. The exchange crafted for this group was similar to that of the Skeptics, but it was framed it terms of a greater focus on putting those we are trying to help in a more dominant position to influence policy and service delivery. This approach appealed to the Objectors, as they also shared a fundamental desire to ensure that services and interventions were designed and delivered to meet peoples' real needs and felt this was currently not happening as much as it should.

Strategy: Media Channels

In an environment in which social marketing was not well understood, it was important to tell a simple and consistent story about what social marketing is and the impact it could have. A key tactic across all the key target groups was to emphasize face-to-face and personal communication. Research indicated that all the target groups had a preference for personal face-to-face communication as well as for information tailored to their specific needs. Face-to-face communication was deemed an effective approach to constantly gathering further direct market intelligence to feed into the review findings. Face-to-face meetings were held, and over 15,000 people heard in person

about social marketing from members of the review team at conferences, workshops, seminars, and other forms of meeting.

An early task was to develop simple "models" and descriptors drawn from the international literature, together with learning materials and case studies. A *customer triangle model* (see Figure 14.2) and a *total process planning* tool were developed along with *social marketing benchmark criteria*, a management checklist, and a number of other resources. These materials were used consistently to build a shared understanding of what social marketing was and was not. All of these materials are available from www.nsmcentre .org.uk.

Figure 14.2 The Customer Triangle, Increasing Understanding of the Social Marketing Process

In addition, appropriate media and channels for communication were developed for each target group and the subgroups within them. For example, targeted politicians received a mixed approach of regular face-to-face and written briefings, opportunities to input their views to developing recommendations, the opportunity to visit real-life examples of social marketing interventions, opportunities to sit in on speeches about social marketing, and help and encouragement to make their own speeches about social marketing. It was also recognized that politicians are influenced to some extent by professional journals, periodicals, and general mass media. Therefore, all of these channels were targeted to ensure that there was a steady drip of social marketing articles, letters, and editorial comment about social marketing from a variety of sources.

Senior policy advisers and civil servants were provided with personal briefings and policy papers to help them brief politicians and increase their own understanding of social marketing. Training courses and tailored learning material and events were also developed for them. These senior officials were engaged in a number of working and discussion groups. The review team was also invited to input social marketing thinking into a wide range of health service policy areas and nonhealth policy areas.

Practitioners and professional associations were engaged through their publications and learning networks. A large number of seminars, workshops, conferences, and speeches were given over 18 months to inform, raise awareness, and debate the nature and use of social marketing. Professional associations were encouraged to inform and disseminate understanding about social marketing.

Results

When social marketing is applied to influencing policy and strategy and professional behavior, the behavioral measures are focused on observable change in policy, strategy, and the behavior of officials, practitioners, and organizations. The national review of social marketing in England was published in June 2006. The Department of Health almost immediately accepted all of its recommendations. In addition to the achievement of this objective, other selected behavioral change indicators included the following:

- The National Social Marketing Centre was launched by Minister for Public Health Caroline Flint in December 2006.
- Public Health policy teams at national, regional, and local levels were building social marketing principles into their planning and delivery. There was a strategy shift to ensure that all future health campaigns will be informed by social marketing principles.
- Social marketing principles were incorporated into the new health strategy for England launched in 2007 called Health Challenge England.
- Ten social marketing demonstration sites were funded and established across England.
- The Department of Health reorganized its communication, marketing, and policy functions.
- A population life course segmentation research project was funded to guide national policy.
- The Department of Health is developing a strategic policy approach to putting people's needs at the center of all policy, including the delivery of health care services.
- The Prime Minister's Strategy unit in February 2007 published *Building on Progress,* a set of policy recommendations for the next phase of public sector reform. This key policy document recommended that a social marketing development fund should be established

by the Treasury to encourage the use of social marketing within the public sector.

- Over 2,000 practitioners have signed up to a national social marketing network.
- Over 6,000 practitioners attended training courses and seminars on social marketing.
- An academic network representing 10 universities has been established to develop curricular and research capacity on social marketing.
- A national social marketing standards group has been formed to develop standards of good practice and a common competencies framework.

- Regional public health groups are allocating large amounts of their budgets to social marketing programs.
- Professional associations are reviewing their competencies requirements to include social marketing.

In addition to the above outcomes, a wide range of other government departments and agencies are now seeking to apply social marketing principles to their work. The European Union (EU) commissioned the review team to brief them about social marketing and has subsequently expressed interest in helping to spread good practice in social marketing across Europe.

PROMOTION: SELECTING COMMUNICATION CHANNELS

This chapter is intended to familiarize you with the numerous options you have for getting your messages to your target audience. It also offers eight factors to help you choose ones that will be the most effective and efficient for reaching and inspiring your target audience. You will be faced with making decisions regarding (a) choosing types of communication channels, (b) selecting specific media vehicles within these broader types, and (c) determining timing for communications. A brief explanation of each follows (see Box 14.1).

Communication Types

Communication channels, also referred to as media channels, can be categorized by whether they are *mass, selective,* or *personal.* Each approach may be appropriate, depending on communication objectives. Many campaigns and programs may warrant all three, as they are mutually reinforcing.

Mass media channels are called for when large groups of people need to be quickly informed and persuaded regarding an issue or desired behavior. There is a need, and perhaps a sense of urgency, for audiences to "know, believe, and/or do something." Typical media types include *advertising, publicity,* and *governmental signage.*

Selective media channels are used in cases where target markets can be reached more cost effectively through targeted media channels and when they need to know more than is available in mass media formats. Typical selective media types include *direct mail, flyers, brochures, posters, special events, telemarketing,* and the *Internet.*

BOX 14.1
Major Social Marketing Communication Channels

A. ADVERTISING (PAID MEDIA AND UNPAID PUBLIC SERVICE ANNOUNCEMENTS)

Broadcast:
  Television
  Radio
  Internet: banner ads
Print:
  Newspaper
  Magazine
Direct Mail:
  Separate mailings
  Paycheck and other stuffers
  Internet/Web sites
Backs of tickets and receipts
Ads on Internet/Web
Ads in Theaters

Outdoor/Out of Home:
  Billboards
  Busboards
  Bus shelter displays
  Subways
  Taxis
  Vinylwrap cars and buses
  Sports events
  Banners
  Postcard racks
  Kiosks
  Restroom stalls
  Truckside advertising
  Airports billboards and signage

B. PUBLIC RELATIONS AND SPECIAL EVENTS

Stories on television and radio
Articles in newspapers and magazines
Op-eds
Public affairs/community relations
Lobbying
Videos
Media advocacy

Special Events:
  Meetings
  Speakers' bureaus
  Conferences
  Exhibits
  Health screenings
  Demonstrations

C. PRINTED MATERIALS

Brochures
Newsletters
Flyers
Posters
Catalogs

Calendars
Envelope messages
Booklets
Bumper stickers
Static stickers

D. SPECIAL PROMOTIONAL ITEMS

Clothing:
  T-shirts
  Baseball hats
  Diapers
  Bibs
Temporary Items:
  Coffee sleeves
  Bar coaster
  Lapel buttons
  Temporary tattoos
  Balloons
  Stickers
  Sports cards

Functional Items:
  Key chains
  Flashights
  Refrigerator magnets
  Water bottles
  Litterbags
  Pens and pencils
  Bookmarks
  Book covers
  Notepads
  Tote bags
Mascots
Door hangers

E. SIGNAGE AND DISPLAYS

Road signs
Signs and posters on government property
Retail displays and signage

(Continued)

(Continued)

F. PERSONAL SELLING AND SOCIAL MEDIA

Face-to-face meetings, presentations, speakers' bureaus   Word of mouth, blogs, personal Web sites
Telephone   Word of Web
Workshops, seminars, and training sessions   Consumer generated media

G. POPULAR MEDIA

Songs
Movie scripts, television, radio programs
Comic books and comic strips
Video games, personal Web sites

Personal media channels are sometimes important to achieve behavior change objectives and include *face-to-face meetings and presentations, blogs, telephone conversations, workshops, seminars, and training sessions.* This approach is most warranted when some form of personal intervention and interaction is required in order to deliver detailed information, address barriers and concerns, build trust, and gain commitment.

Communication Vehicles

Within each of the major communication channels (media types) there are specific vehicles to select. Which TV stations, radio programs, magazines, and bus routes should you choose? At what events should you sign up for a booth? When are road signs warranted? Where should you put your fact sheets?

Communication Timing

Timing elements include decisions regarding months, weeks, days, and hours when campaign elements will be launched, distributed, implemented, and/or aired in the media. Your decisions will be guided by when your audience is most likely to be reached or when you have your greatest windows of opportunity for being heard (e.g., a drinking and driving campaign aimed at teens might be most effective immediately prior to and during prom and graduation nights.)

TRADITIONAL MEDIA CHANNELS

Advertising and Public Service Announcements

Defined formally, advertising is "any paid form of nonpersonal presentation of ideas, goods, or services by an identified sponsor."[3] More commonly, you probably think of one or more of the popular, traditional mass media communication channels such as *television*, *radio*, *newspapers*, *magazines*, *direct mail*, *the Internet*, and a variety of *outdoor* (out-of-home) channels such as billboards, transit signage, and kiosks. In the commercial sector, these advertisements are most often placed (bought) by the organization's advertising or media buying agency.

As a social marketer working for a public sector or nonprofit organization, you will also have opportunities for *unpaid advertising,* something you know of as public service announcements (PSAs). An obvious advantage of PSAs, of course, is the cost (often free, or at least deeply discounted); the disadvantage is that you do not have the same level of control over where the ad will actually appear in the newspaper or magazine or during what program or time of day it will air on television or radio. This perhaps is why some refer to a PSA as "people sound asleep."

There are several tactics you can use to increase your odds of obtaining public service placement of your advertisements and the likelihood they will appear when and where you would like. First, build a relationship with the public affairs or community relations personnel at your local television and radio networks. Know that what they will be most interested in (it's their job) are issues that their listeners and viewing audience care about and ones that their organization has chosen as a community priority. Ensure high quality of your productions, whether for television or radio, as they will consider it a reflection of their organization as well. Be prepared to negotiate. If they can't offer you free placement at times you are targeting, they may have interested corporate sponsors; and if they can't do it free of charge, they may be able to offer a discounted price (e.g., two for the price of one).

Example: Denver Water's Conservation Advertising Campaign

From 2002 to 2006, Denver Water's 1.2 million customers reduced their water usage by about 20% each year. The Denver mayor, however, wanted to continue this trend and announced a partnership in July 2006 to reduce use by 22% a year over the next decade, including a $500,000 advertising campaign intended to help make this happen. The campaign, with the tagline "Use Only What You Need," will appear in community newspapers, magazines, billboards, transit, and other out-of-home media (see Figure 14.3). The ads will also appear in places you might not expect, such as on 20,000 drink coasters that will go to local restaurants and bars, offering water conservation tips such as "Be a real man and dry shave, tough guy."[4]

Public Relations and Special Events

Public relations is distinguishable by its favorable outcome—free visibility for your campaign.[5] Successful activities generate free, positive *mentions of your programs in the media*, most commonly as news and special programming on radio and television, and as stories, articles, and editorial comments in newspapers and magazines. Additional typical efforts in this channel include planning for *crisis communications* (e.g., responding to adverse or conflicting news), *lobbying* (e.g., for funding allocations), *media advocacy* (e.g., working with the media to take on and advance your social issue), and managing *public affairs* (e.g., issue management). Although some organizations hire public relations firms to handle major campaigns, it is more likely that internal staff often handle day-to-day media relations.

Figure 14.3　A Creative Campaign and Use of Outdoor Advertising for Denver Water

Some believe this is one of the more underutilized channels, and yet a well-thought-out program coordinated with other communications-mix elements can be extremely effective. It provides more in-depth coverage of your issue than is often possible with a brief commercial and is often seen as more objective than paid advertising. Tools used to generate news coverage include press releases, press kits, news conferences, editorial boards, letters to the editor, and strong personal relationships with key reporters and editors. Siegel and Doner have several recommended keys to success:

Build relationships with the media by first "finding out who covers what and then working to position yourself and your initiative as an important, reliable source of information so that the reporters will call you when they are running a story on your topic."[6]

Frame the issues with the goals of the media in mind, "to appeal to the broadest number of audience members possible, and . . . tell a compelling story that is relevant to their audience and in the public's interest."[7]

Create news by convening a press conference, special event, or demonstration. Consider a technique mastered by the Center for Science in the Public Interest (CSPI) in which their studies create "news that applies pressure to decision makers. For example, after its analysis of the nutrient content of movie popcorn was reported in the media, many major movie chains began using oils lower in saturated fat or offering air-popped options."[8]

Special events can also generate visibility for your effort, offering advantages of interaction with your target audience, allowing them to ask questions and express attitudes toward your desired behaviors you probably need to hear. They may be a part of a larger public gathering such as a county fair, or they may be ones that you have organized just for your campaign. It might include a demonstration (e.g., car seat safety checks), or it might be a presentation at a community forum or town hall meeting, such as the one in the following example.

Example: Edens Lost & Found: How Ordinary
Citizens Are Restoring Our Great American Cities

It seems there is an exciting new consensus emerging that it is possible to restore America's degraded urban environments and to then plan for future growth with much greater wisdom. With nearly 80% of the U.S. population living in urban environments with insufficient access to open space and public parks, Harry Wiland and Dale Bell of the Media & Policy Center Foundation produced Edens Lost & Found to give this issue more visibility and the effort more support. It is the centerpiece of an extensive public policy campaign to target decision makers in industry and government, engage citizens in the challenge of urban sustainability, and share ideas that have proven effective and can be readily replicated.

The effort includes a 4-hour PBS series that premiered on PBS in May 2006, showcasing extraordinary stories of environmental rebirth. One features a mayor who took the bold step to close an airport runway on the edge of the city in the middle of the night, making way for an oasis of wildflowers, prairie grasses, and trees. Another tells the story of a father who works through his grief after his son's death by transforming an abandoned lot into a public garden. Four cities are featured (Los Angeles, Chicago, Philadelphia, and Seattle), and town hall meetings repeat broadcasts of the series, promote community action guides, and serve to stimulate and sustain community dialogue. Edens Lost & Found's Web site (www.edenslostandfound.org) provides "Starter Kits" for these meetings and helps seek local stakeholders to serve as "Venue Sponsors."[9]

Printed Materials

This is probably the most familiar and utilized communication channel for social marketing campaigns. *Brochures, newsletters, booklets, flyers, calendars, bumper stickers, door hangers, and catalogs* provide opportunities to present more detailed information regarding the desired behavior and the social marketing program. Sometimes, but not as often as you might like, target audiences hold on to these materials, ideally even share them with others. In some cases, special materials are developed and distributed to other key internal and external groups, such as program partners and the media. Included in this channel category are any collateral pieces associated with the program, such as *letterheads, envelopes,* and *business cards.*

Figure 14.4 A Weekly Calendar Intended to Increase Safety Practices on Construction Job Sites

Example: A Calendar to Increase Workplace Safety

With a touch of humor and 52 photos, the Washington State Department of Labor and Industries, Division of Occupational Safety and Health, issued its first 2007 Job Site Calendar, intended to prompt workers to work safely every day (see Figure 14.4). Inspired by a job site foreman, it features accident statistics and perhaps unbelievable, but true, hazards, dangerous conditions, and bad judgment found on construction sites. A news release in December 2006 led to a number of newspaper stories and generated demand for the calendar. The original 4,500 copies went quickly, prompting a second printing of 2,000. All but 100 copies of the calendar were distributed by March 2007.

Special Promotional Items

You can reinforce and sometimes sustain campaign messages through the use of special promotional items, referred to by some in the industry as "trinkets and trash." Among the most familiar are messages on clothing (e.g., T-shirts, baseball hats, diapers, and bibs), *functional items* (e.g., key chains, water bottles, litterbags, pens and pencils, notepads, bookmarks, book covers, and refrigerator magnets), and more *temporary mechanisms* (e.g., bar coasters, stickers, temporary tattoos, coffee sleeves, sports cards, and lapel buttons). Some campaigns, such as the one in the following example, create a treasure chest of these items.

Example: Temporary Tattoos and More for Pooper Scoopers

In Snohomish County, Washington, Dave Ward of the Snohomish County Public Works Department understands the difference between an awareness campaign and a social marketing one. He also understands how important it is to research target audience current attitudes and practices regarding picking up pet waste and to focus on creative strategies to influence very specific, targeted behaviors by solving the customer's problem.

His research among pet owners revealed that 42% picked up their dog's waste regularly and disposed of it properly in the trash; 42% were picking it up regularly but not disposing of it properly (e.g., they were burying it on their property); and 16% were picking it up only sometimes or not at all. To influence more "proper behaviors," the county created concrete and vivid communications: "More than 126,000 dogs live in Snohomish County, producing waste equivalent to a city of 40,000 people. More than 20 tons of dog waste are dropped in Snohomish County backyards every day."

Observation research then helped define the problem even further. Although citizens appeared to be fairly reliable in picking up pet waste on public property such as sidewalks and parks (where they could be seen), they were less judicious in their own backyards.

Ask a dog owner why they don't pick up their dog's waste in their yard and you might hear what Dave did. "When I come home from work at night and let the dog out to go, it's too dark to see where they go." To address this barrier, a free functional promotional item was

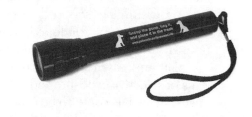

Figure 14.5 A Promotional Item, a Flashlight, That Also Helps Overcome Barriers to "Scooping the Poop" in the Dark

developed, a small flashlight that could be left by the door, serving not only as a way to follow the pet around the yard but also prompt the desired behavior on a regular basis (see Figure 14.5). And to spread the word and recognize these pooper scoopers, another promotional item, a temporary tattoo for the hand with the words "I'm a pooper scooper," was especially popular among youth.[10]

Signage and Displays

Many social marketing campaigns rely on signage and displays to launch and, especially, sustain campaign messages. Examples of those more permanent in nature include *road signs* warning against drinking and driving, reminding people to use a litterbag, and asking motorists to "Move right for sirens and lights." *Signs on government property and establishments regulated by the government* can be used to target messages, such as those in forests asking people to stay on the path, plaques in bars with messages warning about the dangers of alcohol when pregnant, and those at airports urging us to remove computers from our bags before reaching the checkpoint. Displays and signage can also be used at point-of-purchase in *retail environments,* for example, for life vests, tarps for covering pickup loads, energy-saving lightbulbs, and natural pesticides. In this case, signage and special displays will include selling the idea to distribution channel decision makers and coordinating distribution of any special signage and accompanying materials.

NONTRADITIONAL AND NEW MEDIA CHANNELS

Popular Entertainment Media

A less well-known and underused media category employs popular forms of entertainment to carry behavior change messages, including movies, television series, radio programs, comic books, comic strips, songs, theater, video games, and traveling entertainers such as puppeteers, mimes, and poets. Social marketing messages integrated into programming, scripts, and performances have included topics such as drinking and driving, use of condoms, eating disorders, recycling, youth suicide, organ donation, HIV testing, and sudden infant death syndrome.

Alan Andreasen sees this approach as a very effective one in overcoming the problems of selective exposure and selective attention on the part of indifferent target audiences. "This has come to be called the Entertainment Education Approach.[11] It began in the 1960s with a soap opera in Peru called *Simplemente Maria*, which discussed family planning, among other topics."[12] And John Davies, an international social marketing consultant who refers to these initiatives as "edutainment," believes that although they can require substantial budgets, costs might be lowered by selling advertising time to multinational companies that market beneficial, affordable health products such as soap for hand washing, oral rehydration salts for babies, and vitamin/mineral tablets for women.[13]

On a local level, you might try persuading local celebrities popular with the target audience to develop special promotional products (e.g., songs on their CDs), to perform at special events, or to be featured in advertisements. In a national award-winning television spot for Mississippi's antilitter campaign, for example, former First Lady Pat Fordice magically appears in the cab of a pickup truck between two "Bubbas," one of whom has gleefully tossed trash out the window. Pinching the ears of the driver and his offending pal, Fordice admonishes the pair for littering Mississippi highways. The former First Lady continues as a spokesperson and representative of the campaign with the tagline "I'm Not Your Mama! Pick It Up, Mississippi!"[14]

Efforts to make this happen on a large scale, however, are likely to be substantial and may include lobbying and partnership efforts with the entertainment industry. The Centers for Disease Control and Prevention (CDC), for example, often partners with Hollywood executives and academic, public health, and advocacy organizations to share information with writers and producers about the nation's pressing health issues. Knowing that an estimated 88% of people in America learn about health issues from television, they believe prime time and daytime television programs are great outlets for health messages. To facilitate this, they provide tip sheets for TV writers and producers, conduct expert briefing for writers, and respond to inquiries for health information. They arrange expert briefings for an entire writing staff of a TV show, set up one-on-one conversations between a producer and a health expert to explore story line possibilities, and help find real people who deal with health issues firsthand. They also present awards and acknowledgments for exemplary portrayal of health issues, as they did in 2003 when they awarded the Sentinel for Health Award to *The Young and the Restless* for "Neil's Alcoholism."[15]

And another impressive trend is also seen as an opportunity for popular media. By 2007, it is anticipated that video games will surpass movie rental, music, and box office films in terms of time and dollars spent. In fact, in 2005, a Games for Change Conference was held in New York City to inspire organizations to use video games to further social change, and there is now a Web site (www.socialimpactgames.com) that provides a listing and description of over 200 "serious games," including one described in the following example.

Example: Video Games for Asthma

Bronkie the Bronchiasaurus, created by Click Health in 1995, is a Super Nintendo video game designed to improve players' asthma self-management. Players take the role of either Bronkie or Trakie, two dinosaurs who have asthma (see Figure 14.6). To win the game, players must keep their dinosaur's asthma under control while also saving their planet from deadly dust clouds. To make sure Bronkie and Trakie stay in top form, the dinosaurs must be guided to measure and monitor their peak flow (breath strength), take medications as needed, follow a sick day plan, use an inhaler correctly, and avoid asthma triggers such as pollen, dust, smoke, and cold viruses shot through the air by Sneezers. The game has been used successfully in homes,

Figure 14.6 A Video Game Helping to Reduce Asthma Attacks

hospitals, clinic waiting rooms, and asthma summer camps. Studies found that young people with asthma who had the Bronkie video game available to play at home reduced their asthma-related emergency and urgent care visits by 40% on average.[16]

Public Art

You have, no doubt, experienced public art intended to advocate for a cause (e.g., white crosses in a park in protest to a war), attract tourists (e.g., Cows on Parade in Chicago), or raise money for a nonprofit organization (e.g., quilts for AIDS victims). But what about public art intended to actually influence behaviors—behaviors to improve health, safety, or the environment? We think it is another emerging and untapped channel, with unique potentials to sustain behaviors, create media attention, and be seen as a credible messenger. Channel types include *sculptures, exhibits, murals, paintings,* and more—all with a specific intention to inspire and influence behaviors, as it was in the following example.

Example: Green Dollhouses

PHOTO COURTESY OF EMILY HAGOPIAN

Figure 14.7 One of 17 Houses in the Green Dollhouse Exhibit at the Coyote Point Museum in 2005[17]

In 2005, the Green Dollhouse Exhibit at Coyote Point Museum in San Mateo, California, showcased 17 "dishy" doll dwellings demonstrating green building principles, including energy efficiency, water conservation, passive solar design, and more. Architects and design students from around the United States—and as far away as Japan—entered a competition. The host, the Coyote Point Museum, with a mission to provide environmental education, believed these green dollhouses would literally bring home the concepts of conservation and energy efficiency for visitors and museum members. They believed the exhibit would bring the concept to a level that everyone could relate to and provide simple ideas on how to make homes healthier and more ecofriendly. Visitors could also have fun building with "green" materials in the hands-on play area. Themed creations ranged from Monopoly Manor to Animal House to Mod Dollhouse (see Figure 14.7).

Product Integration

In the commercial sector, product placement is a specialty of its own, with marketers finding inventive ways to advertise during actual television programs and movies especially. You probably recognize this when you see a familiar logo on a cup of coffee in an actor's hand or the Swoosh on a star's baseball cap. In the James Bond film *Die Another Day*, for example, 7UP, Aston Martin, Finlandia, VISA, and Omega all spent an estimated $100 million for product placement rights, with some critics nicknaming the film *Buy Another Day*.[18]

More relevant for social marketing is the integration of your desired behaviors into commercial products or their packaging. Sometimes corporations decide "all on their own" to take on an initiative. In the fall of 2006, for example, the toymaker Mattel unveiled Tanner, Barbie's new pet dog. Tanner comes with little brown plastic "biscuits" that he could be fed simply by lifting his tail. When he then "releases them," Barbie can then scoop them up using her new, magnetic pooper-scooper and place them in the little garbage can that is included in the package. More often, the social marketing organization approaches the corporation for support, as Seafood Watch did with Warner Home Video, who then agreed to include the 2007 *Seafood Watch* pocket guide in every copy of the Academy Award–winning animated film *Happy Feet* when millions of DVD copies became available in March 2007.

Social Media

This personal communication channel involves *social channels* made up of friends, neighbors, family members, and associates "talking" to your target audience face to face and via blogs, e-mails, podcasts, YouTube, MySpace—even through demonstrations sometimes called "guerilla marketing" on the street. To underscore its power, one study by Burson-Marsteller and Roper Starch Worldwide found that one influential person's word of mouth tends to affect the buying attitudes of two other people, on average. And yet, that circle of influence jumps even farther to eight when online, which explains why "word of Web" is joining, perhaps even surpassing, "word of mouth" as a powerful channel of influence.[19]

In some cases, positive word of mouth, or buzz, happens in a natural way. A homeowner attends a workshop on natural gardening, for example, and then shares with his neighbor about an easier and safer way to get rid of dandelions. Or a young woman gets an HIV/AIDS test and tells a friend how relieved she is and that it only took 15 minutes. In these cases, the benefits, even features, of desired behaviors get spread and endorsed by credible spokespersons.

More often, especially in the corporate sector, this "buzz" is created and managed. You can begin by *identifying influential individuals.* Malcolm Gladwell, in his book *The Tipping Point,* identifies three key types: *Mavens* are knowledgeable about big and small things, *Connectors* know and communicate with a great number of people, and *Salesmen* have great natural persuasive skills and power.[20] You can also consider *viral marketing or "ideavirus" marketing.* Viral marketing leverages social networks. Seth Godin, in his book *Unleashing the Ideavirus,* proclaims that "marketing by interrupting people isn't cost-effective anymore. You can't afford to seek out people and send them unwanted marketing messages, in large groups, and hope that some will send you money. Instead, the future belongs to marketers who establish a foundation and process where interested people can market to *each other.* Ignite consumer networks and then get out of the way and let them talk."[21]

Web Sites

To increase visibility for your Web site, *search engine marketing* has evolved immensely in the past several years, and many of us are not fully exhausting recommended strategies to increase the visibility of our Web site when someone conducts a Google-type search (e.g., natural gardening). There are paid options to ensure a ranking, often with a "pay per click" fee structure, a strategy that probably makes more business sense in the for-profit sector. There are also numerous unpaid options to improve the chances (ranking) that your site will make the first results page, if not the top of that page. Rankings can be improved by enhancing a Web site's structure, content, and keyword submissions.

Web sites are a critical "touchpoint" for your customer, one that not only impacts awareness and attitudes toward your organization but also makes a difference in whether your audience is inspired and supported to act (e.g., pledge to keep a lawn pesticide-free). Some even believe your Web site could be "the Third Place," a term referring to social surroundings different from the two usual social environments of home and the workplace. Customers of Starbucks, for example, might classify their coffee spot as one of their third places.

To maximize the influence of your Web site, experts advise that you pay attention to (a) your site's ease of navigation, (b) ability to tailor itself to different users, (c) potential for two-way communications, and (d) availability of related links. And be certain to ensure that the "look and feel" of the site is consistent with your desired brand identity.[22] The following is a good example.

Example: A Web Site and Partnership to Protect Watersheds

In April 2006, CBS 11 in Dallas/Fort Worth introduced a Web site to influence citizen behaviors to protect the Upper Trinity River Watershed in North Texas, in partnership with the Environmental Protection Agency, the Texas State Soil and Water Conservation

Figure 14.8   Web Site Encouraging Citizen Stories and Actions

Board, and the North Central Texas Council of Governments. The station's new "e-Life" encourages citizens to share story ideas for on-air coverage; photos of people, places, and wildlife in the watershed; Web links with related information that they will then post; events that can be put on a community calendar; even brochures that they would like posted to e-Life. The site also includes features on a variety of other weather and climate-specific topics, including drought, flooding, and wildfires (see Figure 14.9).[23]

Mobile Phones for "Pull Versus Push" Campaigns

Mobile phones are among the great channels for "pull campaigns," where the customer initiates the action and the marketer responds. These are in contrast to the traditional "push campaigns," where marketing activities are directed toward the customer through various forms of media and other channels. As Don Schultz, a professor at Northwestern University, comments: "Many argue the shift to pull is inevitable. As consumers gain more control of information technology and therefore, the marketplace, there will be a natural tendency for them to acquire the knowledge, information or materials they need, rather than be subjected to the generally untargeted marketing programs pushed toward them through mass marketing. The evidence being cited for the pull scenario is the incredible growth of search-based media forms such as Yahoo!, AOL and the like."[24] The following example represents the possibilities in the social marketing arena.

Example: Wireless AMBER Alerts[25]

Wireless AMBER Alerts™, introduced in May 2006, are text messages that are sent out to subscribers as soon as local law enforcement release an AMBER Alert. The program is sponsored by the National Center for Missing & Exploited Children, the Wireless Foundation, and the U.S. Department of Justice. Messages include information about the child and any known information about the abductor and the abductor's vehicle. Potential audiences are huge, with anyone capable of receiving text messages and whose wireless carrier is a participant in the program able to sign up to receive these alerts. Estimates are that over 93% of all U.S. wireless subscribers are served by the 28 carriers currently participating in the Wireless AMBER Alert program. One year after launch, the program had 322,000 subscribers. With a goal to reach 1 million subscribers, the Ad Council will be helping to accelerate adoption with new PSAs, scheduled to air in late summer and early fall of 2007.

FACTORS GUIDING COMMUNICATION CHANNEL DECISIONS

Clearly, you have numerous channel options available for getting your messages to target audiences. Choices and decisions can be guided by a few important factors, seven of which are described in the following sections, in no particular order, since each one is an important consideration, some even decision makers.

Factor #1: Your Campaign Objectives and Goals

In Step 4 of your planning process, you ideally set a quantifiable goal for changes in behavior, behavior intent, awareness, and/or attitudes. Those measures/targets are now your guide for selecting communication channels.

It makes sense, no doubt, that if you want 50 homes in a neighborhood of 500 homes on a river, for example, to be stream stewards, you will have a very different outreach (communication) strategy than if you wanted 5 million residents of a state to be aware of an E. coli outbreak. Confirming these numbers ahead of time with funders and team members will help you make the case for the strategies that you then propose.

Factor #2: Desired Reach and Frequency

Kotler and Armstrong describe *reach* as "a measure of the percentage of people in the target market who are exposed to the ad campaign during a given period of time" and *frequency* as "a measure of how many times the average person in the target market is exposed to the message."[26] This will be an important decision. For example, a state health department may want radio and television spots to reach 75% of youth aged 12 to 18 living in major metropolitan areas at least nine times during a 2-month campaign. Media representatives will then use computer programs to produce media schedules and associated costs to achieve these objectives. The media planner often looks at the cost of the plan and calculates the cost per contact or exposure (often expressed as the *cost per thousand,* the cost of reaching 1,000 people using the medium).

Factor #3: Your Target Audience

Perhaps the most important consideration when planning media strategies will be the *target market's profile* (demographics, psychographics, geographics, and behaviors) and their *media habits.* This will be especially important when using paid advertising and selecting specific media vehicles such as radio stations, television programs, sections of the newspaper, magazines, and direct mail lists. Ideally, these were identified as "openings" when developing the creative brief. Again, media representatives will be able to provide audience profiles and recommendations. The goal will be to choose general media types, specific vehicles, and the timing most likely to reach, appeal to, and influence target audiences. *Compatibility* of the social marketing program and associated messages will also be key and will contribute to the ultimate impact of the given medium. For example, a message regarding safe gun storage is more strategically aligned with a parenting magazine than one on home decorating, even though both may have readerships with similar demographic profiles. And the timing of this ad would be best linked to special issues on youth violence or campus shootings.

Factor #4: Being There Just in Time

Many social marketers have found that an ideal moment to speak to the target audience is when they are about to choose between alternative, competing behaviors. They are at a fork in the road, and the social marketer wants a last chance to influence this decision. Tactics demonstrating this principle include the following:

- The use of the ♥ on menus signifying a smart choice for those interested in options that are low in fat, cholesterol, and/or calories
- The familiar forest fire prevention signs that give updates on the current level of threat for forest fires in the park
- A message on the backs of diapers reminding parents to turn their infants over, onto their backs, to sleep
- The idea of encouraging smokers (in the contemplation stage) to insert their child's photo under the wrappers of cigarette packs
- A sign at a beach that makes the benefit of a life vest clear (see Figure 14.9)
- A key chain for teens with the message "You Don't Have to Be Buzzed to Be Busted"
- A handmade tent card next to a napkin holder suggesting customers take only what they need

Factor #5: Being There "In The Event Of"

Communicators also want to prepare for events that are likely to motivate target audiences to listen, to learn more, and to alter their behaviors. Examples would include events such as an earthquake, a teen suicide in a small community, the listing of an endangered species, threats of drought and power blackouts, a famous female entertainer diagnosed with AIDS, a governor injured in an automobile accident and not wearing a seatbelt, a college student sexually assaulted after a rave party, or a politician diagnosed with prostate cancer. Events such as these often affect levels of awareness and belief relative to costs and benefits associated with behavior change. The amount of time it will take to learn about

Figure 14.9 A Sign at a Beach Shows the Benefit of a Life Vest

and prepare a home for a potential earthquake seems minor compared with suffering the costs and losses in a real earthquake. Though such events are often tragic, the silver lining is that target audiences in the precontemplation stage are often moved to contemplation, even action, and the social marketer can take advantage of the momentum created by heightened publicity and the need for practical information. Just as public relations professionals prepare for crisis communications, the social marketer also wants to prepare for these *opportunity communications* (see Figure 14.10).

Figure 14.10   Practical Behaviors Presented in a Popular Magazine After a Crisis[29]

Factor #6: Integrated Marketing Communications

Experience of commercial sector marketers routinely investing millions of dollars in marketing communications has led many companies to adopt the concept of *integrated marketing communications* (IMC), "where a company carefully integrates and coordinates its many communication channels to deliver a clear, consistent, and compelling message about the organization and its products."[28]

With integrated marketing communications, you achieve consistency in the use of slogans, images, colors, font types, key messages, and sponsor mentions in all media vehicles and customer touchpoints. It means that statistics and facts used in press releases are the same as those in printed materials. It means that television commercials have the same tone and style as radio spots and that print ads have the same look and feel as the program's Web site.[29]

In addition, IMC points to the need for a graphic identity and perhaps even a statement or manual describing graphic standards. The integrated approach also addresses the need for coordination and cooperation between those developing and disseminating program materials and, finally, calls for regular audits of all customer touchpoints.

Benefits of an integrated approach are significant, with (a) increased efficiencies in developing materials (e.g., eliminating the need for frequent debates over colors and typefaces and incremental costs for developing new executions) and (b) increased effectiveness of communications, given their consistent presentation in the marketplace.

Example: Friends Don't Let Friends Drive Drunk

In the early 1990s, the Ad Council and the U.S. Department of Transportation's National Highway Traffic Safety Administration introduced a new campaign encouraging friends to intervene in order to prevent a drunk person from getting behind the wheel. It was originally designed to reach 16- to 24-year-olds, who accounted for 42% of all fatal alcohol-related car crashes.[30] Eighty-four percent of Americans now recall having seen or heard a PSA with the now famous "Friends Don't Let Friends Drive Drunk" tagline. More impressively, nearly 80% report they have taken action to prevent a friend or loved one from driving drunk, and 25% report they have stopped drinking and driving as a result of the campaign.[31] This hard-hitting campaign was instrumental, it is reported, in achieving a 10% decrease in alcohol-related fatalities between 1990 and 1991—the single largest 1-year drop in alcohol-related fatalities ever recorded.[32]

Figure 14.11   Magazine Insert for a Memorable Campaign[33]

Communication channels have been consistent in their use of the tagline, emotional themes, and memorable stories of "innocent victims" and have included PSAs produced for TV, radio, print, out-of-home, and online media outlets (see Figure 14.12).

Factor #7: Knowing Advantages and Disadvantages of Media Type

Media decisions should also be based on advantages and limitations of each unique media type and should take into consideration the nature and format of key messages established in the creative brief. For example, a brief message such as "Choose a designated driver" can fit on a key chain or bar coaster, whereas a complex one such as "How to talk with your teen about suicide" would be more appropriate in a brochure or on a special radio program. Table 14.1 presents a summary of advantages and limitations for each of the major advertising categories.

Table 14.1   Profiles of Major Media Types

Medium	Advantages	Disadvantages
Newspapers	Flexibility, timeliness, good local market coverage, broad acceptability, high believability	Short life, poor reproduction quality, small pass-along audience
Television	Good mass-market coverage; low cost per exposure; combines sight, sound, and motion; appealing to the senses	High absolute costs, high clutter, fleeting exposure, less audience selectivity
Direct Mail	High audience selectivity, flexibility, allows personalization	Relative high cost per exposure, "junk mail" image
Radio	Good local acceptance, high geographic and demographic selectivity, low cost	Audio only, fleeting exposure; low attention ("the half-hear" medium); fragmented audiences
Magazines	High geographic and demographic selectivity, credibility, and prestige, high-quality reproduction, long life and good pass-along readership	Long ad purchase lead time, high cost, no guarantee of position
Outdoor	Flexibility, high repeat exposure, low cost, low message competition, good positional selectivity	Little audience selectivity, creative limitations
Internet	High selectivity, low cost, immediacy, interactive capabilities	Small, demographically skewed audience; relatively low impact; audience controls exposure
Sales Promotions	Attention-getting, stronger and quicker buyer response, incentives adding value	Short life, potential image of "trinkets and trash"
Public Relations	High credibility, ability to catch prospects off guard, reaching prospects preferring to avoid salespeople and advertisements	Less audience reach and frequency
Events & Experiences	Relevance, high involvement and active engagement, and more "soft sell"	Less audience reach, high cost per exposure
Personal Selling	Effective for understanding consumer objections and for building buyer preference, conviction, action, and relationships	Audience resistance, high cost

SOURCE: Adapted from Kotler, P., & Armstrong, G. (2001). *Principles of Marketing,* p. 553. Upper Saddle River, NJ: Prentice Hall. Reprinted with permission.

Factor #8: Your Budget

Even when all other factors are considered, resources and funding may very well have the final say in determining communication channels. In the ideal scenario, as we have discussed, media strategies and associated budgets are based on desired and agreed-upon campaign goals (e.g., reach 75% of youth at least nine times). In reality, plans are more often influenced by budgets and available funding sources. For example, first estimates of a draft media plan to achieve the above goal may indicate that costs for the desired reach and frequency exceed actual and fixed budgets. In this (all too common) scenario, you will need to prioritize and allocate funding to media types and vehicles judged to be most efficient and effective. In some cases, it may then be necessary and appropriate to reduce campaign goals (e.g., reach 50% of youth at least nine times) and/or create a phased approach to campaign implementation (e.g., achieve the reach and frequency goals in half the state).

ETHICAL CONSIDERATIONS WHEN SELECTING COMMUNICATION CHANNELS

Options for communication channels are numerous, and several factors for consideration have been identified in this chapter, including audience profile and campaign resources. Ethical considerations will also be a factor. Does the end justify the means in a case in which antiabortionists block the entrance to clinics and threaten the lives of doctors? Or what about a case in which activists threaten (but do not physically harm) a woman wearing a fur coat? Considerable mention was made of channels involving access to computers, e-mails, and the Internet. What about the fact that many target audiences don't have this access, even skills, to fully utilize and benefit from these new media campaigns?

And here's one to ponder. Is it wrong to advertise for a kidney donor? In April 2007, a column in the *National Review Online* mentioned the existence of a Web site that introduces patients needing an organ to humanitarians willing to donate one (MatchingDonors.com). One physician is evidently waging a campaign against such Web sites, believing the practice is unethical and should be illegal, as it "bypasses" the national organ donor list. Proponents of the Web site argue that those on the organ donor list only get organs harvested from cadavers and that there are currently 70,000 people waiting for a kidney and that half of those on this list will die while waiting.[34]

Chapter Summary

Communication channels, also referred to as media channels, can be categorized as one of three types: mass, selective, or personal. *Mass media* channels are called for when large groups of people need to be quickly informed and persuaded regarding an issue or desired behavior; *selective* channels are used when target markets can be reached more cost effectively through targeted channels such as direct mail and the Internet; *personal channels* are more costly but sometimes warranted in order to achieve behavior change objectives.

Traditional communication channels, like the label implies, are ones you are probably most familiar with and exposed to:

- Advertising and PSAs
- Public relations and special events
- Printed materials
- Special promotional items
- Signage and displays

You were encouraged to consider nontraditional channels and new media options, ones that may be more successful in "catching your audience by surprise." They may also be ones where your audience will spend more time considering your messages:

- Popular entertainment media
- Public art
- Product integration
- Social media
- Web sites
- Mobile phones for "pull versus push" campaigns

Eight factors were presented to guide your selection of communication types, vehicles, and timing:

Factor #1: Your Campaign Objectives and Goals

Factor #2: Desired Reach and Frequency

Factor #3: Your Target Audience

Factor #4: Being There Just in Time

Factor #5: Being There "In the Event Of"

Factor #6: Integrated Marketing Communications

Factor #7: Knowing Advantages and Disadvantages of Media Type

Factor #8: Your Budget

Measuring the Impact of Health Content on Popular TV Shows (2002)

THE HENRY J. KAISER FAMILY FOUNDATION[35]

Although a growing number of social marketers have been working with Hollywood writers and producers to incorporate public health information in their shows, evidence of the effectiveness of this approach is limited. In early 2001, however, an article published in the journal *Health Affairs* presented findings from national surveys conducted by researchers at the Kaiser Family Foundation to actually measure this impact. Their findings are encouraging.

Background

On April 10, 1997, one episode of the NBC drama *ER* briefly addressed emergency contraception through a short vignette about a patient who has been the victim of a date rape and then requests information in the emergency room about what she could do to prevent a pregnancy from the rape. The entire scene lasted about 3 minutes, and the actual discussion about the use of birth control pills for emergency contraception lasted only around 20 seconds.

On February 24, 2000, a short vignette featured a nurse (Carol Hathaway) who sees a teen patient recently diagnosed with cervical cancer. She explains to her that it could be related to the sexually transmitted disease human papillomavirus (HPV).

Working with a writer/producer of *ER* to get advance information about upcoming episodes, researchers at the Kaiser Family Foundation conducted surveys of regular viewers to determine the impact of entertainment media as an information source on health and health policy.

Methodology

Researchers conducted 10 separate national random-sample telephone surveys of regular viewers of *ER*. Surveys were conducted between March 1997 and April 2000 with a total of 3,500 regular *ER* viewers 18 and older (300–500 per survey). (A regular *ER* viewer is anyone reporting they usually watch three out of four new episodes of the show.) Six of the surveys tested whether viewers' awareness of specific health topics increased after the individual episodes of the show (emergency contraception and HPV). Four other surveys conducted throughout the 1997–1998 television season were part of a more general assessment of viewers' interest in health-related story lines and the personal actions they may have taken based on these story lines.

Findings

Awareness of the Emergency Contraception Episode: Viewers' awareness of emergency contraception increased 17 percentage points in the week after the episode aired. Among those surveyed who knew that a woman has options for preventing pregnancy even after having unprotected sex, the number who specifically mentioned that she could take birth control pills (the method mentioned in the show) increased by 23 percentage points. To measure whether these effects persisted over time, a separate sample of *ER* viewers was asked about emergency contraception two and a half months later, by which time awareness of emergency contraception had decreased to preepisode levels (see Table 14.2).

Awareness of the Human Papilloma Virus Episode: As with the emergency contraception episode, viewers' knowledge rose substantially. Specifically, the proportion of viewers who said they had heard of HPV nearly doubled in the week after the episode aired, from 24% to 47% of regular viewers. In addition, the proportion who could correctly define HPV and who were aware of its link to cervical cancer tripled. However, as was the case with the episode on emergency contraception, the increased level of awareness was not sustained over time.

Viewer Response to Health Content: Another issue addressed in the surveys was whether *ER* episodes led viewers to take any action with respect to health issues. Slightly more than half of regular viewers said that in addition to being entertained by *ER,* they also learned about important health issues from watching the show. Similarly, about half (51%) said they talked with family and friends about the health issues addressed on the show. A third of viewers said that they had gotten information from *ER* that helped them make choices about their own or their family's health care. About one in five said they had gone to other sources to find additional information about a health issue because of something they saw on *ER.* And one in seven viewers (14%) said they had contacted a doctor or health care provider about a health problem because of something they saw on *ER.*

Viewer Interest in Health-Related Story Lines: Viewers indicated substantial interest in

Table 14.2   Percentage of Regular ER Viewers Who Have Heard of HPV

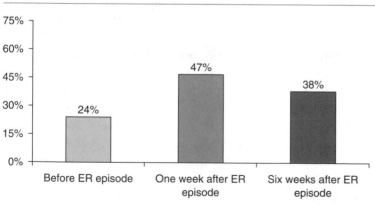

SOURCE: Kaiser Family Foundation Survey of *ER* Viewers on HPV and Cervical Cancer, February–April 2000.

the health-related story lines on *ER,* particularly when the story was centered on a personal drama involving one of the main characters of the show. However, the more abstract policy-oriented health story lines were of less interest to viewers.

Discussion

Although these surveys document that some viewers want to and do learn about health topics from entertainment television, they highlight that repetition of messages is the key to increased comprehension and longer-term retention among audiences. It also has implications that dramatically depicting health-related issues through entertainment television may be a mechanism to inform the public about key health topics. On the other hand, it seems worth the effort to try to make the content as accurate and science-based as possible and to take advantage of opportunities to convey public health messages that can improve health and sometimes save lives.

Part V

MANAGING SOCIAL MARKETING PROGRAMS

CHAPTER 15

Developing a Plan for Monitoring and Evaluation

Marketing is a learning game. You make a decision. You watch the results. You learn from the results. Then you make better decisions.[1]

—Philip Kotler

Now you've reached a step you may not be eager for—developing a plan for monitoring and evaluation. If this is true for you, your experiences and conversations may be similar to those people making the following common laments:

- My administrators and additional funders think it's nice I can report on how many PSAs we ran and how many hits we got to our Web site, but I can see it in their eyes. It's not enough. They want to know how many more people got an HIV/AIDS test as a result of our efforts. And actually, that's not even enough. What they really want to know is how many positives did we find and how much did it cost us to find each one.
- You think that's hard. In my line of work, they want to know if the fish are any healthier.
- Most of the evaluation strategies I've looked at could cost as much as the small budget I have for this campaign. I honestly can't justify it. And yet, everyone seems to want it.
- Quite frankly, my concern is with the results. What if it's bad news—that we didn't reach our goal? They like the plan, are going to fully fund it, and trust that we know what we're doing. Bad news could dampen any further work like this.

In this chapter's opening highlight, you'll read how one program director addresses these challenges, developing an evaluation approach for a youth suicide prevention program that she can stand behind and others respect.

MARKETING HIGHLIGHT

Youth Suicide Prevention (2007)

SUE EASTGARD, MSW, DIRECTOR
Youth Suicide Prevention Program of Washington

Background

On the weekend of Martin Luther King's holiday, Trevor Simpson drove north to the Tulalip Indian Reservation from his home in Edmonds, Washington. He went alone; he went without others knowing where he was going or why. In the quiet of the night, Trevor hung himself with the battery cable of his car.

Trevor was a popular student at Edmonds-Woodway High School. He was intelligent, earning a 3.9 grade point average. He was an athlete, playing halfback for the school's football team and coaching his younger brother's soccer team. He was adored by his parents and extended family. So why did he take his own life?

In 2003 there were 4,232 youth (10–24 years of age) completed suicides in the United States. Many, many more young people made suicide attempts that resulted in emergency room visits and hospitalizations. Boys and young men are much more likely to end their lives by suicide, while girls and young women make more attempts. Among ethnic groups, Native American young people have the highest rates of suicide.

Depression is a significant component of most suicidal deaths. Depression is a chemical imbalance—you can be born with it or you can develop it as a result of situational crises. Depression in children and adolescents looks different than it does in adults; irritability, anxiety, hypersensitivity to criticism, and physical complaints are common symptoms of depression for young people. Sadly, many depressed teens do not get diagnosed or do not receive adequate treatment.

About 80% of the time, depressed teens exhibit clues or warning signs about their thoughts of suicide. Trevor asked his friend Monica the day before he died, "If you were going to kill yourself, how would you do it?" In hindsight we can probably appreciate that Trevor was trying to talk about suicide, but unfortunately Monica did not know that talking about suicide was a warning sign. Trevor also gave his favorite baseball cap to his friend Jason, indicating that he was going to get another one. Jason admired Trevor's hat and was pleased to accept it as a sign of friendship. Had Jason known that giving away prized possessions was another sign, he would have reacted differently. In addition to these "clues," we need to also be watchful for a preoccupation with death, a hopeless mood, increased drug and alcohol use, and a change in normal activities. Prior suicidal behavior is also an important factor, as past behavior influences present and future behavior.

Target Audiences

The Youth Suicide Prevention Program (YSPP) is committed to reducing suicidal behaviors in Washington State by raising public awareness, by providing training, and by supporting communities to take action. Educational presentations to identify the warning signs and helpful intervention strategies are delivered to *parents, teachers, coaches,* and *mentors*. In middle and high schools across the state, student prevention teams facilitate learning for their *peers* regarding depression and how to help a friend who may be at risk of suicide. Formal training on suicide assessment and intervention is held for *professional caregivers*. YSPP also works with *coalitions* to plan and implement local suicide prevention efforts.

Desired Behaviors

Three behaviors are promoted to target audiences concerned that a youth is suicidal. The first way to be helpful to suicidal teens is to *show that you care*: ask how they are doing, listen to their feelings, and avoid giving advice or demanding that they "get over it." It is important that we attempt to understand their frustrations, their worries, their problems. As adults we usually have a capacity for greater perspective—thank goodness! Suicidal teens typically do not want to die; they want to find a solution to their problems.

The second intervention strategy is to *ask the question*. If you suspect young people may be at risk of suicide, it is important to ask directly and calmly, "Are you thinking about harming yourself, about dying?" This question will not plant the idea of suicide in their brain; it will actually give permission—if the thoughts

are present—to talk about them. Giving permission to talk about suicide can relieve pressure; not talking about suicide can leave adolescents feeling hurt and more alone.

If the answer to the question about suicide is yes *or* you are concerned that it is, then it is time to *get help*, the third intervention strategy. Help might mean calling a hotline or talking to a school counselor, coach, or favorite teacher. It is important not to leave suicidal youths alone.

Results

The mission of YSPP is to reduce the incidence of suicidal behaviors by building public awareness, offering training, and supporting communities to tackle the problem locally.

To build awareness we support peer-to-peer programming in middle and high schools across the state. While students do not always know whether their efforts have made a difference in the statistics related to suicidal behavior, they know that isolation and bullying are two behaviors that can enhance the risk of depression and suicide. As one student-participant said, "I have no idea if we saved any lives, but no one sits by themselves at lunch anymore." The peer-to-peer campaign messages might include "Be a Lifesaver" or "Take your friend by the hand before their hand takes their life."

In addition to student education, YSPP talks with caregivers—parents, scout leaders, pastors, educators, and soccer coaches—about adolescent depression and suicide. We reach out to the public through our Web site as well as through brochures, posters, newspaper articles, and TV and radio interviews. We work to address the stigma that gets in the way of seeking help in a time of crisis.

YSPP is providing training to frontline gatekeepers. We believe that learning how to intervene in a suicidal situation is as important as learning CPR; suicide intervention can be seen as psychological first aid. Our training workshops develop competencies in four areas: attitudes, knowledge, intervention, and resources. We adopt a highly interactive, applied learning approach ensuring that the participant comes away with skills and not just extensive notes written on a tablet but never looked at again.

Finally, we work to strengthen community safety nets for our kids. If every community built a stronger support system for youth, perhaps fewer young people would fall through the cracks. As one community advocate said, "We want to change the incredible sadness into an energy that would be usable and positive and actually do something." YSPP works to promote cooperation and collaboration between mental and physical health resources and families. We advocate for the early identification of children's mental health issues and encourage families to seek help, rather than avoid it. We support the accreditation and incorporation of local crisis hotlines into the national Lifeline— 1-800-273-TALK. We provide technical assistance and consultation for local groups that want to address the problems of depression and hopelessness in their community.

Results

Every suicide prevention program needs to include evaluation activities that help to determine the efficacy of the services. Given the complexity of the issue (and the cost of doing research), it may be impractical, even impossible, to determine whether a program is responsible for a decrease or increase in mortality and morbidity rates. We can, however, answer questions related to changes in attitudes, skills, and knowledge.

Research shows, for example, that more exposure to suicide prevention training creates a greater likelihood that students will use the three critical skills of "show you care, ask about suicide, and get help." As a result, we attempt to answer the following questions in order to evaluate our activities:

- Did training increase the likelihood that a teacher will be able to accurately assess and intervene with suicidal youth?
- Were there more referrals to the school counselor as a result of a curriculum focused on enhancing help-seeking behaviors?
- Did parents who have attended an educational presentation feel more comfortable asking young people directly about suicide?
- Can more youth identify the warning signs for suicide after the introduction of a curriculum than before?

Knowledge and skills gained by training participants at the close of a 2-day workshop persisted after 3 months and in some instances even persisted at 9 and 12 months. Over 35% of training participants reported contact with one or more suicidal youth and were referring youth to a wide range of resources. As a result of training, participants reported more comfort in helping a suicidal person, along with more confidence that they would try to help and a greater feeling of competence when actually helping.

STEP #8: DEVELOPING A PLAN FOR MONITORING AND EVALUATION

We recommend that you take time to develop a plan for monitoring and evaluating your social marketing effort before creating your budget in Step 9 and implementation plan in Step 10. You will want your final budget to include funding for this critical activity and your implementation plan to include action items to ensure it happens.

This chapter will guide you in determining these funding needs and identifying related activities. It is intended to help by outlining components of a monitoring and evaluation plan, posed in the form of questions you'll want to answer in a sequential way, starting with the toughest one, of course:

- Why are you conducting this measurement?
- What will you measure?
- How will you conduct these measurements?
- When will these measurements be taken?
- How much will it cost?

One distinction is important to clarify up front: the difference between the term *monitoring* and the term *evaluation*.

Monitoring refers to measurements that are conducted sometime after you launch your social marketing effort but before it is completed. Its purpose is to help you determine whether you need to make midcourse corrections that will ensure that you reach your ultimate marketing goals. Remember the VERB Summer Scorecard campaign mentioned in Chapter 2 encouraging tweens to monitor their physical activity and try new ways to be physically active throughout the summer? Program managers might be eager to know in July how the tweens are doing toward the goal to get 24 squares stamped by the end of the summer. Are the partners, such as public pools, honoring the special promised deals? Are parents being supportive of the effort? Methods to conduct monitoring in this particular case might simply involve talking with a few kids, partners, and parents on the phone and then making recommendations for any increased or new activities to support the kids during the rest of the summer.

Evaluation, on the other hand, is a measurement and final report on what happened, answering the bottom-line question: Did you reach your goals for changes in behaviors, knowledge, and attitudes? What percentage of tweens completed all 24 squares, and how does this compare to the plan's goal? Additional questions are also likely to be addressed in the evaluation. Were activities implemented on time and on budget? Were there any unintended consequences that will need to be addressed now or in future similar projects? Which program elements worked well to support outcomes? Which ones didn't? Was there anything missing? What will you do differently next time, if there is a next time?[2]

WHY ARE YOU CONDUCTING THIS MEASUREMENT?

Your purpose for this measurement often shapes what you measure, how you measure, and when. Consider the differing implications for your plan for each of the following potential reasons for your effort:

- To fulfill a grant requirement
- To do better the next time we conduct this same campaign
- To (hopefully) get continued, even increased funding
- To help us decide how to prioritize and allocate our resources going forward
- To alert us to midcourse corrections we need to make in order to achieve goals

For a Grant Requirement: Sometimes the nature of the monitoring and/or evaluation will be predetermined by specifications in a grant. Consider an example where a city receives a grant from a state department of transportation (DOT) to increase the use of pedestrian flags in the city's eight crosswalks in a downtown corridor. Assume the DOT is hoping that this city's campaign strategies are successful and that these strategies can then be shared by DOT with other cities in the state. The campaign's evaluation plan will certainly include measuring levels of flag usage before and after the campaign. And the funder will need to be assured that the data were collected using a systematic, reliable, and verifiable methodology, one that could be replicated in other cities as well.

To Do Better Next Time: What if, instead, you are sincerely interested in measuring what happened so that you can improve results in your next similar effort. Perhaps it is a pilot and you want to evaluate the campaign elements to decide what worked well and should be repeated, what could be improved, and what elements should be "dropped" next time around. Imagine a countywide effort to reduce smoking around children in cars and that a pilot the first year is to help determine what elements of the campaign should be used when rolled out in Year 2 countywide. The pilot includes a packet of materials sent home from school with children in the elementary schools and contains a secondhand tobacco smoke information card, a plug to replace the cigarette lighter, a smoke-free pledge card, and an air freshener with the campaign's slogan, "Please Smoke Outside." Follow-up surveys with parents will then measure changes in levels of smoking around their child in the car as well as parents' ratings on which of the materials in the packet they noticed, used, and said were influential. Imagine further that the results indicated that some of the parents thought the air freshener would reduce the harmful effects of the smoke, so they didn't change their habits. This finding, of course, would then lead the county to eliminate this $1.50 item when rolled out countywide.

To Get Support for Continued Funding: Often the purpose of an evaluation is to persuade funders to reinvest in the project to sustain it into the future. As would be imagined, key to this will be to identify criteria the funders will use to make their decisions and to then create an evaluation plan that includes measures that will provide this information. Consider the Road Crew case in Wisconsin mentioned in Chapter 9, the one describing a service using limousines and other luxury vehicles to pick up people at their home, business, or hotel, take them to the bars of their choice and home at the end of the evening—all for about $15–$20 an evening. A key statistic funders for this program were interested in was a cost benefit analysis, and the program's evaluation methodology provided just that. It showed an estimated $15,300 cost per crash avoided compared with a savings to all those impacted by a crash of $610,000.

To Help Determine Resource Allocation: Management may also, or instead, want to use an evaluation effort to help decide how resources should be allocated in the future. In King County, Washington, for example, the Department of Natural Resources and Parks wanted an evaluation survey to help decide which of some 30 community outreach efforts should receive more funding and which, perhaps, should be pulled back. This objective led to a plan to measure household behaviors that each of these 30 programs sought to influence (e.g., leave grass clippings on the lawn). Those programs with the greatest potential market opportunity for growth were then considered first for increased support, with market opportunity determined by the percentage of households doing the behavior sometimes, but not on a regular basis (the in action stage of change) or not doing the behavior at all but considering doing it (the contemplation stage of change).

To Decide If Course Corrections Are Needed: This purpose will lead to a monitoring effort, measuring sometime after an effort launches, but before completion, to determine whether goals are likely to be met based on how the market is responding. Think back to the *Inconvenient Truth* case on global warming. Given some of the pushback from critics of global warming, it would be interesting to know if the issue should be reframed as "climate protection" or "climate change."

WHAT WILL YOU MEASURE?

What you will measure to achieve your evaluation purpose is likely to fall into one or more of three categories: *outputs, outcomes,* and *impacts.* As you will read, required efforts and rigor vary significantly by category.

Output/Process Measures

The easiest and most straightforward measures are those describing your campaign's outputs, sometimes referred to as process measures. This measure focuses on quantifying your marketing activities as much as possible. They are distinct from outcome measures, those focusing on target audience response to these activities. Many are available in your records and databases.[3]

- **Numbers of Materials Distributed:** This measure refers to numbers of mailings, brochures, flyers, key chains, bookmarks, booklets, and coupons handed out. Note this does not indicate whether they were read or used—only that they were distributed.

- **Reach and Frequency:** Reach refers to the number of different people or households exposed to a particular image or message during a specified period of time. Frequency is the number of times within this time frame, on average, that the target audience was exposed to the communication.

- **Media Coverage:** Measures of media and public relations efforts, also referred to as earned media, may include reporting on numbers of *column inches* in newspapers and magazines, *minutes on television and radio* news and special programs, and *people in the audience* attending a planned speaker's events. Efforts are often made to determine and report what this coverage would have cost if it had been paid for.

- **Total Impressions/Cost per Impression:** This measurement combines information from several categories, such as reach and frequency, media exposure, and material dissemination. Typically these numbers are combined to create an estimate of the total number of people in the target market who were exposed to campaign elements. Taking this to the next level of rigor, *to achieve a cost per impression, total campaign costs associated with this exposure can then be divided by the estimated number of people exposed to the campaign.* For example, consider a statewide campaign targeting mothers to increase children's fruit and vegetable consumption; the campaign may have collected exposure information from media buys (e.g., parenting magazines) and any additional efforts (e.g., messages on grocery bags). Let's assume they were able to estimate that 100,000 mothers were exposed to these campaign efforts and that the associated costs were $10,000. Their cost per impression would be $10. These statistics can then be used over time to compare the cost efficiency of varying strategies. Suppose, for example, that in a subsequent campaign, efforts reached 200,000 mothers after funds were redirected to sending messages from child care and preschools, thus reducing the cost per impression to $5.

- **Implementation of Program Elements:** An audit of major activities planned and implemented (or not) may shed light on campaign outputs and outcomes. Did you do everything you planned to do? Did you complete activities on time and on budget? This audit can help address the tendency many of us have to expect campaign goals to be achieved, even though we did not implement all planned activities or spend originally allocated funds in planned time frames.

Outcome Measures

Measuring outcomes are a little more rigorous, as you are now assessing customer response to your outputs, most likely involving some type of primary research surveys. Ideally, these measures were determined by the goals you established in Step 4, the specific measurable results you want your program to achieve—one or more of the following types:

- **Changes in Behavior:** This may be measured and stated in terms of a *change in percentage* (e.g., adult binge drinking decreased from 17% to 6%), a *percentage increase or decrease* (e.g., seatbelt usage increased by 20%), and/or a *change in numbers* (e.g., 40,000 new households signed up for food waste recycling bins, increasing the total number of households participating from 60,000 to 100,000).

- **Changes in Behavior Intent:** This measure might be appropriate for campaigns with minimal exposure or when campaigns have been running for only short periods of time. It may be the most appropriate measure for campaigns targeting those in the precontemplation stage, when the social marketer's goal is to move them to contemplation and then (eventually) to the action stage.

- **Changes in Knowledge:** This may include changes in awareness of important *facts* (e.g., five drinks at one sitting is considered binge drinking), *information* (e.g., an estimated 75,000 people are on waiting lists for organ transplants), and *recommendations* (e.g., eat five or more servings of vegetables and fruit daily for better health).

- **Changes in Belief:** Typical indicators include *attitude* indicators (e.g., my vote doesn't count), *opinions* (e.g., native plants are not attractive), and *values* (e.g., tanning is worth the risk).

- **Responses to Campaign Elements:** Here you may be counting *calls to an 800 number* (e.g., for a booklet on natural gardening), *redemption of coupons* (e.g., for a bike helmet), *mail or Internet orders or requests for more information* (e.g., for a free consultation on home earthquake preparedness), *purchase of tangible objects* that were promoted (e.g., number of new low-flow toilets sold or energy-saving lightbulbs compared with numbers in prior year), and *services provided* (e.g., number of blood pressure checks given at a mall event), or *participation rates* (e.g., number of coupons for home emergency kits redeemed).

- **Campaign Awareness:** Though not necessarily an indicator of impact or success, measures of awareness of campaign elements provide some feedback on the extent to which the campaign was noticed and recalled. Measurements might include levels of *unaided awareness* (e.g., what you have seen or heard lately in the news about legal limits for blood alcohol levels while driving); *aided awareness* (e.g., what have you seen or heard lately in the news about our state's new 0.08% legal limit); or *proven awareness* (e.g., where did you read or hear about this change in the law).

- **Customer Satisfaction Levels:** Customer satisfaction levels associated with service components of the campaign provide important feedback for analyzing results and for planning future efforts (e.g., ratings on levels of satisfaction with counseling at the Women, Infants, and Children [WIC] program clinics).

- **Partnerships and Contributions Created:** Levels of participation and contributions from outside sources are significant and represent positive responses to your campaign, even though they may not be a reflection of the impact on your target audience behaviors. These may include numbers of and hours spent by volunteers, partners, and coalition members participating in the campaign, as well as amounts of cash and in-kind contributions received from foundations, media, and businesses.

- **Policy Changes:** A legitimate campaign goal may focus on causing an important change in *policies* or *infrastructures* that will encourage and/or support behavior change. In the interest of oral health for children, for example, efforts have paid off in some communities persuading grocery stores to remove candy and gum from checkout lanes.

Impact Measures

This measure is the most rigorous, costly, and controversial of all measurement types. In this category, you are attempting to measure the impact that changes in behavior you achieved (e.g., more homeowners using natural fertilizers) have had on the social issue your plan is addressing (e.g., water quality). It would, indeed, be great to be able to report on the following types of impact measures, in addition to outputs and outcomes:

- *Lives saved* (e.g., from reducing drinking and driving)
- *Diseases prevented* (e.g., from increased physical activity)
- *Injuries avoided* (e.g., from safer workplace practices)
- *Water quality improved* (e.g., from taking prescription drugs back to pharmacies)
- *Water supply increased* (e.g., from increased purchases of low-flow toilets)
- *Air quality improved* (e.g., from fewer leaf blowers being used in a community)
- *Landfill reduced* (e.g., from composting food waste)
- *Wildlife and habitats protected* (e.g., from decreases in littering)
- *Animal cruelty reduced* (e.g., from increases in spaying and neutering)
- *Crimes prevented* (e.g., from increases in use of motion sensors for outdoor lighting)

The reality is that not only is this rigorous and costly to determine, it may in fact be inappropriate and inaccurate to try to connect your campaign activities with these impacts, even though they were designed with them in mind.

Several key points can assuage you and others. First, you need to trust, or assume, that the behavior that was chosen for your campaign is one that can have an impact on the issue (e.g., that folic acid can help prevent some birth defects). Second, you may need to wait longer to measure, as there may be a lag between adopting the behavior and seeing the impact (e.g., increased physical activity to lower blood pressure levels). Finally, your methodology for measurement may need to be quite rigorous, controlling for variables that may also be contributing to the social issue (e.g., there may not be an improvement in water quality in a lake if during your campaign period a new manufacturer in the area started polluting the same waters). You will need to be diligent and forthright about whether you believe you can even determine and claim this victory.

How Monitoring and Evaluation Relates to Logic Models

The terms *Output*, *Outcome,* and *Impact* are also used as labels in program evaluation logic models. You may be familiar with ones with labels similar to those used in Table 15.1. In these models, there are usually the additional categories of Inputs and Activities, ones included with Outputs as part of your Process Evaluation. As also noted in the table, Outcomes are more near term and Impacts long term. In reality, there would be multiple mentions in each column and arrows showing relationships between inputs and activities, outputs and short-term outcomes, and short-term outcomes and long-term impacts.

HOW WILL YOU MEASURE?

Our third step in developing an evaluation and monitoring plan is to identify methodologies and techniques that will be used to actually measure indicators established in our first step. Chapter 5 outlined typical research methodologies available to you, a few

Table 15.1   Hypothetical Excerpts From a Logic Model for a Suicide Prevention Program Evaluation

PROCESS EVALUATION			IMPACT EVALUATION	
INPUTS	*ACTIVITIES*	*OUTPUTS*	*SHORT-TERM OUTCOMES*	*LONG-TERM IMPACTS*
Federal, state, and local funding	Identification of greatest suicide risk factors for middle school youth	Youth and families are informed about risk factors and resource availability at community forums	Increased youth and family awareness and knowledge of suicide warning signs	Reduced suicides among teens

of which are most typical for evaluation and monitoring measures. In general, audience surveys will be the primary technique used in measuring outcomes, given the focus on the actual influence you have had on your target audience in terms of behavior, knowledge, and beliefs. Records, contact reports, anecdotal comments, and project progress reports will be the primary sources of data for measuring outputs. Impact measures, on the other hand, may require more scientific or technical surveys.

Quantitative Surveys are needed when reliable data are key to evaluation (e.g., percentage increase in levels of physical activity) and are most commonly conducted using telephone surveys, self-administered questionnaires, and/or in-person interviews. These may be proprietary or shared-cost studies in which several organizations have questions for similar populations. They may even rely on established surveys such as the Behavioral Risk Factor Surveillance System (BRFSS), presented in Chapter 7.

Qualitative Surveys should be considered when evaluation requirements are less stringent or more subjective in nature and include methodologies such as focus groups, informal interviews, and capturing anecdotal comments. Focus groups might be appropriate for exploring with child care providers which components of the immunization tracking kits were most and least useful and why. This information might then refocus efforts for the next kit reprint. Informal interviews might be used to understand why potential consumers walked away from the low-flow toilet display, even after reading accompanying materials and hearing testimonials from volunteers. Anecdotal comments regarding a television campaign might be captured on phone calls to a sexual assault resource line.

Observation Research is often more reliable than self-reported data and, when possible, the most appropriate technique and can be used for evaluating behaviors such as wearing a life vest, washing hands before returning to work, or topping off gas tanks. It may also provide more insight for assessing skill levels and barriers than self-reported data (e.g., sorting garbage and placing it in proper containers or observing a WIC client finding her way around a farmers' market for the first time).

Scientific or Technical Surveys may be the only sure methodology to assess the impact of your efforts. If you are charged with reporting back on the difference your efforts made in reducing diseases, saving lives, improving water quality, and the like, you will need help designing and conducting reliable scientific surveys that not only are able to measure changes in these indicators but can also link these changes to your social marketing campaign.[4]

Control Groups used in combination with quantitative and scientific or technical surveys will further ensure that results can be closely tied to your campaign and program efforts. A drug and alcohol prevention campaign might be implemented in high schools in one community but not in another similar community. Extra precautions can even be taken to ensure the similarity of the control groups by conducting surveys prior to the selection of the groups and then factoring in any important differences. Results on reported drug use in the control group of high schools are then compared with those in the other (similar) communities.

Records and Databases will be very useful for several indicators, particularly those measuring responses to campaign elements and dissemination of campaign materials. This may involve keeping accurate track of number of visits to a Web site and length of time spent, numbers of calls (e.g., to a tobacco quitline), numbers of requests (e.g., for child care references), numbers of visits (e.g., to a teen clinic), numbers of people served (e.g., at car seat inspections), or numbers of items collected (e.g., at a needle exchange). This effort may also involve working with suppliers and partners to provide similar information from their records and databases, such as numbers of coupons redeemed (e.g., for trigger locks), tangible objects sold (e.g., compost tumblers featured in the campaign), or requests received (e.g., organ donation applications processed).

WHEN WILL YOU MEASURE?

Earlier, we distinguished between evaluation and monitoring, referring to final assessments of efforts as *evaluation* and ongoing measurements as *monitoring.* Timing, then, for measurement efforts is likely to happen as follows:

1. *Prior* to campaign launch, sometimes referred to as precampaign or baseline measures

2. *During* campaign implementation, thought of as tracking and monitoring surveys, and may be one time only or over a period of years (i.e., longitudinal surveys)

3. *Postcampaign* activities, referring to measurements taking place when all campaign elements are completed, providing data on short-term outcomes and long-term impact

Baseline measures are critical when campaigns have specific goals for change and future campaign efforts and funders will rely on these measures for campaign assessment. These are then compared with postcampaign results, providing a *pre- and postevaluation* measure. Monitoring efforts during campaigns are often conducted to provide input for changes midstream and to track changes over time. Postcampaign (final) assessments are the most typical points in time for evaluation, especially when resources and tight time frames prohibit additional efforts. A few programs will use all points in time for evaluation, most common when significant key constituent groups or funders require solid evidence of campaign outcomes.

HOW MUCH WILL IT COST?

Costs for recommended monitoring and evaluation activities will vary from *minimal* costs for those that simply involve checking records and databases or gathering anecdotal comments, to *moderate* costs for those involving citizen surveys or observation research, to potentially *significant* costs for those needing scientific or technical surveys. Ideally, decisions to fund these activities will be based on the value they will contribute to your program. If it will assist you in getting support and continued funding for your program, it may be a wise investment. If it helps you refine and improve your effort going forward, there is likely to be a payback in terms of return on your investment. Once a methodology is determined based on your research purpose, you can then assess these potential costs versus potential benefits.

ETHICAL CONSIDERATIONS IN EVALUATION PLANNING

Ethical considerations for monitoring and evaluation are similar to those discussed regarding research and have the most focus on the respondents that are surveyed for the evaluation.

One additional issue worthy of mention is the extent to which you should (or can) measure and report on unintended outcomes (consequences) as well, both positive and negative. For example, many program managers are now reporting concerns with their success in encouraging recycling. Although volumes of materials are being recycled that might otherwise have been put in landfills, managers believe they have significantly increased the use of recyclable materials. Anecdotal comments such as these confirm their fears: "I don't worry about printing extra copies anymore because I'm using recycled paper and I'll put any copies not used in the recycling bin" and "I don't worry about buying small bottles of water to carry around because I can recycle them." As a result, environmentalists in some communities are now beginning to direct more of their efforts to the other two legs of their "three-legged stool": "Reduce use" and "Reuse."

CHAPTER SUMMARY

Key components of an evaluation and monitoring plan are determined by answers to the following questions:

- Why are you conducting this measurement?
- What will you measure?
- How will you conduct these measurements?
- When will these measurements be taken?
- How much will it cost?

Reasons *why* you are measuring will guide your research plan, as methodologies will vary according to your reason for measurement. Is it to fulfill a grant requirement? To do better the next time you conduct this same campaign, to (hopefully) get continued, even increased funding? To help you decide how to prioritize and allocate your resources going forward? Or to alert you to midcourse corrections you need to make in order to achieve goals?

What you will measure to achieve your evaluation purpose is likely to fall into one or more of three categories: outputs, outcomes, impacts. Output measures report on campaign activities, outcomes on target audience responses, and impacts on improvements in social conditions, as a result of targeted behavior changes.

Optional techniques for *measurement* include surveys that are quantitative, qualitative, observational, or scientific/technical in nature, as well as ones that use control groups and rely on records and databases.

You will also determine in this plan *timing* for evaluations, considering opportunities to measure prior to the campaign launch, during campaign implementation, and postcampaign.

Finally, you determine *costs* for your proposed efforts, ones it was suggested should be weighed in light of potential benefits.

RESEARCH HIGHLIGHT

Improving Service Delivery at the Internal Revenue Service (2007)

PETE WEBB
Pacific Consulting Group

Purpose

While the mandate of the Internal Revenue Service (IRS) is to collect tax revenues through the administration and enforcement of tax laws, the IRS's mission statement is "Provide America's taxpayers top quality service by helping them understand and meet their tax responsibilities and by applying the tax law with integrity and fairness to all." Commissioner Mark Everson has said that the IRS's "working equation" for fulfilling its mission is "Service Plus Enforcement Equals Compliance." The provision of high-quality service to taxpayers is a critical element in maximizing the number of citizens who voluntarily comply with desired behaviors—to complete tax returns correctly and pay the right amount of taxes owed on time. Failure to do so creates a societal problem in that tax shortfalls either increase the burden on law-abiding citizens to make up the difference or that important government programs that rely on tax revenues are underfunded or eliminated altogether.

The IRS provides services to taxpayers through a variety of distribution channels. The most heavily used includes a nationwide network of about 450 walk-in tax assistance offices (7 million visits annually), a toll-free 800 number (61 million calls annually), and a Web site (143 million contacts in 2005). Services most sought by taxpayers include getting forms and publications, answering tax law questions, getting refund information, tax return preparation assistance, and getting information about a notice received from the IRS. Despite heavy use of all three service delivery channels, many taxpayers familiar with a particular channel are unaware of how another might better serve their needs. In addition, faced with severe budget constraints, the IRS must improve the efficiency of its services by cutting back on those that cost the most without reducing the overall level of service to taxpayers.

Methodology

To help achieve this goal, research was undertaken to determine the specific attributes of service most important to taxpayers in order to help develop marketing strategies for migrating taxpayers from more expensive to less expensive service delivery channels. (Costs per contact in 2005 were $28.73 for tax assistance centers, $19.46 for toll-free assisted, $.71 for toll-free automated, and $.13 for the Web site.) The audience for this research was all individual taxpayers, numbering approximately 130 million. In addition, Congress has mandated that particular attention be paid to disadvantaged groups—including low-income, handicapped, senior citizen, and limited English proficiency populations—to ensure that strategies developed for the tax-paying population as a whole do not adversely affect any of these groups.

The survey research method employed was choice-based conjoint analysis. This method is growing rapidly in popularity for its realistic portrayal of decisions consumers make among competing alternatives in the marketplace. It presents survey respondents with a number of hypothetical scenarios, each showing several possible choices of service delivery channels with different levels of service on several attributes taxpayers consider important in obtaining the service they need. Respondents evaluate each alternative relative to the others and select the one they would prefer if these were the actual choices they faced in the marketplace. For example, one scenario might look like this:

Each respondent is asked to evaluate 8–10 of these scenarios, each showing a different combination of attribute levels for each of the channel choices. While there are literally thousands of possible combinations of attribute levels, only a small fraction is required in order to determine exactly what is driving each respondent's choices and what those choices would be for any possible combination. Output from the conjoint analysis consists of a numeric rating of the relative importance of each service attribute and the overall preferences for each channel for any combination of attribute levels. This can be expressed at the individual respondent level, for the respondent group as a whole, or for any particular subgroup of respondents of interest.

We determined which particular service attributes to include in the analysis through a series of focus groups with taxpayers from a wide spectrum of geographic and socioeconomic groups. To ensure that the conjoint task was not too difficult for respondents, an initial list of 12–15 attributes was pared to the 4 noted in the example above (research has shown that more than 4 or 5 attributes in the

Table 15.2   Service Delivery Options and Levels of Service

IRS Tax Assistance Method	IRS Office	Toll-Free Line Automated	Web site	Toll-Free Line Assisted
Access Time	To reach office and speak to rep **60 minutes**	To find the right menu choice **3 minutes**	To find the right section **15 minutes**	To speak to rep **5 minutes**
Servicing Time	Once you see rep **5 minutes**	To listen to and understand answer **3 minutes**	To read and understand answer **1 minute**	To get an answer to question **10 minutes**
Hours of Availability	**Regular business hours, evenings, and weekends**	**24 hours, 7 days**	**24 hours, 7 days**	**Regular business hours plus evenings**
Percentage First Contact Resolution	**85%**	**95%**	**75%**	**95%**

conjoint task leads to unrealistic simplification on the part of respondents in order to complete the choice task). For each of these attributes, three levels were presented across the scenarios respondents evaluated. The ranges for each attribute were chosen to reflect the lowest levels taxpayers would consider acceptable, the highest levels the IRS could realistically hope to achieve, and a level somewhere in between.

The survey was administered online using respondents recruited from a panel maintained by a leading market research firm. Respondents completed the survey either online or, for those without computers, using an interactive television set-top box.

Findings

Results of this research proved very favorable to the IRS in terms of its objective of shifting taxpayers from high-cost to low-cost service delivery channels. In particular, the Web site is preferred over either office visits or assisted telephone calls for most information-seeking interactions. In addition, the telephone is preferred to office visits for most transactional interactions.

To achieve the desired migration requires a range of marketing strategies now being developed and implemented by the IRS. The main difference between the results of the conjoint analysis and the behavior currently observed in the marketplace is that the conjoint exercise reflects full awareness on the part of respondents about what each channel can provide on the attributes taxpayers consider important. In actuality, awareness of this information is severely limited. For example, many taxpayers who prefer to go to an IRS office for service have never used the Web or even the toll-free telephone line and therefore have no idea that they could get the same service they do in person—in many instances much quicker. Thus, relative to preferences, the Web site is currently severely underutilized relative to all other channels and the toll-free line is underutilized relative to office visits.

In addition to raising awareness of the capabilities of the Web and the toll-free telephone line (and especially the automated toll-free service), the IRS is considering the use of a range of marketing techniques for achieving their service objectives covering all of the 4Ps. For example:

- Product: Content quality enhancements for the Web site; improved first-contact resolution for the toll-free line
- Price: Charging a fee (or even limiting access) to higher-income taxpayers for interactions with staff at IRS offices
- Place: Reducing wait times for reaching toll-free representatives (especially during the January–April tax season); closing some IRS offices
- Promotion: Promoting the toll-free line and the Web site at IRS offices; promoting the Web site while on hold for a toll-free phone representative

CHAPTER 16

Establishing Budgets and Finding Funding

Corporate and nonprofit partnerships that are "built to last" are invaluable. A meaningful partnership in which the cause is intertwined with each brand's DNA can exponentially enhance the positive impacts on business and society.

—Carol Cone
*Chairman and Founder
Cone LLC*

In this chapter, not only will you read about how to determine and justify budgets for your proposed plans, you will explore options for additional funding. You will read that we encourage you to seriously consider opportunities for corporate support for your initiatives, such as ones mentioned in the opening Marketing Highlight featuring the Go Red for Women campaign. In the ethical considerations section of the chapter, we'll then ask you to think back on your reaction to the following examples of corporate initiatives related to decreasing childhood obesity:

Sesame Street: A press release from the Sesame Workshop in September 2005 presented findings from a research study titled "The Effectiveness of Characters on Children's Food Choices" (the "Elmo/Broccoli Study"). It indicated that "intake of a particular food increased if it carried a sticker of a *Sesame Street* character. For example, in the control group (no characters on either food) 78% of children participating in the study chose a chocolate bar over broccoli, whereas 22% chose the broccoli. However, when an Elmo sticker was placed on the broccoli and an unknown character was placed on the chocolate bar, 50% chose the chocolate bar and 50% chose the broccoli. Such outcomes suggest that the *Sesame Street* characters could play a strong role in increasing the appeal of healthy foods."[1]

Nickelodeon: In an article titled "Regaining the Health of a Nation: What Business Can Do About Obesity," Berry, Seiders, and Hergenroeder mention *Nickelodeon's* initiative to reducing childhood obesity. "In October of 2005, *Nickelodeon* held its 2nd annual Worldwide Day of Play, a part of its larger Let's Just Play initiative. The network went dark for the first time in its 25-year history, from 12 p.m. to 3 p.m., replacing its usual programming with a broadcast message that encouraged kids to go outside and play. More than 60,000 kids registered online to get a number to wear to Day of Play events, and 40,000 kids attended events organized by *Nickelodeon* in selected American cities and abroad."[2]

MARKETING HIGHLIGHT

Go Red for Women (2007)

KRISTIAN DARIGAN, CONE LLC

KATHY ROGERS, AMERICAN HEART ASSOCIATION

CAROL CONE, CHAIRMAN AND FOUNDER, CONE LLC

Background

In 2003, the American Heart Association (AHA) faced a challenge. Cardiovascular disease claimed the lives of nearly 500,000 American women each year, yet women were not paying attention. In fact, many even dismissed it as an "older man's disease." To dispel the myths and raise awareness of heart disease as the number one killer of women, the AHA and Cone LLC created Go Red For Women (GRFW)—a passionate, emotional social movement designed to empower women to take charge of their heart health.

To truly make change and help save lives, the AHA needed more than the limited budget of a nonprofit. To maximize available funds and communications resources, the AHA needed new, stronger relationships with corporate partners, particularly those experienced in targeting and engaging women. The AHA's traditional corporate base had been the largely business to business (B2B) health care industry, but to best reach women within their daily lives, GRFW would need the funds and marketing firepower of the more consumer-facing corporate sector.

Increasing Passion for the Cause: Merging the "White Coat" With the "Red Dress"

To overcome its long-held reputation among consumers as a "stuffy," clinical organization, the AHA adopted the symbol for women and heart disease, the red dress, as the icon for GRFW and the color red as the movement's signature color, creating an immediately identifiable face for the cause. Wrapped in this new look and feel, the AHA issued a simple call to action for women: join the movement and wear red. When women enrolled (via phone, online, or at events), they received a red dress pin and information welcoming them to the movement and showing them how to reduce their risks (see Figure 16.1).

Strategy: Sparking a Movement: Reaching Women Where They Are

To literally flood the market with the urgency and the passion of the cause, the AHA developed GRFW as a diversified movement with outreach in multiple channels. In the first of these channels, retail stores, product promotions were held by corporate sponsors

Figure 16.1 National Wear Red Day Poster Urges Women to Wear Red and Join the Movement

nationwide from Hamilton Beach red kitchen appliances to Swarovski Power of Love jewelry to Kellogg's Smart Start gift with purchase, all with proceeds benefiting GRFW.

Companies celebrated National Wear Red Day, an annual fundraiser held on the first Friday in February. Participating companies received implementation tool kits, and employees were encouraged to donate $5 and wear something red. Individuals were able to visually show their commitment to the cause, raise awareness among their friends, families, and coworkers, and contribute critical funds to the movement.

To build on these national efforts, AHA regional and local offices reached women personally, in their own communities, through Cities Go Red activities, including local

women's luncheons, advocacy efforts, mayoral proclamations, buzz events, and more. Communications and social marketing techniques focused around key annual GRFW push times (February for American Heart Month and Valentine's Day, and May for Mother's Day). From a national call-in day, to billboard and transit public service announcements (PSAs), to life-sized red dress statues, to celebrity spokespersons, the flurry of communications catapulted GRFW into popular culture.

Amidst the flash and hype, the AHA stayed true to its traditions by deeply rooting the cause efforts in science. With the launch of GRFW, the AHA released comprehensive guidelines for treating heart disease in women and continued to update the research as the movement developed. The information was disseminated to consumers via wallet cards and brochures and to physicians via tool kits. This blend of style and substance became the signature of the GRFW movement and attracted consumers, health care professionals, and companies alike.

Strategy: Building Meaningful Partnerships

While the AHA had built solid strategies and executional tactics, the organization knew corporate sponsors would be necessary to amplify its voice in the marketplace and sustain the momentum. To attract companies, Cone first recommended revisions to the AHA's corporate relations policies that would allow companies access to what they wanted most—the AHA logo, with 98% unaided consumer recognition. These revisions included relaxing restrictions to enable use of the GRFW brand (which included the AHA's recognizable heart and torch logo) on packages. Logo-use policies varied among high mission-alignment (e.g., pharmaceutical industry) to low mission-alignment (e.g., consumer goods) to alleviate danger of implied endorsement of the former.

To allow companies of all sizes to participate, enhance the length of new partnerships, and allow companies to customize their support, the team developed tiered sponsorship levels. National sponsors, the highest level, were offered a 3-year contract and visibility throughout national GRFW elements. Supporting sponsors, the second tier, also signed on for a 3-year commitment but received visibility around only certain assets of particular interest. Cause-related marketing sponsorships were offered at a minimum cost of entry for those companies interested in raising funds through product promotions. At the local level, sponsorship packages were sold for Cities Go Red and local luncheons to maximize funds raised and spread grassroots awareness.

Once companies were signed on, the AHA encouraged all partners to activate their sponsorship by weaving the cause into PR, marketing, advertising, Web content, events, collateral, in-store signage, and other activities. The more engaged the sponsors were in the cause, the more their brand was associated with the movement, and the more satisfied they became with their investment.

To maintain these larger, longer-term relationships, the AHA offered enhanced account management, assigning each sponsor a corporate relations staff member to field questions, offer ideas, and act as an internal ambassador to help navigate the administration of the partnership. Staff members were also able to assess and report results and return on investment back to sponsors, keeping them apprised of progress.

Results: Making an Impact: Checking the Numbers

With the enormous aid of corporate dollars, GRFW enjoys continued success, building women's awareness of heart disease as their number one killer to 55% in 2005, up from 34% in 2000. By the end of 2006, more than $60 million had been raised, more than 500,000 women had joined the movement, and 50% of consumers named GRFW as a cause movement that would be important to them in 2007.

The movement has been overwhelmed by companies pledging their support, including current national sponsors Macy's and Merck and supporting sponsors Bayer, Kellogg's, and Campbell's. At the cause-related marketing level, numerous companies participate, including Swarovski Crystal, Day-Timer, Key Bank, Flooring America, Hamilton Beach, Brighton Collectibles, V8, and Yankee Candle. Hundreds of other companies and health organizations have joined at the local level.

In addition to monetary support, companies volunteered their marketing assets to drastically raise awareness. Highlights include Macy's Shop for a Cause Day, employee engagement, and national ad placements; Kellogg's $35 million in-kind TV and print advertising with celebrity partner Sela Ward; Campbell's online Red Dress community and auction, celebrity partner Lorraine Bracco, and ad purchase and on-air messaging on the popular primetime show *Deal or No Deal*.

This wave of corporate support helped to greatly increase GRFW's impact, alerting countless women of their risk and empowering them to love their hearts. The AHA's sophisticated recruitment and retention of corporate sponsors allowed for what was originally a limited budget to expand, giving GRFW a prominent place in women's hearts in a short period of time. By continuing to work through multiple consumer channels and welcoming corporate sponsors to become fully engaged in the movement, the AHA hopes to further raise awareness and substantially reduce heart disease in American women (see Figure 16.2).

Figure 16.2 The Go Red Heart Checkup Urges Women to "Know Their Numbers" and Their Risk of Heart Disease

STEP #9: ESTABLISHING BUDGETS

Step 9, the budgeting process, is "where the rubber hits the road." You are now ready to identify price tags for strategies and activities that you have identified in your plan. Once this number is totaled, you will evaluate this potential cost by referring to anticipated benefits from targeted levels of behavior change, compare this with current funding levels, and, if needed, identify potential additional resources. This chapter will take you through each of these budgeting phases.

DETERMINING BUDGETS

In the commercial as well as nonprofit and public sectors, several approaches are often cited as possibilities to consider for determining marketing budgets.[3] The following three have the most relevance for social marketing:

The *affordable method*. Budgets are based on what the organization has available in the yearly budget or on what has been spent in prior years. For example, a county health department's budget for teen pregnancy prevention might be determined by state funds allocated every 2 years for the issue, and a local blood bank's budget for the annual blood drive might be established each year as a part of the organizational budgeting process.

The *competitive-parity method*. In this situation, budgets are set or considered on the basis of what others have spent for similar efforts. For example, a litter campaign budget might be established on the basis of a review of media expenses from other states that have been successful at reducing litter using mass media campaigns.

The *objective-and-task method.* Budgets are established by (a) reviewing specific objectives, (b) identifying the tasks that must be performed to achieve these objectives, and (c) estimating the costs associated with performing these tasks. The total is the preliminary budget.[4] For example, the budget for a utility's marketing effort for recycling might be based on estimated costs, including *staffing* a new telephone service center for questions on what can be recycled; *plaques* for recognizing homeowner participation; and *promotional strategies,* including television ads, radio spots, statement stuffers, and flyers. These total costs are then considered in light of any projections in increased revenues and decreased costs for the utility.

The most logical of these approaches, and one consistent with our planning process, is the objective-and-task method. In this scenario, you will identify costs related to your marketing mix strategy (product, price, place, and promotion) as well as evaluation and monitoring efforts. This becomes a preliminary budget, one that is based on what you believe you need to do in order to achieve the goals established in Step 4 of your plan. (In subsequent sections of this chapter, we discuss options to consider when this preliminary budget exceeds currently available funds, including sources to explore for additional funding, as well as the potential for revising strategies and/or reducing behavior change goals.)

More detailed descriptions of typical costs associated with implementing the marketing plan follow. A brief example is included to further illustrate the nature of identifying strategies with budget implications. In this example, assume a hospital has developed a draft marketing plan to decrease the number of employees commuting to work in single-occupant vehicles (SOVs). The campaign *objective* is to influence employees to use public transportation, car pools, van pools, or walk or bike to work, with a *goal* to decrease the number of SOVs on campus by 10% (100 vehicles) over a 12-month period. The hospital is motivated by a desire to build a new wing, an effort that will require land use permits granted, in part, based on impacts on traffic congestion in the surrounding neighborhoods.

Product-related costs are most often associated with producing or purchasing any accompanying *tangible objects* and developing or enhancing associated *services* needed to support the behavior change. Costs may include those that are direct costs for providing these goods and services or may be indirect ones, such as staff time. Product-related cost considerations for the hospital will include the need to lease additional vans from the county's transit system, install new bike racks, and construct several additional showers for employee use if marketing goals are in fact met. Incremental service charges as a result of increased efforts might include costs for temporary personnel to provide ride share matching or to build and maintain a special online software program for ride sharing.

Price-related costs include those associated with incentives, recognition programs, and rewards. In some cases, it includes net loss from sales of any goods and services associated with the marketing effort. Price implications for the hospital may be for incentives, including cash incentives for carpooling, reduced rates for parking spots close to the building, free bus passes, and costs for occasional free taxi rides home promised to staff if they need to stay late. The draft plan also includes providing recognition pins for name tags, a strategy anticipated to make members of the program "feel good" as well as spread the word about the program to other employees during meetings, in the cafeteria, and the like. They might also decide to reward those who have stuck with the program for a year with a free iPod, to make their ride home on the bus or in the van more pleasant and encourage others to stick with the program.

Place-related costs are related to providing new or enhanced access or delivery channels, such as telephone centers, online purchasing, extended hours, and new or improved locations. There may be costs related to distribution of any tangible objects associated with the program. In our example, there may be costs for creating additional parking spots for car pools close to the main entrance of the hospital or for staffing a booth outside the cafeteria for distributing incentives and actual ride share sign-up.

Promotion-related costs are those associated with costs for developing, producing, and disseminating communications. Promotional-related costs in this case might include costs for developing and producing fact sheets on benefits, posters, special brochures, and transportation fairs.

Evaluation-related costs include estimated costs for any planned measurement and tracking surveys. In this case, there might be costs for conducting a baseline and follow-up survey that measures employee awareness of financial incentives and ride share matching programs, as well as any changes in attitudes and intentions related to alternative transportation.

JUSTIFYING THE BUDGET

First, consider how those in the commercial marketing sector look at marketing budgets—it's all about the return on the investment. We begin with a story from *Kotler on Marketing*, one that illustrates the marketing mindset, as well as a potential budget analysis:

> The story is told about a Hong Kong shoe manufacturer who wonders whether a market exists for his shoes on a remote South Pacific island. He sends an *order taker* to the island who, upon cursory examination, wires back: "The people here don't wear shoes. There is no market." Not convinced, the Hong Kong shoe manufacturer sends a *salesman* to the island. This salesman wires back: "The people here don't wear shoes. There is a tremendous market."
>
> Afraid that this salesman is being carried away by the sight of so many shoeless feet, the Hong Kong manufacturer sends a third person, this time a *marketer.* This marketing professional interviews the tribal chief and several

of the natives, and finally wires back: "The people here don't wear shoes. However they have bad feet. I have shown the chief how shoes would help his people avoid foot problems. He is enthusiastic. He estimates that 70 percent of his people will buy the shoes at the price of $10 a pair. We probably can sell 5,000 pairs of shoes in the first year. Our cost of bringing the shoes to the island and setting up distribution would amount to $6 a pair. We will clear $20,000 in the first year, which, given our investment, will give us a rate of return on our investment (ROI) of 20 percent, which exceeds our normal ROI of 15 percent. This is not to mention the high value of our future earnings by entering this market. I recommend that we go ahead."[5]

Consider, then, the marketing budget as an investment, one that will be judged based on *outcomes* (levels of behavior change) relative to financial *outputs*. Theoretically, what you want to calculate are your costs for the targeted levels of behavior change and then compare this with the potential economic value of these behaviors influenced. The following examples are the types of simple, but not necessarily easy, questions you would want to answer for yourself and others:

- What is it worth in terms of medical and other societal costs for a health department to find 50 HIV-positive men in one city as a result of their testing efforts in gay bathhouses? How does that compare with the proposed marketing budget of $150,000 to support this effort? Is each "find" worth at least $3,000 ($150,000 ÷ 50)?

- What is the economic value of a 2% increase in seatbelt usage in a state? How many injuries and deaths would be avoided, and how do savings in public emergency and health care costs compare with a $250,000 budget for promotional activities proposed to achieve this increase?

- How does a budget of $100,000 for a state department of ecology to influence and support remodelers and small contractors to post their materials on an online exchange Web site compare with the value of 500 tons of materials being diverted from the landfill the first year—the goal in their marketing plan?

- If a county's campaign to increase spaying and neutering of pets is anticipated to persuade 500 more pet owners this year, compared to last year, how does a budget of $50,000 sound? Is it worth $100 for each "litter avoided"?

You may be surprised how grateful (even delighted) colleagues, funders, and management will be when you provide estimates on these returns on investment. This is only possible when you have established specific, measurable, attainable, relevant, and time sensitive (S.M.A.R.T.) goals for behavior changes, developed calculated strategies to support these goal levels, and then determined a budget based on each marketing-related expense.

FINDING SOURCES FOR ADDITIONAL FUNDING

What if the costs for the marketing activities you propose—ones you believe are needed in order to reach the agreed-upon goal—are more than is currently available in your agency's budget? Before reducing the goals, you have options for additional funding to explore.

Government Grants and Appropriations

Federal, state, and local government agencies are the most common sources of funds and grants for social marketing efforts. Potential sources, especially for nonprofit organizations, include national, state, and local departments of health, human services, transportation, ecology, traffic safety, natural resources, fish and wildlife, parks and recreation, and public utilities.

Example: In 2002, the Centers for Disease Control and Prevention (CDC) awarded Dr. Christina Economos, an assistant professor at Tufts University, a $1.5 million grant for a community-based obesity intervention in Somerville, Massachusetts, a Boston suburb. At the time, it was believed to be the first controlled experiment to demonstrate the value of a communitywide effort. Over a period of 5 years, this town of 78,000 implemented a variety of strategies, many that included additional grants, partnerships, and support from key community leaders. Many restaurants switched to low-fat milk and smaller portion sizes and received recognition as Shape Up partners. The school district nearly doubled the amount of fresh fruit at lunch, thanks in part to a donation of fresh produce from Whole Foods. To encourage more walking to school, crosswalks that had been hard to find due to faded paint received a fresh coat of longer-lasting reflective paint, and school crossing guards were reassigned to areas where children were more likely to walk to school. And a grant from the Robert Wood Johnson Foundation helped fund an extension of a bike path that will eventually go all the way to Boston. The CDC grant also paid for refrigerated display cases, food processors, and fruit juicers to make serving fresh fruits and vegetables easier for the kitchen staff. In classrooms, teachers taught nutrition and exercise curriculums developed by Tufts, with fun activities such as taste tests for the fruit or vegetable of the month. And the research indicates the experiment is working. During the 2003–2004 school year, Somerville schoolchildren gained less weight than children in two nearby communities used as a control group. In 2007, the program is reaching more than children in the community, with a Department of Homeland Security grant providing fitness equipment at fire stations and chefs to train the firefighters about nutrition and healthy meals.[6]

Nonprofit/Foundations

There are more than 67,000 active independent corporate, community, and grant-making foundations operating in the United States alone (2004), with missions to contribute to many of the same social issues and causes addressed by social marketing efforts.[7] Kotler and Andreasen identify four major relevant groups: *family foundations*, in which funds are derived from members of a single family (e.g., Bill and Melinda Gates Foundation); *general foundations,* usually run by a professional staff awarding grants in many different fields of interest (e.g., Ford Foundation); *corporate foundations*, whose assets are derived primarily from the contributions of a for-profit business (e.g., Bank of America Foundation); and *community foundations,* set up to receive and manage contributions from a variety of sources in a local community, making grants for charitable purposes in a specific community or region.[8]

Example: The I Am Your Child Foundation (IAYC) received a $1 million gift from the Bill and Melinda Gates Foundation in November 2000 to support a *national public awareness and engagement campaign to make early childhood development a top priority in the United States.* Working with renowned early childhood development leaders, key policy-makers, and media partners, IAYC provides parents, teachers, health professionals, and other caregivers with information, technical assistance, and support; their goal is to ensure that every child gets a healthy start in life and enters school ready to learn. With this support, IAYC will expand its national program of dissemination and will form alliances with several states to make research-based information available to new parents on a voluntary basis. The state campaigns will have opportunities to use IAYC's educational video series and accompanying print materials as a centerpiece.[9]

Advertising and Media Partners

Advertising agencies often provide pro bono services to support social causes with contributions ranging from consulting on media buying and creative strategies to actually developing and producing advertising campaigns. Several factors motivate their choices, including opportunities to contribute to issues in the community, give their junior staff more experience, have more freedom to call the shots in developing creative strategies, and make new and important business contacts.[10]

The Ad Council, formed in 1942 as the War Ad Council to support efforts related to World War II, has played a significant role in producing, distributing, promoting, and evaluating public service communication programs. Familiar campaigns include Smokey Bear's "Only You Can Prevent Forest Fires," "Friends Don't Let Friends Drive Drunk," and McGruff the Crime Dog's "Take a Bite Out of Crime." Each year the council supports approximately 40 campaigns to enhance health, safety, community involvement, strengthening families, and protecting the environment, chosen from several hundred requests from nonprofit organizations and public sector agencies. Factors used for selection include criteria that the campaign is noncommercial, nondenominational, and nonpolitical in nature. It also needs to be perceived as an important issue and one that is national in scope. When a proposal is selected, the council then organizes hundreds of professional volunteers from top advertising agencies, corporations, and the media to contribute to the campaign.[11]

Television and radio stations are often approached to provide free or discounted ("two for one") airtime for campaigns with good causes. Even more valuable, they may also be interested in having their sales force find corporate sponsors for campaigns, who then pay for media placement (e.g., for a campaign promoting bicycling, a media partnership between an outdoor equipment retailer, a health care organization, and a local television station). In this win-win-win situation, the social marketing campaign gets increased frequency and guaranteed placement of ads on programs that appeal to their target audience; the local corporations get to "do good" and "look good" in the community; and the television or radio stations get paid, versus public service advertising.

Coalitions and Other Partnerships

Many social marketing campaigns have been successful, at least in part, due to the resources and assistance gained from participating in coalitions and other similar partnerships. Coalition members may be able to pool resources to implement larger-scale campaigns. Networks of individual coalition members can provide invaluable distribution channels for campaign programs and materials (e.g., the local department of license offices airs a traffic safety video in the lobby, where a captive audience awaits their number to be called).

Example: In the late 1990s, the Academy for Educational Development (AED), with funding and a cooperative agreement with the Environmental Protection Agency (EPA) Office of Mobile Sources, undertook a challenge to get America's youth involved in the reduction of vehicle miles traveled (VMT). The premise was that by reducing VMT, kids nationwide could do something proactive to help improve air quality in their communities. Thus, Let Kids Lead was created. Three sites across the nation—Boston, Kansas City, and Tampa—were pilot sites for the program. Each had the goal of creating a replicable and sustainable program for involving youth and their families in reducing VMT. In addition to the students, partners in these communities included local governmental agencies, coalitions, councils, commissions, school district administrators, teachers, professional associations, corporations, and concerned citizens. Student activities ranged from conducting surveys, developing catalogs, organizing marches, and making presentations at public meetings to sustainable and ongoing programs, including forming clubs and participating in curriculum development and adaptation. In terms of concrete results, in Boston, the kids got buses rerouted; in Tampa, the American Lung Association fostered clubs for kids working on pollution; and in Kansas City, kids mapped new routes for bikes and walking trails. Going forward, training and program materials have been developed by AED to support other communities nationwide to "let the kids lead."[12]

Corporations

As Kotler and Lee describe in their book *Corporate Social Responsibility: Doing the Most Good for Your Company and Your Cause,* three trends in corporate giving are noteworthy, especially for social marketers. First, the good news is that giving is on an upward trend, with a report from Giving USA indicating that giving by for-profit corporations has risen from an estimated $9.6 billion in 1999 to $13.77 billion in 2005.[13] Second, there is an increased shift to strategic versus obligatory giving, with a desire, even expectation, for "doing well and doing good." More and more corporations are picking a few strategic areas of focus that fit their corporate values. They are selecting initiatives that support their business goals, choosing issues more closely related to their core products, and more interested in opportunities to meet marketing objectives, such as increased market share, market penetration, or building a desired brand identity.[14] And this brings us to the third relevant trend. Many corporations are discovering (and deciding) that supporting social marketing initiatives and campaigns can be one of the most beneficial of all corporate social initiatives, especially for supporting their marketing efforts. In an article titled "Best of Breed" in the *Stanford Innovation Review* in the spring of 2004, Kotler and Lee describe why corporations find this so attractive:

- It can support brand positioning (e.g., Subway partnering with the American Heart Association to influence healthy eating).
- It can create brand preference (e.g., Pampers' support of the SIDS Foundation to influence parents and caregivers to put infants to sleep on their back).
- It can build traffic in stores (e.g., Best Buy's recycling events at store locations).
- It can increase sales (e.g., Mustang Survival partnership with Children's Hospital and Regional Medical Center helping the company capture a share of the toddler market).
- It can have a real impact on social change, and consumers make the connection (e.g., 7-Eleven participating in the Don't Mess With Texas litter prevention campaign that has helped decrease litter by more than 50% in that state).[15]

Corporations have several ways to support your campaigns, ones described in the following sections: cash grants and contributions, cause-related marketing campaigns, in-kind contributions, and providing use of their distribution channels.

Cash Grants and Contributions

Cash contributions from corporations (as opposed to their foundations) are awarded for a variety of purposes, including sponsorship mentions in communications, potential for building traffic at retail or Internet sites, and opportunities for visibility with key constituent groups.

Example: Child Care Resources is a nonprofit organization in Washington State providing information and referral assistance to families seeking child care, training and assistance for child care providers, and consulting and advocacy for quality child care. In the mid-1990s, SAFECO, an insurance company based in Seattle, provided a generous grant to Child Care Resources to strengthen the ability of child care providers to promote and track immunizations of children in their care. Formative research with child care providers provided input for developing training and a kit of materials that included immunization tracking forms, posters, flyers, stickers, door hangers, and brochures for parents, with refrigerator magnets and immunization schedules (see Figure 16.3). In partnership with numerous local and state health agencies, Child Care Resources developed and disseminated more than 3,000 kits to child care providers in the first year of the grant. An evaluation survey among approximately 300 of the providers indicated that 94% felt the materials helped them encourage parents to keep their children's immunizations up-to-date. The grant was extended for a second year, and trainings and kit distribution were taken statewide under the direction of the Washington State Child Care Resource and Referral Network.

Cause-Related Marketing

Cause-related marketing (CRM) is an increasingly popular strategy with a win-win-win proposition. In the typical scenario, a percentage of sales of a company's product is devoted to a nonprofit organization (e.g., at one time a percentage of sales of Evian bottled water was contributed to the World Wildlife Fund). The strategy is based on the premise that buyers care about the civic virtue and caring nature of companies. When market offerings are similar, buyers have been shown to patronize the firms with the better civic reputations. Carefully chosen and developed programs help a *company* achieve strategic marketing objectives (e.g., sell more product or penetrate new markets) and demonstrate social responsibility, with an aim of moving beyond rational and emotional branding to "spiritual" branding. At the same time, CRM raises funds and increases exposure for a *social issue or cause* and gives *consumers* an opportunity to be involved in improving the quality of life.[17] Well-known partnerships include programs such as American Express and Charge Against Hunger, Yoplait yogurt and breast cancer, and Lysol and Keep America Beautiful. National surveys indicate that the majority of consumers would be influenced to buy, or even switch and pay more for brands, when the product supports a cause, especially when product features and quality are equal. However, if the promotion rings hollow, customers may be cynical; if the charitable contribution doesn't amount to much or the promotion doesn't run

Figure 16.3 Door Hanger Used at Child Care Centers to Remind Parents to Check Immunization Status[16]

long enough, customers may be skeptical; if the company chooses a cause of less interest to their customers, it will gain little; and if the company chooses a cause and other causes feel miffed, it may lose out.

In-Kind Contributions

For some corporations, in-kind donations are even more appealing than cash contributions. Not only do they represent opportunities to offload excess products or utilize "idle" equipment such as for printing, they also provide opportunities to connect consumers with the company's products and to connect the product with the organization's cause. The following example illustrates this opportunity well.

Example: Drowning is the second leading cause of unintentional injury death for children in the United States. In Washington State alone, 90 children under the age of 15 drowned from 1999 to 2003. Sadly, in too many cases, drowning deaths could have been avoided if the child had been wearing a properly fitted life jacket. Although Washington State regulations require that children 12 years and younger wear a properly sized U.S. Coast Guard–approved life jacket on any boat under 19 feet, not all children are wearing life jackets or ones that are properly fitted. In 1992, Mustang Survival, a life vest manufacturer, made a 3-year commitment to a partnership that included Children's Hospital and Regional Medical Center and other members of a drowning prevention coalition. In addition to contributing free life jackets for special events, they also provided financial support, discount coupons, bulk buy programs, and in-kind printing (see Figure 16.4). Financial support was used to develop a parent's guide, children's activity booklet, and an interactive display. Their support of the program continues more than 10 years later.

Figure 16.4   Coupon Used to Promote Life Vest Use[18]

Use of Distribution Channels

Companies can provide tremendous visibility and support for your efforts by giving you space in their stores, such as making room for car seat safety checks at car dealers, flu shots at grocery stores, and pet adoptions at pet stores. In some cases, it can have a profound impact, as it did in the following example.

Example: The EPA estimates that in 2007, citizens in the United States will generate 2 million tons of e-waste, or "tech trash"—old or obsolete cellular phones, rechargeable batteries, ink jet cartridges, televisions, computer components, monitors, appliances, and so on. The good news is that many of these materials can be conveniently recycled, even refurbished, at Best Buy stores, the largest U.S. retailer of consumer electronics. Just inside the door of every single U.S. Best Buy store, you can find free recycling drop-off kiosks for cell phones, rechargeable batteries, and ink jet cartridges. In partnership with the EPA, Best Buy also hosts and/or sponsors a series of weekend recycling events at its store parking lots across the United States. In 2006 alone, more than 20 million pounds of e-waste were recycled through Best Buy programs.

APPEALING TO FUNDERS

The same principles we have outlined for influencing target audiences are applicable for influencing potential funders as well. They could be viewed simply as another type of target audience and the same steps and customer orientation are called for:

- Begin by identifying and prioritizing segments (potential funders) who represent the greatest opportunities for funding your program. Several criteria may guide this prioritization, with a special focus on organizations where you have existing contacts and relationships, common areas of focus and concern, and similar target audiences, publics, or constituent groups.

- Formulate clear, specific potential requests you have for them.

- Spend time deepening your understanding of the funders' wants, needs, and perspectives. What are potential benefits and concerns with your proposal? Who is the competition, and what advantages and disadvantages do you have?

- On the basis of this information, refine and finalize your specific request. Your preliminary inquiries, for example, may reveal that a large request (risking the "door in your face") may in fact make it more likely that you will receive funding for a smaller one.

- Develop a strategy using all elements of the marketing mix, a proposal that (a) articulates clear value for the funder (what's in it for them) and benefits to the cause (target audiences), (b) addresses concerns and barriers, (c) ensures a smooth and responsible administrative process, and (d) provides assurance of measurable outcomes.

It is helpful for you to keep in mind that corporations evaluating an opportunity to support a social marketing effort are likely to consider the following questions:

- Is there a natural bond between the cause and the company?
- Is it an issue that our target market cares about?
- Is there an opportunity for staff to be involved?
- Can we own or at least dominate the position of corporate partner?

- Can we stick with the program for at least 2 to 3 years?
- Is there synergy with our current distribution channels?
- Does it provide enhanced media opportunities?
- Can we develop an optimal donation model that provides sales incentives at an economically feasible per-unit contribution?
- Will we be able to absolutely measure our return on investment?

REVISING YOUR PLAN

What happens if funding levels are still inadequate to implement the desired plan? In this familiar scenario, you have several options to make ends meet:

Develop Campaign Phases: Spread costs out over a longer period of time, allowing for more time to raise funds or to use future budget allocations. Options for phasing could include targeting only one or a few target markets the first year; launching the campaign in fewer geographic markets; focusing on only one or a few communication objectives (e.g., using the first year for awareness building or preparing some strategies the first year and others in subsequent years); or implementing some strategies the first year and others in subsequent years (e.g., waiting until the second year to build the demonstration garden using recyclable materials).

Strategically Reduce Costs: Options might include *eliminating strategies and tactics* with questionable potential impact; *choosing less expensive options* for noncritical executional strategies (e.g., using black and white instead of four colors for brochures or lower-grade paper); and where feasible, *bringing some of the tasks in-house* (e.g., the development and dissemination of news releases and organizing special events).

Adjust Goals: Perhaps the most important consideration is the potential need to return to Step 4 and adjust your goals. Clearly, in situations where you have chosen to spread campaign costs over a longer period of time, goals will need to be changed to reflect new time frames. In other situations where time frames cannot be adjusted and additional funding sources have been explored, you may need to eliminate one or more key strategies (e.g., television may not be an option, even though it was identified as key to reach and frequency objectives). In this scenario, you will then need to adjust the goal (e.g., reach 50% of the target audience instead of 75% that television was anticipated to support). You are encouraged to then return to your managers, colleagues, and team members with frank discussions for the need to adjust preliminary goals so that "promises" are honest and realistic.

ETHICAL CONSIDERATIONS WHEN ESTABLISHING FUNDING

Ethical considerations regarding budgets and funding are probably familiar and include issues of responsible fiscal management, reporting, and soliciting of funds. Consider, though, the following additional dilemmas that could face a social marketer. What if a major tobacco company wanted to provide funding for television spots for youth tobacco prevention but didn't require the company's name to be placed in the ad? Is that okay with you? What if a major lumber and paper manufacturer wanted to provide funding for a campaign promoting recyclable materials and wanted the name of the company associated with the campaign? Any concerns? What if a fast-food chain wanted to be listed as a sponsor of magazine ads featuring the food guide pyramid? Is it okay to accept pro bono work from an advertising agency for a counter-alcohol campaign if the parent company has clients in the alcohol industry? In the opening of this chapter, you read about two corporate initiatives to help decrease childhood obesity (the *Sesame Street* and *Nickelodeon* projects). What did you think? Did you think they were well intended and a smart move on their part? Or were you put off in some way?

Chapter Summary

Preliminary budgets are best determined by using the *objective-and-task method,* in which budgets are established by (a) reviewing specific objectives, (b) identifying the tasks that must be performed to achieve these objectives, and (c) estimating the costs associated with performing these tasks. These costs will include those related to developing and implementing elements of the marketing mix, as well as funds needed to support the evaluation and monitoring plan. And to justify them, you were encouraged to quantify the intended outcomes you are targeting for these outputs to produce.

When preliminary budgets exceed current funding, several major sources for additional funds were identified: government grants and appropriations, nonprofit organizations and foundations, advertising and media partners, coalitions and other partnerships, and corporations. You were also encouraged to consider more than cash grants and contributions from corporations, with cause-related marketing initiatives, in-kind contributions, and the use of their distribution channels as excellent opportunities as well.

If proposed budgets still exceed funding sources even after exploring additional sources, you can consider creating campaign phases, strategically reducing costs, and/or adjusting campaign goals established in Step 7.

CHAPTER 17

Creating an Implementation Plan and Sustaining Behavior

Behavior change is the cornerstone of sustainability. As such, social marketing has a critical role to play in assisting with the transition to a sustainable future.

—Doug McKenzie-Mohr
Environmental Psychologist

We envision a world where people are healthy and safe, protecting the environment and contributing to their communities. We have written this book for the thousands of current and future practitioners on the front line who are responsible for influencing public behaviors that will help create this reality.

After reading the prior 16 chapters, we hope you see social marketing as a process with a customer-centric focus and a toolbox with more than messages, ones we think you'll need to get the job done. You'll read in this final chapter about the importance of creating a detailed implementation plan to ensure accountability as well as sustainability. We hope you appreciate the rigor involved to achieve success and that you picked up on principles that will help ensure your desired outcomes—ones worth repeating and reviewing:

- Take advantage of prior and existing successful campaigns.
- Start with target markets most ready for action.
- Promote single, simple, doable behaviors.
- Identify and remove barriers to behavior change.
- Bring real benefits to the present.
- Highlight costs of competing behaviors.
- Search for and include tangible objects and services in your campaign, ones that will help your target audience perform the behavior.
- Consider nonmonetary incentives in the form of recognition and appreciation.
- Make access easy.
- When appropriate, have a little fun with your messages.
- Use media channels at the point of decision making.
- Try for social and entertainment media channels.
- Get commitments and pledges.
- Use prompts for sustainability.
- Track results and make adjustments.

And we think this familiar quote from Margaret Mead introduces our final Marketing Highlight, and its author, well: "Never doubt that a small group of thoughtful, committed citizens can change the world; indeed, it is the only thing that ever has."

Turn it Off: An Anti-Idling Campaign (2007)

DOUG MCKENZIE-MOHR, PHD
Environmental Psychologist

Background

Each day millions of motorists unnecessarily idle their vehicle engines. For example, it is estimated that Canadians idle their vehicles an average of 5 to 10 minutes every day and that at any given time 56% of Canadian motorists are idling their engines when parked and sitting in their vehicles. Natural Resources Canada (NRCan) reports that if motorists reduced their idling by 5 minutes per day, Canadians would reduce their annual carbon monoxide emissions by over 1 million tons and over $1.7 million CDN would be saved each and every day (assuming an average gasoline cost of $.95 per liter).

With the support of Catherine Ray at NRCan and David Dilks of Lura Consulting, I developed a pilot project to reduce the extent to which Canadians idle their vehicles. This project utilized community-based social marketing.[1] Community-based social marketing is based on five steps: (1) carefully selecting the behavior to be targeted, (2) identifying the barriers and benefits to the action, (3) developing a strategy to overcome the barriers and enhance the perceived benefits, (4) piloting the strategy, and finally, (5) implementing on a broad scale. Following this process, we began by conducting barrier and benefit research, which involved conducting Canada-wide focus groups and survey research. This research identified several barriers to reducing idling as well as one significant perceived benefit. Regarding barriers, Canadians believed they should idle their vehicles for longer than 3 minutes before it was more fuel efficient to turn their engines off and then at a later time restart them (NRCan reports that the actual threshold is 10 seconds). Furthermore, they believed that it was necessary to warm their engines before driving (it is actually better for a vehicle to be driven to warm it up than to idle it) and that turning an engine off and on repeatedly would harm the starter. In addition, motorists reported forgetting to turn their engines off when parked and sitting in their vehicles. An effective anti-idling program would have to address each of these barriers as well as emphasize the reported benefit of enhancing air quality by turning off an engine when parked.

Objectives and Strategies

This pilot project sought to decrease both the frequency and duration of motorists idling their vehicle engines. The project involved staff approaching motorists at Toronto schools and Toronto Transit Commission Kiss and Ride parking lots and speaking with them about the importance of turning off their vehicle engines when parked and sitting in their vehicles.

Approached motorists were provided with an information card (see Figure 17.1), and signs reminding motorists to turn off their engines were posted at both the schools and the Kiss and Ride sites (see Figure 17.2). As part of the conversation, each motorist was asked to make a commitment to turn off the vehicle engine when parked. To assist motorists in remembering to turn off their engines, they were asked to place a sticker on their front windshields. The sticker served both as a prompt to turn off their engines and facilitated the development of community norms with respect to engine idling (the sticker, which was static-cling, could be pulled off, was transparent, and was placed

on the front windshield of the vehicle with the graphic and text viewable from both inside and outside the vehicle). Over 80% of the motorists who were asked to make a commitment to turn off their engine did so, and 26% placed the sticker on their front window (see Figure 17.3).

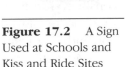

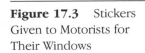

Figure 17.2   A Sign Used at Schools and Kiss and Ride Sites

Figure 17.3   Stickers Given to Motorists for Their Windows

You can use energy more wisely and help improve air quality by turning off your engine when parked.

Conserve energy – You'll help reduce needless greenhouse gas emissions.

Breathe easier – You'll breathe more easily by combatting problems like poor air quality and smog.

Save money – You'll save over 80 litres of gasoline per year if you reduce your idling by only 10 minutes a day.

Idling for over 10 seconds uses more fuel than restarting your engine.

idling gets you
NOWHERE

Natural Resources Canada   Ressources naturelles Canada   Canada

Figure 17.1   These Information Cards Outline the Benefits of Reduced Engine Idling and Are Suitable for Distribution at Schools and Other Community Locations[2]

Results

This project had three separate conditions. Two Kiss and Ride sites and two schools served as controls and received none of the above materials. In a second condition, two Kiss and Ride sites and two schools received only the signs. Finally, in the third condition, the personal conversations, which involved providing an information card and the sticker described above, were used in conjunction with signs. Note that the signs alone, which is what most municipalities would gravitate toward using, were completely ineffective. Motorists in the sign-only condition were no more likely to turn off their engines than were those in the control group. However, the combination of signs, stickers, and information cards (third condition) dramatically affected idling. In this condition, there was a 32% reduction in idling and over a 70% reduction in the duration of idling. These results are based on over 8,000 observations of vehicles in the various parking lots. With the support of NRCan, this pilot project was subsequently implemented across two Canadian cities, Mississauga and Sudbury, with similar results. Most important, NRCan has made the materials from the project freely available to communities so that they can quickly and inexpensively implement their own anti-idling campaigns. As a consequence, municipalities across North America have implemented anti-idling programs based upon this case study.

For further information, visit the Government of Canada's Idle Free Zone Web site (http://oee.nrcan.gc.ca/transportation/personal/idling.cfm). This site provides further details on delivering effective anti-idling programs as well as downloadable materials that can be used in a local program.

STEP #10: CREATING AN IMPLEMENTATION PLAN

For some, the implementation plan *is* the marketing plan, one that will reflect all prior decisions and is considered your final major step in the planning process. It functions as a concise working document to share and track planned efforts. It provides a mechanism to ensure you and your team do what you said you wanted to do, on time, and within budgets. It provides the map that charts your course, enabling timely feedback when you have wavered or need to take corrective actions. It is not the evaluation plan, although it incorporates evaluation activities. It is also not the same as a marketing plan for an entire program or organization, as the emphasis in this book has been on developing a marketing plan for a specific social marketing campaign.

Kotler and Armstrong describe *marketing implementation* as "the process that turns marketing strategies and plans into marketing actions in order to accomplish strategic marketing objectives."[3] They further summarize that many managers think that *doing things right* (implementation) is just as important as *doing the right things* (strategy). In this model, both are viewed as critical to success.

Key components to a comprehensive implementation plan include addressing the classic action-planning elements of what will be done, by whom, when, and for how much.

- *What will we do?* Key activities necessary to execute strategies identified in the marketing mix and the evaluation plan are captured in this document. Many were reviewed and then confirmed in the budgeting process activity and will be incorporated in this section.
- *Who will be responsible?* For each of these major efforts, you will identify key individuals and/or organizations responsible for program implementation. In social marketing programs, typical key players include *staff* (e.g., program

coordinators), *partners* (e.g., coalition members or other agencies), *sponsors* (e.g., a retail business or the media), *suppliers* (e.g., manufacturers), *vendors* (e.g., an advertising agency), *consultants* (e.g., for evaluation efforts), and other internal and external publics, such as *volunteers, citizens,* and *lawmakers.*

- *When will it be done?* Time frames are included for each major activity, typically noting expected start and finish dates.
- *How much will it cost?* Expenses identified in the budgeting process are then paired with associated activities.

Most commonly, these plans represent a minimum of 1-year activities and, ideally, 2 or 3 years. In terms of format, options range from simple plans included in executive summaries of the marketing plan to complex ones developed using software programs. Box 17.1 presents a summary of one section of a social marketing plan developed in 2006 for the Mental Health Transformation Grant Social Marketing Initiative in Washington State, a section focusing on influencing policymakers.

BOX 17.1

A Social Marketing Plan for Eliminating the Mental Health Stigma: Special Section for Influencing Policymakers

1.0 Background, Purpose, and Focus

The purpose of this initiative is to reduce the stigma surrounding mental illness and the barriers it creates in the work setting, at home, within the health care system, and in the community. The focus is on increasing the understanding that people with mental illness can and do recover and live fulfilling and productive lives.

2.0 Situation Analysis

2.1 SWOT Analysis:

Strengths: Statewide transformation initiative with executive support, multiagency work-group commitment, and marketing task group with strong consumer participation; recent legislative action on mental health issues, including: PACT teams, parity, and increased funding for children's mental health

Weaknesses: Limited budget, unrealistic expectations for a communications solution, and lack of consensus on the use of social marketing

Opportunities: Grant funding, governor endorsement, emerging coalitions, provider interest and support, and political curiosity

Threats: Competing projects/staff time limitations, constituent expectation that "campaign" can be all things to all people, and skepticism that marketing is a legitimate method for social change

2.2 This initiative will be built around the framework set forth by Patrick Corrigan, professor of psychiatry at Northwestern University, whose research suggests a target-specific stigma change model, identifying and influencing groups who have the power to change stigma and support adoption of the recovery model. Policymakers, the focus of this section of the plan, were identified as one of three priority audiences and will be addressed in Year 3 of the social marketing initiative. The full marketing plan includes sections targeting consumers and providers.

3.0 Target Market Profile

- State legislators who are responsible for state-level policies and funding
- State agency officials who set reimbursement rules for the types of services that can be covered

- Local elected officials who are responsible for local policies and allocating funds to regional service providers

4.0 Marketing Objectives and Goals

4.1 We want this plan to influence policymakers to

- Pass legislation that enables "recovery" and "mental health transformation."
- Reallocate existing funds to put more resources into recovery, resulting in a decreased need for crisis intervention.
- Interpret regulations affecting people with mental illness using "recovery" lens.
- Ensure adequate funding to support recovery-oriented mental health services, including consumer participation.
- Support the provision of employment of opportunities for consumers.
- Eliminate stigmatizing language and views and adopt a language and process that promotes recovery.

4.2 Goals

- Conduct a minimum of four speaking engagements with local elected officials.
- Conduct a minimum of six speaking engagements with state legislators.
- Conduct a minimum of five speaking engagements with state agency officials.
- Increase understanding that people with mental illness can and do recover and lead fulfilling lives in the community.
- Decrease need for crisis intervention by increasing funding for recovery-oriented and self-help services.
- Modify regulations to allow reimbursement for recovery-oriented and peer-led programs.
- Decrease stigmatizing language.

5.0 Target Market Barriers, Benefits, and the Competition

5.1 Barriers

Perceived barriers to desired behaviors include (a) lack of knowledge about mental illness and funding/resource issues, (b) uncertainty that successful recovery is how the consumer defines it, and (c) uncertainty that recovery-oriented treatment systems can be devised where people with mental illness pose no greater violence risk to the community than people without mental illness.

5.2 Motivators

Potential motivators include: consumer success stories and proof that the recovery model works and is an efficient way to spend tax dollars.

(Continued)

(Continued)

5.3 Competing Behaviors

Responding to public fear and belief in stereotypes, providing funding for crisis intervention before funding recovery-oriented self-help programs.

6.0 Positioning Statement

We plan to develop a speakers' bureau consisting of providers and consumers of mental health services that will educate policymakers about recovery and serve as living examples of success. We want them to view these speaking engagements as an opportunity to hear success stories from consumers and as a good source of information about mental health issues, including recovery and stigma. We will also develop white papers, in partnership with consumers and providers, and want policymakers to see these as a credible source of information about mental illness, recovery and resiliency, and stigma, and as a source of empirical evidence that the recovery model works, can be economical, and is a good investment.

7.0 Marketing Mix Strategies (4Ps)

7.1 Product

Core: Increased knowledge of mental illness and Washington's Mental Health Transformation Project

Actual: Adopt recovery model best practices and support funding for recovery-oriented and peer-led services.

Augmented: Strategic speaking engagements and presentations highlighting consumer success stories and the recovery model; white papers on the transformation effort in Washington State

7.2 Price

Speaking engagements and white papers will be free. Media coverage will address public fear and instill hope for recovery. Advocacy awards will honor policy "heroes" who contribute to recovery and the breaking down of myths and stereotypes.

7.3 Place

Speaking engagements will be scheduled at locations and times throughout the state that are convenient for policymakers. White papers will be available on the Internet and downloadable for print. Hard copies will be mailed out individually and available at speaking engagements.

7.4 Promotion

Speaking engagements will be promoted in association newsletters, on Listservs and at sessions at related conferences. White papers will be promoted via direct mail. A news bureau will be used to publicize awards, conduct editorial board meetings to discuss mental health transformation, and stimulate feature stories. Availability of speakers' bureau will be promoted through ongoing conversations with elected officials and their staff.

8.0 Evaluation Plan

Purpose and Audience for Evaluation: Speakers' bureau evaluation will measure change in policymaker knowledge of mental illness and recovery, change in belief that people with mental illness can live fulfilling lives in the community, disposition toward changing regulations and funding to support recovery-oriented services, and actual changes in policies, regulations, and funding. The marketing team will use evaluation findings to determine continuation, improvement, and expansion of speakers' bureau and policymaker strategies.

Output measures include number of speaking engagements conducted, number of white papers distributed, number of news articles and editorials printed, news stories aired, and editorial board meetings conducted.

Outcome measures include number of policymakers at speaking engagements, visits to Web site, increased knowledge about mental illnesses, increased knowledge about Washington's Mental Health Transformation Project, and decreased stigmatizing attitudes and beliefs by policymakers attending speaking engagements.

How and when to measure: Pre- and postworkshop questionnaires by speakers' bureau participants and audience members. Tracking of policy, regulation, and funding changes. Media monitoring for number of letters to the editor, retractions of stereotypical portrayals, features stories on recovery, and media coverage of award recipients.

9.0 Budget

Budget estimate is for Year 3 for speakers' bureau and news bureau aimed at three target audiences—consumers, providers, and policymakers—and does not include all planned activities for Year 3. The project is funded by a Mental Health Transformation State Incentive Grant from the Substance Abuse and Mental Health Services Administration, U.S. Department of Health and Human Services.

(Continued)

(Continued)

Speakers' bureau	$70,000
Recovery and stigma materials (print and web)	$20,000
News bureau	$15,000
Professional education	$10,000
Management & coordination	$20,000
Total for speakers' and news bureaus	$135,000

10.0 Implementation Plan

Key Activities	Responsibility/Lead	Timing	Budget
Project coordination and oversight	DOH	Ongoing	$30,000
Speakers' bureau coordination and scheduling	Washington Institute for Mental Illness Research and Training Finalize schedule 4 speaking engagements	First quarter Quarterly	$70,000
Continuing availability of recovery and stigma materials in print and on the web	DOH	Ongoing (started in Year 2)	$10,000
Policy white papers	Mental Health Transformation staff w/DOH	1st Quarter: Draft for review 2nd Quarter: Finalize and print 2nd-4th Quarter: Publicity and distribution	(Included in project coordination)

Update and publicize online training calendar	Washington Community Mental Health Council	Ongoing (started in Year 2)	In-kind
Promote advocacy awards	DOH with transformation partners	Ongoing (started in Year 2)	Included in project
News bureau	Contractor TBD Media monitoring and response to stereotypical or stigmatizing coverage Generate coverage of advocacy award honorees and their personal stories	Ongoing (started in Year 2)	$20,000

SOURCE: Heidi Keller and Daisye Orr, Office of Health Promotion, Washington State Department of Health, with Washington's Mental Health Transformation Project, Office of the Governor, 2006.

PHASING

As mentioned earlier in our discussion on budgeting in Chapter 16, when funding levels are inadequate to implement the desired plan, one tactic to consider is to spread costs over a longer period of time, allowing more time to raise funds or use future budget allocations. Natural options include creating phases that are organized (driven) by some element of the marketing plan: *target markets, geographic areas, campaign objectives, campaign goals, stages of change, products, pricing, distributional channels, promotional messages,* or *media channels*. The following provide examples of situations when a particular framework might be most appropriate.

Phases Organized by Target Market

In a differentiated strategy in which several market segments are targets for the campaign, each phase could concentrate on implementing strategies for a distinct segment. This would provide a strong focus for your efforts, as well as increase resources behind them. For the intimate partner violence campaign described in the case from Australia, a potential phasing might proceed as follows:

Phase 1: Male perpetrators in the contemplation stage of change

Phase 2: Intermediaries such as male counselors who perpetrators will be referred to

Phase 3: Female victims

Phases Organized by Geographic Area

Phasing by geographic area has several advantages. It may align with funding availability as well as offer the ability to pilot the campaign, measure outcomes, and then make important refinements prior to subsequent implementation. Most important, by using this option, you will also be implementing all of the strategic elements you chose for the marketing mix. You will just be concentrating them in one or a few geographic areas. Thinking back on the tween VERB Scorecard case, a campaign phased by geographic area might look like the following:

Phase 1: Pilot VERB Scorecard in Lexington, Kentucky

Phase 2: Roll out to other communities in Kentucky

Phase 3: Roll out to other communities around the country

Phases Organized by Objective

In a situation in which a campaign has identified important objectives related to knowledge and beliefs as well as behavior, campaign phases can be organized and sequenced to support each objective. The litter prevention campaign in Washington State used this strategy, allowing more time to gain support of partners (e.g., law enforcement), secure sponsors (e.g., fast-food restaurants), and establish important infrastructures (e.g., broad distribution channels for litterbags and incorporating questions on fines for litter in driver's education tests). In this example, phases reflect the process of moving target audiences from awareness to action—over time.

Phase 1: Creating awareness of laws and fines

Phase 2: Altering beliefs that "no one's watching" or cares, by implementing a toll-free hotline for reporting littering

Phase 3: Changing littering behavior

Phases Organized by Goal

Campaigns may have established specific benchmarks for reaching interim goals, in which case, activities and resources would then be organized to support desired outcomes. The advantage of this framework is that funders and administrators "feel good" that the program will achieve targeted goals—eventually. Similar to phasing by geographic area, this approach does not require altering the marketing strategy you developed for the program. For Singapore's Healthier Restaurant Program, for example, goals for restaurant participation in offering healthy options on their menu might have been targeted as follows:

Phase 1: 50 restaurants in Singapore participate in the program

Phase 2: 100 restaurants are enrolled

Phase 3: 150 restaurants are enrolled

Phases Organized by Stage of Change

In keeping with objectives of moving audiences through stages of change, it may make the most sense to phase a campaign effort by first targeting those "most ready for action" and then using this momentum to move on to other markets. In a campaign encouraging food waste composting, for example, efforts might be made to set up demonstration households in neighborhoods with eager volunteers who can then be supported and promoted to spread the word to neighbors. In this case, phases might appear as follows:

Phase 1: Promote to households with consistent participation in all curbside recycling (maintenance segment)

Phase 2: Promote to households participating only in paper and glass curbside recycling (in action segment)

Phase 3: Promote to households that had responded to and inquired about information in past but are not regular curbside recyclers (contemplator segment)

Phases Organized by Service or Tangible Object Introductions or Enhancements

When new or improved services and tangible objects have been identified for a program plan, it may be necessary, even strategic, to introduce these over a period of time. A Women, Infants, and Children (WIC) program clinic, for example, might phase the introduction of service enhancements by starting with those perceived to have the most potential impact on increased use of farmers' markets and then move on to those providing added value:

Phase 1: Counselor training and support materials

Phase 2: Market tours and transportation vouchers

Phase 3: Clinic classes on freezing and canning

Phases Organized by Pricing Strategies

A program may plan a pricing strategy in which significant price incentives are used early in the campaign as a way to create attention and stimulate action. In subsequent phases, efforts may rely on other elements of the marketing mix, such as improved distribution channels or targeted promotions. In the case of a utility promoting energy-efficient appliances, pricing strategies might change over time as follows:

Phase 1: Rebates for turning in old appliances

Phase 2: Discount coupons for energy-efficient appliances

Phase 3: Pricing similar to competing appliances and increased emphasis on *contribution to the environment*

Phases Organized by Distribution Channels

A campaign relying heavily on convenience of access might begin with implementing distribution channels that are the quickest, easiest, or least expensive to develop and then move on to more significant endeavors over time. In the case describing access to family planning services in Nepal, for example, distribution channels have progressed over time:

Phase 1: Family planning services only available at health posts

Phase 2: Services available at health fairs

Phase 3: Mobile units traveling to remote villages

Phases Organized by Messages

When multiple campaign messages are needed to support a broad social marketing program (e.g., decreasing obesity), behavior change may be facilitated by introducing messages one at a time. This can help your target adopter spread costs for change over a period of time, as well as feel less overwhelmed (self-efficacy). The Ad Council's Small Steps campaign for the U.S. Department of Health and Human Services mentioned earlier could phase its 100 recommended actions in the following clustered way:

Phase 1: *Steps at Work:* Walk during your lunch hour. Get off a stop early and walk. Walk to a coworker's desk instead of e-mailing or calling them.

Phase 2: *Steps When Shopping:* Eat before grocery shopping. Make a grocery list before you shop. Carry a grocery basket instead of pushing a cart.

Phase 3: *Steps When Eating:* Eat off smaller plates. Stop eating when you are full. Snack on fruits and vegetables.

Phases Organized by Media Channels

At the time of onset of major threats such the avian flu, mad cow disease, or terrorist attacks, you may need to first reach broad audiences in a very short period of time. Once this phase is complete, efforts may shift to more targeted audiences through more targeted media channels. For avian flu, for example, we might see media channels in a country progress as follows:

Phase 1: Mass communication channels: news stories on TV, radio, and in newspapers

Phase 2: Selective channels: posters and flyers (e.g., hand-washing signs in restrooms)

Phase 3: Personal contact: health care workers making visits to poultry farmers

Phases Organized by a Variety of Factors

In reality, it may be important, even necessary, to use a combination of phasing techniques. For example, campaign target markets may vary by geographic area (e.g., farmers are more important target markets for water conservation in rural than in urban communities). As a result, different communities may have different target market phasing in their campaigns. As most practitioners will attest, campaigns will need to be meaningful to their specific communities or they will not receive the necessary support for implementation.

Phase 1: Rural communities target farmers and urban communities target large corporations for water conservation

Phase 2: Rural communities target businesses, and urban communities target public sector agencies

Phase 3: Rural communities and urban communities target residential users

SUSTAINABILITY

At this point in the planning process, most strategies have been identified and scheduled to support desired behavior change objectives and goals. It is a worthwhile exercise, however, to give last-minute considerations to any additional tactics to include in the plan that will keep your campaign visible and behavior change messages prominent after ads go off the air and the news stories die down. In addition, are there other mechanisms you could include in the campaign that will help your target audience sustain their behavior over the long term? In keeping with our stages of change theory and model, you should be specifically interested in ensuring that those in the action stage don't return to contemplation and that those in the maintenance stage don't return to irregular actions. In the following sections, ideas including the use of prompts, commitments, and public spaces are presented.

Sustaining Behaviors

Prompts

In their book *Fostering Sustainable Behavior*, McKenzie-Mohr and Smith offer insights, guidelines, tools, and checklists for the social marketer to consider for supporting continued behavior change. They describe prompts as "visual or auditory aids which remind us to carry out an activity that we might otherwise forget. The purpose of a prompt is not to change attitudes or increase motivation, but simply to remind us to engage in an action that we are already predisposed to do."[4] They recommend making the prompts noticeable and self-explanatory and presenting them as close in time and space as possible to the targeted behavior. They also suggest that we encourage positive behaviors rather than avoid harmful ones. "Anchoring" is similar to prompting, where the desired behavior (e.g., flossing) is "anchored," or closely linked, to a current established behavior (e.g., brushing your teeth). Examples of both are illustrated in Table 17.1.

Commitments

Gaining commitments from target adopters has also proven surprisingly effective. "Individuals who agreed to a small initial request were far more likely to agree to a subsequent larger request."[5] Examples include a backyard wildlife sanctuary program in which the homeowner signs the application promising to follow the natural gardening guidelines or a client at a WIC clinic who signs a receipt for farmers' market coupons stating that she is interested in using these in the next 3 months. Evidently, McKenzie-Mohr and Smith report, "When individuals agree to a small request, it often alters the way they perceive themselves."[6] A note from a mother with a teen girl to the editor of the *China Times*, for example, described an agreement the two reached to reduce their quarreling. The mother and daughter, evidently at odds over privacy matters, made an agreement that "they will discuss sex issues at home regularly; the mother will stop peeking into her daughter's diary and mails; and the daughter will not have a boyfriend in high school." It was reported further that keeping this agreement has evidently greatly helped to improve their relationship.[7]

Sustaining Campaign Efforts

If you are working in the public sector, you have numerous opportunities for sustained visibility, as you often have access to public places and signage at public agencies. Those working on traffic safety can negotiate for signage on roadways; those working on flu prevention have access to public restrooms for signage reminding people to wash their hands; those working on pedestrian safety can negotiate for tougher tests

Table 17.1   Sustaining Behaviors and Campaign Efforts

Issue	*Using Prompts to Sustain Behavior*
Tobacco cessation	Electronic alerts during vulnerable times in the day that signal, "Come on, you can do it."
Binge drinking	Small posters in bar restroom stalls showing someone bending over "the porcelain god"
Physical activity	Wearing a pedometer to make sure you get 10,000 steps a day
Unintended pregnancies	Keeping a condom in a small case on a key chain
Fat intake	Detailed data on food labels indicating fat grams and percentage of calories
Fruits and vegetables	Placing fruits and vegetables in glass bowls at eye level in refrigerators
Water intake	Stickers at water coolers saying, "Have you had your 8 glasses today?"
Breastfeeding	Pediatricians encouraging a nursing mom to continue breastfeeding at the 6-month checkup
Breast cancer	Shower nozzle hanger reminding about monthly breast self-exams
Folic acid	Keeping vitamin pills by the toothbrush as an established habit
Immunizations	Mailings recognizing and reminding when a child's immunization is due
Diabetes	Using a beeper as a reminder for blood glucose monitoring
Car seats	Keeping a car seat in all cars used frequently by a child
Drinking and driving	Making breathalyzers available in bars
Booster seats	Air fresheners for cars with reminders about booster seats
Drowning	Providing loaner life vests for toddlers at public beaches
Smoke alarms	Placing reminder stickers in planning calendars for checking batteries in smoke alarms
Waste reduction	Label on a bathroom towel dispenser suggesting, "Take only what you need. Towels are trees."
Food waste composting	Stickers on recycling containers recognizing a homeowner who also composts food waste
Reducing use	Messages at coffee stands suggesting that "the regulars" bring their own cups
Air pollution	Stickers inside car doors reminding car owners when it is time to get their tires inflated
Organ donation	Lawyers asking their clients who are organ donors if they have talked to their families about their wishes

when getting drivers' licenses; and those working on decreasing secondhand tobacco smoke can work with school districts to send home "smoke-free home" pledge cards with the children. These are resources and opportunities that many in commercial marketing would envy and most would have a hard time paying for.

SHARING AND SELLING YOUR PLAN

Several techniques will help increase buy-in, approval, and support for your plan. First, include representatives from key internal and external groups on the planning team. Consider those who have a role in approving the plan, as well as those key to implementation. For a litter prevention campaign with an emphasis on enforcement, it would be critical that a member of the state patrol have input in the planning process; to increase WIC clients' use of farmers' markets, it would be important to have a representative from the farmers' market association present, especially to hear the results of research with clients on their experiences shopping at the market; and a city developing a pedestrian safety plan will benefit from having a police officer, an engineer, someone from the communications department, someone from local businesses, and a citizen at the planning table.

Second, share a draft plan with decision makers and those key to implementation, prior to finalizing your plan. Identify their concerns and address them. Be prepared to share the background data that led to your recommended strategies, and be prepared to compromise or modify a strategy based on their feedback. And surprise them with the targeted quantifiable goals you are proposing and how you plan to evaluate and report on your campaign outcomes.

Finally, once the plan is finalized, consider developing and disseminating a concise summary of the plan. It could be as simple as a one-pager that presents the purpose, focus, target audience, objectives, key strategies, and evaluation plan. Where warranted, it could even be a more portable format such as a wallet-sized card or a more accessible one such as on your agency's Web site. Your intention is to position your campaign effort as one that is evidence based, strategically developed, and outcome driven.

ETHICAL CONSIDERATIONS WHEN IMPLEMENTING PLANS

In most of the chapters in this book, we have presented ethical considerations related specifically to each phase in the planning process. To highlight final considerations when developing an implementation plan and to summarize ethical considerations in general, we present the American Marketing Association member code of ethics, published on their Web site (www.MarketingPower.com), in Box 17.2. Many of the principles apply to social marketing environments, with themes similar to those we have highlighted, including *Do no harm, Be fair, Provide full disclosure, Be good stewards, Own the problem, Be responsible,* and *Tell the truth.*

BOX 17.2
ETHICAL NORMS AND VALUES FOR MARKETERS

Preamble

The American Marketing Association commits itself to promoting the highest standard of professional ethical norms and values for its members. Norms are established standards of conduct that are expected and maintained by society and/or professional organizations. Values represent the collective conception of what people find desirable, important and morally proper. Values serve as the criteria for evaluating the actions of others. Marketing practitioners must recognize that they not only serve their enterprises but also act as stewards of society in creating, facilitating and executing the efficient and effective transactions that are part of the greater economy. In this role, marketers should embrace the highest ethical norms of practicing professionals and the ethical values implied by their responsibility toward stakeholders (e.g., customers, employees, investors, channel members, regulators and the host community).

General Norms

1. Marketers must do no harm. This means doing work for which they are appropriately trained or experienced so that they can actively add value to their organizations and customers. It also means adhering to all applicable laws and regulations and embodying high ethical standards in the choices they make.

2. Marketers must foster trust in the marketing system. This means that products are appropriate for their intended and promoted uses. It requires that marketing communications about goods and services are not intentionally deceptive or misleading. It suggests building relationships that provide for the equitable adjustment and/or redress of customer grievances. It implies striving for good faith and fair dealing so as to contribute toward the efficacy of the exchange process.

3. Marketers must embrace, communicate and practice the fundamental ethical values that will improve consumer confidence in the integrity of the marketing exchange system. These basic values are intentionally aspirational and include honesty, responsibility, fairness, respect, openness and citizenship.

Ethical Values

Honesty—*to be truthful and forthright in our dealings with customers and stakeholders. We will tell the truth in all situations and at all times.*

(Continued)

(Continued)

- We will offer products of value that do what we claim in our communications.
- We will stand behind our products if they fail to deliver their claimed benefits.
- We will honor our explicit and implicit commitments and promises.

Responsibility—*to accept the consequences of our marketing decisions and strategies.*

- We will make strenuous efforts to serve the needs of our customers.
- We will avoid using coercion with all stakeholders.
- We will acknowledge the social obligations to stakeholders that come with increased marketing and economic power.
- We will recognize our special commitments to economically vulnerable segments of the market such as children, the elderly and others who may be substantially disadvantaged.

Fairness—*to try to balance justly the needs of the buyer with the interests of the seller.*

- We will represent our products in a clear way in selling, advertising and other forms of communication; this includes the avoidance of false, misleading and deceptive promotion.
- We will reject manipulations and sales tactics that harm customer trust.
- We will not engage in price fixing, predatory pricing, price gouging or "bait-and-switch" tactics.
- We will not knowingly participate in material conflicts of interest.

Respect—*to acknowledge the basic human dignity of all stakeholders.*

- We will value individual differences even as we avoid stereotyping customers or depicting demographic groups (e.g., gender, race, sexual orientation) in a negative or dehumanizing way in our promotions.
- We will listen to the needs of our customers and make all reasonable efforts to monitor and improve their satisfaction on an ongoing basis.
- We will make a special effort to understand suppliers, intermediaries and distributors from other cultures.
- We will appropriately acknowledge the contributions of others, such as consultants, employees and coworkers, to our marketing endeavors.

Openness—*to create transparency in our marketing operations.*

- We will strive to communicate clearly with all our constituencies.
- We will accept constructive criticism from our customers and other stakeholders.

- We will explain significant product or service risks, component substitutions or other foreseeable eventualities that could affect customers or their perception of the purchase decision.
- We will fully disclose list prices and terms of financing as well as available price deals and adjustments.

Citizenship—*to fulfill the economic, legal, philanthropic and societal responsibilities that serve stakeholders in a strategic manner.*

- We will strive to protect the natural environment in the execution of marketing campaigns.
- We will give back to the community through volunteerism and charitable donations.
- We will work to contribute to the overall betterment of marketing and its reputation.
- We will encourage supply chain members to ensure that trade is fair for all participants, including producers in developing countries.

Implementation

Finally, we recognize that every industry sector and marketing subdiscipline (e.g., marketing research, e-commerce, direct selling, direct marketing, advertising) has its own specific ethical issues that require policies and commentary. An array of such codes can be accessed through links on the AMA Web site. We encourage all such groups to develop and/or refine their industry and discipline-specific codes of ethics to supplement these general norms and values.

SOURCE: American Marketing Association. (2004). Reprinted with permission. Retrieved from www.Marketing Power.com.

Chapter Summary

Developing an implementation plan is Step 10, the final step in this marketing plan model. It turns strategies into actions and is critical to *doing things right,* even if you've planned *the right things.* Implementation plans function as a concise working document that can be used to share and track planned efforts. It provides a mechanism to ensure that we do what we said we would do, on time, and within budgets. Key components of the plan include the following: What will you do? Who will be responsible? When will it be done? How much will it cost?

Formats for plans vary from simple plans incorporated in the executive summary of the marketing plan to complex plans using software programs. The ideal plan identifies activities over a period of 2 to 3 years.

Plans are often presented in phases, usually broken down into months or years. Several frameworks can be used to determine and organize phases, including *target markets, geographic areas, campaign objectives, campaign goals, stages of change, products, pricing, distribution channels, promotional messages,* and *media channels.* Often it will be a combination of these factors.

Typical strategies to sustain visibility for your campaign, as well as target adopter behaviors, include the use of prompts, commitments, and existing infrastructures. Tactics and mechanisms include signage, stickers, mailings, electronic reminders, labels on packaging, and taking advantage of public places and agency partnerships.

Several techniques were mentioned to increase buy-in, approval, and support for your plan. First, include representatives from key internal and external groups on the planning team. Second, share a draft plan with decision makers and those key to implementation, prior to finalizing your plan. Third, once the plan is finalized, consider developing and disseminating a concise summary of the plan. It could be as simple as a one-pager that presents the purpose, focus, target audience, objectives, key strategies, and evaluation plan.

Appendix A

Social Marketing Planning Worksheets

STEP 1: PROVIDE BACKGROUND, PURPOSE, AND FOCUS FOR PLAN

1.1 Summarize key *background* information leading to the development of this plan.
(e.g., Increased Rates of Teen Pregnancies, Decreased Salmon Populations)

_____

_____

_____

_____

_____

1.2 What is the campaign *purpose*, the intended impact (benefit)?
(e.g., Reduced Teen Pregnancies, Protection of Salmon Habitats)

_____

_____

_____

_____

_____

1.3 What is the campaign *focus*?
(e.g., Teen Abstinence, Residential Gardening Practices)

_____

_____

_____

_____

_____

Refer to Chapter 5 for Detailed Descriptions of Process

STEP 2: CONDUCT A SITUATION ANALYSIS

Internal Factors

2.1 What internal *strengths* will your plan maximize?
(e.g., resources, expertise, management support, internal publics, current alliances and partnerships, distribution channels)

_____

_____

2.2 What internal *weaknesses* will your plan minimize?
(e.g., resources, expertise, management support, internal publics, current alliances and partnerships, distribution channels)

_____

_____

External Forces

2.3 What external *opportunities* will your plan take advantage of?
(e.g., external publics and cultural, technological, demographic, natural, economic, and political/legal forces)

_____

_____

2.4 What external *threats* will your plan prepare for?
(e.g., external publics and cultural, technological, demographic, natural, economic, and political/legal forces)

_____

_____

Prior and Similar Efforts

2.5 What findings from *prior and similar efforts* are noteworthy, those of yours and others?

_____

_____

Refer to Chapter 5 for Detailed Descriptions of Process

STEP 3: SELECT TARGET AUDIENCES

3.1 Describe the *primary target audiences* for your program/campaign in terms of size, problem incidence and severity, and relevant variables, including demographics, psychographics, geographics, behaviors, and/or stages of change:

_____

_____

_____

_____

_____

_____

_____

3.2 If you have *additional important target audiences* that you will need to influence as well, describe them here:

_____

_____

_____

_____

_____

_____

_____

Refer To Chapter 6 for Detailed Descriptions of Process

STEP 4: SET OBJECTIVES AND GOALS

Objectives

4.1 Behavior Objective:
What, very specifically, do you want to influence your target audience to *do* as a result of this campaign or project?

_____

_____

_____

4.2 Knowledge Objective:
Is there anything you need them to *know*, in order to act?

_____

_____

_____

4.3 Belief Objective:
Is there anything you need them to *believe*, in order to act?

_____

_____

_____

Goals

4.4 What quantifiable, measurable goals are you targeting? Ideally, these are stated in terms of *behavior change*. Other potential targeted goals are ones for campaign awareness, recall and/or response, and changes in knowledge, belief, or behavior intent levels.

_____

_____

_____

Refer to Chapter 7 for Detailed Descriptions of Process

STEP 5: ANALYZE TARGET AUDIENCES AND THE COMPETITION

Barriers

5.1 Make a list of *barriers* your audience may have to adopting the desired behavior. These may be physical, psychological, skills, knowledge, awareness, attitudes, and so on.

1.	
2.	
3.	
4.	
5.	
6.	
7.	
8.	
9.	
10.	

Benefits

5.2 What are the key *benefits* your target audience will be motivated by?

Competition

5.3 What are the major competing *alternative behaviors*?

5.4 What *benefits* do your audiences associate with these behaviors?

5.5 What *costs* do your audiences associate with these behaviors?

Refer to Chapter 8 for Detailed Descriptions of Process

STEP 6: CRAFTING A DESIRED POSITIONING

Positioning Statement

6.1 Write a statement similar to the following, filling in the blanks:
"We want [TARGET AUDIENCE] to see [DESIRED BEHAVIOR] as [DESCRIPTIVE PHRASE] and as more important and beneficial than [COMPETITION]."

_____

_____

_____

_____

_____

_____

_____

_____

_____

_____

_____

_____

_____

_____

_____

_____

Refer to Chapter 9 for Detailed Descriptions of Process

STEP 7: DEVELOP MARKETING STRATEGIES

7.1 Product: Design the Product Platform

7.1.1 What is the *core* product, the major perceived benefit, your target audience wants from performing the behavior that you will highlight? (Choose one or a few from those identified in 5.2.)

_____

_____

7.1.2 What is the *actual* product, the desired behavior?
(Refer back to your behavior objective in 3.1 and refine/finalize here.)

_____

_____

Relative to the *augmented* product (tangible objects and services):

7.1.3 Are there any *new tangible objects* that will be included in program and campaign efforts?

_____

_____

7.1.4 Are there any *improvements* that need to be made to existing tangible objects?

_____

_____

7.1.5 Are there any *new services* that will be included in program and campaign efforts?

_____

_____

7.1.6 Are there any *improvements* that need to be made to existing services?

_____

_____

Refer to Chapter 10 for Detailed Descriptions of Process

7.2   Price: Fees & Monetary Incentives and Disincentives

7.2.1   If you will be including tangible objects and services in your campaign, what, if anything, will the target audience have to *pay* for them?

_____

_____

_____

7.2.2   Will there be any *monetary incentives* for target markets (e.g., coupons, rebates)?

_____

_____

_____

7.2.3   Will there be any *monetary disincentives* you will highlight (e.g., fines, increased taxes)?

_____

_____

_____

7.2.4   Will you use any *nonmonetary incentives* (e.g., recognition, reward)?

_____

_____

_____

7.2.5   Will you use any *nonmonetary disincentives* (e.g., negative visibility)?

_____

_____

_____

Refer to Chapter 11 for Detailed Descriptions of Process

_____

Step 7: (Continued)

Step 7: (Continued)

7.3 Place: Making Access Convenient

As you determine each of the following, look for ways to make locations closer and more appealing, to extend hours, and to be there at the point of decision making.

7.3.1 *Where* will you encourage and support your target audience to *perform the desired behavior* and *when*?

_____

_____

_____

7.3.2 *Where* and *when* will the target market acquire any related tangible objects?

_____

_____

_____

7.3.3 *Where* and *when* will the target market acquire any associated services?

_____

_____

_____

7.3.4 Are there any groups or individuals in the distribution channel that you will target to support efforts?

_____

_____

_____

Refer to Chapter 12 for Detailed Descriptions of Process

7.4 Promotion: What Will You Say, Who Will Say It, How, and Where?

Messages

7.4.1 What key messages do you want your campaign to communicate to target audiences?

_____

_____

_____

Messengers

7.4.2 Who will deliver the messages and/or be the perceived sponsor?

_____

_____

_____

Creative Strategy

7.4.3 Summarize, describe, or highlight elements such as logos, taglines, copy, visuals, colors, script, actors, scenes, and sounds in broadcast media.

_____

_____

_____

Communication Channels

7.4.4 What communication channels will you use?

_____

_____

_____

Refer to Chapters 13 and 14 for Detailed Descriptions of Process

STEP 8: DEVELOP A PLAN FOR
EVALUATION AND MONITORING

8.1 What is the *purpose* of this evaluation? Why are you doing it?

_____

_____

8.2 *Who* is the evaluation being conducted for? Who will you present it to?

_____

_____

8.3 *What goals* from Step 4 will be measured?

_____

_____

8.4 *What techniques and methodologies* will be used to conduct these measures?

_____

_____

8.5 *When* will these measurements be taken?

_____

_____

8.6 *How* will measurements be reported and to whom?

_____

_____

Refer to Chapter 15 for Detailed Descriptions of Process

STEP 9: DETERMINE BUDGETS AND FIND FUNDING SOURCES

9.1 What costs will be associated with *product*-related strategies?

_____

_____

9.2 What costs will be associated with *price*-related strategies?

_____

_____

9.3 What costs will be associated with *place*-related strategies?

_____

_____

9.4 What costs will be associated with *promotion*-related strategies?

_____

_____

9.5 What costs will be associated with *evaluation*-related strategies?

_____

_____

9.6 If costs exceed currently available funds, what potential additional funding sources can be explored?

_____

_____

Refer to Chapter 16 for Detailed Descriptions of Process
For an electronic version of this plan, visit www.socialmarketingservice.com

STEP 10: COMPLETE AN IMPLEMENTATION PLAN

10.1 Will there be phases to the campaign? How will they be organized (i.e., by market, objectives, activities)?

_____

_____

_____

_____

_____

_____

_____

10.2 For each phase, what will be done, who will be responsible, when will it be done, and for how much?

_____

_____

_____

_____

_____

_____

_____

Refer to Chapter 17 for Detailed Descriptions of Process

Appendix B

Social Marketing Resources

Compiled by Mike Newton-Ward, Social Marketing Consultant, North Carolina Division of Public Health, and Turning Point Social Marketing National Excellence Collaborative. He thanks participants on the Georgetown Social Marketing Listserv for additional suggestions.

CD-ROM-Based Planning Tools

CDCynergy-Social Marketing Edition Version 2 CD-ROM-based software to help you plan, implement, and evaluate social marketing initiatives. Contains over 700 resources, such as consultant videos, best practice case studies, templates, and journal articles. Purchase online at http://www.tangibledata.com/CDCynergy-SOC

Web Sites

A Goodman: Good Ideas for Good Causes	http://www.agoodmanonline.com/red.html
AED, Social Marketing and Behavior Change	http://www.aed.org/SocialMarketingandBehaviorChange/
AED, Center for Social Marketing and Behavior Change	http://csmbc.aed.org/index.htm
American Evaluation Association	http://www.eval.org/
American Marketing Association	http://www.marketingpower.com
Association of Consumer Research	http://www.acrwebsite.org
Australia and New Zealand Marketing Academy	http://www.anzmac.org
Center for Advanced Studies in Nutrition and Social Marketing	http://socialmarketing-nutrition.ucdavis.edu
Center of Excellence for Public Sector Marketing	http://www.publicsectormarketing.ca/home_e.html
Centers for Disease Control and Prevention, Division of Nutrition and Physical Activity, Index of Qualitative Research	http://www.cdc.gov/nccdphp/dnpa/qualitative_research/index.htm
Centers for Disease Control and Prevention, Division of Nutrition and Physical Activity, Social Marketing Resources	http://www.cdc.gov/nccdphp/dnpa/socialmarketing/index.htm

Claritas: PRIZM Geocoding System	http://www.claritas.com
Community-Based Social Marketing	http://www.cbsm.com/
George Washington University, School of Public Health and Health Services, Public Health Communication and Marketing (Under Resources: Case Studies Quarterly Lecture Series Free Publications)	http://www.gwumc.edu/sphhs/departments/pch/phcm/index.cfm
Harvard Business School *Working Knowledge* Newsletter	http://hbswk.hbs.edu/forms/newsletter.html
The Institute for Social Marketing, University of Stirling, Scotland	http://www.ism.stir.ac.uk/
MRS Market Research	http://www.marketresearch.org.uk/index.htm
National Cancer Institute Health Behavior Constructs: Theory, Measurement and Research	http://cancercontrol.cancer.gov/brp/constructs/index.html
National Center for Health Marketing, Centers for Disease Control and Prevention	http://www.cdc.gov/healthmarketing/
National Centre for Health Marketing, Department of Health, United Kingdom	http://www.nsmcentre.org.uk
Nielsen Buzzmetrics	http://nielsenbuzzmetrics.com/
Population Services International (PSI)	http://www.psi.org
Social Marketing Downunder (New Zealand, Australia and South Pacific)	http://socialmarketing.co.nz
Social Marketing Institute	http://www.social-marketing.org/
The Social Marketing Network, Health Canada	http://www.healthcanada.gc.ca/socialmarketing
The Social Marketing Place	http://social-marketing.com/
Social Marketing Services, Inc. (to request electronic version of worksheets in Appendix A)	http://socialmarketingservice.com
SRI Consulting Business Intelligence: VALS Segmentation System	http://www.sric-bi.com/
Stanford Social Innovation Review	http://ssireview.org
Stanford University Persuasive Technology Lab	http://captology.stanford.edu/
Tangible Data.com (URL on which to order copies of CDCynergy-Social Marketing Edition CD-ROM planning tool)	http://www.tangibledata.com/CDCynergy-SOC

Tools of Change	http://www.toolsofchange.com/
Turning Point Social Marketing National Excellence Collaborative	http://socialmarketingcollaborative.org/smc/
University of Lethbridge (Canada), Faculty of Management	http://www.uleth.ca/man/research/centres/csrm/related.shtml

E-Learning Tools

Applying the BEHAVE Framework	http://www.coregroup.org/working_groups/behave/CORE_Welcome.htm
CDCynergy-Social Marketing Edition online	http://www.orau.gov/cdcynergy/soc2web/default.htm
The National Training Collaborative for Social Marketing, USF Health, University of South Florida	http://hsc.usf.edu/medicine/ntcsm/TLM/present/index/index.htm
Social Marketing E-Learning Tool	http://www.hc-sc.gc.ca/ahc-asc/activit/marketsoc/tools-outils/index_e.html

Electronic Media

The basics of social marketing	http://socialmarketingcollaborative.org/smc/pdf/Social_Marketing_Basics.pdf
Evaluating nutrition and physical activity social marketing campaigns: a review of the literature for use in community campaigns	http://socialmarketing-nutrition.ucdavis.edu/Downloads/SamuelsSMC.pdf
Free-range thinking	http://www.agoodmanonline.com/newsletter/index.html
The manager's guide to social marketing	http://socialmarketingcollaborative.org/smc/pdf/Managers_guide.pdf
Promoting nutrition and physical activity social marketing: current practices and recommendations	http://socialmarketing-nutrition.ucdavis.edu/Downloads/ALCALAYBELL.PDF
Social marketing and public health: lessons from the field	http://socialmarketingcollaborative.org/smc/pdf/Lessons_from_field.pdf
Social marketing lite	http://www.aed.org/ToolsandPublications/upload/Social%20Marketing%20Lite.pdf
Storytelling as best practice: how stories strengthen your organization, engage your audience, and advance your mission	http://www.agoodmanonline.com/publications/storytelling/index.html
Theory-at-a-glance	http://www.cancer.gov/PDF/481f5d53-63df-41bc-bfaf-5aa48ee1da4d/TAAG3.pdf
Why bad ads happen to good causes, and how to ensure that they don't happen to yours	http://www.agoodmanonline.com/bad_ads_good_causes/index.html

Blogs and Wikis

On Social Marketing and Social Change   http://socialmarketing.blogs.com/
(the Social Marketing Blog)

The Social Marketing Place Blog   http://www.social-marketing.com/blog/

Social Marketing Wetpaint/Wiki Site   http://socialmarketing.wetpaint.com/

Search Engines

Google Scholar   http://www.google.com/scholar

HealthComm Key   http://cfusion.sph.emory.edu/PHCI/Users/LogIn.cfm

Books

Andreasen, A. (1995). *Marketing Social Change: Changing Behavior to Promote Health, Social Development, and the Environment.* San Francisco: Jossey-Bass.

Andreasen, A. (Ed.). (2001). *Ethics in Social Marketing.* Washington, DC: Georgetown University Press.

Andreasen, A. (2001). *Marketing Research That Won't Break the Bank: A Practical Guide to Getting the Information You Need* (2nd ed.). San Francisco: Jossey-Bass.

Andreasen, A. (2006). *Social Marketing in the 21st Century.* Thousand Oaks, CA: Sage.

Basil, D. Z., & Wimer, W. W. (2007). *Social Marketing: Advances in Research & Theory.* Binghamton, NY: Haworth Press.

Bearden. W. O., & Netemeyer, R. G. (1999). *Handbook of Marketing Scales* (2nd ed.). Thousand Oaks, CA: Sage.

Buros Institute. (2005). *The Sixteenth Mental Measurements Yearbook.* Lincoln, NE: Author.

Donovan, R., & Henley, N. (2003). *Social Marketing Principles and Practice.* Victoria, Australia: IP Communications.

Galdwell, M. (2000). *The Tipping Point: How Little Things Can Make a Big Difference.* Boston: Little, Brown.

Glanz, K., Rimer, B. K., & Lewis, M. L. (2002). *Health Behavior and Health Education: Theory, Research, and Practice.* San Francisco: Jossey-Bass.

Hastings, G. (2007). *Social Marketing: Why Should the Devil Have All the Best Tunes?* Oxford, England: Butterworth-Heinemann.

Kotler, P., & Lee, N. (2007). *Marketing in the Public Sector: A Roadmap for Improved Performance.* Philadelphia: Wharton School.

Kotler, P., & Lee, N. (2008). *Social Marketing: Influencing Behaviors for Good.* (3rd ed.). Thousand Oaks, CA: Sage.

Kreuger, R. A., & Casey, M. A. (2000). *Focus Groups: A Practical Guide for Applied Research* (3rd ed.). Thousand Oaks, CA: Sage.

Locke, C. (2001). *Gonzo Marketing: Winning Through Worst Practices.* Cambridge, MA: Perseus.

Maibach, E., & Parrott, R. L. (Eds.). (1995). *Designing Health Messages.* Thousand Oaks, CA: Sage.

McKenzie-Mohr, D., & Smith, W. (1999). *Fostering Sustainable Behavior: An Introduction to Community-Based Social Marketing.* Gabriola Island, British Columbia, Canada: New Society.

Morrison, M., Haley, E., Sheehan, K. B., & Taylor, R. E. (2002). *Using Qualitative Research in Advertising: Strategies, Techniques, and Applications.* Thousand Oaks, CA: Sage.

Prochaska, J. O., Norcross, J., & DiClemente, C. (1995). *Changing for Good: A Revolutionary Six-Stage Program for Overcoming Bad Habits and Moving Your Life Positively Forward.* New York: Collins.

Siegel, M., & Lotenburg, L. D. (2007). *Marketing Public Health: Strategies to Promote Social Change* (2nd ed.). Boston: Jones & Bartlett.

Weinreich, N. K. (1999). *Hands-On Social Marketing: A Step-by-Step Guide.* Thousand Oaks, CA: Sage.

Listservs and E-Mail Digests

*Dispatches: Insights on Business Development
from the Marketing Front (E-mail digest), Brand
Development Network International*

To subscribe, send an e-mail to loriv@bdn-intl.com or call 800-255-9831.

Fostering Sustainable Behavior Listserv

To subscribe, send an e-mail to web@cbsm.com with "subscribe" in the subject.

Georgetown Social Marketing Listserv

To subscribe, send an e-mail message to LISTPROC@LISTPROC.GEORGETOWN.EDU. In the body of the message write: "subscribe SOC-MKTG [your name]" and type your actual name in place of "your name."

Journals and Magazines

Advertising Age

Crain Communications, Inc.
http://adage.com/

American Journal of Health Behavior

American Academy of Health Behavior
http://131.230.221.136/ajhb/

Brand Week

VNU, Inc.
http://www.brandweek.com/bw/subscriptions.jsp

Health Marketing Quarterly

Haworth Press
http://www.haworthpress.com/store/product.asp?sku=J026

Journal of Consumer Research

University of Chicago Press
http://www.journals.uchicago.edu/JCR

Journal of Health Communication

Taylor and Francis
http://www.tandf.co.uk/journals/titles/10810730.html

Journal of Marketing

American Marketing Association
http://www.marketingpower.com/content1053.php

Journal of Nonprofit & Voluntary Sector Marketing

John Wiley & Sons
http://www.wiley.com/WileyCDA/WileyTitle/productCd-NVSM.html

Journal of Public Policy and Marketing

American Marketing Association
http://www.marketingpower.com./content1056.php

Social Marketing Quarterly

Taylor and Francis
http://www.tandf.co.uk/journals/titles/15245004.html
http://www.socialmarketingquarterly.com/

Conference Opportunities

1. *Social Marketing in Public Health Annual Conference*

June, University of South Florida, Clearwater Beach, Florida
Contact:
Continuing Professional Education
University of South Florida College of Public Health
813-974-9684

To view and download registration information, go to
http://www.cme.hsc.usf.edu/smph/index.html
To view and download materials from previous conferences, go to
http://www.cme.hsc.usf.edu/smph/presentations.html

2. *Social Marketing Advances in Research
and Theory (SMART) Conference (biennial)*

University of Lethbridge, Faculty of Management
Calgary, Alberta, Canada
To be added to conference mailing list:
Send an e-mail request to sr@uleth.ca
To view and download materials from previous conferences go to
http://www.uleth.ca/man/research/centres/csrm/conferences/smart/2006

Journal Articles and Dedicated Issues

Andreasen, A. (2002). "Marketing Social Marketing in the Social Change Marketplace," *Journal of Public Policy & Marketing, 21,* 3–13.

Bloom, P. N., & Novelli, W. D. (1981). "Problems and Challenges in Social Marketing," *Journal of Marketing, 45,* 79–88.

Kotler, P., & Lee, N. (2004, Spring). "Best of Breed: Corporate Social Marketing," *Social Innovations Review,* 14–23.

Kotler, P., & Zaltman, G. (1971). "Social Marketing: A Planned Approach to Social Change," *Journal of Marketing, 35,* 3–12.

McCormack Brown, K. R. (Ed.). (2004). "Social Marketing" [Special issue], *Eta Sigma Gamma Health Monograph Series 1*(1).

Pechmann, C. (Ed.). (2002). "Special Issue on Social Marketing Initiatives," *Journal of Public Policy & Marketing, 21*(1).

Rothschild, M. (1999). "Carrots, Sticks, and Promises: A Conceptual Framework for the Management of Public Health and Social Issue Behaviors," *Journal of Marketing, 63,* 24–37.

Smith, W. A. (1998). "Forget Messages . . . Think About Structural Change First," *Social Marketing Quarterly, 4*(3), 13–19.

Smith, W. A. (1998). "Marketing With No Budget," *Social Marketing Quarterly, 5*(2), 6–11.

Wiebe, G. D. (1952). "Merchandizing Commodities and Citizenship on Television," *Public Opinion Quarterly, 15,* 679–691.

Chapter Notes

Chapter 1

1. Personal communication, 2006.
2. Personal communication, 2006.
3. Andreasen, A. R. (1995). *Marketing Social Change: Changing Behavior to Promote Health, Social Development, and the Environment* (p. 7). San Francisco: Jossey-Bass.
4. French, J., & Blair-Stevens, C. (2005). *Social Marketing Pocket Guide*. London: National Social Marketing Centre of Excellence.
5. Reprinted with permission of RockTheVote.org.
6. American Marketing Association. (2007). Retrieved 7/31/07 from http://www.marketing power.com/mg-dictionary.php?SearchFor=marketing&Searched=1
7. Donovan, R., & Henley, N. (2003). *Social Marketing: Principles and Practices*. Melbourne, Australia: IP Communications.
8. Provided by National Archives and Records Administration, Washington, DC.
9. Kotler, P., & Zaltman, G. (1971, July). "Social Marketing: An Approach to Planned Social Change," *Journal of Marketing, 35*, 3–12.
10. Bagozzi, R. P. (1978, March-April). "Marketing as Exchange: A Theory of Transactions in the Marketplace," *American Behavioral Science,* 535–556.
11. Smith, W. (2002, Summer). "Social Marketing and Its Potential Contribution to a Modern Synthesis of Social Change," *Social Marketing Quarterly 8*(2), 46.
12. Hornik, R. (2002, Summer). "Some Complementary Ideas About Social Change," *Social Marketing Quarterly, 8*(2), 11.
13. Marchione, M. (2006). "Doctors Test Anti-Smoking Vaccine." Retrieved 7/31/07 from http://www.foxnews.com/printer_friendly_wires/2006Jul27/0,4675,TobaccoVaccine,00.html
14. Teinowitz, I. (2006, December 4). "Pediatricians Demand Cuts in Children-Targeted Advertising," *Advertising Age*. Retrieved 12/4/06 from http://adage.com/print?article_id=113558
15. Environmental Defense. (2006). "Starbucks Paper Project." Retrieved 10/9/06 from http://www.environmentaldefense.org/article.cfm?contentid=791
16. World Health Organization, Tobacco Free Initiative. (2003). Statistics for the year 2000 and published in the HNP Discussion Paper No. 6, Economics of Tobacco Control Paper No. 6, The World Bank.
17. Andreasen, A. R. & Kotler, P. (2003). *Strategic Marketing for Non-Profit Organizations* (6th ed., p. 490). Upper Saddle River, NJ: Prentice Hall.
18. Andreasen, A. R. (2006). *Social Marketing in the 21st Century* (p. 11). Thousand Oaks, CA: Sage.
19. Kotler, P., & Lee, N. (2006). *Marketing in the Public Sector: A Roadmap for Improved Performance*. Upper Saddle River, NJ: Wharton School.

20. Synthesis of personal communications to authors, including comments in year 2000 from Social Marketing Listserv participants.

21. Kotler, P., & Roberto, E. (1989). *Social Marketing: Strategies for Changing Public Behavior* (p. 26). New York: Free Press.

Chapter 1 Table Notes

a. CDC Behavioral Risk Factor Surveillance System (BRFSS). (2005). Prevalence Data Section. Retrieved 10/20/06 from http://apps.nccd.cdc.gov/brfss/

b. CDC, BRFSS. (2005). Prevalence Data Section. Retrieved 10/20/06 from http://apps .nccd.cdc.gov/brfss/

c. March of Dimes: Drinking Alcohol During Pregnancy. Survey data for 1999. Retrieved 10/20/06 from http://www.marchofdimes.com/professionals/681_1170.asp

d. CDC, BRFSS. (2005). Prevalence Data Section. Retrieved 10/20/06 from http://apps .nccd .cdc.gov/brfss/

e. CDC Morbidity and Mortality Weekly Report (MMWR). Youth Risk Behavior Surveillance–United States, 2005. June 9, 2006/Vol.55/No. SS-5.

f. Fleming, P., Byers, R. H., Sweeney, P. A., Daniels, D., Karon J. M., and Janssen, R. S., 2002. "HIV Prevalence in the United States, 2000 (Abstract #11, 9th Conference on Retroviruses and Opportunistic Infections: February 2002)."

g. CDC, BRFSS. (2005). Prevalence Data Section. Retrieved 10/20/06 from http://apps .nccd.cdc.gov/brfss/

h. CDC, BRFSS. (2005). Prevalence Data Section. Retrieved 10/20/06 from http://apps .nccd.cdc.gov/brfss/

i. CDC. 2003 National Immunization Survey.

j. CDC, Press Release July 26, 2005: BRFSS. (2004). Prevalence Data Section. Retrieved 10/20/06 from http://apps.nccd .cdc.gov/brfss/

k. CDC, BRFSS. (2004). Prevalence Data Section. Retrieved 10/20/06 from http://apps .nccd.cdc.gov/brfss/

l. Colon Cancer Alliance: http://www.ccalliance.org/cca/media/factsfigures.html

m. 2004 March of Dimes survey conducted by The Gallup Organization. Retrieved 10/20/06 from http://www.medicalnewstoday.com/medicalnews.php?newsid=13625

n. CDC Press Release, July 26, 2005: "Childhood Immunization Rates Surpass Healthy People 2010 Goal."

o. CDC Morbidity and Mortality Weekly Report (MMWR). Youth Risk Behavior Surveillance – United States, 2005. June 9, 2006/Vol.55/No. SS-5.

p. CDC, BRFSS. (2004). Prevalence Data Section. Retrieved 10/20/06 from http://apps.nccd.cdc .gov/brfss/

q. American Diabetes Association: All About Diabetes. Retrieved 10/20/06 from http://www.diabetes.org/about-diabetes.jsp

r. American Heart Association. High Blood Pressure Statistics 2002. Retrieved 10/20/06 from http://www.americanheart.org/presenter.jhtml?identifier=2139

s. National Eating Disorders Association. Retrieved 10/20/06 from http://www.edap.org/nedaDir/files/documents/PressRoom/CollegePoll_9-28-06.doc

t. CDC, BRFSS. (2005). Prevalence Data Section. Retrieved 10/20/06 from http://apps .nccd.cdc.gov/brfss/

u. National Highway Traffic Safety Administration. Report dated August 30, 2005. Retrieved on 10/20/06 from http://www .ncsl.org/print/transportation/cellphoneup805.pdf

v. National Highway Traffic Safety Administration. Report dated May 2004, Retrieved October 10, 2006 from www.nhtsa.dot.gov

w. National Safe Kids Campaign. "Headed for Injury: An Observational Survey of Helmet Use Among Children Ages 5 to 14 Participating in Wheeled Sports." May 2004. Retrieved 10/20/06 from http://www.usa.safekids.org/content_documents/ACFC7.pdf

x. Safe Kids USA: "Preventing accidental injury. Injury Facts, Motor Vehicle Occupant Injury" Retrieved 11/20/06 from http://www.usa.safekids.org/tier3_cd.cfm?content_item_id= 1133&folder_id=540

y. CDC Morbidity and Mortality Weekly Report (MMWR). Youth Risk Behavior Surveillance–United States, 2005. June 9, 2006/Vol.55/No. SS-5

z. World Waterpark Association. "Be Water-Aware During National Water Safety Week." Retrieved 11/20/06 from http://www.waterparks.org/news_detail.asp?itemId=206

aa. Mental Health Journal. "Domestic Violence Statistics: Prevalence and Trends." Retrieved 11/20/06 from http://www.therapistfinder.net/Domestic-Violence/Domestic-Violence-Statistics.html

bb. SafeKids. "Facts About Unintentional Firearm Injuries to Children." Retrieved 11/20/06 from http://www.usa.safekids.org/content_documents/Firearm_facts.pdf

cc. CDC Morbidity and Mortality Weekly Report (MMWR). Youth Risk Behavior Surveillance–United States, 2005. June 9, 2006/Vol.55/No. SS-5

dd. National Fire Protection Association. "Smoke Alarms." Retrieved 11/20/96 from http://www.nfpa.org/categoryList.asp?categoryID=278&URL=Research%20&%20Reports/Fact% 20sheets/Fire%20protection%20equipment/Smoke%20alarms

ee. CDC. "National Center for Injury Prevention and Control." Retrieved 11/20/06 from http://www.cdc.gov/ncipc/factsheets/adultfalls.htm

ff. About Pittsburgh, PA. "Happy Birthday Mr. Yuk." Retrieved 11/20/06 from http://pitts burgh .about.com/b/a/253770.htm

gg. EPA. "Municipal Solid Waste-Recycling." Retrieved 11/20/06 from http://www.epa.gov/ epaoswer/non-hw/muncpl/states.htm

hh. Public Broadcasting System (PBS). Bill Moyers Reports: "Earth on the Edge." (2001, June). *Discussion Guide,* p. 4. Retrieved 10/10/01 from http://www.pbs.org/earthonedge/

ii. Gore, A. (2006). *An Inconvenient Truth (*p. 316). New York: Rodale.

jj. Northwest Coalition for Alternatives to Pesticides. "Pesticide Use Reporting Program." Retrieved 1/31/07 from http://www.pesticide.org/PUR.html

kk. EPA. At Home. Retrieved 1/29/07 from http://epa.gov/climatechange/wycd/home.html

ll. U.S. Census Bureau 2000. Retrieved 1/31/07 from http://www.census.gov/prod/ 2004pubs/c2kbr-33.pdf

mm. EPA. At Home. Retrieved 1/29/07 from http://epa.gov/climatechange/wycd/home.html

nn. Van Cleef, L. (2001, April). http://www.informationweek.com/breakaway/835/landfill.htm

oo. Smokey Bear. "Only You." Retrieved 1/31/07 from http://www.smokeybear.com/ couldbe.asp

pp. Oregon State Web Site. "Renewable Resources of Energy." Retrieved 1/31/07 from http://www.oregon.gov/ENERGY/RENEW/inform.shtml

qq. CigaretteLitter.Org. (2001). "Facts About Cigarette Butts and Litter." Retrieved 9/19/2001 from http://www.cigarettelitter.org

rr. Watson, T. USATODAY.com "Dog waste poses threat to water." Published June 7, 2002. 1/6/2002 http://www.usatoday .com/news/science/2002-06-07-dog-usat.htm

ss. United Network for Organ Sharing. Retrieved 1/31/07 from http://www.unos.org/

tt. American Red Cross. 50 Quick Facts. Retrieved 1/31/07 from http://www.givelife2.org/sponsor/quickfacts.asp

uu. *Federal Election Commission.* Retrieved 1/31/07 from http://www.infoplease .com/ipa/A0781453.html

vv. Reading Research, Parent Reading. Retrieved 1/31/07 from http://www.m2fbooks.com/research

ww. Bureau of Justice Statistics. Press Release: Identity Theft, 2004. Retrieved 1/31/07 from http://www.ojp.usdoj.gov/bjs/pub/press/it04pr.htm

xx. American Human Protecting Animals: Care & Issues: Spay and Neuter. "Why Spay or Neuter Your Pet?" Retrieved 1/31/07 from http://www.americanhumane.org/site/PageServer?pagename=pa_care_issues_spay_neuter

Chapter 2

1. National Center for Health Statistics (NCHS). (2005). "Prevalence of Overweight Among Children and Adolescents: United States, 1999–2002." Retrieved 8/1/07 from http://www.cdc.gov/nchs/products/pubs/pubd/hestats/overwght99.htm

2. Hedley, A. A., Ogden, C. L., Johnson, C. L., Carroll, M. D., Curtin, L. R., & Flegal, K. M. (2004). "Overweight and Obesity Among U.S. Children, Adolescents, and Adults, 1999–2002," *Journal of the American Medical Association, 291*(23), 2847–2850.

3. Hill, J. O., Wyatt, H. R., Reed, G. W., & Peters, J. C. (2003). "Obesity and the Environment: Where Do We Go From Here?" *Science, 229*, 853–855.

4. Strauss, R., Rodzilsky, D., Burack, G., & Colin, M. (2001). "Psychosocial Correlates of Physical Activity in Healthy Children," *Archives of Pediatric and Adolescent Medicine, 155*(8), 897–902.

5. Sothern, M., Loftin, M., Suskind, R., Udall, J., & Blecker, U. (1999). "The Health Benefits of Physical Activity in Children and Adolescents: Implications for Chronic Disease Prevention," *European Journal of Pediatrics, 158,* 271–274.

6. Centers for Disease Control and Prevention. (2006, June 9). "Youth Risk Behavior Surveillance—United States, 2005. Surveillance Summaries," *Morbidity and Mortality Weekly Report, 55*(SS-5).

7. Huhman, M., Potter, L. D., Wong, F. L., Banspach, S. W., Duke, J. C., & Heitzler, C. D. (2005). "Effects of a Mass Media Campaign to Increase Physical Activity Among Children: Year-1 Results of the VERB Campaign," *Pediatrics, 116,* 277–284.

8. Bretthauer-Mueller, R., Berkowitz, J. M., Thomas, M., McCarthy, S., Green, L. A., Melancon, H., et al. (Under review). "Catalyzing Community Action Within a National Media Campaign: VERB™ Community and National Partnerships," *American Journal of Preventive Medicine.*

9. Kotler, P., & Keller, K. L. (2005). *Marketing Management* (12th ed., pp. 15–23). Upper Saddle River, NJ: Prentice Hall.

10. Drucker, P. F. (1973). *Management: Tasks, Responsibilities, Practices* (pp. 64–65). New York: Harper & Row.

11. Kotler P., & Keller, K. L. (2005). *Marketing Management* (12th ed., pp. 27–29).

12. Parker-Pope, T. (2006, September 5). "Passing the Ball: Hip Campaign That Got Kids to Be Active Looks for Its Next Move," *Wall Street Journal,* p. D1.

13. Kotler, P., & Lee, N. (2006). *Marketing in the Public Sector* (pp. 283–284). Upper Saddle River, NJ: Wharton School.

14. Washington State Department of Ecology. (2006). "Litter Campaign." Retrieved 10/10/06 from http://www.ecy.wa.gov/programs/swfa/litter/campaign.html

15. Washington State Department of Ecology. (2005, March). *Washington 2004 State Litter Study—Litter Generation and Composition Report.* Olympia, WA: Author.

16. Ries, A., & Trout, J. (1986). *Positioning: The Battle for Your Mind* (p. 2). New York: Warner Books.

17. Kotler, P., & Lee, N. (2006). *Marketing in the Public Sector* (p. 113).

18. Courtesy of Washington State Department of Ecology.

19. Ibid.

20. Ibid.

21. Andreasen, A. (2002). *Marketing Research That Won't Break the Bank*. San Francisco: Jossey-Bass.

22. Message posted to Social Marketing Institute's Social Marketing Listserv. (2006, March 16).

23. Ibid.

24. Ibid.

Chapter 3

1. Academy for Educational Development. (2006). "Ten Promises to Terry: Towards a Social Marketing Manifesto," *Social Marketing Quarterly, 7*(2), 59.

2. Food Standards Agency. (2000). *National Diet and Nutrition Survey of Young People Aged Four to 18 Years.* London: HMSO Food Standards Agency. Retrieved from http://www.food .gov.uk/multimedia/webpage/academicreview

3. U.K. Department of Health. (2003). "Obesity: Defusing the Health Time Bomb." In *Health Check: On the State of the Public Health. Annual Report of the Chief Medical Officer, 2002* (pp. 36–45). London: Author.

4 Mulrow, C. D. (1994). "Rationale for Systematic Reviews," *British Medical Journal, 309*(6954), 597–599.

5. Boaz, A., Ashby, D., & Young, K. (2002). *Systematic Reviews: What Have They Got To Offer Evidence Based Policy and Practice* (Working Paper 2). ESRC UK Centre for Evidence Based Policy and Practice, Queen Mary, University of London.

6. Young, B. (2003). "Advertising and Food Choice in Children: A Review of the Literature" (Report prepared for the Food Advertising Unit). Retrieved from http://www.fau.org.uk/brian_ youngliteraturereview.pdf

7. Paliwoda, S., & Crawford, I. (2003). "An Analysis of the Hastings Review." Commissioned by the Food Advertising Unit (FAU) for the Advertising Association. Retrieved 6/19/06 from http://www.adassoc.org.uk/hastings_review_analysis_dec03.pdf

8. Food Standards Agency. (2003). "Safe Food and Healthy Eating for All." Retrieved 12/06 from http://www.food.gov.uk/multimedia/webpage/academicreview; Food Standards Agency. (2003). "Outcome of the Review Exercise on the Paliwoda and Crawford Paper: An Analysis of the Hastings Review: 'The Effects of Food Promotion on Children.'" Retrieved from http://food .resultspage.com/search?p=R&srid=S2%2d2&lbc=food&w=paliwoda&url=http%3a%2f%2f www%2efood%2egov%2euk%2fmultimedia%2fpdfs%2fpaliwodacritique%2epdf&rk=1&uid=17 1613895&sid=2&ts=v2&rsc=qFgSz0DVJSuCqC5T&method=and&mainresults=mt%5fmainre sults%5fyes

9. Ibid.

10. Food Standards Agency. (2003). "Outcome of the Review Exercise on the Paliwoda and Crawford Paper."

11. Paliwoda, S., & Crawford, I. (2003). *An Analysis of the Hastings Review*. (Commissioned by the Food Advertising Unit for the Advertising Association) Retrieved 6/19/06 from http://www.adassoc.org.uk/hastings_review_analysis_dec03.pdf

12. Office of Communications. (2006). "New Restrictions on the Television Advertising of Food and Drink Products to Children." Retrieved 11/28/06 from http://www.ofcom.org.uk/media/ news/2006/11/nr_20061117

13. Other references: Food Standards Agency. *National Diet and Nutrition Survey of Young People Aged Four to 18 Years;* Hastings, G. (2007). *Social Marketing: Why Should the Devil Have All the Best Tunes?* Oxford, England: Elsevier; Hastings, G., Stead, M., McDermott, L., Forsyth, A., MacKintosh, A., Rayner, M., et al. (2003). *Review of Research on the Effects of Food Promotion to Children—Final Report and Appendices* (Prepared for the Food Standards Agency). Stirling, England: Institute for Social Marketing. Retrieved from http://www .ism.stir.ac.uk

14. City of Austin. (n.d.). "Scoop the Poop: Dogs for the Environment." Retrieved 10/23/06 from http://www.ci.austin.tx.us/watershed/wq_scoop.htm

15. Ibid.

16. Kotler, P., & Lee, N. (2006). *Marketing in the Public Sector* (p. 199). Upper Saddle River, NJ: Wharton School.

17. Puget Sound Blood Center. (n.d.). Retrieved 10/23/06 from http://www.psbc.org/home/ index.htm

18. Reprinted with permission of Puget Sound Blood Center.

19. Kotler & Lee, *Marketing in the Public Sector,* p. 200.

20. National Crime Prevention Council. (2006). "Take a Bite Out of Cyber Crime." Retrieved 10/24/06 from http://www.bytecrime.org/index.html

21. Ibid.

22. Kotler & Lee, *Marketing in the Public Sector,* pp. 201–202.

23. Rothschild, M. (2003, June). Plenary Presentation. 13th Annual Social Marketing in Public Health Conference, University of South Florida, Tampa, FL.

24. Camit, M. (2002). "Smoke Alarms Wake You Up If There's a Fire: A Smoke Alarm Campaign Targeting Arabic, Chinese, and Vietnamese Communities in New South Wales," *Social Marketing Quarterly, 8*(1), 52–54.

25. The Humane Society, Tacoma and Pierce County. (n.d.). "Kittenkaboodle." Retrieved 10/25/2006 from http://thehumanesociety.org/2006/09/kittenkaboodle/

26. Kotler & Lee, *Marketing in the Public Sector*, p. 206.

27. Wiebe, G. D. (1951–1952, Winter). "Merchandising Commodities and Citizenship on Television," *Public Opinion Quarterly, 15,* 579–690.

28. Walking School Bus. (2006). "Starting a Walking School Bus: The Basics." Retrieved 10/26/06 from http://www.walkingschoolbus.org/

29. Ibid.

30. National Highway Traffic Safety Administration. (2006). "Successful School Transportation Safety Programs. Case Study. The Walking School Bus: Bringing Schools and Communities Together to Create Safety Walking Environments for Kids." Retrieved 10/26/06 from http://www .nhtsa.dot.gov/people/injury/buses/GTSS/case4.html

31. United Nations Environment Program. (2006). "Assessing Trade & Environmental Effects of Ecolabels." Retrieved 10/06 from http://www.unep.org/Documents.Multilingual/Default .asp?DocumentID=457&ArticleID=5061&l=en and http://www.unep.fr/shared/docs/publica tions/Ecolabelpap141005f.pdf

32. Ecolabels (2006). "Ecolabelling." Retrieved 10/06 from http://www.envirohelp.co.uk/ ireland/bestpractices/ecolabels.html

33. "Measure of Sustainability Eco-Labeling." (n.d.). Retrieved 8/07 from http://www.canadi-anarchitect.com/asf/perspectivessustainibility/measuresofsustainablity/measuresofsustainablitye colabeling.htm

34. Case Source: Pretti Shridhar, Seattle Public Utilities.

35. Reprinted with permission of Seattle Public Utilities.

36. Kotler & Lee, *Marketing in the Public Sector,* p. 209.

37. U.S. Department of Health & Human Services. (2007, June 4). "Public Service Campaign to Promote Breastfeeding Awareness Launched" [Press release]. Retrieved 4/6/07 from http:// www.hhs.gov/news/press/2004pres/20040604.html

38. U.S. Department of Health and Human Services. (2005). "National Breastfeeding Awareness Campaign: Babies Are Born to Be Breastfed." (n.d.). Retrieved 4/07 from http://www.4woman.gov/breastfeeding/index.cfm?page=campaign

39. The National Women's Health Information Center (womenshealth.gov), a service of the Office on Women's Health in the U.S. Department of Health and Human Services.

40. Health Promotion Board. (n.d.). "Ask for Healthier Food—And Get a Discount." Retrieved 10/31/06 from http://www.hpb.gov.sg/hpb/default.asp?

41. Kotler, P., & Roberto, E. L. (1989). *Social Marketing: Strategies for Changing Public Behavior* (p. 102). New York: Free Press.

42. Case Source: Nancy Lee, Social Marketing Services, Inc.

43. McKenzie-Mohr, D., & Smith, W. (1999). *Fostering Sustainable Behavior: An Introduction to Community-Based Social Marketing* (p. 48). Gabriola Island, British Columbia, Canada: New Society.

44. Environment Canada. (n.d.). "Program: AT&T Telework Program Government of Canada." Retrieved from http://www.fhio-ifppe.gc.ca/default.asp?lang=En&n=A6D35B68-1

45. McKenzie-Mohr & Smith, *Fostering Sustainable Behavior,* p. 61.

46. National Institutes of Child Health and Human Development (NICHD), Back to Sleep Campaign. (n.d.). "Safe Sleep for Your Baby: Ten Ways to Reduce the Risk of Sudden Infant Death Syndrome." Retrieved 10/31/06 from http://www.nichd.nih.gov/publications/pubs/safe_sleep_gen .cfm#backs

47. NICHD, Back to Sleep Campaign. (n.d.). "Pampers Will Print the Back to Sleep Logo Across the Diaper Fastening Strips of Newborn Diapers." Retrieved 10/31/06 from http://www.nichd.nih .gov/sids/pampers.cfm

48. NICHD, Back to Sleep Campaign. "Safe Sleep for Your Baby."

49. Case Source: National Eating Disorders Association.

Chapter 4

1. Andreasen, A. R. (2002). *Marketing Research That Won't Break the Bank* (pp. 6–11). San Francisco: Jossey-Bass.

2. Kotler, P., & Armstrong, G. (2001). *Principles of Marketing* (9th ed., p. 140). Upper Saddle River, NJ: Prentice Hall.

3. Ibid.

4. Ibid.

5. Andreasen, A. R. (1995). *Marketing Social Change: Changing Behavior to Promote Health, Social Development, and the Environment* (p. 120). San Francisco: Jossey-Bass.

6. Ibid., p. 127.

7. Washington Traffic Safety Commission. "Seat Belts." Retrieved 11/03/06 from http://www.wtsc.wa.gov/seat_belts.html

8. Kotler & Armstrong, *Principles of Marketing* (9th ed.), p. 141.

9. Lefebvre, C. (2007, January 21). Message posted to Social Marketing Listserv.

10. Kotler & Armstrong, *Principles of Marketing* (9th ed.), p. 152.

11. Ibid., p. 146.

12. Ibid., p. 144.

13. Kotler, P., & Lee, N. (2007). *Marketing in the Public Sector: A Roadmap for Improved Performance* (p. 259). Upper Saddle River, NJ: Wharton School.

14. Cho, H., & Witte, K. (2005). "Managing Fear in Public Health Campaigns: A Theory-Based Formative Evaluation Process," *Health Promotion Practice, 6*(4), 483–490.

15. Witte, K. (1992). "Putting the Fear Back Into Fear Appeals: The Extended Parallel Process Model," *Communication Monographs, 59,* 329–349.

16. Cho, H., & Witte, K. "Managing Fear in Public Health Campaigns."

17. Ibid., pp. 484–489.

18. Andreasen, *Marketing Social Change,* p. 101.

19. Simons-Morton, B., Haynie, D., Crump, A., Eitel, P., & Saylor, K. (2001). "Peer and Parent Influences on Smoking and Drinking Among Early Adolescents," *Health Education & Behavior, 23*(1), 95–107.

20. Johnston, L. D., O'Malley, P. M., & Bachman, J. G. (1995). *National Survey Results on Drug Use From the Monitoring the Future Study, 1975-1994: Vol. 1. Secondary School Students* (NIH Pub. No. 95-4206). Rockville, MD: U.S. Department of Health and Human Services, National Institute on Drug Abuse.

21. Andreasen, *Marketing Research That Won't Break the Bank.*

22. Ibid., p. 75.

23. Ibid., p. 108.

24. Ibid., p. 120.

25. Ibid., p. 167.

Chapter 4 Table Notes

a. Kotler, P., & Armstrong, G. (2001). *Principles of Marketing* (9th ed., p. 140). Upper Saddle River, NJ: Prentice Hall.

b. Ibid., p. 146.

c. *Webster's New World Dictionary*. (1980). Cleveland, OH: William Collins; Senter, R. J. (1969). *Analysis of Data: Introductory Statistics for the Behavioral Sciences.* Glenview, IL: Scott, Foresman; Andreasen, A. R. (2002). *Marketing Research That Won't Break the Bank*. San Francisco: Jossey-Bass; Rumsey, D. (2003). *Statistics for Dummies.* Indianapolis, IN: Wiley; Kotler & Armstrong, *Principles of Marketing* (9th ed.); Ellen Cunningham of Cunningham Environmental Consulting.

Chapter 5

1. Majithia, R. (2006, June 9). "Report Finds HK's Bad Air Claims a Heavy Toll," *South China Morning Post,* p. 1.

2. Qide, C. (2004, April 1). "Campaign to Teach Kids About Road Safety," *China Daily.* Retrieved 11/20/06 from http://www.chinadaily.com.cn/english/doc/2004-04/01/content_319588.htm.

3. *People's Daily Online*. (2005, June 17). "China Focus: Energy Conservation Highlighted at Level of National Strategy." Retrieved 11/27/06 from http://english.people.com.cn/200506/17/eng20050617_190751.html

4. Quanlin, Q. (2006, May 30). "Campaign Aims to Smoke Out Young Addicts," *China Daily,* pp. 1, 5.

5. Feng, Z. (2006, May 30). "Current Anti-Smoking Efforts Failing to Make an Impact," *China Daily,* p. 1.

6. Ibid.

7. Qi, L. (2006, May 29). "Pets Bring Host of Problems," *China Daily*, p. 5.

8. Feng, Z. "Current Anti-Smoking Efforts Failing to Make an Impact," pp. 1, 5.

9. Holder, K. (2006). "China Road," *UCDAVIS Magazine Online.* Retrieved 11/28/06 from http://www-ucdmag.ucdavis.edu/current/feature_2.html

Chapter 6

1. World Health Organization (WHO). (2002). *World Report on Violence and Health.* Geneva, Switzerland: Author.

2. Donovan, R. J., & Vlais, R. (2005). *VicHealth Review of Communication Components of Social Marketing/Public Education Campaigns Focusing on Violence Against Women.* Melbourne, Australia: Victorian Health Promotion Foundation.

3. Englander, E. K. (2003). *Understanding Violence.* Hillsdale, NJ: Lawrence Erlbaum.

4. Prochaska, J. O., & DiClemente, C. C. (1984). *The Transtheoretical Approach: Crossing the Traditional Boundaries of Therapy.* Homewood, IL: Dow-Jones/Irwin.

5. Donovan, R. L., & Henley, N. (2003). *Social Marketing: Principles and Practice.* Melbourne, Australia: IP Communications.

6. Donovan, R. J., Francas, M., Paterson, D., & Zappelli, R. (2000). "Formative Research for Mass Media-Based Campaigns: Western Australia's 'Freedom from Fear' Campaign Targeting Male Perpetrators of Intimate Partner Violence," *Health Promotion Journal of Australia, 10*(2), 78–83.

7. Donovan & Henley, *Social Marketing.*

8. Gondolf, E. W. (2002). *Batterer Intervention Systems: Issues, Outcomes and Recommendations.* Thousand Oaks, CA: Sage.

9. Donovan, R. J., Paterson, D., & Francas, M. (1999). "Targeting Male Perpetrators of Intimate Partner Violence: Western Australia's 'Freedom From Fear' Campaign," *Social Marketing Quarterly, 5*(3), 127–143.

10. Cant, R., Downie, R., Fisher, C., Henry, P., & Froyland, I. (2002). *Evaluation of Perpetrator Programs for Mandated and Voluntary Participants in Western Australia.* Perth, Australia: Centre for Research on Women, Family and Domestic Violence Unit.

11. Donovan, R. J., Gibbons, L., Francas, M., & Zappelli, R. (2006). "Impact on Callers to a Men's Domestic Violence Helpline," *Australian and New Zealand Journal of Public Health, 30*(4), 384–385.

12. Kotler, P., & Armstrong, G. (2001). *Principles of Marketing* (p. 265). Upper Saddle River, NJ: Prentice Hall.

13. Ibid., p. 244.

14. Ibid., pp. 253–259.

15. Ibid., p. 259.

16. Prochaska, J., & DiClemente, C. (1983). "Stages and Processes of Self-Change of Smoking: Toward an Integrative Model of Change," *Journal of Consulting and Clinical Psychology, 51,* 390–395.

17. Prochaska, J., Norcross, J., & DiClemente, C. (1994). *Changing for Good* (pp. 40–56). New York: Avon Books.

18. Ibid., pp. 40–41.

19. Ibid.

20. Ibid., pp. 41–43.

21. Ibid., p. 43.

22. Ibid., p. 44.

23. Ibid., p. 45.

24. Ibid., p. 46.

25. Ibid., p. 47

26. "The Spiral of Change" from *Changing for Good* by James O. Prochaska, John C. Norcross, and Carlo C. DiClemente. Copyright © 1994 by James O. Prochaska, John C. Norcross, and Carlo C. DiClemente. Reprinted by permission of HarperCollins Publishers Inc.

27. Kotler, P., & Roberto, E. L. (1989). *Social Marketing: Strategies for Changing Public Behavior* (pp. 119, 126–127). New York: Free Press.

28. PRIZM NE. (n.d.). "The New Evolution in Segmentation." Retrieved 1/2/07 from http://www.claritas.com/claritas/Default.jsp?ci=3&si=4&pn=prizmne

29. SRI Consulting Business Intelligence (SRIC-B1); www.sric.bi.com/VALS.

30. Kotler & Roberto, *Social Marketing,* p. 149.

31. Andreasen, A. R. (1995). *Marketing Social Change: Changing Behavior to Promote Health, Social Development, and the Environment* (p. 148). San Francisco: Jossey-Bass.

32. Ibid., pp. 177–179.

33. Kotler & Armstrong, *Principles of Marketing,* pp. 265–268.

34. Ibid., p. 266.

35. Glynn, M., & Rhodes, P. (2005, June 14). *Estimated HIV Prevalence in the United States at the End of 2003.* Presented at the National HIV Prevention Conference, Atlanta, GA.

36. Centers for Disease Control and Prevention (CDC). (2003). "Advancing HIV Prevention: New Strategies for a Changing Epidemic—United States, 2003," *Morbidity and Mortality Weekly, 52*(15), 329–332.

37. CDC. (2004). "HIV/AIDS Among Women: HIV/AIDS Fact Sheet." Retrieved 2/24/06 from http://www.cdc.gov/hiv/pubs/facts/women.htm

38. Glynn & Rhodes, *Estimated HIV Prevalence in the United States at the End of 2003.*

39. CDC. (2005). "Advancing HIV Prevention: Interim Technical Guidelines for Selected Interventions." Retrieved 2/24/06 from http://www.cdc.gov/hiv/topics/prev_prog/AHP/resources/guidelines/AHPIntGuidfinal.pdf

40. Shepherd, M., Pollard, W., Bonds, M., & Anderton, J. (2001). *KNOW NOW! A Social Marketing Campaign for Increasing Awareness of HIV Status.* Presentation at the National HIV Prevention Conference, Atlanta, GA.

41. U.S. Census Bureau. (2003). "Marital Status of People 15 Years and Over, by Age, Sex, Personal Earnings, Race and Hispanic Origin, Black Only." Retrieved 1/15/05 from http://www.census.gov/population/socdemo/hh-fam/cps2003/tabA1-black.pdf

42. CDC. (2004). "HIV/AIDS Among Women" [HIV/AIDS Fact Sheet]. Retrieved 2/24/06 from http://www.cdc.gov/hiv/pubs/facts/women.htm

43. CDC, Behavioral Risk Factor Surveillance System (BRFSS). (2003). Retrieved from http://www.cdc.gov/brfss

44. CDC, BRFSS. (2000). Retrieved from http://www.cdc.gov/brfss

45. CDC. (2002). "HIV Testing Survey" [HIV/AIDS Special Surveillance Report 5]. Atlanta, GA: Author.

46. CDC, BRFSS. (2003).

47. U.S. Department of Labor. (2005). "Women as Major Health Care Consumers: Fact Sheet." Retrieved 1/15/05 from http://www.dol.gov/ebsa/newsroom/fshlth5.html

Chapter 7

1. Gore, A. (2006). *An Inconvenient Truth* (p. 305). New York: Rodale.

2. Courtesy of Paramount Pictures.

3. *An Inconvenient Truth.* (2006). "The Science: What Is Global Warming?" Retrieved 1/31/07 from http://www.climatecrisis.net/thescience/

4. Ibid.

5. Ibid.

6. *An Inconvenient Truth.* (2006). "Ten Things to Do." Retrieved 8/10/07 from http://www.climatecrisis.net/pdf/10things.pdf

7. Kerry, J. (2006, December 13). "*An Inconvenient Truth* House Parties" e-mail.

8. Project Smart. (n.d.). Smart Goals. Retrieved 8/11/07 from http://www.projectsmart.co.uk/smart-goals.html

9. Dillard, J., Hunter, J., & Burgoon, M. (1984). "Sequential Request Persuasive Strategies: Meta-Analysis of Foot-in-the-Door and Door-in-the-Face," *Human Communication Research, 10*, 461–488; Dillard, J. (1991). "The Current Status of Research on Sequential-Request Compliance Techniques," *Personality and Social Psychology Bulletin, 17,* 282–288

10. Ibid.

11. © March of Dimes Birth Defects Foundation, 1999. Reprinted with permission.

12. ODPHP, DHHS, *Healthy People 2010 Initiative.*

13. Office of Disease Prevention and Health Promotion (ODPHP), Department of Health and Human Services is the Coordinator of the Healthy People 2010 Initiative. Information retrieved 10/1/01 from http://www.health.gov/healthypeople/LHI/lhiwhat.htm

14. CDC, BRFSS. (2000). Retrieved 3/23/01 from http://www.cdc.gov/nccdphp/brfss/at-a-gl.htm

Chapter 7 Table Notes

a. Survey data is from a folic acid telephone survey conducted by the Gallup Organization, commissioned by the March of Dimes, and supported by the Centers for Disease Control and Prevention. Goal is for nonpregnant women.

Chapter 8

1. Public Safety Canada. (n.d.). "Discussion Paper: National Disaster Mitigation Strategy." Retrieved from http://www.publicsafety.gc.ca/prg/em/ndms/discussionsnac-en.asp

2. Ekos Research Associates. (2005, March). "Exploring Canadians' Attitudes Towards Safety and Security." Retrieved from http://epe.lac-bac.gc.ca/100/200/301/pwgsc-tpsgc/poref/public_safety_emergency/2004/2004-1416-e.pdf

3. GPC Public Affairs. (2005, December). "Are Canadians Prepared for an Emergency?" Retrieved from http://epe.lac-bac.gc.ca/100/200/301/pwgsc-tpsgc/por-ef/public_safety_emergency/2005/2005-1468/index.html

4. Ibid.

5. Ibid.

6. Ibid.

7. Ekos Research Associates. (2005, May). *Security Monitor.* Retrieved from http://www.ekos.com/studies/default.asp

8. Ibid. "Exploring Canadians' Attitudes Towards Safety and Security."

9. GPC Public Affairs. "Are Canadians Prepared for an Emergency?"

10. Ipsos-Reid Canada. (2007, March). *Public Safety and Emergency Preparedness Canada 2006-7 Advertising Evaluation.* Target audience findings are based on a small sample (n = 123), directional use only. Retrieved from http://epe.lac-bac.gc.ca/100/200/301/pwgsc tpsgc/por-ef/public_safety_canada/2007/264-06/index.html. Changes cited are based on a comparison of data from 2005 GPC study and Custom Wave 1 survey from the 2006–2007 Ipsos-Reid. These are all custom reports commissioned by Public Safety Canada. For further information, please contact por-rop@ps-sp.gc.ca

11. Bagozzi, R. P. (1978, March–April). "Marketing as Exchange: A Theory of Transactions in the Marketplace," *American Behavioral Science,* 535–556.

12. Kotler, P. (1972, April). "A Generic Concept of Marketing," *Journal of Marketing,* 46–54.

13. Kotler, P., & Levy, S. J. (1969, January). "Broadening the Concept of Marketing," *Journal of Marketing,* 10–15.

14. See Bagozzi, R. P. (1974). "Marketing as an Organized Behavioral System of Exchange," *Journal of Marketing, 38,* 77–81; Bagozzi, R. P. (1978, March–April). "Marketing as Exchange: A Theory of Transactions in the Marketplace," *American Behavioral Science,* 536–556.

15. McKenzie-Mohr, D. (n.d.). "Community Based Social Marketing: Quick Reference." Retrieved 1/30/07 from http://www.cbsm.com/Reports/CBSM.pdf

16. America's Blood Centers (ABC). (2006). "About ABC." Retrieved 12/28/06 from http://www.americasblood.org/go.cfm?do=Page.View&pid=29#research

17. Kotler, P., & Lee, N. (2006). *Marketing in the Public Sector: A Roadmap for Improved Performance* (p. 199). Upper Saddle River, NJ: Wharton School.

18. Smith, B. (2003). "Beyond 'Health' as a Benefit," *Social Marketing Quarterly, 9*(4), 22–28.

19. Key Findings from America's Blood Centers' Nationwide Survey on Blood Donation, 2001. Summary information provided by Brightline Media of Arlington, Virginia. Mike Broder, President, and Eric Wilk, Research Manager.

20. Reprinted with permission of Puget Sound Blood Center. Photo by Craig Harrold.

21. Peattie, S., & Peattie, K. (2003). "Ready to Fly Solo? Reducing Social Marketing's Dependence on Commercial Marketing Theory," *Marketing Theory Articles, 3*(3), 365–385.

22. McKenzie-Mohr, D., & Smith, W. (1999). *Fostering Sustainable Behavior* (p. 5). Gabriola Island, British Columbia, Canada: New Society.

23. National Cancer Institute. (2006). "Most Americans Do Not Know When or How Often to Get Cancer Screening Tests." Retrieved 8/4/06 from http://www.cancer.gov/newscenter/press releases/HINTS

24. Andreasen, A. R. (1995). *Marketing Social Change: Changing Behavior to Promote Health, Social Development, and the Environment* (pp. 108–109). San Francisco: Jossey-Bass.

25. March of Dimes. (2001). "Folic Acid and the Prevention of Birth Defects: A National Survey of Pre-pregnancy Awareness and Behavior Among Women of Childbearing Age, 1995–2001" [Executive Summary, conducted by the Gallup Organization]. Retrieved 10/2/01 from http://www.modimes.org/Programs2/FolicAcid/Health_Professionals.htm

26. Personal communication. (2001).

27. McCormack Brown, K. R. (1999). "Health Belief Model." Retrieved 4/2/01 from http://www.hsc.usf.edu/-kmbrown/Health_Belief_Model_Overview.htm

28. National High Blood Pressure Education Program (NHBPEP). (2001). As cited in National Institutes of Health, National Heart, Lung, and Blood Institute's Web site. Retrieved 9/18/01 from http://hin.nhlbi.nih.gov/nhbpep_kit_about_m.htm

29. National Institutes of Health, National Heart, Lung, and Blood Institute. (2001). "Taking Action to Control High Blood Pressure." Retrieved 1/19/01 from http://www.nih.gov/health/hbp tifl/3.htm

30. Ibid.

31. Ibid.

32. Ajzen, I. (1991). "The Theory of Planned Behavior." *Organizational Behavior and Human Decision Processes, 50*, p. 179–211.

33. Fishbein, M., summarizing Bandura (1986, 1989, 1999) in *Developing Effective Behavior Change Intervention* (p. 3). As summarized by the Communication Initiative, "Summary of Change Theories and Models. Slide 5." Retrieved 4/2/01 from http://www.com minit.com/power_point/change_theories/sldoo5.htm

34. Andreasen, A. R. (1995). *Marketing Social Change: Changing Behavior to Promote Health, Social Development, and the Environment* (pp. 266–268). San Francisco: Jossey-Bass.

35. Fishbein, *Developing Effective Behavior Change Intervention,* p. 3.

36. Washington Department of Health. (2006). From Draft Social Marketing Plan. Ilene Silver, lead project manager.

37. Institutional Review Board. (2007). Retrieved 1/16/07 from Wikipedia: http://en.wikipedia .org/wiki/Institutional_Review_Board

38. Marzio Della Santa has a PhD in public finance and a master of public health. After 2 years with Arthur Andersen as a change enablement expert, he began working as a project manager in 2000 for *Rete sanitaria*, an initiative to introduce an e-health network in the Ticino Canton (Switzerland).

39. François Lagarde (MA) is a Canadian social marketing consultant to several organizations in the health, philanthropy, development aid, environment, and housing fields. He is also an associate professor in the Faculty of Medicine of the University of Montreal, where he teaches social marketing in the health administration and public health programs.

Chapter 9

1. Ries, A., & Trout, J. (1982). *Positioning: The Battle for Your Mind* (p. 3). New York: Warner Books.

2. Ibid., pp. 7–8.

3. Rothschild, M. L., Mastin, B., & Miller, T. W. (2006). "Reducing Alcohol Related Crashes Through the Use of Social Marketing," *Accident Analysis and Prevention, 38*(6), 1218–1230.

4. Adapted from Kotler, P., & Keller, K. L. (2005). *Marketing Management* (12th ed., p. 320). Upper Saddle River, NJ: Prentice Hall.

5. Ibid.

6. Ibid., pp. 312–313.

7. King County Emergency Management. (2006). "3 Days, 3 Ways, Are You Ready?" Retrieved 1/19/07 from http://www.govlink.org/3days3ways/

8. Transportation Security Administration. (n.d.). "311 for Carry-Ons." Retrieved 1/19/07 from http://www.tsa.gov/assets/pdf/311-credit-card.pdf

9. Photo courtesy of the Produce for Better Health Foundation.

10. Produce for Better Health Foundation. (2005, November 30). "Fruit and Vegetable Consumption on the Rise for First Time in Nearly 15 Years." Retrieved 1/19/07 from http://www.5aday.com/html/press/pressrelease.php?recordid=159

11. Washington State Department of Health. (2007). "Tobacco Quit Line." Retrieved 1/22/07 from http://www.quitline.com/

12. Case Source: Kocher, K. W., & cR Kommunikation AG, Zurich. (1993). *The STOP AIDS Story, 1987–1992* (1st ed.). STOP AIDS Campaign of the Swiss AIDS Foundation and the Federal Office for Public Health. Images retrieved from http://tecfa.unige.ch/tecfa/research/humanities/ AIDS-campaign/campaign-themes.html

13. Reprinted with permission of The Swiss AIDS Foundation and the Federal Office for Public Health.

14. Campanile, C. (2007, January 8). "COVERUP: CITY'S OWN CONDOMS." *New York Post*. Retrieved 1/17/2007 from http://www.nypost.com

15. U.S. Environmental Protection Agency. (2006). "How Many Light Bulbs Does It Take to Protect the Environment and Save $30?" Retrieved from http://yosemite.epa.gov/opa/admpress.nsf/7c02ca8c86062a0f85257018004118a6/64a3072475dc5045852571fd005a9ab3!OpenDocument

16. Reprinted with permission of Pilgrim Plastics, Brockton, MA.

17. Sun Microsystems. (2007). "DIAL 311." Retrieved 1/22/2007 from http://www.sun.com/about-sun/media/features/311.html

18. Smith, B. (1999, June). "Social Marketing: Marketing With No Budget," *Social Marketing Quarterly, 5*(2), 7–8.

19. From *Newsweek,* 10/2/00 © 2000 Newsweek, Inc. All rights reserved. Reprinted by permission. Photograph © Nicole Rosenthal.

20. D.A.R.E. America. (n.d.). "The New D.A.R.E. Program. Substance Abuse and Violence Prevention." Retrieved 1/22/07 from http://www.dare.com/home/newdareprogram.asp

21. Ibid.

22. Kotler, P., & Armstrong, G. (2001). *Principles of Marketing* (9th ed., p. 301). Upper Saddle River, NJ: Prentice Hall.

23. Produce for Better Health Foundation. (n.d.). "5 A Day the Color Way." Retrieved 1/29/07 from http://www.5aday.com/html/colorway/colorway_home.php

24. Substance Abuse and Mental Health Services Administration. (2005). Results from the *2004 National Survey on Drug Use and Health* (Office of Applied Studies, NSDUH Series H-27, DHHS Publication No. SMA 05-4061). Rockville, MD: Author. Retrieved from http://oas.samhsa.gov/NSDUH/2k4nsduh/2k4Results/2k4Results.pdf

25. Photo by Pete Stone. Reprinted with permission of Arnold Worldwide.

Chapter 10

1. Kotler, P., & Keller, K. L. (2005). *Marketing Management* (12th ed., p. 372). Upper Saddle River, NJ: Prentice Hall.

2. Ibid.

3. Kotler, P., & Armstrong, G. (2001). *Principles of Marketing* (9th ed., p. 294). Upper Saddle River, NJ: Prentice Hall.

4. Ibid.

5. Reprinted with permission of Centers for Disease Contol and Prevention's Media Campaign Resource Center.

6. Kotler, P., & Roberto, E. L. (1989). *Social Marketing: Strategies for Changing Public Behavior* (p. 155). New York: Free Press; Assael, H. (1981). *Consumer Behavior and Marketing Action.* Boston: Kent.

7. Salmon Friendly Gardening program materials were developed by Seattle Public Utilities. Reprinted with permission.

8. Kotler & Roberto, *Social Marketing,* p. 156.

9. Wiebe, G. D. (1951–952). "Merchandising Commodities and Citizenship on Television," *Public Opinion Quarterly, 15*, 679–691 (at p. 679).

10. Kotler, P., & Zaltman, G. (1971). "Social Marketing: An Approach to Planned Social Change," *Journal of Marketing, 35*, 3–12.

11. Monterey Bay Aquarium. (2006, November 2). "Dire Warning About Future of Seafood Lends New Urgency to Making Better Choices" [Press release].

12. Ibid.

13. Equator Initiative. (2000, January). "Play Pumps—South Africa." Retrieved 11/17/2005 from http:www.tve.org/ho/doc.cfm?aid=535; "Why Pumping Water Is Child's Play." (2005, April 25). BBC News. Retrieved 2/6/07 from http://news.bbc.co.uk/1/hi/world/africa/4461265.stm

14. Chakravorty, B. (1992, April/May). "Smokeless Tobacco Substitute Tested With Southern Illinois Youth." *Public Health Reports.* As quoted in *Social Marketing Quarterly* (1996), "Product Substitution for Social Marketing of Behavior Change: A Conceptualization," p. 5.

15. Ibid., p. 5.

16. Ibid., p. 10.

17. Ibid., pp. 9–10.

18. Kotler & Roberto, *Social Marketing,* pp. 155–157.

19. Kotler & Armstrong, *Principles of Marketing* (9th ed.), p. 301.

20. U.S. Environmental Protection Agency (EPA). (2006, June 6). [Press release]. Retrieved from http://www.epa.gov/watersense and U.S. EPA Web site, http://www.epa.gov/cgi-bin/epa printonly.cgi

21. The Food Stamp National Media Campaign, OMB Blanket Clearance No. 0584-0524.

22. American Dietetic Association (ADA). (1998); Intersociety Professional Nutrition Education Consortium (IPNEC). (1998); Keithley, Keller, & Vazquez. (1996); National Center for Health Statistics. (1993).

23. Reprinted with permission of Beverly Schwartz.

24. Since the Food Stamp Program is federally mandated, only an act of Congress can change the name of the program.

Chapter 10 Table Notes

a. Kotler, P., & Armstrong, G. (2001). *Principles of Marketing* (9th ed., p. 300). Upper Saddle River, NJ: Prentice Hall.

b. Kotler & Armstrong, *Principles of Marketing* (9th ed.), p. 299.

Chapter 11

1. Bueckert, D. (2007). "Federal Budget Hammers Gas-Guzzlers, Leaves Kyoto in the Air." *Canoe Network–CNEWS.* Retrieved 3/20/07 from http://cnews.canoe.ca/CNEWS/Canada/2007/03/19/3783431-cp.html

2. Health Promotion Board, Singapore Research & Strategic Planning Division. (2004). *Report of the National Nutrition Survey.* Please see page 61 of http://www.hpb.gov.sg/data/hpb .home/files/edu/NNS%20Report_Final(Merged).pdf

3. Kotler, P., & Armstrong, G. (2001). *Principles of Marketing* (p. 371). Upper Saddle River, NJ: Prentice Hall.

4. O'Connor, R., Fix, B., Celestino, P., Carlin-Menter, S., Hyland, A., & Cummings, K. M. (n.d.). "Financial Incentives to Promote Smoking Cessation: Evidence from 11 Quit and Win Contests." Retrieved 3/10/07 from http://www.ncbi.nlm.nih.gov/entrez/query.fcgi?cmd=Retrieve&db=pubmed&dopt=Abstract&list_uids=16340515&query_hl=6&itool=pubmed_docsum

5. Rosenberg, T. (2006, November 16). "How to Fight Poverty: 8 Programs That Work," *New York Times*. Retrieved 3/9/07 from http://www.globalaidsalliance.org/mediaclips/New_York_Times_November_16_2006.cfm

6. Ibid.

7. Ibid.

8. Ibid. This article cites this resource as well: Dr. Ruth Levine, "Millions Saved: Proven Successes in Global Health," a project of the Center for Global Development and the Disease Control Priorities Project.

9. Information in this example is from Harborview Injury Prevention and Research Center, University of Washington, Seattle. Retrieved 10/01/01 from http://www.hiprc.org

10. Kotler, P., & Roberto, E. L. (1989). *Social Marketing: Strategies for Changing Public Behavior*. New York: Free Press, citing Fox, K. F. (1980). "Time as a Component of Price in Social Marketing." In R. P. Bagozzi, et al. (Eds.), *Marketing in the '80s* (pp. 464–467). Chicago: American Marketing Association.

11. Ibid.

12. Kotler & Roberto, *Social Marketing,* pp. 182–183, citing Gemunden, H. G. (1985). "Perceived Risk and Information Search: A Systematic Meta-Analysis of the Empirical Evidence," *International Journal of Research in Marketing, 2,* 79–100.

13. Andreasen, A. R. (2006). *Social Marketing in the 21st Century* (p. 153). Thousand Oaks, CA: Sage.

14. Ibid., p. 102.

15. Reusablebags.com. (n.d.). "Facts and Figures Regarding the True Cost of Plastic Bags." Retrieved 3/13/07 from http://www.reusablebags.com/facts.php?id=1&display=print

16. Planet Ark. (2007, February 22). "Ireland to Raise 'Green' Tax on Plastic Bags." Retrieved 3/13/2007 from http://www.planetark.com/avantgo/dailynewsstory.cfm?newsid=40454

17. Ibid.

18. BBC News. (2002, August 20). "Irish Bag Tax Hailed Success." Retrieved 3/13/2007 from http://news.bbc.co.uk/1/hi/world/europe/2205419.stm

19. City of Tacoma. (2007). "The Filthy 15." Retrieved 3/21/07 from http://www.cityoftacoma.org/Page.aspx?nid=167

20. Copyright © 2001 by Washington State Office of Superintendent of Public Instruction.

21. Ibid.

22. Ibid.

23. Students received creative and production assistance from Cynthia Hartwig (creative director), Shelley Baker (art director at Cf2gs Advertising), Marlene Liranzo (Mercer Island High School teacher), Gary Gorland (Teen Aware program manager), and Nancy Lee (consultant).

24. Kotler & Roberto, *Social Marketing,* pp. 176–177.

25. National Highway Traffic Safety Administration. (2007). "Traffic Safety Facts." Retrieved 3/21/07 from http://www-nrd.nhtsa.dot.gov/Pubs/810690.PDF

26. Alabama Department of Economic and Community Affairs, Law Enforcement/Traffic Safety Division. (2006, September 30). "Evaluation of 2006 Click It or Ticket." Prepared by Pevear, J., III, Alabama Department of Public Health & *CARE* Research & Development Laboratory, and by Parrish, A. S., & Wright, K., Computer Science Department, University of Alabama, Tuscaloosa. Retrieved 3/21/07 from http://care.cs .ua.edu/docs/2006%20CIOT.pdf

Chapter 12

1. Kane County Environmental Management. (2006). "Kane County Recycles." Retrieved 2/11/07 from www.co.kane.il.us/Environment/recycle/facts.htm

2. Watson, T. (2002, June 6). "Dog Waste Poses Threat to Water," *USA Today*. Retrieved 2/11/07 from http://www.usatoday.com/news/science/2002-06-07-dog-usat.htm

3. Healthy People 2010. (n.d.). "Progress Review Tobacco Use." Retrieved 2/11/07 from http://www.healthypeople.gov/Data/2010prog/focus27/default.htm

4. Nathan, H. M., Conrad, S. L., Held, P. J., McCullough, K. P., Pietroski, R. E., Siminoff, L. A., et al. (2003). "Organ Donation in the United States," *American Journal of Transplantation, 3*(4), 29–40. Retrieved 2/11/07 from http://www.blackwell-synergy.com/links/doi/10.1034/j.1600 6143.3.s4.4.x/full/?cookieSet=1

5. Information from *SmileMobile* brochure, an effort of the Washington State Dental Association the Washington Dental Service Foundation, and Delta Dental Washington Dental Service. (n.d.). *Smilemobile*, retrieved from http://www.deltadentalwa.com/WDSFoundation/ WDSFoundationSmileMobile.aspx?DView=WDSFoundation_SmileMobile

6. Reprinted with permission from Washington Dental Service Foundation, *Making Dental Care for Children More Accessible*.

7. U.S. Census Bureau. (2004, November). "Current Population Survey." Retrieved from http://www.census.gov/Press-Release/www/releases/archives/CB05-73Table2.xls

8. Wright, J. (2004, November 23). "Mail-in Ballots Give Oregon Voters Control," *Seattle Post-Intelligencer.* Retrieved from http://seattlepi.nwsource.com/opinion/200682_ore gonvote23.html

9. Ibid.

10. DanceSafe. (2006). Retrieved 2/14/07 from http://www.dancesafe.org/

11. Ibid.

12. Ibid.

13. Ibid.

14. Healthy Transportation Network. (n.d.). "Safer Streets, Sidewalks and Trails." Retrieved from http://www.healthytransportation.net/view_resource.php?res_id=7&cat_type=improve and Michelle Mowery, Bicycle Program Manager LADOT, Los Angeles, CA. Retrieved from http://www.healthytransportation.net/categories.php?type=improve

15. Rubenstein, E., & Kalina, S. (n.d.). "The Adoption Option: Choosing and Raising the Right Shelter Dog for You." Retrieved 2/17/07 from http://www.phsspca.org/store/ choosingadog.htm

16. Sacramento Society's Prevention of Cruelty to Animals (SSPCA). (n.d.). "Pets on the Net." Retrieved 10/31/01 from http://www.sspca.org/adopt.html

17. http://www.sspca.org/ContactUs.html.

18. American Heart Association. (2006, October 6). "President Clinton and American Heart Association Announce Joint Agreement Between Alliance for a Healthier Generation and Food Industry Leaders to Set Healthy Standards for Snacking in School. Landmark Agreement Signed by Leading Food Manufacturers: Campbell Soup Company, Dannon, Kraft Foods, Mars and PepsiCo," *Association News.* Retrieved 2/17/07 from http://www.americanheart.org/presenter .jhtml?identifier=3042692

19. National Conference of State Legislatures. (2005, March 1). "Vending Machines in Schools." Retrieved from http://www.ncsl.org/programs/health/vending.htm

20. The Food Trust. (n.d.). "School Food & Beverage Reform." Retrieved 8/21/07 from http://www.thefoodtrust.org/php/programs/school.food.beverage.reform.php

21. National Conference of State Legislatures. (2005, March).

22. National Conference of State Legislatures. (2006, January 5). "Childhood Obesity—2005 Update and Overview of Policy Options." Retrieved 2/18/07 from http://www.ncsl.org/pro grams/health/ChildhoodObesity-2005.htm

23. Dawdy, P. (2006, September 27). "Broke as a Smoke: Powerful State Legislators Explore Ditching the 25-Foot Rule as Barkeeps Struggle to Weather a Butt-Free Recession," *Seattle Weekly.* Retrieved 2/19/07 from http://www.seattleweekly.com/2006-09-27/news/broke-as-a-smoke.php

24. Washington's Tobacco Prevention and Control Program. (2006, March). "Secondhand Smoke." Retrieved 2/19/07 from http://www.doh.wa.gov/tobacco/fact_sheets/secondhandfacts.htm

25. Bott, J. (1999, April 28). "Karmanos Site to Offer Mammograms at Mall," *Detroit Free Press.* Retrieved from http://www.freep.com/news/health/qkamra28.htm (Reprinted with permission).

26. Kowal, J. (2004, January 2). "Rapid HIV Tests Offered Where Those at Risk Gather: Seattle Health Officials Get Aggressive in AIDS Battle by Heading to Gay Clubs, Taking a Drop of Blood and Providing Answers in 20 Minutes," *Chicago Tribune.* Retrieved from http://www.aegis.com/news/ct/2004/CT040101.html

27. Kotler, P., & Lee, N. (2006). *Marketing in the Public Sector* (p. 97). Upper Saddle River, NJ: Wharton School.

28. Personal communication. (2007, March). Data from the HIV/AIDS Program, Public Health–Seattle & King County.

29. The survey was designed by Cunningham Environmental Consulting in consultation with WCRC and Northwest Research Group. It was included in a January 2006 edition of SoundStats™, a regularly scheduled omnibus survey fielded by Northwest Research Group. The sample included 400 households in King County. The overall margin of sampling error for the survey is plus or minus 5%. Full survey results are available online at http://wastenotwashington .org/Pharmsurvey.pdf

30. This is a project of the Local Hazardous Waste Management Program in King County, Snohomish County Solid Waste Management Division, Seattle-King County Public Health, Northwest Product Stewardship Council, Washington Citizens for Resource Conservation, and Washington State Department of Ecology, and advised by the Washington Board of Pharmacy. For more information, please contact Emma Johnson, Project Facilitator, Washington State Department of Ecology, (425)649-7266, ejoh461@ecy.wa.gov.

31. Kotler, P., & Roberto, E. L. (1989). *Social Marketing: Strategies for Changing Public Behavior* (p. 162). New York: Free Press.

32. Coughlan, A. T., & Stern, L. W. (2001). "Market Channel Design and Management." In D. Iacobucci, et al. (Eds.), *Kellogg on Marketing* (pp. 247–267). New York: John Wiley & Sons.

33. Ibid., p. 250.

34. Gladwell, M. (2000). From *The Tipping Point: How Little Things Can Make a Big Difference* (pp. 203–206), Copyright by Malcolm Gladwell. Boston: Little, Brown. (By permission of Little, Brown and Company, Inc.)

Chapter 13

1. Adapted from Kalisa, N., Uwabakurikiza, P., Kyagambiddwa, S., Wijnants, J., & Collens, S. (2007). "*Urunana*-Radio Health Communication: A Case Study From Rwanda." In M. Siegel & L. D. Lotenberg (Eds.), *Marketing Public Health: Strategies to Promote Social Change* (2nd ed.). Boston: Jones & Bartlett.

2. Ministry of Finance and Economic Planning. (2002). *Rwanda Poverty Reduction Strategy Paper (PRSP)*. Kigali, Rwanda: Author.

3. UNICEF. (2005). *State of the World's Children Report*. New York: Author.

4. Ministry of Finance and Economic Planning. (2002). *Rwanda National Census*. Kigali, Rwanda: Author.

5. Health Unlimited Rwanda. (2005). *Baseline Survey Report of the Urunana/Umuhoza Rural Extension Project 2005–2008*. Kigali, Rwanda: Author.

6. Health Unlimited Rwanda Well Women Media Project. (2005). *Preliminary Evaluation of the Urunana KAP Monitoring Data: Statement of Major Findings (September 2002–July 2005)*. Kigali, Rwanda: Author.

7. Ibid.

8. Kotler, P., & Keller, K. L. (2005). *Marketing Management* (12th ed., p. 536). Upper Saddle River, NJ: Prentice Hall.

9. Reeves, R. (1960). *Reality in Advertising*. New York: Knopf.

10. Siegel, M., & Doner, L. (1998). *Marketing Public Health: Strategies to Promote Social Change* (pp. 332–333). Gaithersburg, MD: Aspen.

11. Ibid., p. 321.

12. Reprinted with permission of Harborview Injury Prevention and Research Center.

13. Crowley, A. E., & Hoyer, W. D. (1994, March). "An Integrative Framework for Understanding Two-Sided Persuasion," *Journal of Consumer Research*, 561–574.

14. Kotler, P. (1976). *Marketing Management* (3rd ed., pp. 334–335). Upper Saddle River, NJ: Prentice Hall.

15. Siegel & Doner, *Marketing Public Health*, pp. 314–315.

16. Obama, B. (2006, December 1). "Race Against Time—World AIDS Day Speech." Retrieved 4/11/07 from http://obama.senate.gov/speech/061201-race_against_time_world_aids_day_speech/index.html

17. Kelman, H. C., & Hovland, C. I. (1953). "Reinstatement of the Communication in Delayed Measurement of Opinion Change," *Journal of Abnormal and Social Psychology, 48*, 327–335. As cited in Kotler & Keller, *Marketing Management* (12th ed.), p. 546.

18. Moore, D. J., Mowen, J. C., & Reardon, R. (1994, Summer). "Multiple Sources in Advertising Appeals: When Product Endorsers Are Paid by the Advertising Sponsor," *Journal of*

the Academy of Marketing Science, 234–243. As cited in Kotler & Keller, *Marketing Management* (12th ed.), p. 546.

19. Montana Meth Project. (n.d.). Retrieved 3/26/07 from http://www.montanameth.org/About_Us/index.php

20. McKenzie-Mohr, D., & Smith, W. (1999). *Fostering Sustainable Behavior* (p. 101). Gabriola Island, British Columbia, Canada: New Society.

21. Roman, K., & Maas, J. M. (1992). *How to Advertise* (2nd ed.). New York: St. Martin's.

22. Kelly, K., Comello, M., & Slater, M. (2006). "Development of an Aspirational Campaign to Prevent Youth Substance Use: Be Under Your Own Influence," *Social Marketing Quarterly,* 7(2), 14–25.

23. Campaign tagline and materials may not be used without permission from Nori Comello: ncomello@lamar.colostate.edu

24. Reprinted with permission of Maria Leonora Comello.

25. Siegel & Doner, *Marketing Public Health,* pp. 335–336.

26. Sternthal, B., & Craig, C. S. (1974). "Fear Appeals: Revisited and Revised," *Journal of Consumer Research, 3,* 23–34. As summarized in P. Kotler & E. L. Roberto. (1989). *Social Marketing: Strategies for Changing Public Behavior* (p. 198). New York: Free Press.

27. Hale, J. L., & Dillard, J. P. (1995). "Fear Appeals in Health Promotion Campaigns: Too Much, Too Little, or Just Right?" In E. Maibach & R. Parrott (Eds.), *Designing Health Messages: Approaches From Communication Theory and Public Health Practice* (pp. 65–80). Thousand Oaks, CA: Sage.

28. Image courtesy of www.adbusters.org.

29. Reprinted with permission of Children's Hospital and Regional Medical Center, Seattle, Washington.

30. McKenzie-Mohr & Smith, *Fostering Sustainable Behavior,* p. 101.

31. Ibid., p. 85.

32. Ibid., p. 86.

33. Burn, S. M. (1991). "Social Psychology and the Stimulation of Recycling Behaviors: The Block Leader Approach," *Journal of Applied Social Psychology, 21,* 611–629.

34. Source: Washington Department of Health.

35. Ad Council. (2006). Retrieved from http://www.adcouncil.org/default.aspx?id=54

36. Author photo.

37. Kotler, P., & Armstrong, G. (2001). *Principles of Marketing* (9th ed., p. 548). Upper Saddle River, NJ: Prentice Hall.

38. Carducci, V. (n.d.). "The Big Idea." Retrieved 3/28/07 from http://www.popmatters.com/books/reviews/h/how-brands-become-icons.shtml

39. Kotler & Armstrong, *Principles of Marketing* (9th ed.), p. 548.

40. Porter Novelli. (2006). "'The Big Idea': Death By Execution." Retrieved 3/28/07 from http://www.porternovelli.com/site/pressrelease.aspx?pressrelease_id=140&pgName=news

41. Spangenberg, E. R., Sprott, D. E., Grohmann, B., & Smith, R. J. (2003, July). "Mass-Communicated Prediction Requests: Practical Application and a Cognitive Dissonance Explanation for Self-Prophecy," *Journal of Marketing,* 47–62. Retrieved from http://www.atyponlink.com/AMA/doi/abs/10.1509/jmkg.67.3.47.18659

42. Guido, M. (2004, Spring). "A More Effective Nag," *Washington State Magazine,* 7.

43. Ibid.

44. MOST of Us. (n.d.). "What Is Social Norms Marketing?" Retrieved 3/29/07 from http://www.mostofus.org/

45. The 2005 Partnership Attitude Tracking Survey (PATS), conducted by the Partnership for a Drug-Free America, found that 83% of teens in 6th through 12th grades in the United States believe there is *great risk in taking methamphetamine regularly,* compared to 93% of Montana teens.

46. The Drug Testing Index, published by Quest Diagnostics as a public service for government, media, and industry, has been considered a benchmark for national trends since its inception in 1988.

Chapter 14

1. TravelSmart. (n.d.). www.GettingAround Portland.org. Retrieved 11/10/2006 from http://www.portlandonline.com/transportation/index.cfm?c=36370

2. Kaiser Family Foundation. (2007, January 25). "MtvU and Kaiser Family Foundation Launch Search for Best Video Game Concept to Reduce Spread of HIV/AIDS" [Press release]. Retrieved from http://www.kff.org/hivaids/phip012507nr.cfm and http://DarfurisDying.com

3. Kotler, P., & Keller, K. (2005). *Marketing Management* (12th ed., p. 546). Upper Saddle River, NJ: Prentice Hall.

4. Dunn, J. (2006, July 13). "Denver Water's Ads Already Working Conservation Angle," *Denver Post.* Retrieved 4/22/07 from http://www.denverpost.com/portlet/article/html/frag ments/print_article.jsp?articleId=4043. Ads developed by Sukle Advertising and Design.

5. Kotler, P., & Lee, N. (2006). *Marketing in the Public Sector* (p. 152). Upper Saddle River, NJ: Wharton School.

6. Siegel, M., & Doner, L. A. (1998). *Marketing Public Health: Strategies to Promote Social Change* (p. 393). Gaithersburg, MD: Aspen.

7. Ibid., p. 394.

8. Ibid., p. 396.

9. Wiland, H., & Bell, D. (Producers). (2006). *Edens Lost & Found* [Television series]. Additional information at http://www.edenslostandfound.org/

10. For more information go to http://www.petwaste.surfacewater.info

11. Rogers, E. M., et al. (1989). *Proceedings From the Conference on Entertainment Education for Social Change.* Los Angeles: Annenberg School of Communications.

12. Andreasen, A. R. (1995). *Marketing Social Change: Changing Behavior to Promote Health, Social Development, and the Environment* (p. 215). San Francisco: Jossey-Bass.

13. Davies, J. (n.d.). "Preventing HIV/AIDS with Condoms: Nine Tips You Can Use." Retrieved 4/12/07 from http://www.johndavies.com/johndavies/new2html/9tips_print.htm

14. Keep America Beautiful. (n.d.). "I'm Not Your Mama: Mississippi's War Against Highway Litter." Retrieved 4/13/07 from http://www.kab.org/aboutus2.asp?id=642

15. Centers for Disease Control and Prevention. (n.d.). "Entertainment Education: Overview." Retrieved 10/10/2006 from http://www.cdc.gov/communication/entertainment_edu cation.htm

16. Social Impact Games. (n.d.). "Entertaining Games With Non-Entertainment Goals." Retrieved 4/12/07 from http://www.socialimpactgames.com/modules.php?op=modload&name= News&file=article&sid=116&mode=thread&order=1&thold=0

17. The Green Dollhouse Project. (2005, September 20). "New Exhibit Makes Child's Play of Building Green" [Press release]. Retrieved 4/12/07 from http://www.greendllhouse .org/pr_092005.shtml. (Partners with Green Dollhouse Project included Sustainable San Mateo County, San Mateo County RecycleWorks Green Building Program, *Sunset* magazine, San Francisco Design Center, & Jennifer Roberts, author of *Good Green Homes*.) Photo courtesy of Emily Hagopian.

18. Weaver, J. (2002, November 17). "A License to Shill," *MSNBC News*. Retrieved from http://www.msnbc.msn.com/id/3073513/

19. Kotler & Keller, *Marketing Management* (12th ed.), p. 548.

20. Gladwell, M. (2000). *The Tipping Point: How Little Things Can Make a Big Difference.* Boston: Little, Brown.

21. Godin, S. (2000). "Unleashing the Ideavirus." Dobbs Ferry, NY: Do You Zoom.

22. Kotler & Keller, *Marketing Management* (12th ed.), p. 613.

23. CBS 11. (n.d.). "CBS 11 Launches 'e-life' Website." Retrieved 4/20/07 from http://cbs11tv.com/press/local_story_114170135.html

24. Schultz, D. (2006, August 15). "IMC Is Do or Die in New Pull Marketplace," *Marketing News,* p. 7.

25. Ad Council. (n.d.). "Wireless Amber Alerts, Campaign Description." Retrieved 4/20/07 from http://www.adcouncil.org/default.aspx?id=354

26. Kotler, P., & Armstrong, G. (2001). *Principles of Marketing* (p. 552). Upper Saddle River, NJ: Prentice Hall.

27. Photo by Richard Lee. Reprinted with permission of *Detroit Free Press*. Text from *Newsweek* 3/13/00 © 2000 Newsweek, Inc. All rights reserved. Reprinted with permission.

28. Kotler & Armstrong. *Principles of Marketing,* pp. 513–517.

20. Ibid.

30. Ad Council. (n.d.). "Drunk Driving Prevention (1983–Present)." Retrieved 4/18/07 from http://www.adcouncil.org/default.aspx?id=137

31. Ibid., "Campaign Description."

32. Ibid.

33. Courtesy of the U.S. Department of Transportation and the Ad Council.

34. Satel, S. (2007, April 13). "Is It Wrong to Advertise for Organs?" *National Review Online,* p. 16.

35. This material is excerpted with permission from the Henry J. Kaiser Family Foundation. (2002, June). "The Impact of TV's Health Content: A Case Study of *ER* Viewers." Survey snapshot [Publication #3230]. Retrieved from http://www.kff.org/entmedia/3230-index.cfm

Chapter 15

1. Kotler, P. (1999). *Kotler on Marketing: How to Create, Win and Dominate Markets* (p.185). New York: Free Press.

2. Kotler, P., & Lee, N. (2006). *Marketing in the Public Sector: A Roadmap for Improved Performance* (p. 266). Upper Saddle River, NJ: Wharton School.

3. Ibid., pp. 268–269.

4. Ibid., p. 272.

Chapter 16

1. Sesame Workshop. (2005, September 20). "If Elmo Eats Broccoli, Will Kids Eat It Too?: Atkins Foundation Grant to Fund Further Research" [Press release]. Retrieved from http://www.sesameworkshop.org/aboutus/inside_press.php?contentId=15092302

2. Berry, L. L., Seiders, K., & Hergenroeder, A. (2006). "Regaining the Health of a Nation: What Business Can Do About Obesity," *Organizational Dynamics, 35*(4), 341–356.

3. Kotler, P., & Armstrong, G. (2001). *Principles of Marketing* (pp. 528–529). Upper Saddle River, NJ: Prentice Hall.

4. Ibid., p. 529.

5. Kotler, P. (1999). *Kotler on Marketing* (p. 31). New York: Free Press.

6. Parker-Pope, T. (2007, May 10). "As Child Obesity Surges, One Town Finds Way to Slim," *Wall Street Journal*, pp. 1, 15.

7. Foundation Center. (2006). "Number of Grantmaking Foundations by Type, 1975 to 2004." Retrieved 5/3/07 from http://foundationcenter.org/findfunders/statistics/pdf/02_found_growth/03_04.pdf

8. Kotler, P., & Andreasen, A. (1991). *Strategic Marketing for Nonprofit Organizations* (p. 285). Englewood Cliffs, NJ: Prentice Hall.

9. Source: Press Room—Bill & Melinda Gates Foundation. (2000). "I Am Your Child Foundation Receives $1 Million Grant from the Bill and Melinda Gates Foundation." Retrieved 6/8/01 from http://www.gatesfoundation.org/pressroom/release.asp?PRindex-325.

10. Pringle, H., & Thompson, M. (1999). *Brand Spirit: How Cause-Related Marketing Builds Brands*. New York: John Wiley; Earle, R. (2000). *The Art of Cause Marketing*. Lincolnwood, IL: NTC Business Books.

11. Ad Council. (2001). Retrieved 10/10/01 from www.adcouncil.org & www.adcouncil.org/body_about.html

12. Smith, W., & Benstein, R. (1999). *Let Kids Lead*. Washington, DC: Academy for Education Development.

13. Kotler, P., & Lee, N. (2006). *Corporate Social Responsibility: Doing the Most Good for Your Company and Your Cause* (p. 4). New York: John Wiley.

14. Ibid., p. 9.

15. Ibid., pp. 119–129.

16. Materials developed by Child Care Resources and SAFECO Insurance.

17. Pringle & Thompson, *Brand Spirit: How Cause Related Marketing Builds Brands*; Earle, *The Art of Cause Marketing*.

18. Reprinted with permission of Children's Hospital and Regional Medical Center, Seattle, Washington.

Chapter 17

1. McKenzie-Mohr, D., & Smith, W. (1999). *Fostering Sustainable Behavior: An Introduction to Community-Based Social Marketing* (2nd ed.). Gabriola Island, British Columbia, Canada: New Society.

2. Natural Resources Canada.

3. Kotler, P., & Armstrong, G. (2001). *Principles of Marketing* (p. 71). Upper Saddle River, NJ: Prentice Hall.

4. McKenzie-Mohr & Smith, *Fostering Sustainable Behavior,* pp. 46–81.

5. Ibid., p. 61.

6. Ibid., p. 48.

7. "ChinaScene: From Widely Read Chinese Media." (2006, May 27–28). *China Daily,* p. 3.

Name Index

Subject Index

About the Authors

Philip Kotler is the S. C. Johnson & Son Distinguished Professor of International Marketing at the J. L. Kellogg Graduate School of Management, Northwestern University, Evanston, Illinois. Kellogg was voted the Best Business School for 6 years in *Business Week's* survey of U.S. business schools. It is also rated as the Best Business School for the Teaching of Marketing. Professor Kotler has significantly contributed to Kellogg's success through his many years of research and teaching there.

He received his master's degree at the University of Chicago and his PhD degree at MIT, both in economics. He did postdoctoral work in mathematics at Harvard University and in behavioral science at the University of Chicago.

Professor Kotler is the author of *Marketing Management: Analysis, Planning, Implementation and Control,* the most widely used marketing book in graduate business schools worldwide; *Principles of Marketing; Marketing Models; Strategic Marketing for Non-Profit Organizations; The New Competition; High Visibility; Social Marketing; Marketing Places; Marketing for Congregations; Marketing for Hospitality and Tourism; The Marketing of Nations;* and *Kotler on Marketing.* He has published over 100 articles in leading journals, several of which have received best article awards.

Professor Kotler was the first recipient of the American Marketing Association's (AMA) Distinguished Marketing Educator Award (1985). The European Association of Marketing Consultants and Sales Trainers awarded him their prize for Marketing Excellence. He was chosen as the Leader in Marketing Thought by the Academic Members of the AMA in a 1975 survey. He also received the 1978 Paul Converse Award of the AMA, honoring his original contribution to marketing. In 1995, the Sales and Marketing Executives International (SMEI) named him Marketer of the Year.

Professor Kotler has consulted for such companies as IBM, General Electric, AT&T, Honeywell, Bank of America, Merck, and others in the areas of marketing strategy and planning, marketing organization, and international marketing.

He has been Chairman of the College of Marketing of the Institute of Management Sciences, Director of the American Marketing Association, Trustee of the Marketing Science Institute, Director of the MAC Group, former member of the Yankelovich Advisory Board, and a member of the Copernicus Advisory Board. He is a member of the Board of Governors of the School of the Art Institute of Chicago and a member of the Advisory Board of the Drucker Foundation. He has received honorary doctoral degrees from Stockholm University, University of Zurich, Athens University of Economics and Business, DePaul University, the Cracow School of Business and Economics, Groupe H.E.C. in Paris, the University of Economics and Business Administration in Vienna, the Catholic University of Santo Domingo, and the Budapest School of Economic Science and Public Administration.

He has traveled extensively throughout Europe, Asia, and South America, advising and lecturing to many companies and organizations. This experience expands the scope and depth of his programs, enhancing them with an accurate global perspective.

Nancy Lee, MBA, is President of Social Marketing Services, Inc. in Seattle, Washington, and an adjunct faculty member at the University of Washington, Seattle University, and the University of South Florida, where she teaches social marketing and marketing in the public sector. With more than 25 years of practical marketing experience in the public and private sectors, Ms. Lee has held numerous corporate marketing positions, including Vice President and Director of Marketing for Washington State's second largest bank and Director of Marketing for the region's Children's Hospital and Medical Center.

Ms. Lee has consulted with more than 100 nonprofit organizations and has participated in the development of more than 100 social marketing campaign strategies for public sector agencies. Clients in the public sector include the Centers for Disease Control and Prevention (CDC), Environmental Protection Agency (EPA), Washington State Department of Health, Office of Crime Victims Advocacy, county Health and Transportation Departments, Department of Ecology, Department of Fisheries and Wildlife, Washington Traffic Safety Commission, City of Seattle, and Office of Superintendent of Public Instruction. Campaigns developed for these clients targeted issues listed below:

- Health: teen pregnancy prevention, HIV/AIDS prevention, nutrition education, diabetes prevention, adult physical activity, tobacco control, arthritis diagnosis and treatment, immunizations, dental hygiene, senior wellness, and eating disorder awareness
- Safety: drowning prevention, underage drinking and driving, youth suicide prevention, binge drinking, pedestrian safety, and safe gun storage
- Environment: natural gardening, preservation of fish and wildlife habitat, recycling, trip reduction, water quality, and water and power conservation

She has conducted social marketing workshops for more than 1,000 public sector employees involved in developing public behavior change campaigns in the areas of health, safety, and the environment. She has been a keynote speaker on social marketing at conferences for improved water quality, energy conservation, family planning, nutrition, recycling, teen pregnancy prevention, and tobacco control.

Ms. Lee has coauthored three other books with Philip Kotler: *Social Marketing: Improving the Quality of Life* (2002), *Corporate Social Responsibility: Doing the Most Good for Your Company and Your Cause* (2005), and *Marketing in the Public Sector: A Roadmap for Improved Performance* (2006). She has also contributed articles to the *Stanford Social Innovation Review*, *Social Marketing Quarterly,* and *The Public Manager.*